DIPLOMA

MARKETING PLANNING AND CONTROL

First edition October 1991

ISBN 0 86277 688 0

British Library Cataloguing-in-Publication Data

A catalogue record for this book
is available from the British Library

Published by

BPP Publishing Limited
Aldine House, Aldine Place
London W12 8AW

Printed in England by
DACOSTA PRINT
35/37 Queensland Road
London N7 7AH
(071) 700 1000

We would like to extend our thanks to Ms Angela Hatton for the valuable contribution she has made to this first edition of this text.

We are grateful to the Chartered Institute of Marketing, the Institute of Chartered Secretaries and Administrators, the Chartered Association of Certified Accountants and the Chartered Institute of Management Accountants for permission to use past examination questions. The suggested solutions have been prepared by BPP Publishing Limited.

CONTENTS

PREFACE

The Diploma awarded by the Chartered Institute of Marketing is a management qualification which puts a major emphasis on the practical understanding of marketing activities. At the same time, the Institute's examinations recognise that the marketing professional works in a fast changing organisational, economic and social environment.

BPP Publishing Limited has extensive experience in producing study material for a wide variety of professional examinations, and leads in these markets. So we are delighted to offer this new range of books, written specifically to the CIM syllabuses, to lecturers and candidates.

Marketing Planning and Control is one of the two compulsory CIM Diploma papers. It is compulsory as the marketing professional is expected to be a *manager*. Knowledge and skills in planning and control, together with an appreciation of the role of marketing in the corporate structure, are essential ingredients of managerial competence in this field.

This text has been written to give precise and comprehensive coverage of the *Marketing Planning and Control* syllabus, reproduced on pages (vii) to (ix), in the light of past examinations of which an analysis is given on pages (ix) to (xi). Each of the chapters in the text covers a major area of the syllabus in a clear and user friendly style. You are encouraged to test acquired knowledge at the end of each chapter and throughout the text you are referred to illustrative questions, with full suggested solutions, on which to practise. The text thus equips you with all the knowledge and skills you need in the examination room.

BPP's Study Texts are noted for their thorough coverage of the syllabus and user friendly style. Moreover, they are reviewed and updated each year. BPP's study material, at once clear, comprehensive and up to date, is thus the ideal investment that students aspiring to the Diploma can make for examination success.

BPP Publishing Ltd
October 1991

Should you wish to send us any comments about this text, please turn to page 353.

INTRODUCTION

SYLLABUS

Aims and objectives

To provide students with an appreciation of the process and concepts of management

To ensure all students are aware of the major aspects of the planning and control elements of the marketing management function

By the end of their study students will be able:

1 to understand and be able to evaluate the contribution of marketing management to corporate management and strategy;

2 to have a detailed knowledge of the planning process and its application to marketing;

3 to formulate short and medium term marketing plans in a structured manner and with reference to particular short, practical case situations;

4 to understand how the marketing mix can be tailored in its detail to the wants/needs of identified market segments and its use as both a strategic and tactical instrument in a highly competitive environment;

5 to identify information requirements for marketing management, planning and control (including its contribution to corporate planning), and have a knowledge of the means of acquiring this information, its costs and limitations. Identify information needs for forecasting in the short and longer term;

6 to understand the contribution made by marketing research to planning decisions and control and be able to evaluate and select from the methodologies available against given criteria;

7 to have an appreciation of the current range of analytical models and techniques relevant to marketing planning and control and understand their practical use; and

8 to adapt the principles of marketing planning and control for organisations operating in services rather than marketing products and also for the smaller business.

Content

(a) *Introduction to planning and control: the management process*

The nature of management
- The management process
- Timing considerations

Relationships between marketing and corporate strategy

The basis of planning and control
- The cycle of control
- Strategic, tactical and contingency planning

Organisational effectiveness

(b) *Where are we now? Strategic and marketing analysis*

Audits and analysis
- Marketing audits
- SWOT analysis
- Ratio analysis
- Productivity analysis

Management and marketing information systems
- Marketing research

(c) *Where do we want to be? Strategic direction and strategy formulation*

Mission and objectives

Structural, market and environmental analysis

Segmental and competitor analysis

Other approaches:
- Product portfolio and life cycle analysis
- Experience curves
- PIMS
- Growth matrix
- Gap analysis

Marketing research

Critical success factors

Sales, profit and technological forecasting

(d) *How might we get there? Strategic choice*

Resource allocation

Controllable v uncontrollable variables

Programming and modelling
- Ansoff matrix
- Buyer behaviour models
- Diffusion models
- Boston matrix

Strategic deployment of the marketing mix
- Products and services
- Pricing
- Promotion
- Distribution

Marketing research

(e) *Which way is best? Strategic evaluation*

Criteria for choice evaluation

Modelling approaches
- Experimentation
- Test marketing
- Competitive response
- Matrix analysis
- Short-run financial - CPV analysis
- Long-run financial - NPV analysis

(f) *How can we ensure arrival? Strategic implementation and control*

Problem areas and organisational considerations

Social control

Management control
- Budgets
- Networks
- Performance evaluation
- Ratio analysis
- Variance analysis
- Corrective responses

Auditing

The format of the examination paper

The examination is divided into two sections. Section I is a compulsory minicase carrying 50% of the available marks. In section II candidates are required to answer three questions from eight, each carrying equal marks.

Analysis of past papers

This brief analysis of the last five examination papers should help you to see the scope of recent examination questions. However you should note that the analysis is only broadly indicative of the types of topic areas examined, particularly as a new senior examiner was appointed in 1990.

June 1991

Section I (Compulsory minicase - choose one of two)
1. Report on implications of results of image research for future marketing strategy
2. Information required for a medium term marketing plan

Section II (Three questions to be answered)
3. The problems of developing a strategic approach to marketing
4. Life style segmentation
5. The value of the product life cycle to the marketing strategist
6. Marketing strategies to challenge market leaders and how to defend against them
7. Factors to be taken into account when pricing a new product
8. The family life cycle and family influences upon behaviour
9. The implications for retailers and manufacturers of increased retail concentration
10. Use of ratios to monitor the implementation of marketing plans

INTRODUCTION

December 1990

Section I (Compulsory minicase - choose one of two)
1. The implications of market research results for marketing planning and control decisions
2. Information required for a medium term marketing communications plan

Section II (Three questions to be answered)
3. Explain contributions made to corporate planning by the marketing information system, product life cycle and SWOT analysis
4. Effect of concern about environmental issues on markets and market segmentation
5. Criteria for deciding whether to increase distribution penetration
6. Use of the marketing information system to assist in sales forecasting and decisions on marketing budgets
7. Concept testing v test marketing in new product development
8. Using the DMU for marketing planning and control in an industrial concern
9. Stages in the buying process of a government authority
10. Effect of a joint venture on marketing planning and control procedures

June 1990

Section I (Compulsory minicase)
1. Presentation of a plan to market physiotherapy services to businesses

Section II (Three questions to be answered)
2. Differences between strategic, tactical and contingency planning
3. Effect of inaccurate sales forecasting on planning and control of pricing and promotion
4. Market segmentation: contribution of lifestyle and psychographic variables
5. Use of marketing information system to reveal causes of falling profitability
6. Using marketing research in promotional planning and control
7. Criticism of PLC approach to product planning
8. Criteria for screening a new launch idea
9. Difficulties in controlling the marketing plan in franchise operations

December 1989

Section I (Compulsory minicase)
1. Report stating advantages and disadvantages of product development and market development and recommended control techniques

Section II (Three questions to be answered)
2. Effect of political, legal and sociological change on marketing mix variables
3. Criteria to determine marketing research method and whether to use an agency
4. Using a marketing information system in marketing mix decisions
5. Critical evaluation of the use of a variety of models and techniques in controlling achievement of marketing plans
6. Effect of a joint venture on marketing planning and control procedures
7. The difficulties in planning and controlling pricing
8. Full marketing audit compared with SWOT analysis
9. Value of sales forecasting from a marketing planning and control viewpoint

June 1989

Section I (Compulsory minicase)
1. Describe the marketing segmentation, planning and control implications of a given situation

Section II (Three questions to be answered)
2. The contribution of marketing planning and control to corporate planning
3. Criteria for selecting target market segments
4. Sources of marketing information to become more marketing orientated
5. Managing the marketing mix: comparison of public and private sector
6. Marketing models to aid decision taking
7. Controlling the element of price in the marketing mix
8. Criteria for deciding which new retailers to approach
9. State and appraise effectiveness of controls used in implementation of marketing plans

Writing examination answers

In the July 1991 issue of *Marketing success* (the CIM student publication), the senior examiner highlighted the most common reasons why candidates fail.

(a) Candidates fail to write an answer relevant to the context of the question set, but produce 'off the peg' practised answers instead.

This subject cannot be tackled as a series of facts or techniques to be learned in isolation. Instead they form of a 'toolbox' of concepts and techniques to be understood, developed and used, both at work and in the examination. You need to reinforce the material learned here with your own experiences and examples.

(b) Answers are either too theoretical or too anecdotal.

As with all the Diploma subjects, the CIM examiners are assessing your practical appreciation of marketing management as well as your theoretical knowledge of the subject. Answers need to be practical, with an emphasis on realistic and credible solutions, supported by the relevant theory and illustrated with examples.

(c) The minicase represents a different set of pitfalls. Candidates sometimes spend too little time on this half of the paper. Impractical and unrealistic recommendations and failure to answer the questions asked will earn few marks.

A minicase is a practical scenario which forces candidates to analyse a situation and make clear recommendations. It commands half of the available marks, so it should take about half of your examination time. At least 25 (out of 50) marks are necessary to pass the minicase part of the paper. The minicase is a very different examination format from essay type questions and you will need to practise it. There is a chapter at the end of this study text to familiarise you with the necessary examination technique.

INTRODUCTION

How to use this text

This study text has been developed to guide you through the required syllabus in a logical way. You should work through each part of the text in order.

Each part is divided into chapters which deal with the individual subjects in the syllabus. At the end of each chapter you will find a number of short questions which test your knowledge of the material which you have just read.

If you can provide complete answers to each of these short questions then you should try the relevant illustrative questions(s) for the chapter. These are located towards the back of the text and the relevant question number(s) is indicated at the end of each chapter.

When you have checked your solution against ours and have understood the reasons for any differences then you are ready to proceed to the next chapter or part of the text.

This systematic approach will ensure that you have a thorough understanding of each aspects of the syllabus before you move on to a fresh one.

PART A

THE MANAGEMENT PROCESS: INTRODUCTION TO PLANNING AND CONTROL

Chapter 1

THE NATURE OF MANAGEMENT

This chapter covers the following topics.

1. The role and functions of managers
2. Understanding the organisation
3. Ensuring organisational effectiveness

1. THE ROLE AND FUNCTIONS OF MANAGERS

1.1 The process of managing and the functions of management have been analysed many times, in various ways and by various writers, who have taken the view that:

- management is an operational process, which can be understood by a close study of management functions; and

- the study of management should lead to the development of certain principles of good management, which will be of value in practice.

1.2 Management theory and studies often recognise two distinct parts to management.

- Managing *the process*, ie forecasting, planning, monitoring and controlling

- Managing *the people* encompassing motivation, leadership, delegation etc and relationship management in general both within the organisation and with groups outside it.

1.3 The CIM planning and control syllabus focuses on the processes of planning, although it is essential that you recognise that producing plans is one thing, successful implementation is another. The internal marketing of plans is a critical element in their successful implementation and we will be examining this in a later chapter. Other CIM subjects have developed the 'people' aspects of the management function, for example under sales and selling topics, managing the sales force has been examined and you should draw on this prior knowledge and your personal experience when working through this syllabus.

The classical view of management

1.4 The ideas of Henri Fayol, the French industrialist and management theorist working in the early decades of this century, were one of the first systematic approaches to defining the manager's 'job'.

According to Fayol, the process of management consists of five functions.

(a) *Planning*. This involves selecting objectives and the strategies, policies, programmes and procedures for achieving the objectives, either for the organisation as a whole or for a part of it. Planning might be done exclusively by line managers who will later be responsible for performance; however, *advice* on planning decisions might also be provided by 'staff' management who do not have 'line' authority for putting the plans into practice. Expert advice is nevertheless a part of the management planning function.

(b) *Organising*. This involves the establishment of a structure of tasks, which need to be performed to achieve the goals of the organisation, grouping these tasks into jobs for an individual, creating groups of jobs within sections and departments, delegating authority to carry out the jobs, providing systems of information and communication and co-ordinating activities within the organisation.

(c) *Commanding*. This involves giving instructions to subordinates to carry out tasks over which the manager has authority for decisions and responsibility for performance.

(d) *Co-ordinating*. This is the task of harmonising the activities of individuals and groups within the organisation, which will inevitably have different ideas about what their own goals should be. Management must reconcile differences in approach, effort, interest and timing of these separate individuals and groups. This is best achieved by making the individuals and groups aware of how their work is contributing to the goals of the overall organisation.

(e) *Controlling*. This is the task of measuring and correcting the activities of individuals and groups, to ensure that their performance is in accordance with plans. Plans must be made, but they will not be achieved unless activities are monitored, and deviations from plan identified and corrected as soon as they become apparent.

1.5 Several writers followed Fayol with broadly similar analyses of management functions. Other functions which might be identified, for example, are *staffing* (filling positions in the organisation with people), *leading* (unlike commanding, 'leading' is concerned with the interpersonal nature of management) and acting as the *organisation's representative* in dealing with other organisations (an ambassadorial or public relations role).

Note the changing emphasis from classical to human relations ideas: many theorists now reject Fayol's concept of 'commanders', arguing instead that managers should approach the same function by being *communicators, persuaders* and *motivators*.

This is very much the view of those who advocate the internal marketing of plans whereby employees are treated as 'customers of change'.

1.6 Another important role not included in Fayol's model is the sustaining of corporate values, ie the creation and maintenance of the *culture* of the organisation. Recent influential management books (for example *In Search of Excellence* by Peters and Waterman) have suggested that this is the vital role of management in today's business environment, since it determines how planning, organising, control and the other functions are carried out.

> 'A company is more than a legal entity engaged in the production and sale of goods and services for profit. It is also the embodiment of the principles and beliefs of the men and women who give it substance, it is characterised by guiding principles which define its view of itself and describe the values it embraces. Such values have, for our company, existed implicitly for very many years - (the company) is what it is and as good as it is because a great many individuals over a long period of time have contributed their own best efforts to preserving and enhancing the values that cause it to endure.'
>
> *Ethics and Operating Principles Handbook*, United Biscuits plc

The approach of Peter Drucker

1.7 Peter Drucker worked in the 1940s and 1950s as a business advisor to a number of US corporations, and was also a prolific writer on management. Drucker (in *The practice of management*) adds explicitly to Fayol's analysis the function of *communication*. It is a manager's task to communicate ideas, orders and results to different people, both within and outside the organisation. Communication is essential for planning, organising, motivating and controlling.

1.8 Drucker grouped the *operations* of management into five categories.

- *Setting objectives* for the organisation. Managers decide what the objectives of the organisation should be, and quantify the targets of achievement for each objective. They must then communicate these targets to other people in the organisation.

- *Organising the work*. The work to be done in the organisation must be divided into manageable activities and manageable jobs. The jobs must be integrated into a formal organisation structure, and people must be selected to do the jobs.

- *Motivating employees* and communicating information to them to enable them to do their work.

- *The job of measurement*. Management must:
  (i) establish objectives or yardsticks of performance for every person in the organisation;
  (ii) analyse actual performance, appraise it against the objectives or yardsticks which have been set, and analyse the comparison;
  (iii) communicate the findings and explain their significance both to subordinate employees and to superiors.

- *Developing people*. The manager 'brings out what is in them or he stifles them. He strengthens their integrity or he corrupts them'.

All managers perform all five of these operations, no matter how good or bad a manager they are. A bad manager performs these functions badly, whereas a good manager performs them well.

1.9 Drucker has also argued that the management of a *business* has one overriding function - *economic performance*. In this respect, the business manager is different from the manager of any other type of organisation. Management of a business can only justify its existence and the legitimacy of its authority by the economic results it produces, however significant the non-economic results which occur as well.

1.10 Drucker described the jobs of management within this basic function of economic performance as follows.

(a) *Managing a business*. The purposes of a business are:
  (i) to create a customer, and
  (ii) innovation. (This is a very important concept for the modern business environment in conditions of change and competitive pressure. It emphasises the *entrepreneurial* aspect of management - even in traditional organisations like banks).

(b) *Managing managers*. The requirements here are:
  (i) management by objectives;
  (ii) proper structure of managers' jobs;
  (iii) creating the right spirit in the organisation;
  (iv) making a provision for the managers of tomorrow;
  (v) arriving at sound principles of organisation structure.

(c) *Managing the worker and work.*

1.11 Drucker called attention to the fact that these three jobs of management are carried out within a *time dimension.*

(a) Management must always consider both the short-term and longer-term consequences of their actions. A business must be kept profitable into the long-term future, but at the same time, short term profitability must be maintained to avoid the danger that the long term will never be reached. The cause of many business failures is cash flow problems rather than an inherent lack of profitability.

(b) Decisions taken by management are for the future, and some have a very long 'planning horizon': the time between making the decision and seeing the consequences of that decision can be substantial. For example a decision to develop market opportunities in China or Japan may take a number of years to implement and still longer to achieve profitable sales.

Managerial 'roles'

1.12 Another way of looking at the manager's job is to observe what managers actually do, and from this to draw conclusions about what 'roles' they play or act out. This is known as the *managerial roles* approach.

Henry Mintzberg identified ten managerial roles, which may be taken on as appropriate to the personality of the manager and his subordinates and the nature of the task in hand.

- *Interpersonal roles*

1. Figurehead	performing ceremonial and social duties as the organisation's representative, for example at conferences
2. Leader	of people, uniting and inspiring the team to achieve objectives
3. Liaison	communication with people outside the manager's work group or the organisation

- *Informational roles*

4. Monitor	receiving information about the organisation's performance and comparing it with objectives
5. Disseminator	passing on information, mainly to subordinates
6. Spokesman	transmitting information outside the unit or organisation, on behalf of the unit or organisation

- *Decisional roles*

7. Entrepreneur	being a 'fixer' - mobilising resources to get things done and to seize opportunities
8. Disturbance-handler	rectifying mistakes and getting operations - and relationships - back on course
9. Resource allocator	distributing resources in the way that will most efficiently achieve defined objectives
10. Negotiator	bargaining, for example for required resources and influence

1.13 The mix of roles varies from job to job and situation to situation: a manager will, as it were, put on the required 'hat' for each task. A manager will, however, wear some hats more than others: senior officials (say, the branch manager of a retail store at local level, and the directors and general managers at corporate level) are more likely to be called upon to act as figureheads than sectional managers and supervisors, who will be more concerned with resource allocation and disturbance-handling.

In modern management theories, particular emphasis has been placed on leadership and entrepreneurship, at *all* levels of management. The cultural effects of both work at team as well as organisational level: involving and committing employees to achieving goals, and focusing on creative action and resource mobilisation to get things done.

The managerial job

1.14 What makes a manager's job different from a worker's?

The difference can be expressed in terms of the functions and roles (discussed above) which are the prerogative of management.

However, there are also particular *characteristics* of the managerial job.

1.15 The characteristics of the managerial job include the following.

(a) *A high level of activity.* Managers are very 'busy' in the sense that they tend to perform a high number of separate activities, and have a high number of interpersonal contacts, in the course of a day.

(b) *Discontinuity.* As the number of activities suggests, managers tend not to be able to spend long on single, continuous tasks. They are constantly interrupted by personal contacts and matters arising for their attention: telephone calls, meetings, people bringing information or problems, and 'deskwork' resulting from all of them. Managerial activity tends to be a rather unpatterned mixture of routine/planned and unplanned tasks.

(c) *Variety.* The nature and diversity of the managerial roles mean that managers have more job variety than most of their subordinates, covering differing types of activity including:
(i) paperwork (dealing with it *and* generating it);
(ii) telephone calls (taking and making);
(iii) meetings (formal - especially in more senior posts - and informal)
(iv) interpersonal contacts - (internal and - especially in senior and marketing posts - external).

For each of these types of activity, the potential range of matters to be dealt with - ie job *content* - is extremely wide, since it is management's responsibility to handle the unforeseen and discretionary areas of business as well as the routine.

(d) *Separation* from the location and detail of operational work. The more senior the manager, the less he or she will be involved 'at the coal face' (relying on feedback through subordinates) and the more time will be spent outside the office, the department and even the organisation.

(e) *Talking and thinking.* Managers are expected (and paid) to perform much more 'brain' activity (such as thinking, planning, decision-making and problem-solving) than subordinates. They are not, in other words, expected to be as immediately and visibly productive as workers. In addition, up to 90% of total work time may be taken up in primarily *oral* activity: telephone calls, discussions, meetings etc.

(f) *Time span of discretion.* This was a term devised by Elliot Jaques to describe the amount of time between a decision or action taken by an individual, and the checking up on it and evaluation of it by the individual's superior. Low level employees are frequently monitored - in so far as they are allowed to exercise their own discretion at all - but managers perform actions and take decisions whose consequences may not emerge for a long time.

(g) *Networks.* The more senior a person is - and the more 'broad' their concerns in the organisation - the wider is the network of information in which they participate. Lower employees 'network' with peers in their immediate sphere of work, and with immediate superiors and subordinates. At higher levels, information for decisions, planning and control will be drawn from a wider set of contacts, including many sources outside the organisation.

Being a manager: the views of Handy

1.16 Charles Handy suggested that a definition of a 'manager' or a 'manager's role' is likely to be so broad as to be fairly meaningless. His own analysis of being a manager was divided into three aspects, based on the practice and experience of being a manager.

- the manager as a General Practitioner;
- managerial dilemmas;
- the manager as a person.

1.17 *The manager as a General Practitioner.* A manager is the first recipient of an organisation's health problem and must do the following.

(a) Identify the symptoms in the situation (for example low productivity, high labour turnover, severe industrial relations problems etc).
(b) Diagnose the disease or cause of the trouble.
(c) Decide how it might be dealt with - developing a strategy for better health.
(d) Start the treatment.

1.18 Typical strategies for improving the organisation's health might be as follows.

(a) *People*: changing people, either literally or figuratively, by:

(i) hiring and firing;
(ii) re-assignment;
(iii) training and education;
(iv) selective pay increases;
(v) counselling or admonition.

(b) *The work and the structure*:

(i) re-organisation of reporting relationships;
(ii) re-definition of the work task;
(iii) job enrichment;
(iv) re-definition of roles.

(c) *The systems and procedures*, to amend or introduce:

(i) communication systems;
(ii) reward systems (payment methods, salary guides);
(iii) information and reporting systems;
(iv) budgets or other decision-making systems (for example stock control, debtor control).

1.19 *The managerial dilemmas.* The job of a manager is different from that of a worker, and managers are paid more than workers, because they face constant dilemmas which it is their responsibility to resolve. These dilemmas are as follows.

- *The dilemma of the cultures.* It is the manager's task to decide which 'culture' of organisation and management is required for the particular task and the people involved. As a manager rises in seniority, he will find it necessary to behave in a culturally diverse manner to satisfy the broader requirements of the job and the more diverse abilities, personalities and expectations of his employees. The manager 'must be flexible but consistent, culturally diverse but recognisably an individual with his own identity. Therein lies the dilemma. Those ...... who relapse into a culturally predominant style will find themselves rightly restricted to that part of the organisation where their culture prevails. Middle layers of organisations are often overcrowded with culturally rigid managers who have failed to deal with this cultural dilemma'.

- *The dilemma of time horizons.* This is the problem of responsibility for both the present and the future at the same time. Concentration on short-term success may be at the expense of the evolution and innovation required for survival and growth in the long term.

- *The trust-control dilemma.* This is the problem of the balance between management's wish to control the work for which they are responsible, and the necessity to delegate work to subordinates, implying trust in them to do the work properly. The greater the amount of trust which is placed in subordinates, the less control is retained, which can be risky and stressful. Retaining control implies a lack of trust in subordinates which may create human relations problems. 'The managerial dilemma is always how to balance trust and control'.

- *The commando leader's dilemma.* In many organisations, junior managers show a strong preference for working in project teams, with a clear task or objective, working outside the normal bureaucratic structure of a large formal organisation and then disbanding. Unfortunately, there can be too many such 'commando groups' for the stability of the total organisation. A manager's dilemma is to decide how many entrepreneurial groups should be created to satisfy the needs of subordinates and the demands of the task, and how much bureaucratic organisation structure should be retained for efficiency, consistency and 'safety'.

1.20 *The manager as a person.* Management is developing into a 'semi-profession' and managers expect to be rewarded for their professional skills. The implications for individual managers are that 'increasingly it will come to be seen as the individual's responsibility to maintain, alter or boost their own skills, to find the right market for those skills and to sell them to the appropriate buyer'. Managers must be regarded as individuals in their own right, with their own personal objectives: not as people existing solely within and for the benefit of the organisation.

1.21 Another consequence of this is that the 'traditional' view that an organisation should employ 'raw recruits' and nurture them into its management structure might in future no longer be accepted. 'There will be no obligation to continue to employ the individual when the benefits of his skills begin to be less than their costs'.

1.22 Marketing professionals have perhaps tended to come from a culture which accepts Handy's analysis of mobility. Experience gained from different marketing and sales experiences are very much the accepted currency on a job market where an apprenticeship approach to personal development is still very much the norm.

2. UNDERSTANDING THE ORGANISATION

2.1 An organisation is made up of people who usually have a responsibility for a function or aspect of the operation. Understanding how these various groups are organised and work together is an important element which needs to be taken into account when preparing and implementing plans.

2.2 A great deal of work has been done to analyse both formal and informal relationships in the work environment and to identify the impact of organisation structure on management effectiveness. In this section we will concentrate on the corporate skeleton, the way in which groups and departments are linked together and the way the culture of the organisation can affect planning and the implementation of change.

Work organisations

2.3 Buchanan and Huczynski (*Introduction to Organisational Behaviour*) put forward the following definition of organisation: 'Social arrangements for the controlled performance of collective goals.'

They point out that the difference between organisations (and particularly work organisations) and other social groupings with collective goals (for example the family or the bus stop queue) is:

- the preoccupation with performance; and
- the need for controls.

2.4 In general terms, organisations exist because they can achieve results which individuals cannot achieve alone. By grouping together, individuals overcome limitations imposed both by the physical environment and also their own biological limitations. Chester Barnard (1956) described the situation of a man trying to move a stone which was too large for him:

(a) the stone was too big for the man (environmental limitation) and
(b) the man was too small for the stone (biological limitation).

By forming an organisation with another man, it was possible to move the stone with the combined efforts of the two men together.

2.5 Barnard further suggested that the limitations on man's accomplishments are determined by the *effectiveness* of his organisation.

2.6 In greater detail, the reasons for organisations may be described as follows.

(a) *Social reasons:* to meet an individual's need for companionship.

(b) To *enlarge abilities:* organisations increase productive ability because they make possible both:

(i) specialisation; and
(ii) exchange or sharing

of knowledge, skills, experience etc. Unlike most individuals, organisations have the capacity to achieve the depth of specialisation across a breadth of activity.

(c) To *accumulate knowledge* (for subsequent re-use and further learning).

(d) To *save time* in achieving objectives.

2.7 The need for *controls* arises because organisation is very complex in practice.

(a) Organisations are collections of interacting individuals, occupying different roles but experiencing common membership. However, this embraces a wide variety of behaviours: the relationship between them may be co-operative or coercive; their roles may be ill-defined or clearly-defined, overlapping, conflicting etc.

(b) Organisations are created because individuals need each other in order to fulfil goals which they consider worthwhile. However, one individual's goals may be very different from another's and from those of the organisation as a whole.

(c) Performance must be controlled in order to make best use of human, financial and material resources, for which individuals, groups and organisations compete. In work organisations, management is usually accountable for the use of these resources, for example to the owners of the business. The need for controlled performance leads to a deliberate, ordered environment, allocation of tasks (ie division of labour), specialisation, the setting of standards and measurement of results against them etc. This implies a whole structure of 'power' or 'responsibility' relationships, whereby some individuals control others.

2.8 Barnard described an organisation as a 'system of co-operative human activities' and it is important to be aware of the following.

(a) An organisation consists of members, ie people who inter-react with each other.

(b) The way in which people inter-react is designed and ordered by the organisation structure so as to achieve joint (organisational) objectives. All individuals have their own view of what these organisational objectives are.

(c) Each person in the organisation has their own personal objectives.

(d) The organisational objectives as gauged by an individual need to be compatible with personal objectives of the individual if he is to be a well-integrated member of the organisation.

The task of recognising and reconciling organisational and individual objectives, and making optimal use of resources to achieve both, is the basic task of management.

2.9 Louis A Allen, in his books *Management and Organisation* and *The Management Profession*, tells us that 'organisation' is a mechanism or structure that enables living things to work effectively together. There are three basic elements of organisation.

(a) Division of labour, ie specialisation ('who does what?').
(b) A source of authority, ('who is responsible for seeing that they do it?').
(c) Relationships ('how does it fit in with what everyone else is doing?').

2.10 Formal organisations have an explicit hierarchy of authority in a well-defined structure. Division of labour is more or less fixed in the form of job design, expressed in job specifications. Communication channels for reporting 'upward' as well as passing information and instructions 'downward' are also well-defined.

2.11 The 'bureaucracy' is the purest form of the formal, rational organisation designed on classical principles. It is important to recognise, however, that the structure of an organisation is affected by the people working within it, and an *informal* organisation exists side by side with the formal one.

The informal organisation of a company is so important that a newcomer has to 'learn the ropes' before he can settle effectively into his job, and he must also become 'accepted' by his fellow workers.

2.12 When people work together, they establish social relationships and customary ways of doing things. They form social groups, or cliques (sometimes acting against one another) and they develop informal ways of getting things done - norms and rules which are different from those imposed by the formal organisation.

Social groups, or cliques, may act collectively for or against the interests of their company; the like-mindedness which arises in all members of the group strengthens their collective attitudes or actions.

Whether these groups work for or against the interests of the company depends to some extent on the type of supervision they get. If superiors involve them in decision-making, they are more likely to be management-minded.

2.13 The informal organisation of a company, given an acceptable social atmosphere, can have beneficial effects.

(a) It improves communications by means of a 'grapevine' or 'bush telegraph' system.
(b) It facilitates the co-ordination of various individuals or departments and establishes 'unwritten' methods for getting a job done. These may 'by-pass' communication problems, for example between a manager and subordinate, or lengthy procedures; they may be more flexible and adaptable to required change than the formal ways of doing things.

2.14 However there are disadvantages of the informal structure.

(a) Individuals may put more energy and loyalty into the group than the organisation.
(b) The 'grapevine' tends to operate by distortion and rumour, more than fact.
(c) The group may have objectives (for example having fun) which run counter to organisational requirements.
(d) Close-knit groups tend to feel very 'cosy' and invincible, and can make bad decisions.
(e) Some individuals may be left out of the informal structure, or not have as much influence there as they ought to have according to their position in the formal structure. A manager who is not respected or liked may have his authority undermined by the informal group or leader.

2.15 Management should not ignore the informal organisation as it can, particularly in large organisations, place real limits on formal authority. In such circumstances the ability to implement plans and change can be a real test of the personal skills of the manager. Internal marketing techniques recognise the significance of opinion leaders in the informal organisation and target them as key influencers who the manager must 'sell' decisions to.

2.16 A conclusion might therefore be that management should seek to harness the informal organisation to operate to the benefit of the formal organisation. In practice, however, this will be difficult because unlike formal organisation, which does not change even when individual employees move into and out of jobs (by promotion, transfer, appointment, resignation or retirement etc) most informal organisations depend on individual personalities. If one member leaves, the informal organisation is no longer the same, and new informal organisations will emerge to take its place.

Organisation design or 'structure'

2.17 Organisational design or structure implies a framework or mechanism intended to do the following.

(a) Link individuals in an established network of relationships so that authority, responsibility and communications can be controlled.

(b) Group together (in any appropriate way) the tasks required to fulfil the objectives of the organisation, and allocate them to suitable individuals or groups.

(c) Give each individual or group the authority required to perform the allocated functions, while controlling behaviour and resources in the interests of the organisation as a whole.

(d) Co-ordinate the objectives and activities of separate units, so that overall aims are achieved without 'gaps' or 'overlaps' in the flow of work required.

(e) Facilitate the flow of work, information and other resources required, through planning, control and other systems.

2.18 The advantages of having a formal organisation structure therefore include the following.

(a) Unity or 'congruence' of objectives and effort.

(b) Clarity in expressing objectives.

(c) Control over interpersonal relationships, exercise of authority, use of resources, communication and other systems (for example promotion, planning, reward, discipline), offering predictability and stability for planning and decision making.

(d) Controlled information flow throughout the structure to aid co-ordination and (arguably) employee satisfaction.

(e) The establishment of precedents, procedures, rules and norms to facilitate decision making and interpersonal relations in recurring situations.

2.19 Many factors influence the structural design of the organisation, including the following.

(a) Its *size*. As an organisation gets larger, its structure gets more complex: specialisation and subdivision are required. The process of controlling and co-ordinating performance, and communication between individuals, also grows more difficult as the 'top' of the organisation gets further from the 'bottom' ie with more intervening levels. The more members there are, the more potential there is for interpersonal relationships and the development of the *informal* organisation.

(b) Its *task*, ie the nature of its work. Structure is shaped by the division of work into functions and individual tasks, and how these tasks relate to each other. Depending on the nature of the work, this can be done in a number of ways. The complexity and importance of tasks will affect the amount of supervision required, and so the ratio of supervisors to workers. The nature of the market will dictate the way in which tasks are grouped together: into functions, or sales territories, or types of customer etc.

(c) Its *staff*. The skills and abilities of staff will determine how the work is structured and the degree of autonomy or supervision required. Staff aspirations and expectations may also influence job design, and the amount of delegation in the organisation, in order to provide job satisfaction.

(d) Its legal, commercial, technical and social *environment*. Examples include: economic recession necessitating staff 'streamlining' especially at middle management level; new technology reducing staff requirements but increasing specialisation.

(e) Its *age:* ie the time it has had to develop and grow, or decline, whether it is very set in its ways and traditional or experimenting with new ways of doing things and making decisions.

(f) Its *culture and management style:* how willing management is to delegate authority at all levels, how skilled they are in organisation and communication (for example in handling a wider span of control), whether teamwork is favoured, or large, impersonal structures accepted by the staff etc, whether the company is product or market oriented and what the driving force for change is, for example research and development, increased market share or profit.

Different types of structure

2.20 The grouping of organisational activities (usually in the form of 'departments') can be done in different ways. The most common forms of departmentation are based on the following.

(a) *Function:* this is a widely-used method of organisation. Primary functions in a manufacturing company might be production, marketing, finance and general administration.

Functional organisation is logical and traditional and accommodates the division of work into specialist areas. Apart from the problems which may arise when 'line' management resents interference by 'staff' advisers in their functional area, the drawback to functional organisation is simply that more efficient structures might exist which would be more appropriate in a particular situation.

(b) *Territory*. This method of organisation is suitable when similar activities are carried out in widely different locations. Many sales departments are organised territorially. The branch structure of a bank works in the same way, to offer local provision of services.

The *advantage* of territorial departmentation is better local decision-making at the point of contact between the organisation (for example a salesperson) and its customers. Localised knowledge is put to better use. In a personal service industry like retailing, the close relationship between the local branch and the community will be important - although 'remote' centralised retailing by telephone and post (for example Next Directory) do maintain a share of retail sales.

The *disadvantage* of territorial departmentation might be the duplication of management effort, increasing overhead costs and the risk of dis-integration. For example, a national organisation divided into ten regions might have a customer liaison department at each regional head office.

(c) *Product*. Some organisations group activities on the basis of products or product lines. Functional division of responsibility remains, but under the overall control of a manager with responsibility for the product, product line or brand.

The *advantages* of product departmentation are as follows.

(i) Individual managers can be held accountable for the *profitability* of individual products.

(ii) Specialisation can be developed. For example, sales staff can be trained to sell a specific product in which they may develop technical expertise.

(iii) The different functional activities and efforts required to make and market each product can be co-ordinated and integrated by the product manager.

The *disadvantage* of product departmentation is that it increases the overhead costs and managerial complexity of the organisation.

(d) *Customer or market segment.* Departmentation by customer is commonly associated with marketing departments and selling effort, but it might also be used at the product development stage. Such an approach encourages cross selling across the whole product range and the orientation of activities to meet the needs of client groups.

(e) *Common processes or technology.* The most obvious example is the data processing department of large organisations. Batch processing operations are conducted for other departments at a computer centre (where it is controlled by DP staff) because it would be uneconomical to provide each functional department with its own large mainframe computer.

- *Departmentation by function*

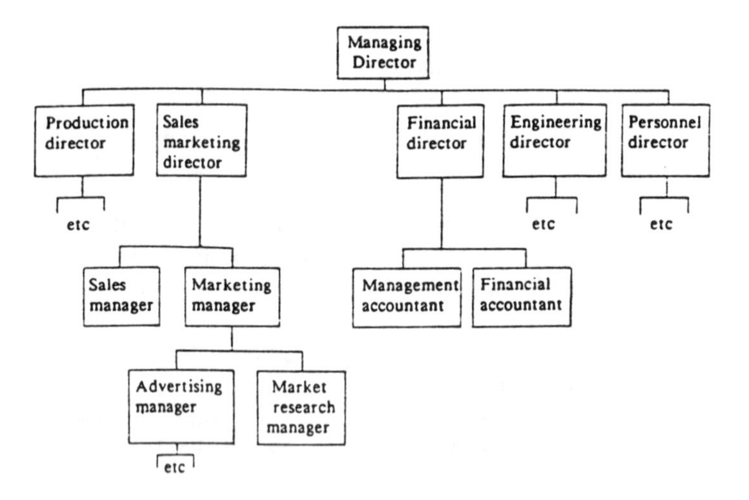

- *Departmentation by territory*

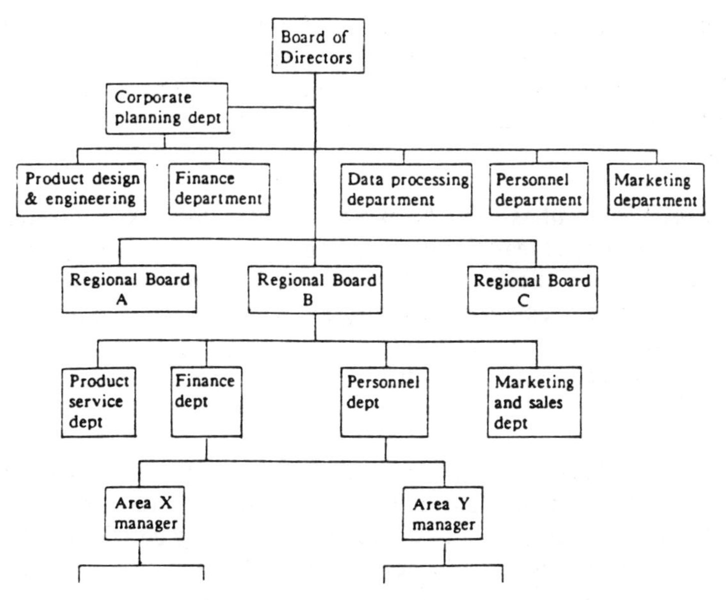

- *Departmentation by product*

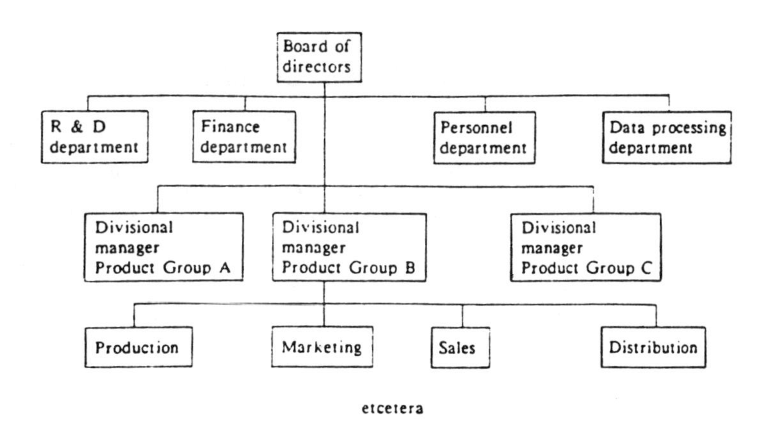

Matrix organisation

2.21 In recent years, the awareness of internal and external influences on organisational structure and operation has contributed to a new emphasis on flexibility and adaptability in organisational design, particularly since the pace of the change in the technological and competitive environment has put pressure on businesses to innovate, to adopt a market orientation.

Part of this shift in emphasis has been a trend towards task-centred structures, for example multi-disciplinary project teams, which draw experience, knowledge and expertise together from different functions to facilitate flexibility and innovation. In particular, the concept of 'matrix' organisation has emerged, dividing authority between functional managers and product or project managers or co-ordinators - thus challenging classical assumptions about 'one man one boss' and the line/staff dilemma.

2.22 Matrix management first developed in the 1950s in the USA in the aerospace industry. Lockheed-California, the aircraft manufacturers, were organised in a functional hierarchy. Customers were unable to find a manager in Lockheed to whom they could take their problems and queries about their particular orders, and Lockheed found it necessary to employ 'project expediters' as customer liaison officials. From this developed 'project co-ordinators', responsible for co-ordinating line managers into solving a customer's problems. Up to this point, these new officials had no functional responsibilities.

With increasingly heavy customer demand, Lockheed eventually created 'programme managers', with full authority for project budgets and programme design and scheduling. This dual authority structure may be shown diagramatically as a management *grid*; for example:

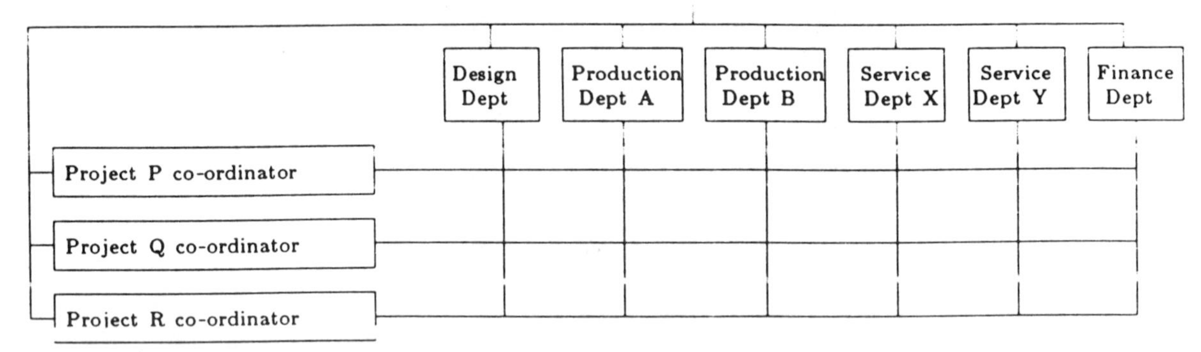

Functional department heads are responsible for the internal organisation of their departments, but project co-ordinators are responsible for the aspects of all departmental activity that affects their particular project.

2.23 The authority of product or project managers may vary from organisation to organisation. J K Galbraith drew up a range of alternative situations, as shown.

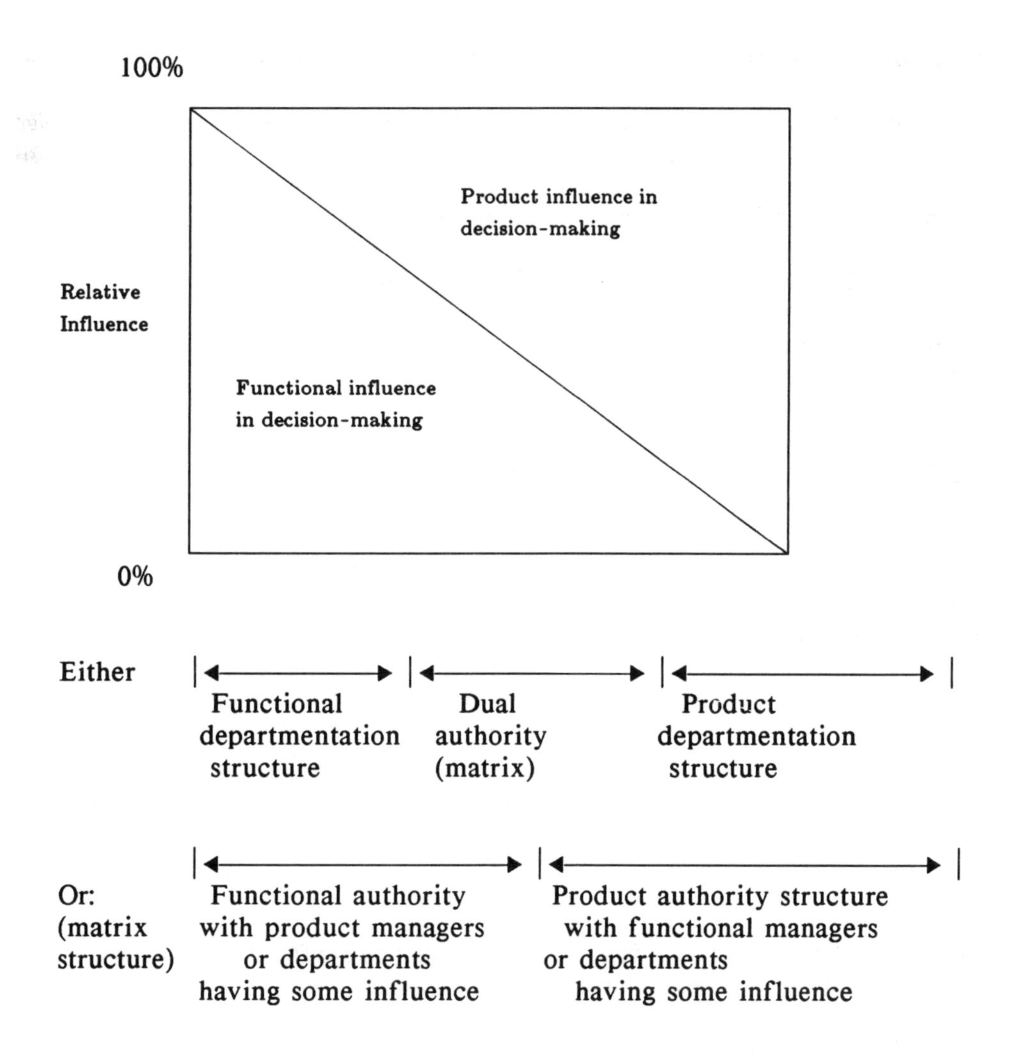

2.24 The *advantages* of a matrix structure are said to be as follows.

(a) Greater flexibility.

(i) *People*. Employees develop an attitude geared to accepting change, and departmental monopolies are broken down.

(ii) *Tasks and structure*. The matrix structure may be short term (as with project teams) or readily amended.

(b) Reorientation. A functional department will often be production-oriented. Product management will create a market orientation.

(c) A structure for allocating responsibility to managers for end results.

(d) Interdisciplinary cooperation and a mixing of skills and expertise.

(e) Arguably, motivation of employees by providing them with greater participation in planning and control decisions.

2.25 The *disadvantages* of matrix organisation are said to be as follows.

(a) Dual authority threatens a conflict between functional managers and product/project managers. Where matrix structure exists it is important that the authority of superiors should not overlap and areas of authority must be clearly defined. A subordinate must know to which superior he is responsible for a particular aspect of his duties.

(b) One individual with two or more bosses is more likely to suffer stress at work.

(c) Matrix management can be more costly, for example product management posts are added, meetings held etc.

(d) It may be difficult for the management of an organisation to accept a matrix structure and the culture of participation, shared authority and ambiguity that it fosters.

2.26 You should be aware that structure has an impact on the culture of the organisation. Attempts to reposition the 'culture' say from product to a more market orientation are often best tackled from a new structure after re-organisation.

This need for a new structure is often implicit in the major case studies and is something you should look out for.

Exercise

Draw a formal organisation chart for a business with which you are familiar. You may be able to obtain a published one if you work for a large organisation.

Now produce a chart of the informal structure and compare the two. *Note:* you will probably find that individuals who marketers refer to as 'gatekeepers': secretaries, personal assistants, reception staff etc are important in the informal communication structure of the organisation. They are often the influencers and advisers who it is important to identify in the process of internal marketing.

---

3. ENSURING ORGANISATIONAL EFFECTIVENESS

3.1 Organisations are much more complex than machines because they are made up of people. Two organisations which are structured similarly on paper will perform very differently. Why?

Organisational culture

3.2 Every organisation is different, as you will readily appreciate if you have worked in more than one. Why is this so? After all, two organisations such as fmcg manufacturers may be similarly structured and involved in similar activities - and *still* be quite unlike to work for or deal with. The concept of organisational 'style' or 'climate' has been developed to explore such differences: the most current term for it is 'culture'.

3.3 Culture may be defined as *the complex body of shared values and beliefs of an organisation.*

Handy sums up 'culture' as 'that's the way we do things round here'. For Schein, it is 'the pattern of basic assumptions that a given group has invented, discovered, or developed, in learning to cope with its problems of external adaption and internal integration, and that have worked well enough to be considered valid and, therefore, to be taught to new members as the correct way to perceive, think and feel in relation to these problems.'

> 'I believe that the real difference between success and failure in a corporation can very often be traced to the question of how well the organisation brings out the great energies and talents of its people. What does it do to help these people find common cause with each other? And how can it sustain this common cause and sense of direction through the many changes which take place from one generation to another?... I think you will find that it owes its resiliency not to its form of organisation or administrative skills, but to the power of what we call *beliefs* and the appeal these beliefs have for its people.'
>
> Watson (IBM) quoted by Peters and Waterman

3.4 All organisations will generate their own cultures, whether spontaneously or under the guidance of positive managerial strategy. The culture will consist of three parts.

(a) The *basic, underlying assumptions* which guide the behaviour of the individuals and groups in the organisation, for example customer orientation, or belief in quality, trust in the organisation to provide rewards, freedom to make decisions, freedom to make mistakes, and the value of innovation and initiative at all levels. Assumptions will be reflected in the kind of people employed (their age, education or personality), the degree of delegation and communication, whether decisions are made by committees or individuals etc.

(b) *Overt beliefs* expressed by the organisation and its members, which can be used to condition (a) above. These beliefs and values may emerge as sayings, slogans, mottos etc. such as 'we're getting there', 'the customer is always right', or 'the winning team'. They may emerge in a richer mythology - in jokes and stories about past successes, heroic failures or breakthroughs, legends about the 'early days', or about 'the time the boss...'. Organisations with strong cultures often centre themselves around almost legendary figures in their history. Management can encourage this by 'selling' a sense of the corporate 'mission', or by promoting the company's 'image'; it can reward the 'right' attitudes and punish (or simply not employ) those who aren't prepared to commit themselves to the culture.

(c) *Visible artefacts*: the style of the offices or other premises, dress 'rules', display of 'trophies', the degree of informality between superiors and subordinates etc.

3.5 'Positive' organisational culture may therefore be important in its influence on the following.

(a) The motivation and satisfaction of employees (and possibly therefore their performance) by encouraging commitment to the organisation's values and objectives, making employees feel valued and trusted, fostering satisfying team relationships, and using 'guiding values' instead of rules and controls.

(b) The adaptability of the organisation, by encouraging innovation, risk-taking, sensitivity to the environment, customer care, willingness to embrace new methods and technologies etc.

(c) The image of the organisation. The cultural attributes of an organisation (attractive or unattractive) will affect its appeal to potential employees, customers etc. For example, the moves of banks to modernise and beautify branch design are meant to convey a 'style' that is up-to-date, welcoming, friendly but business-like, with open-plan welcome areas, helpful signposting, lots of light and plants etc, a significant change from the old days of 'approach with awe', and the authority figure of the traditional bank manager.

Cultural problems and how to change culture

3.6 Not all organisation cultures are so 'positive' in their nature and effect, however. The symptoms of a negative, unhealthy or failing culture (and possibly organisation as a whole) might be any of the following.

(a) No 'visionary' element: no articulated beliefs or values widely shared, nor any sense of the future.

(b) No sense of unity - because no central driving force. Hostility and lack of co-ordination may be evident.

(c) No shared norms of habits, ways of addressing others etc. Sub-cultures may compete with each other.

(d) Political conflict and rivalry, as individuals and groups vie for power and resources and their own interests.

(e) Focus on the internal workings of the organisation rather than opportunities and changes in the environment. In particular, disinterest in the customer.

(f) Preoccupation with the short term.

(g) Low employee morale, expressed in low productivity, high absenteeism and labour turnover, 'grumbling' etc.

(h) Abdication by management of the responsibility for doing anything about the above - perhaps because of apathy or hopelessness.

(i) No innovation or welcoming of change: change is a threat and a problem.

(j) Rigorous control and disciplinary systems have to be applied, because nothing else brings employees into line with the aims of the business.

(k) Lacklustre marketing, company literature etc.

3.7 A pretty depressing picture. So what can be done about it? There are many factors which influence the organisational culture, including the following.

(a) *Economic conditions*
In prosperous times organisations will either be complacent or adventurous, full of new ideas and initiatives. In recession they may be depressed, or challenged. The struggle against a main competitor may take on 'heroic' dimensions.

(b) *Nature of the business and its tasks*
The types of technology used in different forms of business create the pace and priorities associated with different forms of work, for example the hustle and frantic conditions for people dealing in the international money market compared with the studious life of a research officer. Task also to an extent influences work environment, which is an important visual cultural indicator.

(c) *Leadership style*
The approach used in exercising authority will determine the extent to which subordinates feel alienated and uninterested or involved and important. Leaders are also the creators and 'sellers' of organisational culture: it is up to them to put across the vision.

(d) *Policies and practices*
The level of trust and understanding which exists between members of an organisation can often be seen in the way policies and objectives are achieved, for example the extent to which they are imposed by tight written rules and procedures or implied through custom and understanding.

(e) *Structure*
The way in which work is organised, authority exercised and people rewarded will reflect an emphasis on freedom or control, flexibility or rigidity.

(f) *Characteristics of the work force*
Organisation culture will be affected by the demographic nature of the workforce, for example manual/clerical division, age, sex, personality.

3.8 As we have already indicated, it is possible to 'turn round' a negative culture, or to change the culture into a new direction.

(a) The overt beliefs expressed by managers and staff can be used to 'condition' people, to sell a new culture to the organisation, for example by promoting a new sense of corporate mission, or a new image. Slogans, mottos ('we're getting there'), myths etc can be used to energise people and to promote particular values which the organisation wishes to instill in its members.

(b) Leadership provides an impetus for cultural change: attitudes to trust, control, formality or informality, participation, innovation etc will have to come from the top - especially where changes in structure, authority relationships or work methods are also involved. The first step in deliberate cultural change will need to be a 'vision' and a sense of 'mission' on the part of a powerful individual or group in the organisation.

(c) The reward system can be used to encourage and reinforce new attitudes and behaviour, while those who do not commit themselves to the change miss out or are punished, or pressured to 'buy in or get out'.

(d) The recruitment and selection policies should reflect the qualities desired of employees in the new culture. To an extent these qualities may also be encouraged through induction and training.

(e) Visible emblems of the culture, for example design of the work place and public areas, dress code, status symbols etc, can be used to reflect the new 'style'.

Types of culture

3.9 Different writers have identified different types of culture, based on particular aspects of organisation and management.

Charles Handy discusses four cultures and their related structures. He recognises that while an organisation might reflect a single culture, it may also have elements of different cultures appropriate to the structure and circumstances of different units in the organisation. (The customer service or marketing units may, for example, have a more flexible, and dynamic 'style' than administrative units, which tend to be more bureaucratic.)

(a) The *power culture*. Mainly in smaller organisations, where power and influence stem from a central source, through whom all communication, decisions and control are channelled. The organisation, since it is not rigidly structured, is capable of adapting quickly to meet change; however, the success in adapting will depend on the luck or judgement of the key individuals who make the decisions. Political competition for a share of power is rife, and emotional behaviour is encouraged by the 'personality' cult surrounding the leader.

(b) The *role culture* or bureaucracy, reflected in a formal, functional organisation structure. There is limited freedom and creativity in decision making and the organisation is likely to be product oriented.

(c) The *task culture*, reflected in a matrix organisation, in project teams and task forces. The principal concern in a task culture is to get the job done; therefore the individuals who are important are the experts with the ability to accomplish a particular aspect of the task. Such organisations are flexible and constantly changing as tasks are accomplished and new needs arise. Innovation and creativity are highly prized. Job satisfaction tends to be high owing to the degree of individual participation, communication and group identity.

(d) The *person culture*, in an organisation whose purpose is to serve the interests of individuals within it. Organisations designed on these lines are rare, but some individuals may use any organisation to suit their own purposes; to gain experience, further their careers, express themselves etc.

3.10 Dale and Kennedy (*Corporate Cultures*) consider cultures to be a function of the willingness of employees to take risks, and how quickly they get feedback on whether they got it right or wrong.

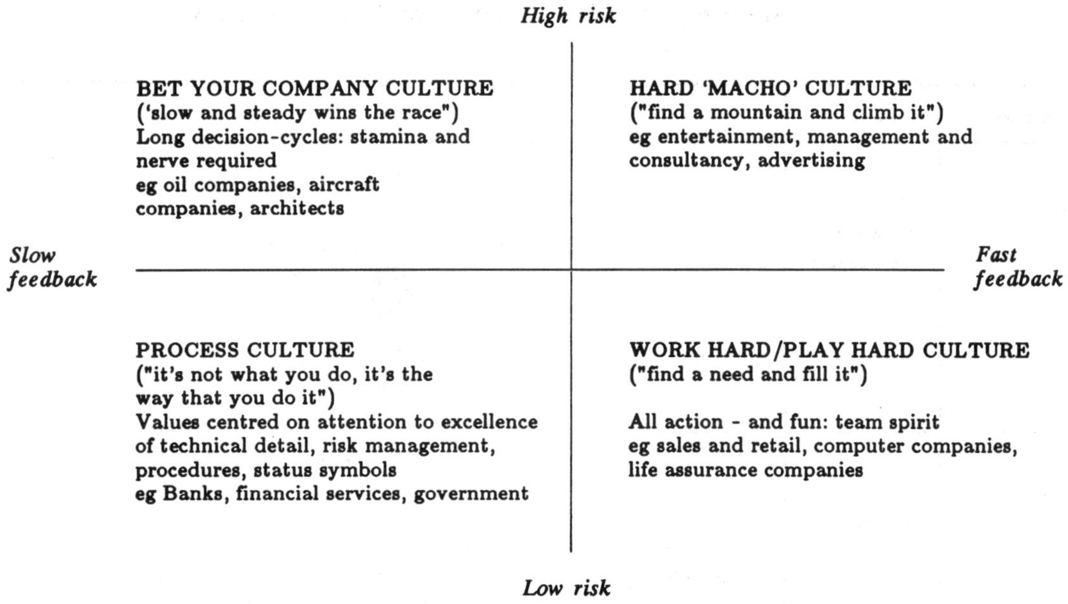

High risk

	BET YOUR COMPANY CULTURE ('slow and steady wins the race") Long decision-cycles: stamina and nerve required eg oil companies, aircraft companies, architects	**HARD 'MACHO' CULTURE** ("find a mountain and climb it") eg entertainment, management and consultancy, advertising
Slow feedback		*Fast feedback*
	PROCESS CULTURE ("it's not what you do, it's the way that you do it") Values centred on attention to excellence of technical detail, risk management, procedures, status symbols eg Banks, financial services, government	**WORK HARD/PLAY HARD CULTURE** ("find a need and fill it") All action - and fun: team spirit eg sales and retail, computer companies, life assurance companies

Low risk

3.11 The diagram on the next page depicts some organisation structures and characteristics. Understanding the characteristics and structure of the organisation is important to the process of planning. It will help you to assess the likely reaction and response to your proposals both from senior managers and subordinates. With this insight you will be able to more accurately forecast the resources required and the time necessary for the implementation of your plans. Case studies will frequently provide you with clues about the organisation and its culture. Recognising these and taking them into account in developing your strategies is an important aspect of the realistic approach the examiners will expect.

For example a company with a risk averse culture is unlikely to adopt a strategy based on speculative land deals and one with a strong religious base to its culture is unlikely to be happy to diversify into casinos or betting shops.

4. CONCLUSION

4.1 The management role has two distinct parts to it, the process and the people. Emphasis in the CIM syllabus is on the process, but the internal marketing of plans is increasingly accepted as critical to the success of the planning process.

4.2 The classical approach to management as characterised by Henri Fayol has given way to the human relations approach more relevant today. Here managers are seen as persuaders and motivators rather than as commanders.

Some organisation structures and characteristics

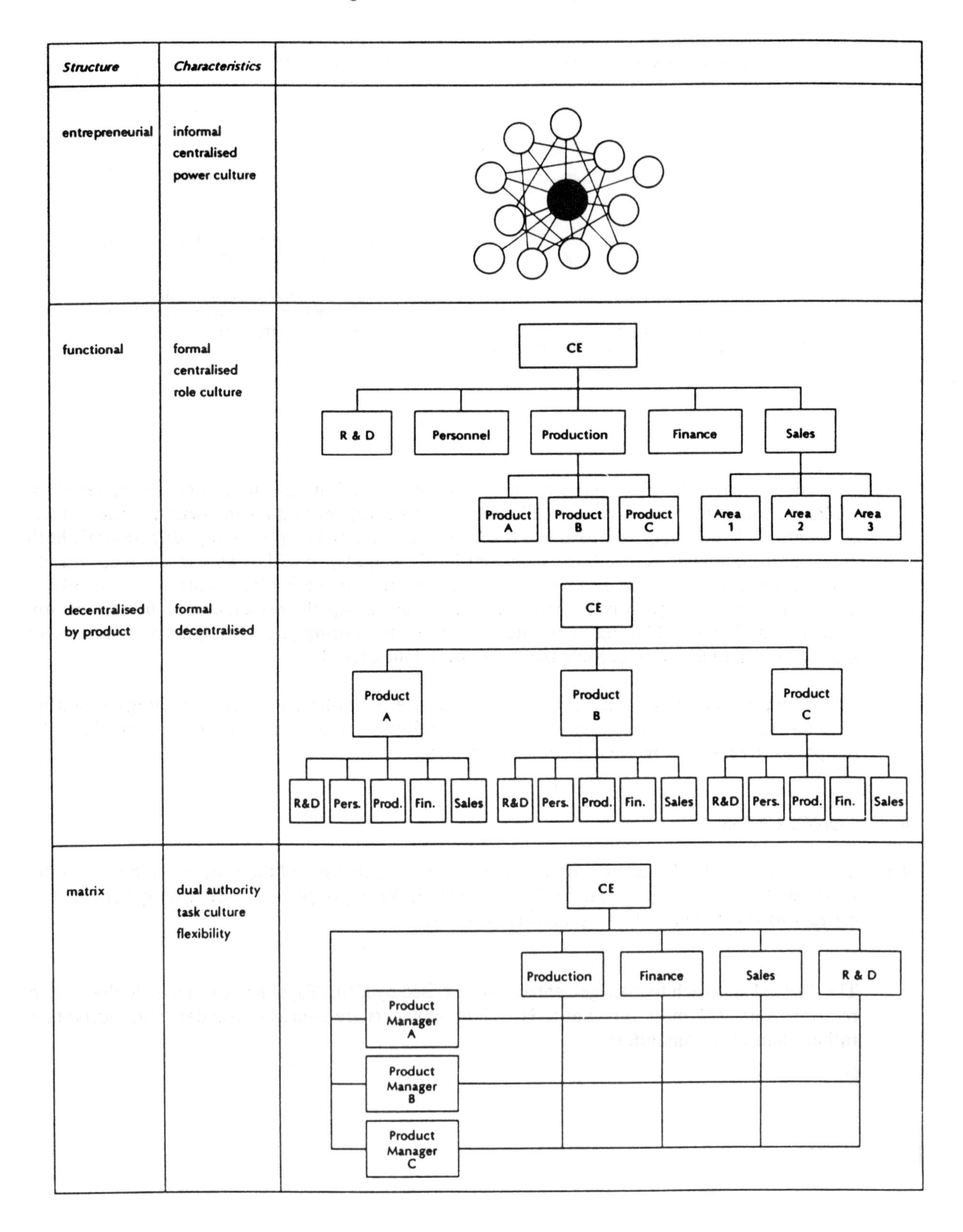

Structure	*Characteristics*
entrepreneurial	informal centralised power culture
functional	formal centralised role culture
decentralised by product	formal decentralised
matrix	dual authority task culture flexibility

4.3 Peter Drucker classified the work of managers into five categories.

(a) Setting objectives.
(b) Organising the work.
(c) Motivating employees.
(d) Measuring performance.
(e) Developing people.

Another view of the work of managers is Charles Handy's description of the manager as a general practitioner responsible for the health of the business.

4.4 Organisations are in effect collections of individuals grouped together in departments or teams responsible for a function or task within the business. These groups have to be linked together if the organisation is to work. How they link together represents the structure of the organisation and exists both formally and informally.

4.5 The design of the formal organisation structure influences both the effectiveness of the operation and its culture. The development of matrix organisation structures reflects the growing recognition of the importance of organisational flexibility and adaptability.

4.6 The style of management and the 'atmosphere' of an organisation reflect its culture. Although intangible, 'the way we do things around here' is fundamentally important in influencing the effectiveness of the business and how it adapts to challenges and changes.

TEST YOUR KNOWLEDGE

The numbers in brackets refer to paragraphs of this chapter

1. List Fayol's five functions of management. Indicate where you would supplement his analysis or disagree with it. (1.4, 1.5, 1.8)

2. What are the dilemmas facing the manager? (1.19)

3. What is meant by the term 'informal organisation'? (2.11, 2.12)

4. What are the disadvantages of the informal structure? (2.14)

5. What factors influence the design of the formal organisation structure? (2.19)

6. What are the advantages of grouping organisational activities on the basis of products? (2.20)

7. What is a matrix organisation and what are its advantages over other organisation structures? (2.21, 2.24)

8. In what ways can the culture of an organisation have an impact on its effectiveness? (3.5)

9. What are the factors which may influence the organisational culture? (3.7)

Now try illustrative question 1

Chapter 2

THE DIMENSIONS OF PLANNING

This chapter covers the following topics.

1. What is planning and control?
2. The planning framework: objectives, strategies and tactics
3. The dimension of time

1. WHAT IS PLANNING AND CONTROL?

What is planning?

1.1 Planning is a fundamental part of the manager's role. It is the dynamic force which helps to drive the organisation forward by co-ordinating resources and channelling them towards the achievement of pre-determined goals.

1.2 Planning does not ensure success, but it does improve the chances of success and reduce the risks of failure. The future cannot be foreseen with certainty and even the best-laid plans will go wrong to a greater or lesser degree. Nevertheless, plans give direction to an organisation. Without plans, events will be left to chance.

Exercise

In business the process of planning is formal, but you are already very skilled in a more informal version of the same activity. Planning is also a fundamental activity in our own personal lives. Take some time to analyse the steps you would take when planning a holiday, a long car journey or a dinner party. Make a note of these. As you work through the remainder of this chapter identify the business parallel to each of your planning steps.

1.3 The rationale for the planning activity is the same in business as it is in your private life. Planning gives us some influence over an uncertain future. By deciding what you want to achieve or what you want to happen in the future, you can take logical steps which will help you to achieve this goal. By building on your current planning competences you should find that the principles and techniques for business planning will soon become second nature to you.

1.4 If individuals and groups within an organisation are to be effective in working for the achievement of the organisation's objectives, they need to know what it is that they are expected to do. The purpose of planning is:

(a) to decide objectives for the organisation;
(b) to identify alternative ways of achieving them; and
(c) to select from amongst these alternatives for both the organisation as a whole, and also for individual departments, sections and groups within it.

1.5 Planning therefore involves decisions about the following factors.

(a) What to do in the future.
(b) How to do it.
(c) When to do it.
(d) Who is to do it.

1.6 Corporate planning has been variously described as follows.

(a) 'Corporate planning is a comprehensive, future oriented, continuous process of management which is implemented within a formal framework. It is responsive to relevant changes in the external environment. It is concerned with both strategic and operational planning and through the participation of relevant members of the organisation, develops plans and actions at the appropriate levels in the organisation. It incorporates monitoring and control mechanisms and is concerned with both the short and the long term.'

(b) It is 'a systematic and disciplined study designed to help identify the objective of any organisation or corporate body, determine an appropriate target, decide upon suitable constraints, and devise a practical plan by which the objective may be achieved.'
(Argenti 1968)

Is strategic planning necessary?

1.7 Some companies might manage quite successfully without any formal system of corporate planning: perhaps they have just been lucky. It might be argued that strategic planning and formal plans would restrict an organisation's entrepreneurial flair (if it has any). But without a cohesive objective, companies are likely to under-utilise their resources and probably to duplicate them in some respects.

1.8 Long-range planning is particularly important for capital-intensive organisations that have a long lead time between deciding to invest in a new project and the investment coming to fruition and starting to earn money for the organisation.

1.9 The advantages of a formal system of strategic planning may be stated as follows.

(a) As companies increase in size, the *risks* also increase. (Risks would be defined as the potential losses from the inefficient or ineffective use of resources.) Strategic planning can reduce the risks.

(b) Strategic planning gives a sense of purpose to the personnel in the company, leading to an improved quality of management.

(c) It helps to encourage creativity and initiative by tapping the ideas of the management team and showing their contribution to the operation of the plan.

(d) Companies cannot remain static, they have to cope with changes in the environment. A strategic plan helps to chart the future possible areas where the company may be involved and draws attention to the need to keep on changing and adapting, not just to 'stand still' and survive.

(e) Strategic plans are merely stating on paper the departmental objectives which have always existed. They help to make them more effective and workable.

(f) A well-prepared plan drawn up after analysis of internal and external factors - risks and uncertainties - is in the long-term best interests of the company because better-quality decisions will be made (on the whole) and management control can be better exercised.

(g) Long-term, medium-term and short-term objectives, plans and controls can be made consistent with one another.

Strategic planning is organised entrepreneurship

1.10 To quote the businessman, Sir James Goldsmith: 'muddling through is a euphemism for failing to plan forward. It means acting tactically and without strategy; it means confusing the means with the end. If we continue to avoid facing the facts ... the epitaph on the graves of our democracy will be: "They sacrificed the long term for the short term, and the long term finally arrived."'

1.11 Peter Drucker wrote the following.

"Every one of the great business builders we know of - from the Medici to the founders of the Bank of England down to Thomas Watson in our day - had a definite idea, a clear 'theory of the business' which informed his actions and decisions. Indeed a clear, simple and penetrating 'theory of the business' rather than an 'intuition' characterises the truly successful entrepreneur, the man who not only amasses a large fortune but builds an organisation that can endure and grow long after he is gone.

But the individual entrepreneur does not need to analyse his concepts and to explain his 'theory of the business' to others, let alone spell out the details. He is in one person, thinker, analyst and executor. Business enterprise, however, requires that entrepreneurship be systemised, spelled out as a discipline and organised as work."

Strategic planning as 'freewheeling opportunism'

1.12 A second approach to strategic planning is to operate a system whereby opportunities are exploited as they arise, judged on their individual merits and not within the rigid structure of an overall corporate strategy. This approach contrasts with the generally accepted principles of disciplined strategic planning and is sometimes called *freewheeling opportunism* .

1.13 The advantages of this approach are as follows.

(a) Opportunities can be seized when they arise, whereas a rigid planning framework might impose restrictions so that the opportunities are lost.

(b) It is flexible and adaptable. A formal corporate plan might take a long time to prepare and is fully documented. Any sudden, unexpected change (for example a very steep rise in the price of a key commodity) might cause serious disruption, so that the process of preparing a new components plan would be slow. A freewheeling opportunistic approach would adapt to the change more quickly.

(c) It might encourage a more flexible, creative attitude among lower-level managers, whereas the procedures of formal planning might not.

1.14 On the other hand, there are disadvantages to the freewheeling opportunism approach to strategic planning.

(a) It fails to provide a co-ordinating framework for the organisation as a whole, so that there would be a tendency for large organisations to break up into many fragments.

(b) It cannot guarantee that all opportunities are identified and appraised. A well-designed formal system should be more capable of identifying as many opportunities as possible. Strategic planning relies heavily on the creative thinking of its managers to design strategies and a formal system should be more thorough in exploiting this creativity to the full.

(c) It emphasises the profit motive to the exclusion of all other considerations.

1.15 Professor Bernard Taylor in his paper '*New dimensions in corporate planning*' re-iterates the fact that the way strategic planning is practised will vary with circumstances. Fitting the planning 'mode' to the situation will require a good deal of skill and experience.

(a) In a large bureaucratic organisation, this will probably require the introduction of a formal planning system.

(b) In circumstances where growth or innovation are required, it will be important to organise for new projects.

(c) In an uncertain situation with many interest groups involved, it may be advisable to use an incremental or organisational 'learning' process, to improve mutual understanding, to explore the problem, and possibly to evolve a consensus.

(d) If it is necessary to influence decisions in other organisations there may be a need for special arrangements to improve formal and informal contacts, for example through joint committees, liaison officers etc.

(e) Where there is a 'crisis of identity' in the organisation (for example if it is not thought to be socially valuable or if the future of the enterprise is tied up with the creation of a new technology with important social implications) it may be particularly important to re-examine the future role of the enterprise in society.

Barriers to good planning

1.16 Planning is obviously essential and an all-round 'good thing' for the organisation. In practice, however, many managers are reluctant to make formal plans, and prefer to operate without them, dealing with problems only when and if they arise. There may be many reasons for their reluctance to plan.

(a) *A lack of knowledge (or interest) about the purpose and goals of the organisation.* However, unless managers know what the organisation's goals are, and how other departments and sections are trying to work towards those goals, their own efforts might well have the following effects.

(i) They may duplicate the efforts of someone else, thereby causing a waste of time and resources.
(ii) They may conflict with the efforts of someone else.
(iii) They may simply be useless to the organisation.

Good planning encourages the co-ordination of efforts within an organisation.

(b) *A reluctance to be committed to one set of targets.* Planning involves making a choice about what to do, from amongst many different alternative courses of action. Managers might want to keep their options open, especially where the business environment is changing rapidly and the future is (even more than usually) uncertain: they will not want to have specific goals. Whereas this is understandable, and might be feasible in a very small organisation, it is unsatisfactory in any organisation where managers must co-ordinate their efforts and work together for the achievement of organisational goals. Freedom of choice could well be a recipe for *lack* of preparation for environmental changes, and a lack of co-ordinated response to economic, technological, social and political developments etc with which the organisation will be faced.

(c) *A fear of blame or criticism for failing to achieve planned targets.* By setting targets or plans, and later comparing actual performance against plans, it is possible to identify success or failure. When failure is 'punished' in any way (for example in the form of lower salaries or bonuses, thwarted promotion prospects and career ambitions, or even the displeasure of senior managers) managers might resent planning, because planning is the start of a process by which they might later be labelled as failures. The motivation to plan for inefficient performance will also be strong, since the likelihood of 'failure' will then be relatively low.

(d) *A manager's lack of confidence in performing the job efficiently and effectively,* or a lack of confidence in the organisation's senior management to provide the resources needed to achieve planned targets.

For example suppose that the manager of a supermarket branch is asked to plan the target volume of turnover and profits in the next two or three years. The manager might lack confidence in head office to provide enough resources (staff, equipment, product ranges, money for sales promotion etc) to achieve a reasonable targeted performance; or if there were sufficient resources, might doubt his own ability to ensure that the targets are achieved. The manager would then prefer instead not to have any plans or targets at all.

(e) *A manager's lack of information about what is going on in the 'environment'.* Managers need to know about the needs of customers, the nature of their markets and their competition, the strength of public opinion or government pressures, the state of the economy etc. Without such information, they will be unable to make plans for the future which are achievable in view of environmental conditions.

(f) *A manager's resentment of plans made for the department.* Some managers have plans imposed upon them without any prior consultation. If managers are told what to do and what the targets are, they are likely to resist the plan and find reasons why it is not achievable, especially if the politics of the situation and relationships with superiors are already 'sensitive'.

1.17 The barriers to good planning must be overcome.

(a) All levels of staff should be involved (to a greater or less degree) in the planning process. Imposing plans on staff without their participation, or without their opinions being sought, is a barrier to successful planning.

(b) Planners must be provided with the information they need (and access to sources of future information, when it arises) to plan properly. The source of information might be:
(i) outside the organisation, concerning environmental factors;
(ii) inside the organisation, concerning facts about the organisation itself. This information is called 'feedback'.

(c) A system of rewards for successful achievement of plans might be beneficial. However, a system of rewards is also a system of punishment for those managers who fail to earn rewards. The motivational problems of rewards and punishments are not easily overcome, and are likely to be a continual barrier to good planning.

(d) Managers should be taught the virtues of planning and the techniques of good planning. For example they should learn the value of co-ordinating efforts for the achievement of common goals. They should also learn that a subordinate can only be expected to achieve certain targets if given sufficient resources to do the job properly.

What is control?

1.18 Although the framework and process of planning is obviously important, today the emphasis is changing from producing plans to the skills needed to implement them. Managers are likely to be judged by their results, not by their intentions. Given that plans are produced with the intention of achieving a specified goal, progress towards that target and necessary modifications to the plan are an integral and essential element in the dynamic planning process.

1.19 Many managers view planning and controlling as two separate activities. However, Robert N Anthony argued in his book *Planning and control systems: a framework for analysis (1956)* that 'the trouble essentially is that, although planning and control are definable abstractions and are easily understood as calling for different types of mental activity, they do not relate to separable major categories of activities actually carried on in an organisation either at different times, or by different people, or for different situations.'

1.20 All managers often plan and control at the same time. Examples are as follows.

(a) In a budgetary control system, a sales manager might receive an adverse sales volume variance report at the end of May. After investigating the variance, the following actions might be taken.

(i) Inform superiors that sales forecasts for the rest of the year will need to be revised (planning activity).
(ii) Take action in an attempt to improve the current sales effort (control activity).

(b) A supervisor might be displeased with the poor quality or low productivity of an employee in the section and might therefore do the following.

(i) Speak to the employee and try to persuade them to improve performance (control activity).
(ii) Revise the estimate of output for the week (planning activity).
(iii) Tell the employee what job should be worked on next after finishing the current task (planning activity).

1.21 Koontz (1958) wrote:

'Planning and control are so closely interconnected as to be singularly inseparable' and

'The fact that there seem ... to be so many fewer principles of control than principles of planning indicates the extent to which control depends upon planning and how it is largely a technique for assuring that plans are realised.'

The cycle of control

1.22 The basic control process or control cycle has six stages.

(a) Making a plan; deciding what to do and identifying the desired results. Without plans there can be no control.

(b) Recording the plan formally or informally, in writing or by other means, statistically or descriptively. The plan should incorporate standards of efficiency or targets of performance.

(c) Carrying out the plan, or having it carried out by subordinates, and measuring actual results achieved.

(d) Comparing actual results against the plans. This is sometimes referred to as the provision of 'feedback'.

(e) Evaluating the comparison, and deciding whether further action is necessary to ensure the plan is achieved.

(f) Where corrective action is necessary, this should be implemented. Alternatively, the plan itself may need adjusting (for example if targets were unrealistic or have been overtaken by events, or if actual results are *better* than planned).

1.23 Once managers have established clearly quantified objectives the process of control is straightforward, but it is dependent on two things.

(a) Feedback on performance.
(b) Willingness and ability to modify plans in the light of changing circumstances and improved information.

1.24 Without controls the process of planning is a sterile exercise unlikely to help the organisation to achieve success. Planning and control systems must therefore be developed together and seen as two sides of a coin, different and distinguishable but inseparable.

2. THE PLANNING FRAMEWORK: OBJECTIVES, STRATEGIES AND TACTICS

2.1 Clarifying the level of planning within the overall framework of the business plan causes students and managers a great deal of difficulty. The confusion arises because the principles and language of planning are so commonplace that we all use them freely, for example we refer to tactics on the football field and battle plans and strategies in times of war.

Defining the terms

2.2 In whatever context it is used, the terminology of planning has broadly similar meaning.

- *Objectives* are what we are trying to achieve. To be of value they should be quantified over time, for example 'we want to be two goals ahead by half time' or 'we want to have sold 5,000 units by March'. Without quantification objectives are actually much less effective *aims*, which do not lend themselves to control measures.

- *Strategy* is a broad statement of how we intend to achieve our objectives, for example by adopting an attacking strategy on the football field or by using a sales push strategy in the market place.

  Strategy is necessary because there are always alternative approaches to achieving the same objective, for example profits can be increased, by cutting costs or by raising revenue. A clear strategy ensures that the organisation's efforts are all channelled not only in the same direction, but down the same path.

- *Tactics* are the details of the plan, for example we will substitute defender Y with attacker X after 25 minutes or we will increase our sales push with a telesales campaign, operated by an agency and targeted at 6,000 client leads over three months from January.

Clarifying the level

2.3 From the office junior to the managing director, everyone plans their work and decides how best to allocate their resources (possibly only time) to achieve the objectives which have been set. As a result people at all levels of the organisation will talk about their objectives, strategy and tactics. To avoid confusion it is necessary to clarify the level in the organisation at which the individual is working.

2.4 Imagine that you are on a flight of stairs. As you step down from one level to another, the tactics of the higher level becomes the strategy of the lower one.

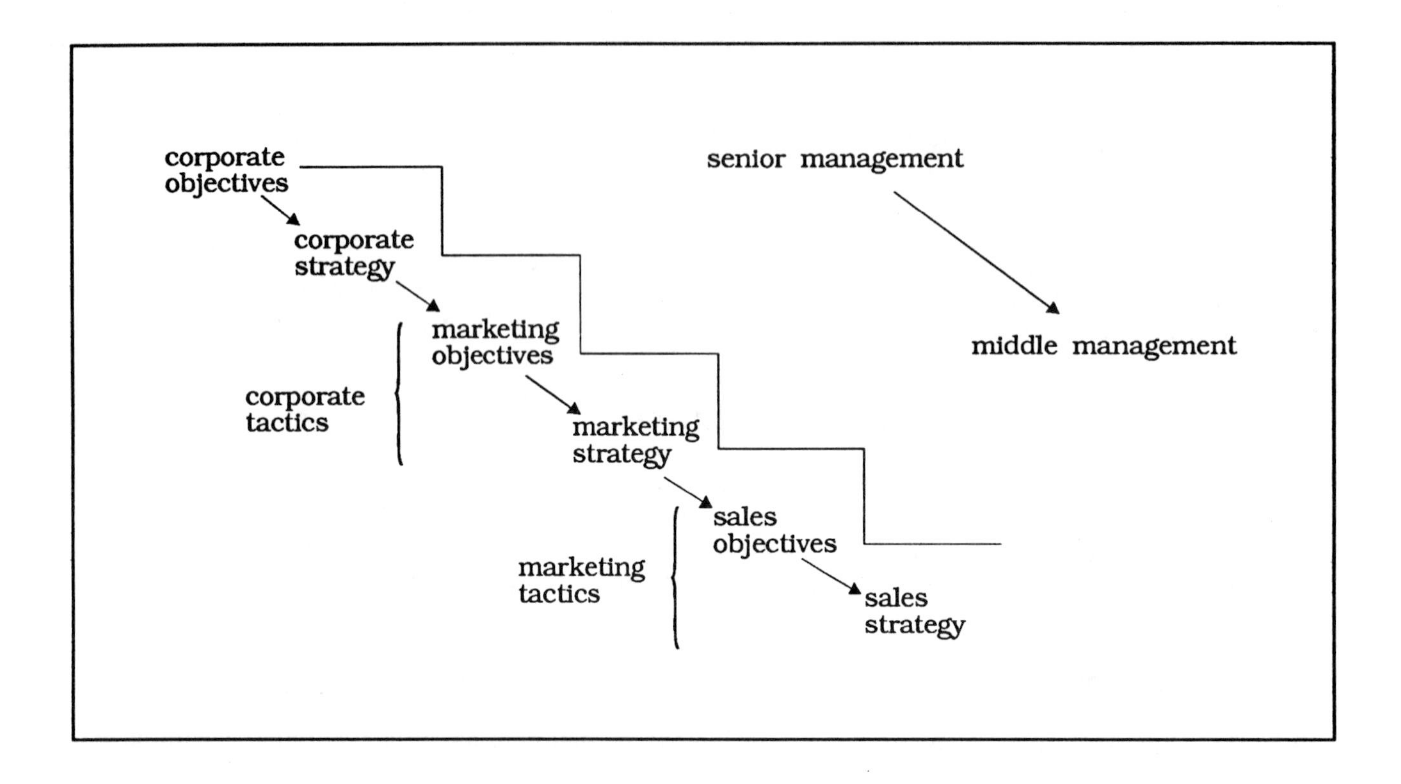

2.5 If you are in any doubt when dealing with planning, start by checking which level of the organisation you are concerned with. As you move down the staircase the process remains the same, but the emphasis changes.

- At corporate level the focus is on the organisation as a whole. Objectives will be expressed in financial terms, for example return on investment or profit, and strategy has to provide direction to the functional areas of the business, for example finance, operations and marketing. The details of implementing this strategy are tactics to the managing director, but represent strategic direction to the functional heads.

- At marketing department level the focus is on the marketing activity. Objectives are shaped against the corporate objectives and strategy and they are expressed in marketing terms, for example market share or sales volume. Marketing strategy indicates how the marketing mix will be set to achieve these objectives and the marketing tactics include details of their implementation. In turn these details are expressed in terms of distribution, research and advertising strategies.

Strategic planning, management control and operational control

2.6 Robert Anthony used three levels or tiers of management decision making as an alternative analysis of planning and control systems.

(a) *Strategic planning:* the process of deciding on objectives of the organisation, on changes in these objectives, on the resources used to attain these objectives and on the policies that are to govern the acquisition, use and disposition of these resources.

(b) *Management control:* the process by which managers assure that resources are obtained and used effectively and efficiently in the accomplishment of the organisation's objectives.

(c) *Operational control:* the process of assuring that specific tasks are carried out effectively and efficiently.

2.7 In spite of the misleading use of the words 'planning' and 'control' in these three titles, each level of decision making includes elements of both planning and control (although perhaps in varying proportions). What clearly exists within the planning framework is a hierarchy of decisions, one level dependent on the other. It is corporate level decision making which establishes the parameters and framework within which all other departments and sections operate to contribute their part to the achievement of the overall picture.

The strategic planning process

2.8 Professor John Higgins has defined *strategic planning* as 'comprehending the environment, and ensuring that the organisation adapts to that environment.'

Strategic planning is a complex process, which involves taking a view of the organisation and of the future that it is likely to encounter, and then attempting to organise the structure and resources of the organisation accordingly.

What does strategic planning involve?

2.9 Johnson and Scholes *(Exploring corporate strategy)* have summarised the characteristics of strategic decisions for an organisation as follows.

(a) Strategic decisions will be concerned with the *scope* of the organisation's activities.

(b) Strategy involves the matching of an organisation's activities to the *environment* in which it operates.

(c) Strategy also involves the matching of an organisation's activities to its *resource capability.*

(d) Strategic decisions therefore involve major decisions about the *allocation* or *re-allocation of resources.*

(e) Strategic decisions will *affect operational decisions*, because they will set off a chain of 'lesser' decisions and operational activities, involving the use of resources.

(f) Strategic decisions will be affected not just by (1) environmental considerations and (2) resource availability, but also by (3) the *values and expectations of the people in power* within the organisation.

(g) Strategic decisions are likely to affect the *long-term direction* that the organisation takes.

(h) Strategic decisions have implications for change throughout the organisation, and so are likely to be *complex in nature.*

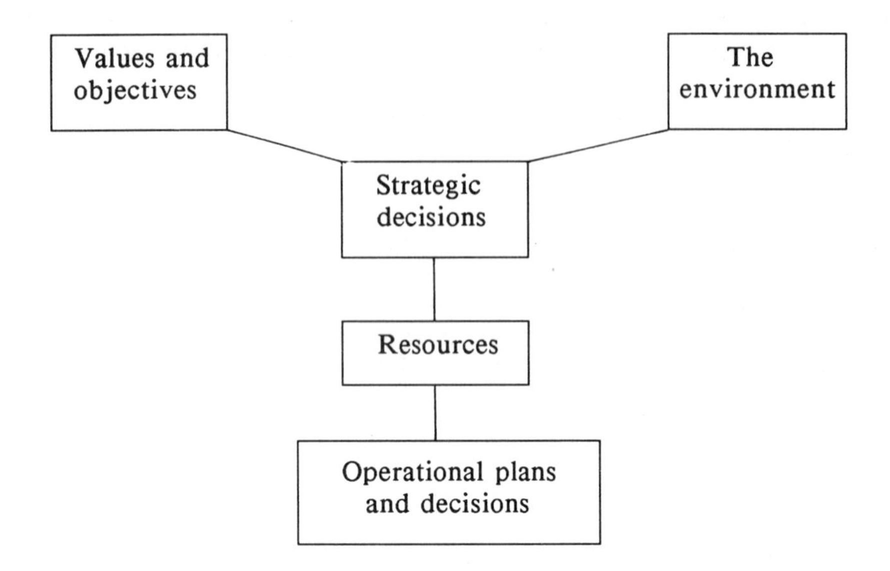

The steps in strategic planning

2.10 Professor JC Higgins of the University of Bradford Management Centre describes the strategic planning process as embracing the following.

(a) Setting corporate/strategic *objectives*. These should be expressed in quantitative terms, with any *constraints* identified.

(b) From (a), establishing targets for corporate performance in terms of return, earnings per share (EPS), sales turnover etc, over the planning period.

(c) *Internal appraisal*, by means of assessing the organisation's current state in terms of resources and performance.

(d) *External appraisal*, by means of a survey and analysis of the organisation's environment.

(e) Forecasting future performance based on the information obtained from (c) and (d), initially as purely *passive extrapolations into the future* of past and current achievements.

(f) Analysing the *gap* between the results of (b) and (e).

(g) Identifying and evaluating various strategies to reduce this 'performance gap' in order to meet strategic objectives.

(h) Choosing between alternative strategies.

(i) Preparing the final corporate plan, with divisions between short term and long term as appropriate.

(j) Implementing the chosen strategies.

(k) Evaluating actual performance against the corporate plan.

2.11 In the remaining chapters of this study text we will be examining each of the stages of the planning process from analysis of the situation, through decision making to implementation of plans.

2.12 This process of planning is a logical one which should reflect the steps you identified in your personal planning analysis undertaken in the exercise at the beginning of this chapter.

	Activity
Where are we now?	An assessment or audit of the current position or opportunity
Where are we going?	Agreement of quantified objectives
How do we get there?	Identification of the alternative courses of action available to achieve the objective and the selection of the most appropriate strategy
Adding detail to the plan	Developing tactical action plans, including budgets to implement the chosen strategy
Are we on the right track?	Review and modification of the plan as it is implemented and our progress against objectives can be assessed

The focus of planning

2.13 At what management level are you positioned? This is the first question you need to ask yourself when presented with a new planning project or scenario. As we have said, the process and framework of planning is the same whether you are the managing director, marketing manager or sales manager. The focus does differ and it is essential that you keep a clear picture of who you are and what your area of authority is. For example the marketing strategy should include decisions about the positioning of the product range, it should not recommend the purchase of a new factory! It is equally easy for a marketing student when questioned on corporate planning to write extensively on strategy for the marketing mix and give scant attention to operations, finance and organisational considerations.

3. THE DIMENSION OF TIME

3.1 Having established the level and framework of decision making there still remains one of the dilemmas of management which we considered in chapter 1: the time dimension.

3.2 You might recall how important it is that objectives are set against a time frame, but how far ahead should managers be looking?

3.3 Planners must decide what the planning period ought to be. The planning period ought to be the period of time which is most suitable for planning requirements and which enables the decision making and control processes to be most effectively exercised. The most suitable length for the planning period varies with circumstances, for example nuclear fuels or forestry may require many years, but pop and fashion industries could be working in months.

3.4 However a failure to take a long enough view to planning can be risky. Managers who are dominated by the short-term problems and objectives of the business can miss long-term opportunities and/or fail to identify emerging threats. British managers have in the past been accused of taking a short-term view of business and have consequently faired badly compared with competitors, particularly those from the Far East.

Defining the long and short term

3.5 (a) *Long term* is usually five years, but in some industries or for some major capital investment projects (for example the Channel Tunnel project) this time may be seven years or even ten years.

(b) *Short term is* usually annual and forms part of a long-term plan. For example, year 1 of a five year long-term plan is a short-term plan. The results achieved would be evaluated at the end of year 1 and the next short-term plan (and, perhaps, the long-term plan) would be modified.

3.6 The problem is that the further ahead you look the more imprecise planning becomes. Forecasting becomes more uncertain with even key variables like interest rates and employment levels more and more difficult to predict. Long-term plans therefore have to be 'broad brush' pictures of the organisation's future. Modification will be necessary as more information becomes available and managers need to be clear that long-term goals are most likely to be achieved by a series of short-term strategies which may not follow a direct path.

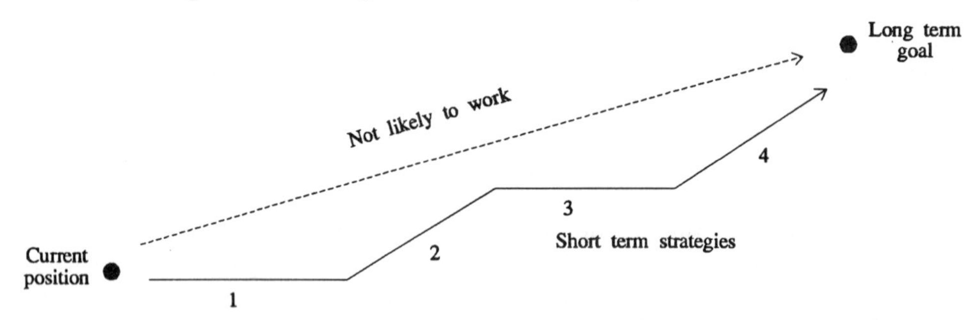

3.7 Long-term planning, even beyond the planning horizon (the furthest time ahead for which plans can be usefully quantified) is still a useful activity as it provides managers with a picture of how the organisation should be developing.

Contingency and scenario planning

3.8 Planning within the planning period but beyond the planning horizon is known as futuristic planning. It has been defined by the Chartered Institute of Management Accountants (CIMA) as follows.

'Planning for that period of time which extends beyond the planning horizon in the form of future expected conditions which may exist in respect of the entity, products/services and environment but which cannot usefully be expressed in quantified terms.

An example would be working out the actions needed in a future with no motor cars.'

3.9 A contingency is an event that is liable, but not certain, to occur. For corporate planners, a contingency is a possible future event which, on the balance of probabilities, they do not expect to happen, but if it were to happen, there would be nothing the organisation's management could do to stop it.

3.10 It is an unhappy fact of commercial life that uncontrollable events do happen. If it is expected to happen, it can be planned for, and since it is provided for in the plan, it would not be a contingency. Contingencies are uncontrollable events which are not provided for in the main plan.

Contingencies which are anticipated events

3.11 Where contingencies are known about, *contingency plans should be prepared in advance* to deal with the situation if and when it arises. Such plans might be prepared in detail, or in outline only, depending on the likelihood that the contingency will become a reality. As an example, a company heavily involved in exporting or importing goods in a competitive market will be susceptible to fluctuations in foreign exchange rates. Although the risks of foreign exchange exposure can be reduced, by matching assets and liabilities in each currency the company deals in, and in the short term by means of forward exchange contracts, the company will almost certainly be unable to eliminate foreign exchange risks over its longer-term corporate planning period. Contingency plans can be prepared to deal with adverse exchange rate movements, by speculating how far rates might alter and calculating the implications of various degrees of change.

3.12 Scenario planning is being used increasingly, particularly by the larger multinational organisations such as Shell. In recognition of the uncertainty of future events management undertake the development of a series of plans against a range of scenarios or 'what if' backgrounds. This investment in planning not only gives managers more experience in the techniques of planning, but also provides organisations with a competitive edge when future events unfold.

3.13 One of the mistakes often made by CIM students is to develop plans which are unrealistic. A frequent factor in this is the failure to consider the time frame of plans, for example objective: to double sales over the next twelve months; student's proposed strategy: to double the sales force.

Reality: such a decision taken and implemented today might increase sales by perhaps 50%, but not the required 100%. This is because the plan fails to consider the time lags and practical issues involved in implementing the strategy. Recruitment, selection and training of the additional sales team is likely to take at least six months to complete. The additional sales team will therefore only be effective for about half a year.

4. CONCLUSION

4.1 Planning is a fundamental activity of business and personal life. Its function is to co-ordinate resources to increase the chances of achieving pre-determined objectives.

4.2 Planning involves making decisions about what has to be done, how and when it should be done and who should do it. An integral part of the planning process is control. If plans are to be successful then systems must be established for their modification in the light of outcomes.

4.3 There are a number of barriers to planning which senior management must tackle if they wish to establish a successful planning culture within their organisation.

4.4 It is important to recognise the hierarchical level of planning and control decisions, because decision makers can only make plans or take control action within the sphere of the authority that has been delegated to them. It is particularly important to bear in mind the time span of decisions and the importance of the potential consequences of individual decisions.

4.5 Understanding planning is dependent on your clarification of the level of planning being considered. The process is always the same but the focus changes as you move through the planning hierarchy.

4.6 Organisations must take a long-term as well as a short-term view of their business if they are to thrive in a rapidly changing business environment.

TEST YOUR KNOWLEDGE

The numbers in brackets refer to paragraphs of this chapter

1. What is the purpose of planning? (1.4)
2. What are the main barriers to good business planning? (1.16)
3. How would you go about ensuring good planning takes place in a business? (1.17)
4. Why are controls important in the planning process? (1.23)
5. What is the distinction between:
   - aims and objectives
   - strategy and tactics? (2.2)
6. What is the focus of a plan at:
   - corporate level
   - marketing department level? (2.5)
7. Why should managers be concerned with the long term? (3.4)
8. How would you distinguish between the long and short term? (3.5)
9. What is meant by the term planning horizon? (3.7)
10. How would you define:
    - futuristic planning (3.8)
    - scenario planning? (3.12)

Now try illustrative questions 2 and 3

Chapter 3

ENVIRONMENTAL INFLUENCES ON PLANNING

This chapter covers the following topics.

1. EXTERNAL INFLUENCES ON PLANNING

1.1 Business plans cannot be produced in a vacuum. They must be developed within the context of the wider environment in which the organisation is operating. They need to take into account the opportunities and threats which are emerging as these external factors change. To ensure this appropriateness of plans, the first critical step in planning entails a thorough assessment of the relevant environment. This situational audit ensures that subsequent plans are relevant and realistic and achievable for the organisation.

1.2 External influences do impact on both corporate and marketing plans and it is important that you are able to do the following.

(a) Recognise the influences of the environment on an organisation.

(b) Identify how environmental changes, in any given situation, might create threats, opportunities and organisational problems - and how management should respond to the changes.

Exercise 1

Choose a business/market with which you are familiar. How has it changed over the last five years? Produce a list of all the external factors (things which the organisation cannot control) which have had a significant impact on the operation in that time. Refine your list as you work through the rest of this chapter.

What is the environment?

1.3 The term 'environment' is very broad. It covers all the economic, political, social, cultural, legal, technological and demographic influences in the countries an organisation operates in, as well as the influences of customers and competitors in the organisation's 'markets'. All these factors share the same characteristic: they have an impact on the performance of the organisation, but they cannot be controlled by management.

1.4 Strategic planners must therefore take account of environmental influences, and try to estimate what these might be, in order to produce plans that are realistic and achievable. Given the continual changes in the environment, this is by no means an easy task. M E Porter (*Competitive strategy*) has written the following.

> 'The essence of formulating competitive strategy is relating a company to its environment.' and
>
> 'Every industry has an underlying structure or set of fundamental economic and technical characteristics ... The strategist must learn what makes the environment tick.'

1.5 When you answer an examination question which is a case study problem, you might be expected to think about the *specific* environmental influences that might be relevant to the particular situation.

1.6 Although both in minicases and in the major analysis and decision case study you are restricted to using only the information provided, you are expected to bring to bear your general knowledge and general business and marketing awareness. This is particularly evident when dealing with case examples set in an international context where you are expected to have a knowledge of the major environmental parameters in other countries.

1.7 This chapter will describe in general terms the environmental variables which planners need to consider and evaluate before developing their plans. How these variables impact on the business will be unique to that particular operation and so you need to think about them in context.

Exercise 2

Choose an industrial product, a consumer durable, a fast moving consumer good, and a service business. For each of them identify how you think the environmental factors identified in the following paragraphs might affect a business operating in that market.

---

2. THE ECONOMIC ENVIRONMENT

2.1 The state of the economy affects all organisations, both commercial and non-commercial.

The rate of growth in the economy is a measure of the overall change in demand for goods and services. Growth is an indication of increases in demand. For example an increase in gross national product per head of the population might result in a greater demand for private cars and less demand for public transport, or a greater demand for certain domestic consumer goods, such as video recorders, dishwashers and compact disc players.

However, if there are regional variations in the rate of growth then demand will be different in different geographic segments of the market.

2.2 Other economic influences on an organisation include the following.

(a) *At a regional or national level*

(i) The rate of inflation.
(ii) Unemployment and the availability of manpower.
(iii) Interest rates.
(iv) The balance of trade and foreign exchange rates.
(v) The level and type of taxation.
(vi) The propensity to save within the community.
(vii) The availability of credit.

(b) *At an international level*

(i) Comparative growth rates, inflation rates, interest rates and wage rates in other countries.
(ii) The extent of protectionist measures against imports.
(iii) The nature and extent of exchange controls in various countries.
(iv) The development of international economic communities such as the European Community and the prospects of international trade agreements between countries.
(v) The levels of corporate and personal taxation in different countries.

2.3 Obviously, in general terms, the state of the economy will influence the planning process for organisations which operate within it. In times of boom and increased demand and consumption, the overall planning problem will be to satisfy the demand. Conversely, in times of recession, the emphasis will be on cost-effectiveness, continuing profitability, survival and competition. Whether the organisation is in a buyers' market or a sellers' market will also have an important bearing on strategic plans.

Economists can contribute to the strategic planning process with economic forecasts and information about economic trends.

Economic trends - regional, national and international

2.4 Three levels of economic trend analysis need to be considered; regional (area) trends, national trends and international trends.

2.5 A company's *local* geographical environment is important. It might be located in a growth area full of modern thriving industry, such as Milton Keynes. Or it may be located in an area of urban decay like parts of the North East, Clydeside or Merseyside. The economic future of the area will affect wage rates, availability of labour, disposable income of local consumers, unemployment, the provision of roads and other services etc. As an example of this, you might consider the implications of the M25, London's orbital motorway. Planners were concerned that its development would favour greenbelt areas around London and reinforce inner city decay.

2.6 *National* economic trends which can be of interest to strategic planners are the prospects for national economic growth and growth in national income per head of population, population growth and changing demographic trends, trends in price inflation, unemployment, international trade, the balance of payments and taxation levels. These are factors over which an organisation has no direct control, but which should be 'exogenous' variables (ie external, or arising from outside) in the organisation's strategic plans.

2.7 National economic trends must be viewed within the context of *world trends*. Although world trends might seem remote to the small or medium-sized business, they can in fact have an important influence on the future of any company with plans to trade abroad, whether in buying imports or selling as exporters.

2.8 There are four economic groupings within the world.

Category	*Characteristic*
Western democracies (including Japan)	Stable economic growth although variable between different countries; politically, fairly stable; low population growth; low growth in basic industries; emphasis more on high technology industries, service industries (for example leisure) and personal care; increased market segmentation and choice for the consumer.
Eastern Europe and USSR	Bias toward heavy industry, but technologically backward, and undergoing economic upheaval. This varies from individual country to country, but 'perestroika' in the USSR, reinforced now by the failed coup and attempts in Poland and Hungary to move towards free market economies, with privatisation of many state industries, have created major potential new opportunities (and risks) for Western organisations.
Less developed countries (LDCs)	Living standards are low, with little hope of improvement; rising population; low education standards; inadequate infrastructure of roads, telecommunications, financial markets etc.
Developing nations	Fast growth in GNP; low wages by Western standards; consumer goods are scarce; infrastructure being provided; income and wealth unevenly distributed; possibly politically unstable; often high rates of inflation and severe problems with repayment of debts to foreign banks.

2.9 At present, trade between the groups is severely distorted. The less developed countries in particular suffered from the explosion in oil prices in 1973/74 and 1979, because they were unable to raise money from exports to pay the high cost of their oil imports. The developing countries represent a serious threat to the Western economies because of low wage rates and high industrial discipline (for example Singapore, Taiwan, South Korea) although some (Brazil, Mexico etc) have serious international debt problems that have restricted their economic growth in the 1980s. Communist China, on the other hand, represents a great opportunity, with its expanding economy and huge potential markets, although political circumstances might slow down the development of Chinese markets by the West and Japan.

2.10 Argenti identifies one particular factor which translates world trends and national trends down to the level of the small and medium-sized company, and that is the implication of economic trends upon organisation size itself. Two developments in particular seem evident.

(a) For standard, basic goods in mass markets, there is a trend towards larger organisations, with a few companies supplying virtually the entire world demand (for example motor cars).

(b) At the other end of the size spectrum, there is a continuing emergence of products and services with an individual personal appeal, leading to product differentiation and market segmentation. Here the trend may well be towards small company operations and greater specialisation.

Economic change

2.11 The economic environment changes continually. World trade and national economies go through cycles of growth and recession. Interest rates and foreign exchange rates fluctuate. Some countries achieve substantial growth over a long period of time (for example Japan) whereas others have been in relative decline for a long time.

2.12 Predicted changes or developments in the economic environment can be vitally important for planning decisions. Here are just two examples.

(a) Courtaulds in the early to mid-1980s recognised that its markets in the Third World countries were going to remain low-growth markets because of the low economic growth that these countries were expected to achieve. As a consequence, the company took a strategic decision to develop more technologically-advanced fibres in order to expand sales and achieve growth in Western European markets instead.

(b) The building of the Channel Tunnel should radically transform the transportation of goods between the UK and mainland Europe, with many more goods now being sent by rail instead of by road and sea, or by air.

The single European market 1992

2.13 You will know that changes to EC rules mean that from 31 December 1992, the 'single European market' will be in existence.

But do you know what the detail of the proposed changes are? Have you thought about how they might affect the future of your own organisation, if at all?

2.14 It may be useful to look briefly at what the 1992 changes will mean.

(a) Certain *technical barriers* to the free movement of goods between countries in the EC will be removed. Technical barriers fragment the market, and force producers to manufacture modified goods, at higher cost, for each separate fragment. There are a number of ways in which the barriers are created.

  (i) Differing national product standards for the quality and safety of goods. These barriers are being eliminated, and harmonised European standards established.

  (ii) Differing food laws, for example on food labelling, and safety and hygiene standards. An EC food harmonisation programme has been introduced.

  (iii) Differing regulations for controlling the access of pharmaceuticals (medicines) to the market. EC proposals for a single market cover licensing new medicines, eliminating disparities in national systems of medicine pricing and the marketing of medicine products.

(b) *Public purchasing*. Public contracts are often lucrative for companies that win them. In the past there has been a tendency for contracts to be awarded by governments to 'national' companies. EC rules will open up the market for goods purchased by governments of member countries, by making sure that all companies in the Community have an equal chance to seek individual public contracts.

(c) *Telecommunications*. The EC is hoping to open up telecommunications markets to greater competition, by eliminating differences in national standards for telecommunications equipment.

(d) *Information technology*. The EC is promoting the creation of a common set of standards for IT equipment (OSI standards), so that IT equipment can be linked and work together, regardless of who manufactures each item.

(e) *Financial services*. There is a continuing process of abolition of national barriers which restrict the provision of financial services between EC countries. Measures include the liberalisation of capital movements, and EC regulations for banks and banking activities.

Similarly, barriers preventing the provision of cross-border insurance services will be removed, and insurance companies in the EC will be able to sell insurance policies to customers in any member country.

(f) *Capital movements*. By 1992, the EC hopes to have achieved the complete liberalisation of capital movements within the Community.

(g) *Transport*. Measures will be taken to liberalise transport services, so as to increase competition and make it easier for companies in one EC country to compete in other EC countries. Liberalisation measures are being applied to road haulage, shipping and civil aviation.

(h) *Professional services*. Professionally-qualified people in one country are currently restricted from practising in another EC country (unless they requalify). These restrictions on the free movement of labour apply to accountants, lawyers and teachers etc. It is proposed to remove them by the end of 1992. The CIM has won European recognition for its Diploma, so you would not be expected to take any further marketing qualification to practise in other European countries, although you may be required to demonstrate your language competence.

Company planning for 1992

2.15 Can you see how these changes should force companies within the EC to assess their planning for 1992 and beyond? Here are just a few ideas. They are intended to illustrate how environmental change has a direct relevance to strategic planning and marketing by individual companies.

2.16 The Department of Trade and Industry listed seven key questions of business strategy, which UK firms (and other EC firms) should face up to, in view of these approaching changes.

(a) How has the market changed for our business?

(b) Should we shift from being a UK firm with a UK market, to a European firm with a European market?

(c) If we became a European firm with a European market, would this alter the *scale of our operations?*

(d) In what ways will we become vulnerable in our existing markets to new or greater competition?

(e) Is our management structure suitable for exploiting new opportunities, and taking defensive measures against new threats?

(f) Should we be seeking mergers or takeovers to strengthen our market position, broaden our product range, or spread our financial risk?

(g) Who in the firm is going to be responsible for making the key decisions about how to exploit the single market opportunities?

2.17 It is worth stressing that this example of the changes in the European Community, to create a single market, is just one example of environmental change. This chapter has developed the example at some length, in order to suggest how you should try to adapt an organisation's planning strategy to changes, either when they occur or as soon as they are foreseen.

3. THE POLITICAL ENVIRONMENT

3.1 Many economic forecasts ignore the implications of a change in government policy, irrespective of whether or not there is a change of government. However, at national level, political influence is significant and not just limited to legislation on trading, pricing, dividends, tax, employment or health and safety (to list but a few).

Politics saw a swing towards more power to shop floor trade unionists during the 1970s, and also a greater liberalising of international trade, creating new markets. The 1980s have seen attempts by the UK government to halt the growing influence of unions, and since the recession in the world's economy in the early part of the decade, calls for protectionist measures in international trade have remained fairly persistent.

3.2 Other areas that are under political influence in a mixed economy include the following.

(a) The government controls much of the economy, being the nation's largest supplier, employer, customer and investor. The slightest shift in political emphasis can decimate a particular market almost overnight. Aerospace and defence are particularly vulnerable to shifts in political decisions and in the UK, current government policy towards both the health service and the railways has serious implications for companies' order books (ie for the firms supplying those industries).

(b) Nationalism: for a variety of reasons, nations wish to 'do their own thing'. The shipping and airline industries have been particularly affected by the desire and insistence of many countries to have their own fleets. Elsewhere, countries are demanding direct equity interests in any foreign company businesses operating in them, to prevent the development of 'robber economies' whereby multinationals plunder the country by taking out all the profits they earn.

Political change

3.3 Given that organisations must operate within a political environment, it is political *change* that complicates the task of predicting future influences, and planning to meet them. It has been suggested, for example, that in the run-up to a general election in the UK, there might be speculative pressures on UK interest rates and the foreign exchange value of sterling, if dealers in the City of London and investors expected a change in the government in power after the election. Companies might therefore make contingency plans about what to do in the event of such a change.

3.4 Some political changes cannot easily be planned for. As an example, there was a strong world-wide political call for economic sanctions against South Africa in mid-1986, with one suggestion being that all British Airways flights to and from South Africa should be banned. British Airways could not develop long-term plans to respond to specific political decisions such as this, but given the likelihood that national airlines will be subjected to political pressures and restrictions, organisations such as British Airways could develop the strategy objective of not relying on a small number of routes for their profitability. In the event of a political ban on a part of its business, an organisation would still be able to fall back on its remaining business without undue worries about profitability and survival.

3.5 Strategic planners ought to be aware of the following.

(a) Whether political change could have a significant impact on their organisation.
(b) What form of influence the political change might have.
(c) What the extent of the consequences of any such change might be.
(d) What is the likelihood of the change taking place.
(e) How the organisation can plan to cope with the change, should it occur - scenario planning.

4. THE SOCIAL AND CULTURAL ENVIRONMENT

4.1 Social change involves changes in the nature, attitudes and habits of society. Social changes are continually happening, and *trends* can be identified. Argenti identifies three components in the relevance of social trends to businesses.

(a) A well-publicised aspect of the changing nature of society in the UK is the fall in the length of working week, the falling demand for labour and so high unemployment in the long term, earlier retirement etc. There have also been changes in housing characteristics, and there are continuing changes in the nature and standard of education.

Rising standards of living may result in wider ownership of automatic dishwashers, microwave ovens, compact disc players and sailing boats. All these changes have implications for sports, leisure and holiday industries. But perhaps the most significant recent social change in the UK has been the emergence of 'green issues' and public concern for the world's environment.

(b) Society's attitude to business and companies: in the UK, increasing social obligations and responsibilities are being heaped on to companies, not least with respect to environmental protection and ethical conduct (towards customers, employees etc). At the present time there is an unresolved debate about Sunday trading, and unresolved issues about the control over 'video nasties' and the regulation of the thriving video industry and the slowly-emerging cable TV industry.

(c) The workforce itself: in the 1960s and 1970s some commentators identified a decline of the 'Calvinistic work ethic' (people no longer believed in working hard to earn their pay). There is evidence that the Thatcher years at least slowed down, if not reversed this trend. There has also been a decline in 'blue collar jobs' and an increasing proportion of people employed hold 'white collar' clerical, supervisory or management jobs. The potential implications to firms of (social) trends among the workforce should be readily identifiable.

4.2 B R Jones (1979) classified the social factors in strategic planning in a slightly different way, as follows.

(a) *Underlying factors:* for example UK population trends, education policy and the educational standards of the workforce, attitudes to acquiring skills.

(b) *People at work:* the labour market, trade unions and work attitudes. These aspects relate to a politically sensitive area in which organisations are very much at the mercy of legislation and political pressures. For example legislation on equal treatment for men and women, on racial discrimination, minimum wages, redundancy pay, unfair dismissals, laws on strike action (for example compulsory strike ballots) and so on.

(c) *Individuals and society:* this category of social factors includes challenge to the existing social order, involvement by junior employees in decisions taken within their organisation, the social responsibility of employers to their employees, income and wealth distribution, and spending patterns.

Consumer credit growth: economic and social implications

4.3 A number of industrial countries have been experiencing a substantial growth in consumer credit in recent years, with credit card lending accounting for much of the growth. A rapid growth in consumer credit can have significant economic and social implications, which could affect the following types of firm.

(a) Firms that provide credit, for example banks, or retail stores with their own in-store credit cards.

(b) Firms that produce goods which are commonly bought with credit finance, for example house builders and property developers, motor car manufacturers, producers of other consumer durable goods.

4.4 The volume of consumer credit varies from country to country, but it may be useful to consider the recent experience of the UK.

(a) Consumer credit grew substantially in real terms during the 1980s. There were two main aspects of this growth.

(i) Credit card borrowing.

(ii) Mortgage borrowing. The mortgage borrowing has risen sharply due to:
(1) higher house prices, but also
(2) 'equity withdrawal', ie people obtaining extra finance for consumption by adding to their existing mortgage, with security provided by the higher market value of their home.

Recession and the slump in house prices in the early 1990s has temporarily slowed down this growth in credit.

(b) Credit cards are also commonly used for transactions purposes, with many cardholders clearing their outstanding balances each month.

(c) Society's attitude to debt appears to have changed. Being in debt, which used to be considered a sign of hardship and so 'socially' undesirable, is now seen much more as the norm. 'Gold cards' issued by credit card companies are in themselves something of a status symbol.

(d) There are signs, however, that consumer credit has expanded too far.

(i) Credit is easy to obtain. Many individuals hold a number of different credit cards and charge cards, including cards issued by retail stores and garages etc.

(ii) There is growing concern about the sizeable number of cardholders who have been unable to service the debts they have built up with their cards, during the recent period of high interest rates.

(e) In spite of this, giving credit is still profitable for financial institutions, despite growing competition in the financial markets and the increased incidence of bad debts.

Cultural changes

4.5 Each society has a certain culture, ie its own attitudes and ways of doing things, and so British culture differs from French culture, which differs from Jamaican culture, or Chinese culture, and so on. Within each society, there are many culture groups. Examples are as follows.

(a) Ethnic and racial cultures.
(b) Religious cultures.
(c) *Corporate cultures.* Most companies have a distinctive culture, which employees, management in particular, are expected to adopt.

Recognition of the different cultural variables is fundamental to any international marketing plan.

4.6 Corporate cultural change is perhaps associated with situations where two or more cultural groups come into contact for the first time. Examples might be as follows.

(a) A large public company might take over a smaller private company.
(b) A multinational company might establish a new subsidiary in a different country.

4.7 The strategic issues in such cultural changes would involve the integration between 'head office' and the subsidiary.

(a) How can employees in an acquired company be taught to adopt the culture of the group that has taken them over?

(b) How can employees in a different country be persuaded to work with ex-patriate senior managers? What concessions, if any, should head office allow to the 'local' culture of the subsidiary's country? How can the problems of language differences be overcome? Reconciliation of corporate cultures is essential if the integration is to succeed.

Again examiners would expect any plans recommended in such a scenario to reflect these issues.

Ethological and social responsibilities

4.8 A business must give some consideration to social trends when developing its corporate plan, but it should do more than simply recognise trends; it should recognise and specify its social responsibilities, or what Argenti calls its ethological responsibilities.

4.9 To this end, Argenti defines *ethos* as 'how a company thinks it should conduct itself in society'. A company should give consideration to the ethics of the following aspects of its operations.

(a) Employment policies (including attitudes to employing and paying women, minority groups, disabled people etc).

(b) Attitudes towards customers, competitors, suppliers, bankers, creditors, the government (national and local), foreign subsidiaries.

(c) Its dealings with foreign governments, especially where those governments have earned disapproval and condemnation from the international community.

(d) Its relationship with environmentalist groups.

(e) Its position in local communities.

4.10 One aspect of social and ethical responsibility is the organisation's effect on the ecology. Historically, it was sufficient for the entrepreneur to exploit natural resources and in doing so, provide wealth. The legacy of such an attitude can be seen, for example, in the blighted

Lower Swansea Valley, still suffering from the 19th century copper smelting industry, and the desolation which is evident in many of the old coal mining areas. It is no longer socially acceptable for firms to be allowed to do lasting damage to the ecology and the environment.

4.11 Long-term planning now requires urgent thinking about stewardship of natural resources. There is concern that many traditional energy sources may soon be exhausted and improved stewardship must be implemented. There are restrictions on the use of oil and gas for electricity generation in the United States, notably the state of Florida. As natural resources disappear, the demands of adequate stewardship will inevitably gather momentum.

4.12 Concern for the ecological environment is one of the most notable developments in recent years, and organisations are having to plan for change, for example spend money on developing products and production methods that are less damaging and harmful. The emerging demands for environmentally friendly products have resulted in new product/market opportunities for 'green' consumers, often at premium prices.

5. THE LEGAL AND TECHNOLOGICAL ENVIRONMENT

The legal environment

5.1 Organisations operate within a framework of laws, which is very broad in scope. For example laws may affect an organisation in the following ways.

(a) How an organisation does its business, for example the law of contract, laws on unfair selling practices and the safety of goods, the law of agency and so on. Occasionally, there are laws to restrict price increases, and legislation on promotional activities.

(b) How an organisation treats its employees (employment law, trade union law etc).

(c) How an organisation deals with its owners and gives information about its performance (for example the Companies Act).

(d) Criminal law.

5.2 Changes in UK law are often predictable. A government will publish a green paper discussing a proposed change in the law, before issuing a white paper and passing a bill through Parliament. Whenever a change in the law is a possibility, and if it is likely to have an impact on what an organisation can do, plans should be formulated about what to do if the change takes place.

The technological environment

5.3 Technological change is rapid, and organisations must adapt themselves to it. Technological change can affect the activities of organisations as follows.

(a) *The type of products or services that are made and sold.* For example, consumer markets have seen the emergence of home computers, compact discs and satellite TV; industrial markets have seen the emergence of custom-built microchips, robots and local area networks for office information systems; government markets have seen space rockets, space shuttles and equipment for the USA's Star Wars defence system. Technological changes can be relatively minor, such as the introduction of tennis and squash rackets with graphite frames, fluoride toothpaste and turbo-powered car engines.

(b) *The way in which products are made.* There is a continuing trend towards the use of modern labour-saving production equipment, such as robots. The manufacturing environment is undergoing rapid changes with the growth of advanced manufacturing technology.

(c) *The way in which services are provided.* For example, high-street banks encourage customers to use 'hole-in-the-wall' cash dispensers, and shops are now using computerised Point of Sale terminals at cash desks.

5.4 The effect of technological change might be as follows.

(a) To cut production costs and other costs of sale, and so (possibly) to reduce sales prices to the customer too.
(b) To develop better quality products and services.
(c) To develop products and services that did not exist before.
(d) To provide products or services to customers more quickly or effectively than before.

5.5 Organisations that operate in an environment where the pace of technological change is very fast must be flexible enough to adapt to change quickly and must plan for change and innovation, perhaps by spending heavily on R & D.

6. THE DEMOGRAPHIC ENVIRONMENT

6.1 Demography is the study of population and population trends. The following demographic factors are important to planners and have an impact on market segmentation.

(a) The rate of growth or decline in a national population and in regional populations.

(b) Changes in the age distribution of the population. In the UK, for example, factors such as longer life expectancy and the post Second World War baby boom are leading to a situation in which there will be an increasing proportion of the national population over retirement age.

(c) The concentration of population into certain geographical areas.

6.2 Demographic change has implications for the following.

(a) What services and products an organisation's customers will want and the size of demand for certain products. In the UK, for example, we might expect the consequences of an ageing population to include greater demand for items such as leisure activities and health care services.

(b) The location of demand. Again, in the UK, there appears to be a gradual population shift out of the inner cities and from the economically-depressed regions towards the more prosperous South East of England.

7. COMPETITION

7.1 The nature of competition is a key element in the environment of commercial organisations. In assessing competition the various factors to be considered can be looked at under three basic headings.

(a) Who are the competitors, how strong are they?
(b) What are the characteristics of the market they compete in?
(c) What are the likely strategies and responses of competitor's to the organisation's strategies?

7.2 Firms must be aware of who their competitors are, and how strong each one of them is. In any market where there is one or more significant competitors, the strategic decisions and marketing decisions by a firm will often be partly a response to what a competitor has done already or else is about to do.

7.3 *Note:* competitors can also be allies, and in many markets there is a mixture of competition and collaboration between companies.

7.4 M E Porter *(Competitive strategy)* identifies five basic forces which influence the state of competition in an industry.

(a) The threat of new entrants to the industry.
(b) The threat of substitute products or services.
(c) The bargaining power of customers.
(d) The bargaining power of suppliers.
(e) The rivalry amongst current competitors in the industry.

7.5 Although these five forces undoubtedly influence the intensity of competition within an industry, you should recognise that firms compete in markets which are not necessarily the same. To that extent the value of Porter's analysis may be limited.

7.6 The intensity of competition will depend on the following factors.

(a) *Whether there is a large number of equally balanced competitors.* Industries with a large number of firms are likely to be very competitive, but when the industry is dominated by a small number of larger firms, competition is likely to be less intense.

(b) *The rate of growth in the industry.* When firms are all benefiting from growth in total demand, their rivalry will be less intense. Rivalry is intensified when firms are competing for a greater market share in a total market where growth is slow or stagnant.

(c) *Whether fixed costs are high.* If fixed costs are high, and variable costs are a relatively small proportion of the selling price, it is often tempting for firms to begin to compete on prices and to sell at prices above marginal cost, even though this may mean a failure to cover fixed costs and make an adequate return in the longer run.

7.7 *The rivalry amongst current competitors in the industry*
The intensity of competitive rivalry within an industry will affect the profitability of the industry as a whole. Competitive actions might take the form of price competition, advertising battles, sales promotion campaigns, introducing new products for the market, improving aftersales service or providing guarantees or warranties.

7.8 Competition can do one of two things.

(a) It can help the industry as a whole to expand, stimulating demand with new products and advertising. In this situation, the industry as a whole will benefit from the competition.

(b) It can leave demand unchanged, in which case individual competitors will simply be spending more money, charging lower prices and so making lower profits, without getting any benefits except maintaining market share.

Competitive moves/response models

7.9 In some competitive market situations (eg oligopoly) firms are influenced by the actions of competitors and are likely:

- to react to the decisions of those competitors;
- to take the response of competitors into account when developing their own strategy.

7.10 Bad or irrational responses by one firm can prevent another's good strategic moves being successful. During the planning stage of strategic development, therefore, managers often have to forecast and assess the responses of competitors.

7.11 The uncertainty of competitor response leaves firms with a dilemma.

- Should they act in the best interests of the *industry*, though that may not maximise their own profits or achievements?

- Should they take aggressive actions which offer, potentially, great rewards but which risk retaliation and thus lower levels of achievement than would be gained by taking the less aggressive first option?

7.12 The analogy of this option can be seen in the classic *prisoner's dilemma* of game theory which you may already be familiar with.

- Two prisoners in jail can choose between staying silent or denouncing the other.
- If both stay silent both will be set free.
- If both denounce each other, both will be hanged.
- If only one denouces his cellmate, he will not only go free but will be given a large reward, whilst the other will be hanged.

Staying silent is obviously the best course for both, but the individual may be tempted to risk a strategy of 'telling' to try and earn the possible reward. Trust and assessment of how the other person will respond are critical to the decision to be made.

7.13 Similarly in an industry, firms which co-operate can make reasonable profits, but a single firm taking an aggressive strategy can do even better, as long as the others do not retaliate.

7.14 If the competitors do retaliate everyone will be worse off than if all had cooperated. Price wars often result in falling profits for all firms. In this 'lose/lose' scenario the only group to benefit are the customers who get the short term advantage of lower prices.

7.15 It can be seen therefore that assessing the likely industry response is an important dimension to the process of strategic planning. There are in essence two aspects.

(a) What moves might others make and how will that affect our business? (What is our response to them?)
(b) How might others react to our strategies? (What is their response to us?)

7.16 Although competitors' specific responses need assessing in the context of an individual strategy, their *general* response is an external factor to the organisation and can therefore legitimately be considered as an opportunity or threat.

7.17 Porter identifies a number of specific competitor responses which can be summarised under three broad categories.

(a) *Neutral moves* are moves which cause no real offence, they are cooperative or at least non threatening.

(i) *Hospitable moves*. These are visible but cause no real threat for example reducing the warranty period on a product range.

(ii) *Blind spot moves*. These are moves not recognised or perceived to be important perhaps because the firm is not felt to be real competition. Timex were not perceived to be a real threat to the Swiss watch industry until it was too late. A competitor's moves into Eastern Europe may be ignored as it is not a market opportunity currently being considered by you.

(b) *Offence moves* are moves likely to improve the firm's position and therefore may elicit a response from competitors. Success of offensive moves is determined by how accurately the firm predicts any likely retaliation. Porter identifies a number of factors the firm needs to assess when predicting the likely retaliation:

- how likely is a reaction?
- how quickly will it happen?
- how effective will it be?
- how tough will it be?
- is it possible to influence the retaliation strategy?

(i) *Superior strength moves*, these come from a privileged position, for example location or technical superiority. The firm must enjoy clear superiority for such a 'brute force' approach to be effective.

(ii) *Asymmetric cost moves*, where matching the move involves a substantial cost. Firms may be prepared to make short term losses to gain strategic advantage.

(c) *Defensive moves* are those made to protect the firm's position, ideally which prevent other firms actually entering into battle.

(i) *Readiness moves* are moves made in anticipation of competition. Pro-active product development, undertaken and communicated to competitors can in effect 'warn them off'.

(ii) *Leverage moves* are moves made so that the firm is ready to retaliate should it be necessary.

7.18 As with all the elements of the external environment which managers need to consider, the nature of competition and the decisions of other firms affect both directly and indirectly the success of the organisation. Good managers and planners are those who do not take the competition for granted. They get to know its characteristics, strengths and weaknesses nearly as well as they know their own.

8. CONCLUSION

8.1 Organisations exist in a wider environment which is constantly changing. These changes can often happen with little warning, as with sudden political unrest and conflicts, for example the Gulf Crisis.

8.2 Although changes in the external environment are outside the control of managers they must be monitored and responded to if the organisation is to maximise the opportunities and minimise the damaging impact of threats.

8.3 The external environment is made up of a number of factors and a complexity of variables which can affect the business. Managers need to know which are critical to their own markets and monitor these carefully.

The impact of environmental change

8.4 The environmental influences on a business are complex and varied, but an awareness of their impact and forecast changes is critical to the survival of any organisation. If planners ignore the external influences on the business they are operating in the dark and the risks of being unprepared for an unexpected environmental threat are immense. The ability to produce plans in the context of a realistic appraisal of the current and forecasted business environment is dependent on adequate information being available to the planners at the right time and in a useable format.

8.5 For your CIM examinations you need to bear in mind that the external factors at corporate level influence how the business operates and the nature of the market. At marketing planning level the main focus of external changes is on how environmental factors influence and change consumer demand.

8.6 Managers who are alert to forecast environmental changes and develop their strategies in advance of these changes are pro-active. These organisations are most likely to thrive and prosper. Those who are forced to change after the event are reactive and run the risk of failing to survive.

8.7 The response of competitors, both in general and to specific strategies must be considered when assessing the opportunities and threats facing the firm.

TEST YOUR KNOWLEDGE

The numbers in brackets refer to paragraphs of this chapter

1. What are the main categories of external influences which affect the organisation? (1.3)
2. Why must you take care when using national economic indicators to assess a market opportunity? (2.1)
3. What are the key economic influences on a firm operating in international markets? (2.2)
4. What are the main changes which the 1992 single market are heralding? (2.14)
5. What sort of questions should planners be asking themselves as a result of these changes in European trade? (2.16)
6. Why do planners need to monitor the political environment? (3.5)
7. How has the growing concern with the environment impacted on business plans? (4.11, 4.12)
8. How does the legislative framework potentially affect an organisation? (5.1)
9. In what three ways does technological change affect business? (5.3)
10. List Porter's five competitive forces in an industry. (7.4)

Now try illustrative question 4

PART B
STRATEGIC AND MARKETING ANALYSIS

Chapter 4

WHERE ARE WE NOW? TOOLS FOR AUDITS AND ANALYSIS

This chapter covers the following topics.

1. CORPORATE POSITION/SITUATION AUDITS

1.1 Plans are devised to help the organisation move from point A to point B. The first essential step in this process is to clarify the location of point A. We need a clear answer to the question, 'Where are we now?'

1.2 We saw in the last chapter the importance of undertaking an environmental audit to ascertain the nature of the external influences on the firm. Equally important is an internal audit to examine the present position of the organisation in terms of its internal strengths and weaknesses.

1.3 Internal factors are classified as the controllable variables which can be influenced by management actions.

1.4 As a marketing manager the controllable elements which need to be assessed would be the 4P's of the marketing mix, but at corporate level the controllable elements are represented by the functional areas of the business. They can be remembered as the five M's.

- Men - its human resources and organisation
- Money - its financial health
- Materials - supply sources and products
- Machines - the production facilities, its fixed assets, capacity etc
- Markets - its reputation, position and market prospects

To this list should be added any intangible resources, for example patents, trademarks, goodwill, development expenditure and so on.

1.5 The information that is gathered might be obtained from the answers to the following list of questions.

(a) *Materials:* Where do they come from? Who supplies them? What percentage of the total cost of sales is accounted for by materials? What are wastage levels? Are new materials being developed for the market by suppliers?

(b) *Labour:* What is the size of the labour force? What are their skills? How much are they paid? What are total labour costs? What proportion of the organisation's added value or sales revenue is accounted for by labour costs? How efficient is the workforce? What is the rate of labour turnover? How good or bad are industrial relations?

(c) *Management:* What is the size of the management team? What are its specialist skills? What management development and career progression exists? How well has management performed in achieving targets in the past? How hierarchical is the management structure?

(d) *Fixed assets:* What fixed assets does the organisation use? What is their current value (on a going concern value and on a break-up value basis)? What is the amount of revenue and profit per £1 invested in fixed assets? How old are the assets? Are they technologically advanced or out of date? What are the organisation's repairs and replacement policies? What is the *percentage fill* in the organisation's capacity? This is particularly important for service industries, such as cinemas, football grounds and trains, where fixed costs are high and resources need to be utilised as much as possible to earn good profits.

(e) *Working capital:* How much working capital does the organisation use? What are the average turnover periods for stocks and debtors? What is the credit policy of the organisation? What credit is taken from suppliers? What is the level of bad debts? How is spare cash utilised by the treasury department? How are foreign exchange transactions dealt with?

(f) *Finance:* What are the company's financial resources? What is its debt ratio and gearing ratio?

(g) *Intangibles.* Intangible items, such as goodwill, reputation, brand names, R & D experience etc, should also be assessed.

1.6 An assessment of a 'random collection' of resources on its own is insufficient for a proper resource audit. Resources are of no value unless they are organised into systems, and so a resource audit should go on to consider how well or how badly resources have been utilised, and whether the organisation's systems are effective and efficient.

1.7 A further aspect of the resource audit should be an assessment of how well resources have been *controlled*. Some resources might be used both efficiently and effectively, but control of the resources could still be poor for the following reasons.

(a) Not enough of the resources were obtained, and even better results could be achieved if more of the resources were obtained and utilised.

(b) Key resources could have been used even more efficiently and effectively if they had been diverted to a different purpose.

Limiting factor

1.8 Every organisation operates under resource constraints. There is never enough money or skilled labour or key components supplies etc. If there is a limiting factor, it must be identified and quantified.

1.9 A limiting factor or *key factor* is defined by CIMA as 'anything which limits the activity of an entity. An entity seeks to optimise the benefit it obtains from the limiting factor. Examples are a shortage of supply of a resource and a restriction on sales at a particular price.'

1.10 *Finance* is always in limited supply, but there could well be other resources or other factors which restrict the effective use of what finance is available. These key factors will limit the ability of the organisation to achieve its objectives. For example, a shortage of skilled labour might put an organisation at a serious disadvantage against competitors and so restrict the ability of the organisation to improve its profitability and return on capital.

1.11 Examples of limiting factors might be as follows.

(a) A shortage of production capacity.
(b) A limited number of key personnel, such as salespeople with technical knowledge.
(c) A restricted distribution network which may be inadequate for a national market coverage.
(d) A very small number of managers with knowledge about finance, or overseas markets.
(e) Inadequate design resources to develop new products or services.

1.12 From your knowledge of finance, you should already be familiar with the idea in budgeting that to maximise short term profitability, it is necessary to use scarce resources in such a way as to maximise the contribution per unit of limiting factor. In the same way, in strategic planning, once the limiting factor has been identified, the planners should seek to make use of the resources it has available so as to contribute most effectively towards the achievement of the organisation's objectives.

Environmental analysis

1.13 The environmental analysis which we have already considered is an extension of a position audit. Instead of getting answers to the question 'Where are we now?' (position audit), environmental analysis asks the question 'What is the environment in which we operate going to be like?'

2. THE MARKETING AUDIT

2.1 It is very easy to confuse marketing planning with corporate level planning and you need to take care to consider at what level in the organisation you are operating. The corporate audit of its product/market strengths and weaknesses and much of its external environment analysis is of course likely to be informed by the marketing audit. The marketing department is probably the most important source of 'bottom up' information, opinions and views which influence the development of the corporate strategy. But the marketing audit also represents the starting point for developing the marketing plan, answering the 'where are we now' question in terms of marketing controllables.

2.2 The marketing audit assesses the strengths and weaknesses of the organisation.

(a) *Products*: range, quality, competitive advantage, stage of the life cycle and technical reputation etc.
(b) *Price*: perceived value for money compared with competitors and price position in the market place.
(c) *Promotion*: image and reputation of the organisation and various products and brands in the market place. Brand loyalty and corporate image.
(d) *Place*: availability of the product, channels of distribution used, waiting lists and the availability of distribution services like credit for end users etc.
(e) *After sales service*: reputation for after sales customer care, provision of spare parts, servicing etc.

2.3 The objective of this internal marketing analysis is to be able to log the company's current market position on a positioning map.

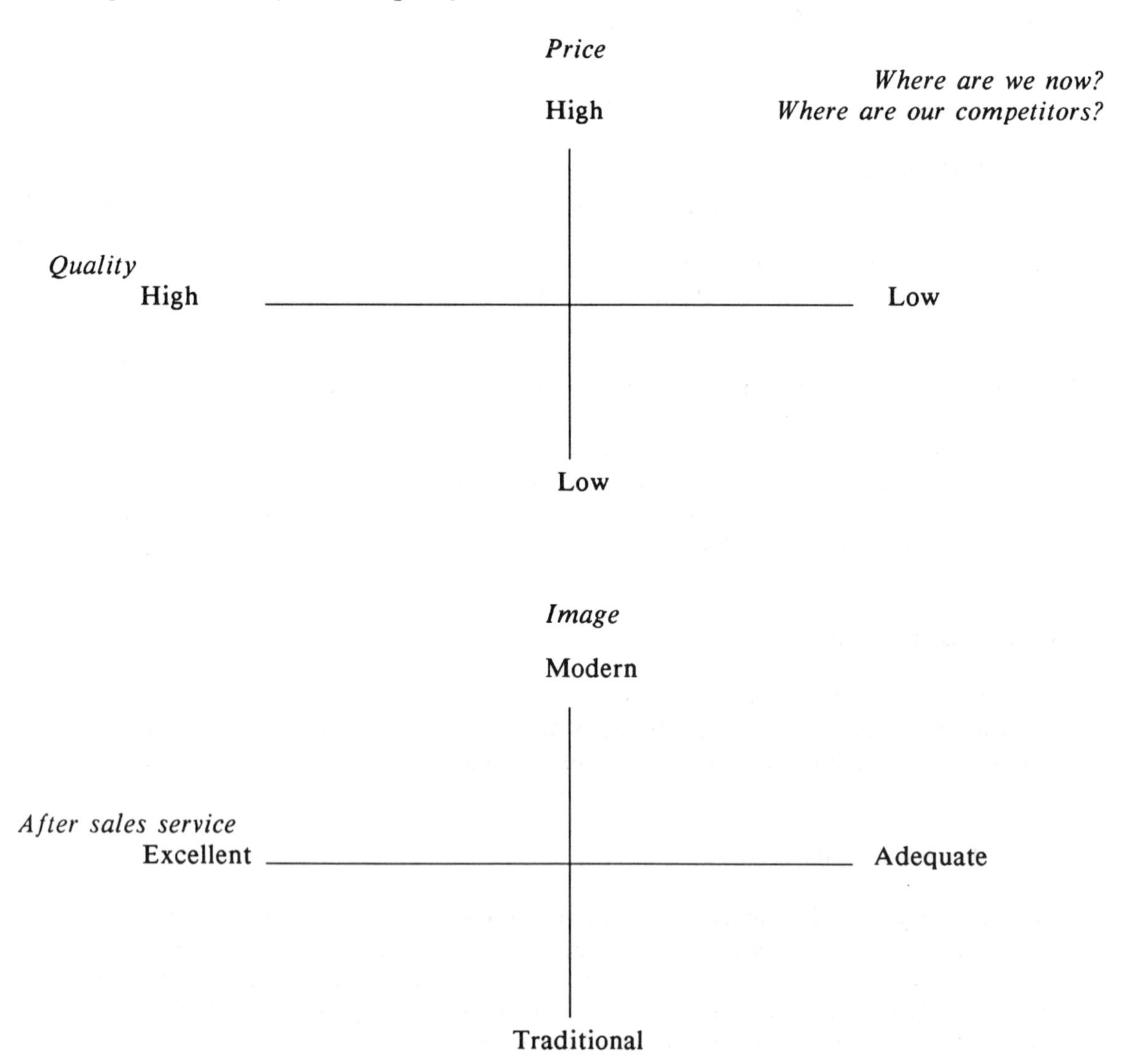

Note: positioning maps are developed on the basis of identifying the most important variables in the customer's choice and need to be produced from the customer's point of view, ie you may believe your product is the fastest on the market and it may actually be the fastest, but what is important is the customer's perception.

2.4 The external factors relevant to the marketing audit are focused on the analysis of competitors and the product/market opportunities and threats facing the firm.

(a) Taking the product overseas, or into new markets, modifying the marketing mix or introducing new products, may be opportunities.

(b) Decreasing demand, new technology or new competitors are clearly threats.

3. USING SWOT ANALYSIS

3.1 Collecting the information about the current position and environment is one thing, but to be of real value to the planners it needs to be assessed. As you have seen there are a number of factors to be considered and turning this collection of facts into a clear picture requires some analysis. One of the most useful tools for sorting information is a SWOT analysis.

3.2 You have probably come across SWOT in other parts of your marketing studies. It stands for strengths, weaknesses, opportunities and threats. One of the most important things to remember is that SWOT analysis is a management tool which you can use in a wide variety of situations. Its value is as a technique to help you sort information. A SWOT analysis can usefully be undertaken at corporate level, marketing or product level or when trying to compare two or more alternative projects or courses of action.

3.3 SWOT analysis is undertaken as part of the preparation in planning. Unless specifically asked for do not present your analysis to the examiners. The quality of your recommendation will reflect the thoroughness of your analysis.

Corporate appraisal/SWOT

3.4 Corporate appraisal has been defined by the CIMA as 'a critical assessment of the strengths and weaknesses, opportunities and threats in relation to the internal and environmental factors affecting an entity in order to establish its condition prior to the preparation of the long-term plan.'

(a) Strengths and weaknesses analysis involves looking at the particular strengths and weaknesses of the organisation itself and its product/service range. It is an *internal appraisal*.

(b) An analysis of opportunities and threats is concerned with profit-making opportunities in the business environment, and with identifiable threats, for example falling demand, new competition, government legislation etc. It is therefore an *external appraisal*.

Internal appraisal: strengths and weaknesses analysis

3.5 As we have already seen, an internal appraisal seeks to identify the following.

(a) Shortcomings in the company's present skills and resources.
(b) Strengths which the company should seek to exploit.

3.6 The strengths and weaknesses analysis is *internal to the company* and intended to shape its approach to the external world. For instance, the identification of shortcomings in skills or resources could lead to a planned acquisition programme or staff recruitment and training.

The strengths and weaknesses part of the SWOT analysis involves looking at the findings of the position audit.

3.7 Typically, the analysis would consider information in the following areas.

(a) *Marketing*

(i) Fate of new product launches - have these a good success record or not, and so is the organisation developing new products successfully?
(ii) Success or failure of advertising campaigns - is the organisation using advertising to good effect? Do the organisation's products each have a unique selling proposition (USP) which is being successfully communicated to potential customers?
(iii) Market shares and market sizes - is the organisation in a strong or weak position?
(iv) Company's standing in growth markets - is the organisation well placed in growth markets, or does it rely on mature or declining markets?
(v) Skills of the sales force and selling techniques used - how good is the success rate of the sales team in winning orders?
(vi) Has the company achieved a superior customer/client service?
(vii) Is the company still sensitive to the needs and demands of customers? Has the company's policy of market segmentation and customer targeting operated successfully?

(b) *Products*

(i) Analysis of sales by market, area, product groups, outlets etc.
(ii) Profit margin and overall profit contribution - are profits for each product good or not?
(iii) Product quality. Does the company place sufficient emphasis on the quality of its work, both in terms of the goods it sells and also in terms of its work processes?
(iv) Age and future life of products - does the company have a good balance between old and new products, and rising, mature and declining products?
(v) Price elasticity of demand of products - is demand price sensitive, and so are prospects for putting up prices poor?

(c) *Distribution*

(i) Delivery service standards - what are delivery lead times, and how do they compare?
(ii) Warehouse delivery fleet facilities - can the delivery fleet cope with demand?
(iii) Geographical availability of products - is the distribution network poor/adequate/ excellent.

(d) *Research and development*

(i) Are R & D projects relevant to future marketing plans?
(ii) The costs of R & D - is R & D spending too little/too much?
(iii) Benefits of R & D in new products/variations on existing products - how good has R & D been?
(iv) R & D workload and schedules. Will we beat our competitor to the new launch?

(e) *Finance*

(i) Availability of short term and long term funds, cash flow - is the organisation in a strong or weak position for further borrowing or cash flow?
(ii) Contribution of each product - how is each product contributing to cash flow?
(iii) Returns on investment.
(iv) Accounting ratios - ratio analysis should help to identify areas of strength or weakness in performance (for example asset turnover ratios, liquidity ratios etc).

(f) *Plant and equipment and other facilities. Production*

(i) Age, value, production capacity and suitability of plant and equipment.
(ii) Valuation of all assets.
(iii) Location of land and buildings, their value, area, use, length of lease, current book value.
(iv) Crucially, has the company succeeded in achieving a 'critical mass' of output capacity, so that it can achieve maximum economies of scale and minimum production costs?

Are assets inadequate? too old? well kept? technologically advanced? Does the organisation have freehold or long leasehold property? If not, does renting or holding short leases on property indicate a potential danger/weakness?

(g) *Management and staff*

(i) Age spread, succession plans.
(ii) Skills and attitudes.
(iii) State of industrial relations, morale and labour turnover.
(iv) Training and recruitment facilities.
(v) Manpower utilisation.

In general, is the management team strong or weak, and in what ways?

(h) *Business management: organisation*

(i) Organisation structure - is this properly suited to the organisation's needs? Is the organisation based on functional divisions (for example production, marketing, finance etc) or product/market profit centres?
(ii) Management style and philosophy - does the management style seem well-suited to the businesses the organisation operates in?
(iii) Communication links - are these adequate?

(i) *Raw material and finished goods stocks*

(i) The sources of supply - is there a single supplier or can supplies be obtained from numerous sources?
(ii) Number and description of items.
(iii) Turnover periods - long or short?
(iv) Storage capacity - adequate? Is there spare capacity?
(v) Obsolescence and deterioration.
(vi) Pilfering etc.

3.8 The appraisal should give particular attention to the following.

(a) *A study of past accounts and the use of ratios.* By looking at *trends*, or by comparing ratios (if possible) with those of other firms in a similar industry, it might be possible to identify strengths and weaknesses in major areas of the business. Ratio analysis is reviewed later in this chapter.

(b) *Product position* and *product-market mix.* This very important area is dealt with later.

(c) *Cash and financial structure.* If a company intends to expand or diversify, it will need cash or sufficient financial standing in order to acquire subsidiaries or for investing in new capacity.

(d) *Cost structure.* If a company operates with high fixed costs and relatively low variable costs, it might be in a relatively weak position with regards to production capacity. High volumes of production and sale might be required to break even. In contrast, a company with low fixed costs might be more flexible and adaptable so that it should be able to operate at a lower breakeven point.

(e) *Managerial ability.* There may be a problem in attempting to assess this and objective measurements should be sought. The danger is that a poor management might overestimate their own ability and incorrectly analyse their weakness as a strength.

3.9 The purpose of the analysis is to express, qualitatively or quantitatively, which areas of the business have strengths to exploit, and which areas have weaknesses which must be improved. Although every area of the business should be investigated, only the areas of significant strength or weakness should warrant further attention.

Summary of significant strengths and weaknesses: an example

3.10 A strengths and weaknesses analysis might come up with the following results.

(a) *Strengths*

(i) Marketing, products and markets:
- products A, B and C are market leaders;
- product D, new product launch, high profit potential;
- good brand images;
- good relations with suppliers and dealers;
- good packaging and advertising appeal.

(ii) Production:
- new factory in North West, fully operational for next year;
- thorough quality inspection standards.

(iii) Finance:
- £0.5 million cash available from internal resources;
- further £2.0 million overdraft facility, so far unused.

(iv) Management and staff:
- high skills in marketing areas of packaging, sales promotion, advertising and sales generally;
- good labour relations, except at one plant which has low productivity.

(b) *Weaknesses*

(i) Marketing:
- products X, Y and Z contribute no profit;
- products P, Q and R are declining and will lose profitability in three years;
- sales of product D are dependent upon a high level of sales of complementary products (for example razor blades and razor);
- no new products, except for D, have been successfully launched in the last two years.

(ii) Research and development:
- no major new products have been derived from R & D for two years. Becoming too dependent on acquisition for additions to product range;
- little control over R & D budget.

(iii) Production:
- plant at most factories has an average age of 8.7 years;
- new developments could threaten ability to compete;
- high level of spoiled goods on lines 3, 7, 9 at one location;
- low productivity on all lines at one plant.

(iv) Management and staff:
- poor labour relations at plant with low productivity;
- senior executives approaching retirement with no clearly recognisable successor;
- success of the organisation too dependent on senior executive charisma.

External appraisal: opportunities and threats analysis

3.11 The internal appraisal highlights areas within the company which are strong and which might therefore be exploited more fully, and weaknesses where some 'defensive' planning might be required to protect the company from poor results.

3.12 An external appraisal is required to identify profit-making opportunities which can be exploited by the company's strengths and also to anticipate environmental threats (a declining economy, competitors' actions, government legislation, industrial unrest etc) against which the company must protect itself.

The external appraisal is the opportunities and threats analysis part of SWOT analysis, and it follows on from the position audit and the environmental analysis.

3.13 For *opportunities* it is necessary to decide the following.

(a) What opportunities exist in the business environment.
(b) What is their inherent profit-making potential.
(c) What are the internal strengths/weaknesses of the organisation, and whether it is capable of exploiting the worthwhile opportunities.
(d) What is the comparative capability profile of competitors and whether these competitors are better placed to exploit these opportunities.
(e) What is the company's comparative performance potential in this field of opportunity.

The opportunities might involve product development, market development, market penetration or diversification. No realistic opportunity should be ignored.

3.14 For *threats* it is necessary to decide the following.

(a) What threats might arise, to the company or its business environment.
(b) How competitors will be affected.
(c) How the company will be affected. Does it have strengths to deal with the threat or do weaknesses need to be corrected so as to survive the threat? Are contingency strategies required?

3.15 Opportunities and threats might relate to the following items.

(a) *Economic:* unemployment, the level of wages and salaries, the expected total market behaviour for products, total customer demand, the growth and decline of industries and suppliers, general investment levels etc. At an international level, world production and the volume of international trade, demand, recessions, import controls, exchange rates etc. must be considered.

(b) *Government:* legislation may affect a company's prospects through the threats/ opportunities of pollution control or a ban on certain products. A law to ban lead in petrol would be a threat to petrol producers and car makers, but at the same time an opportunity for selling lead-free petrol and making cars that use it. Pollution controls offer opportunities for companies that make equipment to prevent or limit pollution. Taxation incentives, rent-free factory buildings, or investment grants might be available for exploitation. Government policy may be to increase expenditure on housing, defence, schools and hospitals or roads and transport and this gives opportunities to private companies and the relevant government organisations alike. Political upheaval might damage market and investment prospects, especially overseas.

(c) *Competitors*

(i) Possible competitors' actions in the future must be considered. It is especially important to identify where competitors are weak in export markets, and where foreign competitors might threaten the industry with cheaper or better imports. British industry in recent years has called for protection against Japanese cars, foreign textiles and imported fish, having been unable to meet the external threat successfully and therefore requiring external assistance from the government. In contrast, manufacturers of lawn mowers successfully identified a threat from Japanese importers and developed competitive new products of their own.

(ii) The company must also decide whether it is under threat of a takeover bid by any other company. A comparison of internal strength and weakness and potential buyers is needed.

A competitive analysis, as described by Porter, would be a part of the SWOT analysis.

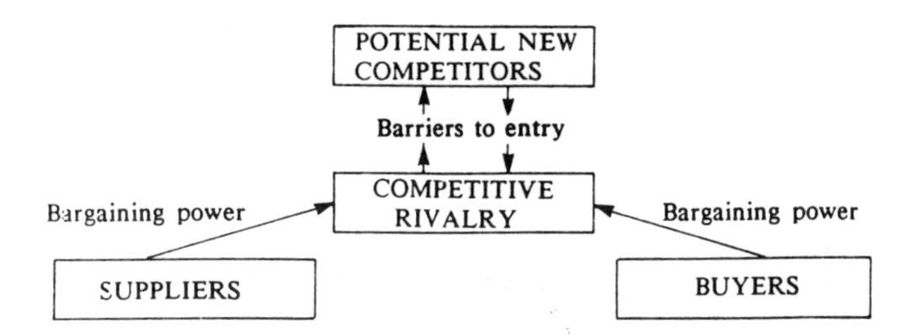

(d) *Technology:* if technological changes are anticipated, there is a possibility of new products appearing, or cheaper means of production or distribution being introduced. The potential of the microchip has far-reaching effects for producers (for example the use of robots), service industries (for example communications and information services), and markets (for example the new products that will be made available for consumers).

(e) *Social*

(i) As we have already discussed, social attitudes will have a significant effect on customer demand and employee attitudes. Attitudes to work are changing, and employees are increasingly unwilling to work in 'dirty' jobs or menial work. Hours of work are shortening, holidays getting longer, and the age of retirement may be lowered. Voluntary early retirement has been a feature in recent years. Inflation in the 1970s and credit cards in the 1980s appear to have encouraged a switch of attitudes to 'spend now, pay later'. This important shift in social attitudes explains the growing interest by many companies in exploiting the leisure and health industry - for example golf clubs and driving ranges, squash, home computers, gambling, holiday items, fitness centres etc.

(ii) Society is also applying pressure to improve the environment, and to reduce noise and pollution.

(iii) Population trends must also be considered. Britain currently has an ageing population so that in future, an increased market will exist among retired people. There are recognised opportunities for growth in the personal pensions market.

(iv) Permanently high unemployment figures will influence the available total spending power of consumers, especially in some of the more depressed regions of the UK.

3.16 Two aspects of the analysis of opportunities and threats which are especially important are as follows.

(a) Trying to identify future *changes*, and the *rate of change*, in the environment and in competition.

(b) Trying to identify *changes in the market*, and preparing *forecasts of prospective sales*, should any of the expected changes occur.

Example: opportunities and threats analysis

3.17 Some years ago, an analysis of opportunities and threats in its industrial environment would have been of some value to strategic planners in the UK paint industry. From 1980, the following four pressures built up on the industry.

(a) The economic recession.
(b) Rising costs of production and marketing.
(c) The fragmentation of the markets for paint products.
(d) New technology.

3.18 As raw material costs rose, paint prices were kept down by intense competition between paint manufacturers, so that profit margins were squeezed. New market segments combined with new technology have forced paint manufacturers to spend heavily on product development - paints for plastics, paints for painting steel coils or aluminium coils on automated production lines, one-coat paints, non-drip paints, and all-weather woodstains are examples of product changes based on new technology. With low profit margins, companies need to have a 15% to 20% share of a market segment to be profitable, but there are still about ten big paint manufacturers in the UK.

3.19 The threats and opportunities in the environment might suggest the following.

(a) There are threats of being taken over by a UK or foreign competitor or opportunities to take over a rival.

(b) Some manufacturers should plan to 'divest' and get out of certain segments of the market. Indeed, ICI, the overall market leader, pulled out of the market for heavy duty paints for agricultural, construction and earth-moving equipment, leaving Macpherson as the dominant market leader in this market segment.

The changes in the paint industry are no doubt still far from over.

Selecting alternative strategies

3.20 The internal and external appraisals of SWOT analysis will be brought together. Potential strategies must now be identified and although it is impossible to legislate in general terms for every case, it is likely that alternative strategies will emerge from the identification of strengths, weaknesses, threats and opportunities. Major strengths and profitable opportunities can be exploited and if there are none, a diversification strategy might become the solution. Major weaknesses and threats should be countered, or a contingency strategy or corrective strategy developed.

3.21 **A cruciform chart is a table listing the significant strengths and weaknesses and opportunities and threats. It can be used to summarise the major conclusions of a SWOT analysis.**

In the example below, the development of potential strategies from the analysis is illustrated.

Strengths £10 million of capital available. Production expertise and appropriate marketing skills.	*Weaknesses* Heavy reliance on a small number of customers. Limited product range, with no new products and expected market decline. Small marketing organisation.
Threats Major competitor has already entered the new market.	*Opportunities* Government tax incentives for new investment. Growing demand in a new market, although customers so far relatively small in number.

3.22 In this simple example, it might be possible to identify that the company is in imminent danger of losing its existing markets and must diversify its products, or its products and markets. The new market opportunity exists to be exploited and since the number of customers is currently few, the relatively small size of the existing marketing force would not be an immediate hindrance. A strategic plan could be developed to buy new equipment and to use existing production and marketing to enter the new market, with a view to rapid expansion. Careful planning of manpower, equipment, facilities, research and development etc. would be required and there would be an objective to meet the threat of competition so as to obtain a substantial share of a growing market. The cost of entry at this early stage of market development should not be unacceptably high.

3.23 In this example, one individual strategy has been identified from our simplified cruciform chart. In practice, a combination of individual strategies will be required with regard to product development, market development, diversification, resource planning, risk reduction etc. Basically, the following three steps are taken.

(a) The difference, or 'gap' between the current position of the firm and its planned targets is estimated.
(b) One or more courses of action (strategy) are proposed.
(c) These are tested for their 'gap-reducing properties'. A course is accepted if it substantially closes the gap between current position and planned position and if it also helps to achieve the social and ethical objectives of the firm.

Examples and exercises in SWOT analysis

3.24 It will help you to get used to the basic thinking that underlies strategic planning if you try a few short exercises in SWOT analysis.

3.25 A good starting point would be the organisation you work for, or one that you are quite familiar with. For example, would you agree with the following analysis of British Coal?

(a) Plenty of home-based coal resources. Projected demand for energy expected to grow into the 21st Century, with much electricity to be supplied from coal burning stations. Oil-burning stations threatened by reducing world resources of oil. Continuing worries about nuclear energy.

(b) New technology reducing the cost of coal extraction in certain fields. Greater productivity.

(c) Good safety record.

(d) Improving profit record.

(e) Relatively high costs of extraction in certain coal fields, and competition from imported coal (Columbia, South Africa, Poland).

(f) Relatively undeveloped export markets.

(g) Recent history of pit closures, redundancies and union troubles.

(h) Environmental problems of acid rain from coal-burning electricity stations, and the 'greenhouse' effect of carbon dioxide in the air. Possibility of legislation in the future, and of social attitudes turning against the use of coal for these reasons.

3.26 As another example, how about Volkswagen, the car manufacturing company? A SWOT analysis back in 1986 might have suggested the following.

(a) An impressive profit recovery from 1984, after the recession in the car market in the early 1980s.

(b) Position as market leader in the European mass car market. The great success of the Golf in Europe as a successor to the Beetle as a big cash earner with a long prospective life cycle.

(c) Large capital investment programme under way.

(d) Recovery of sales in the USA. However, problems with production quality at its USA plant in Pennsylvania (1 million models of the 'Rabbit' (Golf) were recalled because of serious defects). Strong competition in the USA from Japanese cars, and so sales growth prospects limited.

(e) New markets opening in Japan and China.

(f) The remote location of VW's main plant in Germany at Wolfsburg. 'The average distance between Wolfsburg and VW's main components suppliers is 250 miles. That makes it impossible to imitate Toyota's just-in-time production system, with suppliers clustered around the main factory. This, together with West Germany's high labour costs, makes it much harder for VW to compete with its Japanese rivals by cost cutting alone.' (*The Economist*, August 1985)

3.27 Attempt a brief solution to the following example.

Example: SWOT analysis

3.28 Hall Faull Downes Ltd has been in business for 25 years, during which time profits have risen by an average of 3% per annum, although there have been peaks and troughs in profitability due to the ups and downs of trade in the customers' industry. The increase in profits until five years ago was the result of increasing sales in a buoyant market, but more recently, the total market has become somewhat smaller and Hall Faull Downes has only increased sales and profits as a result of improving its market share.

The company produces components for manufacturers in the engineering industry.

In recent years, the company has developed many new products and currently has 40 items in its range compared to 24 only five years ago. Over the same five year period, the number of customers has fallen from 20 to nine, two of whom together account for 60% of the company's sales.

Give your appraisal of the company's future, and suggest what it is probably doing wrong.

Analysis

3.29 A general interpretation of the facts as given might be sketched as follows.

(a) *Objectives:* the company has no declared objectives. Profits have risen by 3% per annum in the past, which has failed to keep pace with inflation but may have been a satisfactory rate of increase in the current conditions of the industry. Even so, stronger growth is indicated in the future.

(b)

Strengths	*Weaknesses*
Many new products developed. Marketing success in increasing market share.	Products may be reaching the end of their life and entering decline. New product life cycles may be shorter. Reduction in customers. Excessive reliance on a few customers. Doubtful whether profit record is satisfactory.
Threats Possible decline in the end-product. Smaller end-product market will restrict future sales prospects for Hall Faull Downes.	*Opportunities* None identified.

(c) *Strengths:* the growth in company sales in the last five years has been as a result of increasing the market share in a declining market. This success may be the result of the following.

(i) Research and development spending.
(ii) Good product development programmes.
(iii) Extending the product range to suit changing customer needs.
(iv) Marketing skills.
(v) Long-term supply contracts with customers.
(vi) Cheap pricing policy.
(vii) Product quality and reliable service.

(d) *Weaknesses*

(i) The products may be custom-made for customers so that they provide little or no opportunity for market development.
(ii) Products might have a shorter life cycle than in the past, in view of the declining total market demand.
(iii) Excessive reliance on two major customers leaves the company exposed to the dangers of losing their custom.

(e) *Threats:* there may be a decline in the end-market for the customers' product so that the customer demands for the company's own products will also fall.

(f) *Opportunities:* no opportunities have been identified, but in view of the situation as described, new strategies for the longer term would appear to be essential.

(g) *Conclusions:* the company does not appear to be planning beyond the short-term, or is reacting to the business environment in a piecemeal fashion. A strategic planning programme should be introduced.

(h) *Recommendations:* the company must look for new opportunities in the longer-term.

(i) In the short term, current strengths must be exploited to continue to increase market share in existing markets and product development programmes should also continue.

(ii) In the longer term, the company must diversify into new markets or into new products and new markets. Diversification opportunities should be sought with a view to exploiting any competitive advantage or synergy that might be achievable.

(iii) The company should use its strengths (whether in R & D, production skills or marketing expertise) in exploiting any identifiable opportunities.

(iv) Objectives need to be quantified in order to assess the extent to which new long-term strategies are required.

A marketing SWOT

3.30 In using a SWOT analysis at marketing level you should follow the same structure, but you must ensure you include under strengths and weaknesses only factors which are within the control of that level of management.

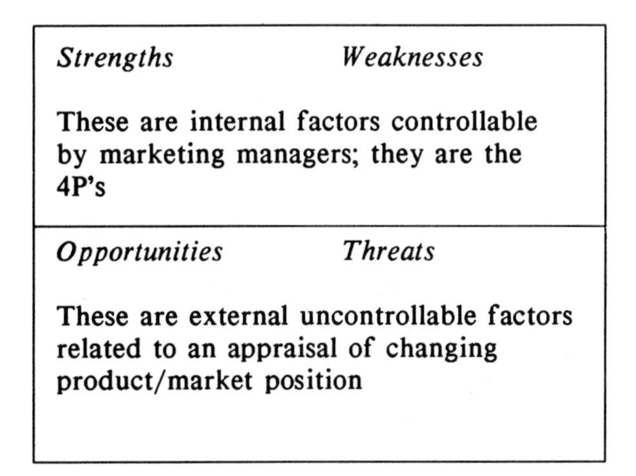
Strengths *Weaknesses*

These are internal factors controllable by marketing managers; they are the 4P's

Opportunities *Threats*

These are external uncontrollable factors related to an appraisal of changing product/market position

3.31 The following schematic should help you to clarify where the audits fit into the various planning levels.

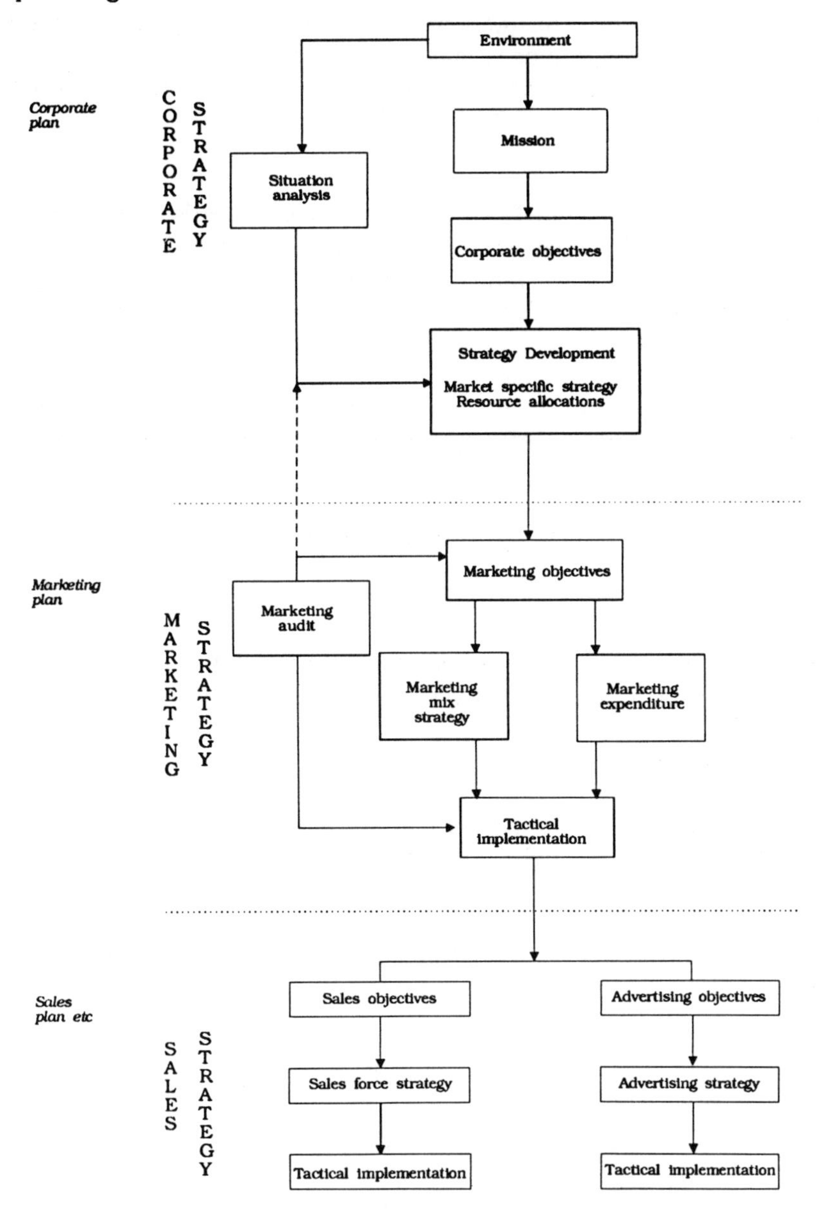

4. USING RATIO ANALYSIS

4.1 Ratio analysis involves comparing one figure against another to produce a ratio, and assessing whether the ratio indicates a weakness or strength in the company's affairs.

The broad categories of ratios

4.2 Broadly speaking, basic ratios can be grouped into five categories.

- profitability and return
- long-term solvency and stability
- short-term solvency and liquidity
- working capital ratios
- shareholders' investment ratios

4.3 It must be stressed that each individual business must be considered separately, and a ratio that is meaningful for a manufacturing company may be completely meaningless for a financial institution. Try not to be too mechanical when working out ratios and constantly think about what you are trying to achieve.

4.4 The key to obtaining meaningful information from ratio analysis is comparison. This may involve comparing ratios over time within the same business to establish whether things are improving or declining, and comparing ratios between similar businesses to see whether the company you are analysing is better or worse than average within its specific business sector.

4.5 It must be stressed that ratio analysis on its own is not sufficient for interpreting company accounts, and that there are other items of information which should be looked at, such as the following.

(a) Comments in the Chairman's report and directors' report.

(b) The age and nature of the company's assets.

(c) Current and future developments in the company's markets, at home and overseas, recent acquisitions or disposals of a subsidiary by the company.

(d) Extraordinary items in the profit and loss account.

(e) Any other noticeable features of the report and accounts, such as post balance sheet events, contingent liabilities, a qualified auditors' report, the company's taxation position, and so on.

In case studies you may well be provided with some of these other items of information so be on the look out for them.

4.6 Although you can use ratio analysis to examine any quantifiable movements over time, for example $\frac{\text{marketing expenditure}}{\text{sales volume}}$, the key financial ratios you need to be comfortable with are in the list which follows. Your financial studies at certificate or graduate conversion level will have already introduced you to this tool of analysis, so in this chapter we will only review the basics.

(a) *Profitability ratios*
  (i) return on capital employed
  (ii) net profit as a percentage of sales
  (iii) asset turnover ratio
  (iv) gross profit as a percentage of sales

(b) *Debt and gearing ratios*
  (i) debt ratio
  (ii) gearing ratio
  (iii) interest cover
  (iv) cash flow ratio

(c) *Liquidity and working capital ratios*
  (i) current ratio
  (ii) quick ratio (acid test ratio)
  (iii) debtor days (average debt collection period)
  (iv) average stock turnover period

(d) *Ordinary shareholders' investment ratios*
  (i) earnings per share
  (ii) dividend cover
  (iii) P/E ratio
  (iv) dividend yield
  (v) earnings yield

4.7 With the exception of the last three ratios, where the share's market price is required, all of these ratios can be calculated from information in a company's published accounts, and from the sort of information you can expect in your analysis and decision case study.

4.8 It is often a good approach to head up a schedule of ratios and statistics. Calculate the ratios in a logical sequence dealing in turn with operating and profitability ratios, use of assets (for example turnover period for debtors and stocks) liquidity and gearing. As you calculate the ratios you are likely to be struck by significant fluctuations and trends. These give you an indication of the company's strengths and weaknesses in each area.

5. PROFITABILITY RATIOS

5.1 In assessing a company's profitability, profit on ordinary activities *before* taxation is generally thought to be a better figure to use than profit after taxation. This is because there might be unusual variations in the tax charge from year to year which would not affect the underlying profitability of the company's operations.

5.2 Another profit figure that should be calculated is PBIT - profit before interest and tax. This is the amount of profit which the company earned before having to pay interest to the providers of loan capital. By providers of loan capital, we usually mean longer-term loan capital, such as debentures and medium-term bank loans, which will be shown in the balance sheet as 'creditors: amounts falling due after more than one year'.

5.3 Profit before interest and tax is therefore:

(a) the profit on ordinary activities before taxation; plus
(b) interest charges on long-term loan capital.

Published accounts do not always give sufficient detail on interest payable to determine how much is interest on long-term finance. Where this information is not provided you may have to make and state an assumption.

Return on capital employed (ROCE)

5.4 It is impossible to assess profits or profit growth properly without relating them to the amount of funds (capital) that were employed in making the profits. It is easy to make profits if you are provided with enough capital. What is important is whether the profit is large enough for the amount of capital which has been employed. The most important profitability ratio is therefore return on capital employed (ROCE), which states the profit as a percentage of the amount of capital employed.

5.5 Profit is usually taken as PBIT, and capital employed is shareholders' capital plus long-term liabilities and debt capital. This is the same as total assets less current liabilities. The underlying principle is that we must compare like with like, and so if capital means share capital and reserves plus long-term liabilities and debt capital, profit must mean the profit earned by all this capital together. This is PBIT, since interest is the return for loan capital.

Thus:

$$\text{ROCE} = \frac{\text{Profit on ordinary activities before interest and taxation (PBIT)}}{\text{Capital employed}}$$

Capital employed = Shareholders' funds plus 'creditors: amounts falling due after more than one year' plus any long-term provision for liabilities and charges.

5.6 What does a company's ROCE tell us? What should we be looking for? There are three comparisons that can be made.

(a) The change in ROCE from one year to the next.

(b) The ROCE being earned by other companies, if this information is available.

(c) A comparison of the ROCE with current market borrowing rates.

(i) What would be the cost of extra borrowing to the company if it needed more loans, and is it earning a ROCE that suggests it could make profits to make such borrowing worthwhile?

(ii) Is the company making a ROCE which suggests that it is getting value for money from its current borrowing?

(iii) Companies are in a risk business and commercial borrowing rates are a good independent yardstick against which company performance can be judged.

5.7 It is easier to spot a low ROCE than a high one, because there is always a chance that the company's fixed assets, especially property, are undervalued in its balance sheet. The capital employed figure might therefore be unrealistically low, leading to a misleadingly high ROCE.

Return on shareholders' capital (ROSC)

5.8 Another measure of profitability and return is the return on shareholders' capital which is:

$$\frac{\text{profit on ordinary activities before tax}}{\text{share capital and reserves}}$$

It is intended to focus on the return being made by the company for the benefit of its shareholders.

5.9 ROSC is not a widely-used ratio, however, because there are more useful ratios that give an indication of the return to shareholders, such as earnings per share, dividend yield and earnings yield, which are described later.

Analysing profitability and return in more detail: the secondary ratios

5.10 We often sub-analyse ROCE, to find out more about why the ROCE is high or low, or better or worse than last year.

5.11 There are two factors that contribute towards a return on capital employed, both related to sales turnover.

(a) *Profit margin.* A company might make a high or low profit margin on its sales. For example, a company that makes a profit of 25p per £1 of sales is making a bigger return on its turnover than another company making a profit of only 10p per £1 of sales.

(b) *Asset turnover.* Asset turnover is a measure of how well the assets of a business are being used to generate sales. For example, if two companies each have capital employed of £100,000 and Company A makes sales of £400,000 per annum whereas Company B makes sales of only £200,000 per annum, Company A is making a higher turnover from the same amount of assets - ie twice as much asset turnover as Company B - and this will help A to make a higher return on capital employed than B. Asset turnover is expressed as 'x times' so that assets generate x times their value in annual turnover. Here, Company A's asset turnover is 4 times and B's is 2 times.

5.12 Profit margin and asset turnover together explain the ROCE and if the ROCE is the primary profitability ratio, these other two are the secondary ratios. The relationship between the three ratios can be shown mathematically.

Profit margin x asset turnover = ROCE

$$\text{ie} \quad \frac{\text{PBIT}}{\text{Sales}} \times \frac{\text{Sales}}{\text{Capital employed}} = \frac{\text{PBIT}}{\text{Capital employed}}$$

5.13 It might be tempting to think that a high profit margin is good, and a low asset turnover means sluggish trading. In broad terms, this is so. But there is a trade-off between profit margin and asset turnover, and you cannot look at one without allowing for the other.

(a) A high profit margin means a high profit per £1 of sales, but if this also means that sales prices are high, there is a strong possibility that sales turnover will be depressed, and so asset turnover is lower.

(b) A high asset turnover means that the company is generating a lot of sales, but to do this it might have to keep its prices down and so accept a low profit margin per £1 of sales.

5.14 Consider the following example.

Company A		*Company B*	
Sales	£1,000,000	Sales	£4,000,000
Capital employed	£1,000,000	Capital employed	£1,000,000
PBIT	£200,000	PBIT	£200,000

These figures would give the following ratios.

$$\text{ROCE} = \frac{200{,}000}{1{,}000{,}000} = 20\% \qquad \text{ROCE} = \frac{200{,}000}{1{,}000{,}000} = 20\%$$

$$\text{Profit margin} = \frac{200{,}000}{1{,}000{,}000} = 20\% \qquad \text{Profit margin} = \frac{200{,}000}{4{,}000{,}000} = 5\%$$

$$\text{Asset turnover} = \frac{1{,}000{,}000}{1{,}000{,}000} = 1 \qquad \text{Asset turnover} = \frac{4{,}000{,}000}{1{,}000{,}000} = 4$$

5.15 The companies have the same ROCE, but it is arrived at in a very different fashion. Company A operates with a low asset turnover and a comparatively high profit margin whereas company B carries out much more business, but on a lower profit margin. Company A could be operating at the luxury end of the market, whilst company B is operating at the popular end of the market (for example Fortnum and Masons v Sainsbury's).

6. LONG-TERM SOLVENCY: DEBT AND GEARING RATIOS

6.1 Debt ratios are concerned with how much the company owes in relation to its size, whether it is getting into heavier debt or improving its situation, and whether its debt burden seems heavy or light.

(a) When a company is heavily in debt banks and other potential lenders may be unwilling to advance further funds.

(b) When a company is earning only a modest profit before interest and tax, and has a heavy debt burden, there will be very little profit left over for shareholders after the interest charges have been paid. And so if interest rates were to go up (on bank overdrafts etc) or the company were to borrow even more, or if profits before interest were to fall, it might soon be incurring interest charges in excess of PBIT. This might eventually lead to the liquidation of the company.

6.2 These are two important reasons why companies should keep their debt burden under control. There are four ratios that are particularly worth looking at.

(a) The debt ratio.
(b) The gearing ratio.
(c) Tnterest cover.
(d) The cash flow ratio.

The debt ratio

6.3 The debt ratio is the ratio of a company's total debts to its total assets.

(a) Assets consist of fixed assets at their balance sheet value, plus current assets.
(b) Debts consist of all creditors, whether amounts falling due within one year or after more than one year.

You can ignore long-term provisions and liabilities, such as deferred taxation.

6.4 There is no absolute guide to the maximum safe debt ratio, but as a very general guide, you might regard 50% as a safe limit to debt. In practice, many companies operate successfully with a higher debt ratio than this, but 50% is nonetheless a helpful benchmark. In addition, if the debt ratio is over 50% and getting worse, the company's debt position will be worth looking at more carefully.

Gearing ratio

6.5 Capital gearing is concerned with a company's long-term capital structure. We can think of a company as consisting of fixed assets and net current assets (ie working capital, which is current assets minus current liabilities). These assets must be financed by long-term capital of the company, which is either:

(a) share capital and reserves (shareholders' funds) which can be divided into:

(i) ordinary shares plus reserves; and
(ii) preference shares;

or
(b) long-term debt capital - ie 'creditors: amounts falling due after more than one year'.

6.6 Preference share capital is not debt. It would certainly not be included as debt in the debt ratio. However, like loan capital, preference share capital has a prior claim over profits before interest and tax, ahead of ordinary shareholders. Preference dividends must be paid out of profits before ordinary shareholders are entitled to an ordinary dividend, and so we refer to preference share capital and loan capital as prior charge capital.

6.7 *The capital gearing ratio* is a measure of the proportion of a company's capital that is prior charge capital. It is measured as:

$$\frac{\text{prior charge capital}}{\text{total capital}}$$

(a) Prior charge capital is capital carrying a right to a fixed return. It will include preference shares and debentures.

(b) Total capital is ordinary share capital and reserves plus prior charge capital plus any long-term liabilities or provisions. In group accounts we would also include minority interests. It is easier to identify the same figure for total capital as total assets less current liabilities, which you will find given to you in the balance sheet.

6.8 As with the debt ratio, there is no absolute limit to what a gearing ratio ought to be. A company with a gearing ratio of more than 50% is said to be high-geared (whereas low gearing means a gearing ratio of less than 50%). Many companies are high geared, but if a high geared company is becoming increasingly high geared, it is likely to have difficulty in the future when it wants to borrow even more, unless it can also boost its shareholders' capital, either with retained profits or by a new share issue.

6.9 A similar ratio to the gearing ratio is the *debt/equity ratio*, which is the ratio of:

$$\frac{\text{prior charge capital}}{\text{ordinary share capital and reserves}}$$

This gives us the same sort of information as the gearing ratio, and a ratio of 100% or more would indicate high gearing.

The implications of high or low gearing

6.10 We must now consider the implications of a company being high or low geared.

Gearing is, amongst other things, an attempt to quantify the degree of risk involved in holding equity shares in a company - risk both in terms of the company's ability to remain in business and in terms of expected ordinary dividends from the company. The problem with a high geared company is that by definition there is a lot of debt. Debt generally carries a fixed rate of interest (or fixed rate of dividend if in the form of preference shares), hence there is a given (and large) amount to be paid out from profits to holders of debt before arriving at a residue available for distribution to the holders of equity. The riskiness will perhaps become clearer with the aid of an example.

	Company A	*Company B*	*Company C*
	£'000	£'000	£'000
Ordinary share capital	600	400	300
Profit and loss account	200	200	200
Revaluation reserve	100	100	100
	900	700	600
6% preference shares	-	-	100
10% loan stock	100	300	300
Capital employed	1,000	1,000	1,000
Gearing ratio	10%	30%	40%

6.11 Now suppose that each company makes a profit before interest and tax of £50,000, and the rate of corporation tax is 30%. Amounts available for distribution to equity shareholders will be as follows.

	Company A	*Company B*	*Company C*
	£'000	£'000	£'000
Profit before interest and tax	50	50	50
Interest	10	30	30
Profit before tax	40	20	20
Taxation at 30%	12	6	6
Profit after tax	28	14	14
Preference dividend	-	-	6
Available for ordinary shareholders	28	14	8

6.12 If in the subsequent year profit before interest and tax falls to £40,000, the amounts available to ordinary shareholders will also fall.

	Company A	*Company B*	*Company C*
	£'000	£'000	£'000
Profit before interest and tax	40	40	40
Interest	10	30	30
Profit before tax	30	10	10
Taxation at 30%	9	3	3
Profit after tax	21	7	7
Preference dividend	-	-	6
Available for ordinary shareholders	21	7	1
Note			
Gearing ratio	10%	30%	40%
Change in PBIT	- 20%	- 20%	- 20%
Change in profit available for ordinary shareholders	- 25%	- 50%	- 87.5%

6.13 The more highly geared the company, the greater the risk that little (if anything) will be available to distribute by way of dividend to the ordinary shareholders. The example clearly displays this fact in so far as the more highly geared the company, the greater the percentage change in profit available for ordinary shareholders for any given percentage change in profit before interest and tax. The relationship similarly holds when profits increase, and if PBIT had risen by 20% rather than fallen, you would find that once again the largest percentage change in profit available for ordinary shareholders (this means an increase) will be for the highly geared company, company C. Try it if you want to be sure! This means that there will be greater volatility of amounts available for ordinary shareholders, and presumably therefore greater volatility in dividends paid to those shareholders, where a company is highly geared. That is the risk. You may do extremely well or extremely badly without a particularly large movement in the PBIT of the company.

6.14 The risk of a company's ability to remain in business was referred to earlier. Gearing is relevant to this. A high geared company has a large amount of interest to pay annually (assuming that the debt is external borrowing rather than preference shares). If those borrowings are 'secured' in any way (and debentures in particular are secured), then the holders of the debt are perfectly entitled to force the company to realise assets to pay their interest if funds are not available from other sources. Clearly the more highly geared a company the more likely this is to occur when and if profits fall.

Interest cover

6.15 The interest cover ratio shows whether a company is earning enough profits before interest and tax to pay its interest costs comfortably, or whether its interest costs are high in relation to the size of its profits, so that a fall in PBIT would then have a significant effect on profits available for ordinary shareholders.

$$\text{Interest cover equals} \quad \frac{\text{profit before interest and tax}}{\text{interest charges}}$$

6.16 An interest cover of 2 times or less would be low, and should really exceed 3 times before the company's interest costs are to be considered within acceptable limits.

Cash flow ratio

6.17 The cash flow ratio is the ratio of a company's net cash inflow to its total debts.

(a) Net cash inflow is the amount of cash which the company has coming into the business from its operations. A suitable figure for net cash inflow can be obtained from the statement of source and application of funds.

(b) Total debts are short-term and long-term creditors, together with provisions for liabilities and charges. A distinction can be made between debts payable within one year and other debts and provisions.

6.18 Obviously, a company needs to be earning enough cash from operations to be able to meet its foreseeable debts and future commitments, and the cash flow ratio, and changes in the cash flow ratio from one year to the next, provide a useful indicator of a company's cash position.

7. SHORT-TERM SOLVENCY AND LIQUIDITY

7.1 Profitability is of course an important aspect of a company's performance and debt or gearing is another. Neither, however, addresses directly the key issue of liquidity.

7.2 Liquidity is the amount of cash a company can put its hands on quickly to settle its debts (and possibly to meet other unforeseen demands for cash payments too). Liquid funds consist of the following.

(a) Cash.

(b) Short-term investments for which there is a ready market, (short-term investments are distinct from investments in shares in subsidiaries or associated companies).

(c) Fixed-term deposits with a bank or building society, for example a six month high-interest deposit with a bank.

(d) Trade debtors (because they will pay what they owe within a reasonably short period of time).

(e) Bills of exchange receivable (because like ordinary trade debtors, these represent amounts of cash due to be received within a relatively short period of time).

7.3 In summary, liquid assets are current asset items that will or could soon be converted into cash, and cash itself. Two common definitions of liquid assets are as follows.

(a) All current assets without exception.
(b) All current assets with the exception of stocks.

7.4 A company can obtain liquid assets from sources other than sales, such as the issue of shares for cash, a new loan or the sale of fixed assets. But a company cannot rely on these at all times, and in general, obtaining liquid funds depends on making sales and profits. Even so, profits do not always lead to increases in liquidity. This is mainly because funds generated from trading may be immediately invested in fixed assets or paid out as dividends. This point should be familiar to you from your earlier studies. A useful ratio that can be derived from the funds statement is:

$$\frac{\text{funds generated from operations}}{\text{total sources of funds}}$$

A low ratio would indicate that the company is heavily dependent on funds from sources other than trading profits.

7.5 The reason why a company needs liquid assets is so that it can meet its debts when they fall due. Payments are continually made for operating expenses and other costs, and so there is a cash cycle from trading activities of cash coming in from sales and cash going out for expenses. This is illustrated by the following diagram.

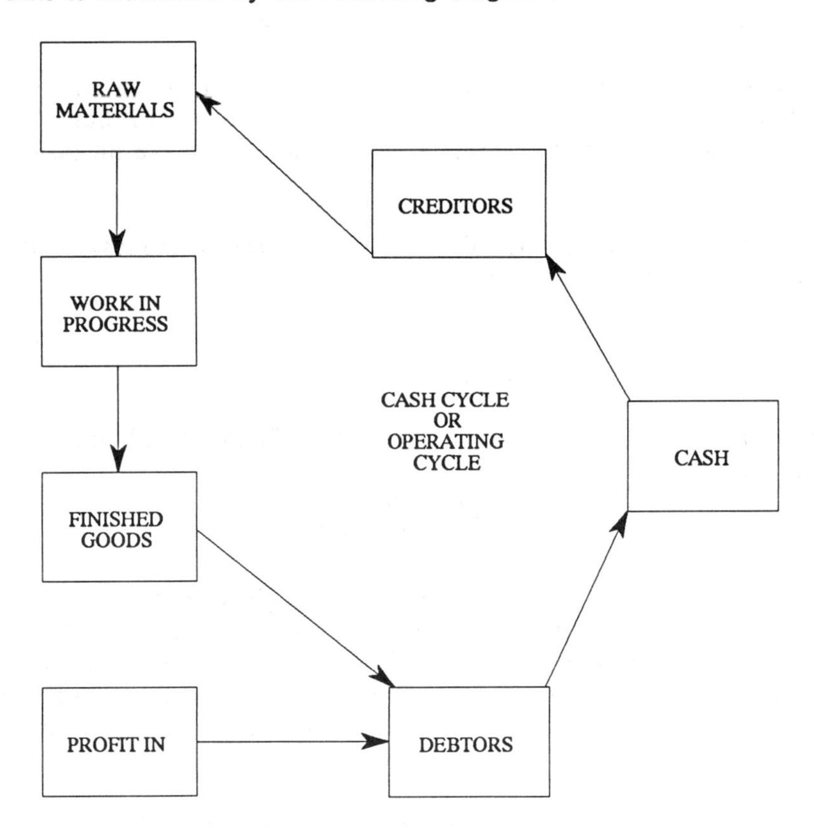

The cash cycle

7.6 To help you to understand liquidity ratios, it is useful to begin with a brief explanation of the cash cycle. The cash cycle describes the flow of cash out of a business and back into it again as a result of normal trading operations.

7.7 Cash goes out to pay for supplies, wages and salaries and other expenses, although payments can be delayed by taking some credit. A business might hold stock for a while and then sell it. Cash will come back into the business from the sales, although customers might delay payment by themselves taking some credit.

7.8 The main points about the cash cycle are as follows.

(a) The timing of cash flows in and out of a business does not coincide with the time when sales and costs of sales occur. Cash flows out can be postponed by taking credit. Cash flows in can be delayed by having debtors.

(b) The time between making a purchase and making a sale also affects cash flows. If stocks are held for a long time, the delay between the cash payment for stocks and cash receipts from selling them will also be a long one.

(c) Holding stocks and having debtors can therefore be seen as two reasons why cash receipts are delayed. Another way of saying this is that if a company invests in working capital, its cash position will show a corresponding decrease.

(d) Similarly, taking credit from creditors can be seen as a reason why cash payments are delayed. The company's liquidity position will worsen when it has to pay the creditors, unless it can get more cash in from sales and debtors in the meantime.

7.9 The liquidity ratios and working capital turnover ratios are used to test a company's liquidity, length of cash cycle, and investment in working capital.

Liquidity ratios: current ratio and quick ratio

7.10 The 'standard' test of liquidity is the current ratio. It can be obtained from the balance sheet, and is the ratio of:

$$\frac{\text{current assets}}{\text{current liabilities}}$$

The idea behind this is that a company should have enough current assets that give a promise of 'cash to come' to meet its future commitments to pay off its current liabilities. Obviously, a ratio in excess of 1 should be expected. Otherwise, there would be the prospect that the company might be unable to pay its debts on time. In practice, a ratio comfortably in excess of 1 should be expected, but what is 'comfortable' varies between different types of businesses.

7.11 Companies are not able to convert all their current assets into cash very quickly. In particular, some manufacturing companies might hold large quantities of raw material stocks, which must be used in production to create finished goods stocks. Finished goods stocks might be warehoused for a long time, or sold on lengthy credit. In such businesses, where stock turnover is slow, most stocks are not very 'liquid' assets, because the cash cycle is so long. For these reasons, we calculate an additional liquidity ratio, known as the quick ratio or acid test ratio.

7.12 The quick ratio, or acid test ratio is:

$$\frac{\text{current assets less stocks}}{\text{current liabilities}}$$

This ratio should ideally be at least 1 for companies with a slow stock turnover. For companies with a fast stock turnover, a quick ratio can be comfortably less than 1 without suggesting that the company should be in cash flow trouble.

7.13 Both the current ratio and the quick ratio offer an indication of the company's liquidity position, but the absolute figures should not be interpreted too literally. It is often theorised that an acceptable current ratio is 1.5 and an acceptable quick ratio is 0.8, but these should only be used as a guide. Different businesses operate in very different ways.

7.14 Don't forget the other side of the coin either. A current ratio and a quick ratio can get bigger than they need to be. A company that has large volumes of stocks and debtors might be over-investing in working capital, and so tying up more funds in the business than it needs to. This would suggest poor management of debtors (credit) or stocks by the company.

8. WORKING CAPITAL RATIOS

Control of debtors and stock

8.1 A rough measure of the average length of time it takes for a company's debtors to pay what they owe is the 'debtor days' ratio, or average debtors' payment period.

8.2 The estimated average debtors' payment period is calculated as:

$$\frac{\text{trade debtors}}{\text{sales}} \times 365 \text{ days}$$

8.3 The figure for sales should be taken as the turnover figure in the profit and loss account. The trade debtors are not the total figure for debtors in the balance sheet, which includes prepayments and non-trade debtors. The trade debtors figure will be itemised in an analysis of the debtors total, in a note to the accounts.

8.4 The estimate of debtor days is only approximate.

(a) The balance sheet value of debtors might be abnormally high or low compared with the 'normal' level the company usually has.

(b) Turnover in the profit and loss account is exclusive of VAT, but debtors in the balance sheet are inclusive of VAT. We are not strictly comparing like with like. (Some companies show turnover inclusive of VAT as well as turnover exclusive of VAT, and the 'inclusive' figure should be used in these cases.)

8.5 Sales are usually made on 'normal credit terms' of payment within 30 days. Debtor days significantly in excess of this might be representative of poor management of funds of a business. However, some companies must allow generous credit terms to win customers. Exporting companies in particular may have to carry large amounts of debtors, and so their average collection period might be well in excess of 30 days.

8.6 The trend of the collection period (debtor days) over time is probably the best guide. If debtor days are increasing year on year, this could be indicative of a poorly managed credit control function (and potentially therefore a poorly managed company).

Stock turnover period

8.7 Another ratio worth calculating is the stock turnover period, or stock days. This is another estimated figure, obtainable from published accounts, which indicates the average number of days that items of stock are held for. As with the average debt collection period, however, it is only an approximate estimated figure, but one which should be reliable enough for comparing changes year on year.

8.8 The number of stock days is calculated as:

$$\frac{\text{stock}}{\text{cost of sales}} \times 365$$

8.9 The reciprocal of the fraction, ie:

$$\frac{\text{cost of sales}}{\text{stock}}$$

is termed the stock turnover, and is another measure of how vigorously a business is trading. A lengthening stock turnover period from one year to the next indicates:

(a) a slowdown in trading; or
(b) a build-up in stock levels, perhaps suggesting that the investment in stocks is becoming excessive.

8.10 Presumably if we add together the stock days and the debtor days, this should give us an indication of how soon stock is convertible into cash. Both debtor days and stock days therefore give us a further indication of the company's liquidity.

Creditors' payment period

8.11 The creditors' payment period can be calculated in a similar way to the debtors' payment period, except using cost of sales instead of sales value.

$$\frac{\text{Trade creditors}}{\text{Cost of sales}} \times 365 \text{ days}$$

Ideally, purchases should be used as the denominator but it is rare to find purchases disclosed in published accounts and so cost of sales serves as an approximation.

Exercise 1

Calculate liquidity and working capital ratios from the accounts of the RMC Group, a manufacturer of products for the construction industry.

	1988	*1987*
	£m	£m
Turnover	2,065.0	1,788.7
Cost of sales	1,478.6	1,304.0
Gross profit	586.4	484.7
Current assets		
Stocks	119.0	109.0
Debtors (note 1)	400.9	347.4
Short-term investments	4.2	18.8
Cash at bank and in hand	48.2	48.0
	572.3	523.2
Creditors: amounts falling due within one year		
Loans and overdrafts	49.1	35.3
Corporation taxes	62.0	46.7
Dividend	19.2	14.3
Creditors (note 2)	370.7	324.0
	501.0	420.3
Net current assets	71.3	102.9

Notes

	1988	1987
1. Trade debtors	329.8	285.4
2. Trade creditors	236.2	210.8

Solution

	1988	1987
Current ratio	$\frac{572.3}{501.0} = 1.14$	$\frac{523.2}{420.3} = 1.24$
Quick ratio	$\frac{453.3}{501.0} = 0.90$	$\frac{414.2}{420.3} = 0.99$
Debtors' payment period	$\frac{329.8}{2,065.0} \times 365 = 58$ days	$\frac{285.4}{1,788.7} \times 365 = 58$ days
Stock turnover period	$\frac{119.0}{1,478.6} \times 365 = 29$ days	$\frac{109.0}{1,304.0} \times 365 = 31$ days
Creditors' payment period	$\frac{236.2}{1,478.6} \times 365 = 58$ days	$\frac{210.8}{1,304.0} \times 365 = 59$ days

8.12 RMC is a manufacturing group serving the construction industry, and so would be expected to have a comparatively lengthy debtors' turnover period, because of the relatively poor cash flow in the construction industry. It is clear that RMC compensates for this by taking a comparable amount of credit from their suppliers (hence the similarity of debtors' and creditors' payment periods).

8.13 It is worth noting that RMC's quick ratio is very little less than the current ratio. This suggests that stock levels are strictly controlled, which is reinforced by the low stock turnover period. It would seem that working capital is tightly managed, to avoid the poor liquidity which could be caused by a high debtors' turnover period and comparatively high creditors.

9. SHAREHOLDERS' INVESTMENT RATIOS

9.1 These are the ratios which help equity shareholders and other investors to assess the value and quality of an investment in the ordinary shares of a company. They are:

(a) earnings per share;
(b) dividend cover;
(c) P/E ratio;
(d) dividend yield;
(e) earnings yield.

9.2 The value of an investment in ordinary shares in a listed company is its market value, and so investment ratios must have regard not only to information in the company's published accounts, but also to the current price.

Earnings per share

9.3 Earnings per share (EPS) is widely used by investors as a measure of a company's performance.

$$\text{EPS} = \frac{\text{profit after tax, minority interests and preference dividend}}{\text{number of ordinary shares in issue}}$$

The EPS monitors the return on each ordinary share. The numerator of the ratio, ie 'profit after tax, minority interests and preference dividend', can be abbreviated to 'earnings'. It is the amount of profit left for ordinary shareholders after all other charges have been paid.

Dividend cover

9.4 Dividend cover is a ratio of:

$$\frac{\text{earnings per share}}{\text{net dividend per (ordinary) share}}$$

It shows what proportion of profit on ordinary activities for the year that is available for distribution to shareholders has been paid (or proposed) and what proportion will be retained in the business to finance future growth. A dividend cover of 2 times would indicate that, ignoring extraordinary items, the company had paid 50% of its distributable profits as dividends, and retained 50% in the business to help to finance future operations. Retained profits are an important source of funds for most companies, and so the dividend cover can in some cases be quite high, indicating that the company has retained a large proportion of their profits for re-investment in the business.

9.5 A significant change in the dividend cover from one year to the next would be worth looking at closely. For example, if a company's dividend cover were to fall sharply between one year and the next, it could be that its profits had fallen, but the directors wished to pay at least the same amount of dividends as in the previous year, so as to keep shareholder expectations satisfied.

P/E ratio

9.6 The P/E ratio (price/earnings ratio) is the ratio of a company's current share price to the earnings per share.

A high P/E ratio indicates strong shareholder confidence in the company and its future, for example in profit growth, and a lower P/E ratio indicates lower confidence.

9.7 The P/E ratio of one company can be compared with the P/E ratios of other companies in the same business sector, or with other companies generally.

Dividend yield

9.8 Dividend yield is the return a shareholder is currently expecting on the shares of a company. It is calculated as:

$$\frac{\text{dividend on the share for the year (\textit{grossed up})}}{\text{current market value of the share (ex div)}} \times 100\%$$

(a) The dividend per share is taken as the dividend for the previous year.

(b) The dividend is inclusive of the tax credit. The net dividend is the amount paid out of the profit and loss account, and the gross dividend is found by multiplying the net dividend by a factor of:

$$\frac{100}{(100 - IT)}$$

IT is the basic rate of income tax. Thus, given a basic rate of income tax of 25%, the gross dividend is the net dividend multiplied by a factor of 100/75.

9.9 Shareholders look for both dividend yield and capital growth. Obviously, dividend yield is therefore an important aspect of a share's performance.

Exercise 2

In the year to 30 September 1988, Saatchi & Saatchi declared an interim ordinary dividend of 7.4p per share and a final ordinary dividend of 8.6p per share. Assuming an ex div share price of 315 pence, what is the dividend yield, given a basic rate of income tax of 25%?

Solution

The net dividend per share is (7.4 + 8.6) = 16 pence

$$\frac{16 \times 100/75}{315} \times 100 \qquad = 6.8\%$$

Earnings yield

9.10 Earnings yield is a performance indicator that is not given the same publicity as the earnings per share, P/E ratio, dividend cover and dividend yield.

It is measured as the earnings per share, grossed up, as a percentage of the current share price.

9.11 The earnings yield attempts to improve the comparison between investments in different companies by overcoming the problem that companies have differing dividend covers. Some companies retain a bigger proportion of their profits than others, and so the dividend yield between companies can vary for this reason. Earnings yield overcomes the problem of comparison because it is not affected by the proportion of earnings which are paid out as dividends.

Exercise 3

	Company P		Company Q	
	£m	£m	£m	£m
Profit on ordinary activities before tax		60.0		6.5
Tax on profit on ordinary activities		20.0		2.4
Profit on ordinary activities after tax		40.0		4.1
Profit attributable to minority interest		2.0		0.4
		38.0		3.7
Extraordinary item				
Before tax	5.0		3.0	
Tax	(1.7)		(1.0)	
	3.3		2.0	
Attributable to minority interest	0.2		0.1	
Attributable to group		3.1		1.9
Profit attributable to shareholders		41.1		5.6
Dividends				
Preference	0.5		-	
Ordinary	20.6		5.4	
		21.1		5.4
Retained profits		20.0		0.2

	Company P	Company Q
Number of ordinary shares	200m	50m
Market price per share	285p	154p
Basic rate of income tax	25%	25%

Compare the dividend yield, dividend cover and earnings yield of the two companies.

Solution

	Company P	Company Q
	£m	£m
Profit on ordinary activities less minority interest	38.0	3.7
Preference dividend	0.5	0
Earnings available for ordinary shareholders	37.5	3.7
Number of shares	200m	50m
Earnings per share	18.75p	7.4p
Ordinary dividend per share	10.3p	10.8p

Dividend cover

Company P: $\frac{18.75}{10.3}$ or $\frac{37.5}{21.1}$ = 1.8 times

Company Q: $\frac{7.4}{10.8}$ or $\frac{3.7}{5.4}$ = 0.7 times

Dividend yield

Company P: $\frac{10.3 \times 100/75}{285} \times 100\%$ = 4.8%

Company Q: $\frac{10.8 \times 100/75}{154} \times 100\%$ = 9.4%

Earnings yield	$\frac{18.75p \times 100/75}{285} \times 100\%$	$\frac{7.4p \times 100/75}{154} \times 100\%$
	= 8.8%	= 6.4%

The dividend yield of Company Q is much higher, but the dividend cover of Company P is greater, and this bigger dividend cover is reflected in the higher earnings yield of Company P. (The dividend cover of Q is less than 1 but because of the extraordinary item in the P & L account, Company Q has managed to pay its dividend out of profits made in the year.)

10. RATIOS FROM VALUE ADDED STATEMENTS

10.1 Value added statements can provide a useful source of information for ratio analysis. The monetary amounts in a value added statement are often accompanied by percentage figures so that it can be seen at a glance how much of the value added has been paid out to each of the contributory groups.

10.2 There are some other interesting ratios which can be calculated from the statement, particularly if the number of the company's employees is known. In a full set of published accounts this will always be known, because its disclosure is a requirement of the Companies Act 1985.

10.3 The possible ratios from a value added statement include the following.

(a) Value added per £1 of capital employed. This is similar to ROCE, except that PBIT is replaced by value added. The formula is:

$$\frac{\text{value added}}{\text{capital employed}}$$

(b) Value added per employee, ie

$$\frac{\text{value added}}{\text{number of employees}}$$

This is a ratio which has been used by some companies as part of productivity agreements. A high ratio would indicate that each employee is making a good contribution to value added.

10.4 Marketing students and unfortunately some professionals are inclined to ignore the quantified and financial aspects of the business world. CIM examiners will not accept financially illiterate students as candidates for a pass at Diploma level. You are therefore strongly recommended to ensure that you are comfortable with the ratio analysis covered in this section.

Exercise 4

Send off for the published accounts of firms operating in your market and analyse their published accounts. Compare different competitors and write a short report on each, indicating their relative strengths and weaknesses.

11. PERFORMANCE/PRODUCTIVITY ANALYSIS

11.1 Ratios for control need not be wholly financial ratios. An organisation can also use quantitative ratios or specially selected cost or revenue performance measures.

Productivity indices (efficiency indices)

11.2 An index of productivity or efficiency can be used to measure performance. Greater productivity should mean lower unit costs. Labour productivity could be measured as follows.

$$\text{Labour productivity} = \frac{\text{'standard' number of hours produced}}{\text{actual number of hours worked}} \times 100\%$$

11.3 When the labour force does a job in exactly the time expected, productivity is 100%. If productivity is better than expected, the index will be higher than 100%. When productivity is lower than expected then the index will be lower than 100%.

11.4 A materials efficiency ratio or a machine efficiency ratio could also be calculated in a similar way.

Example: labour productivity

11.5 A unit of product is expected to take six hours to make. Labour is paid £5 per hour.

During 19X8 the following results were achieved.

Output (units)	3,000 units
Labour cost	16,000 hrs x £5 = £80,000

Required

(a) Calculate the labour productivity ratio for 19X8.

(b) Calculate the actual labour cost per unit, and comment on your result.

Solution

11.6 (a) Productivity ratio

$$= \frac{\text{standard hours produced}}{\text{actual time}} = \frac{3{,}000 \times 6\text{hrs}}{16{,}000\text{ hrs}} \times 100\%$$

$$= 112.5\%$$

(b) Labour cost per unit (actual cost)

$$= \frac{£80{,}000}{3{,}000}$$

$$= £26.67$$

The actual labour cost per unit is less than the budgeted labour cost (6hrs x £5) £30, because labour productivity was higher than budgeted.

Market share

11.7 Market share shows the volume of sales for the organisation's own product as a percentage of total sales for the market as a whole.

11.8 For example, suppose that the total market sales volume for a type of product is expected to be 200,000 units. A company budgets its own sales of the product to be 40,000 units and actual sales are 48,000 units.

$$\text{Budgeted market share} = \frac{40{,}000}{200{,}000} \times 100\% = 20\%$$

$$\text{Actual market share} = \frac{48{,}000}{200{,}000} \times 100\% = 24\%$$

Other performance ratios

11.9 Cost or revenue performance measures may include non-monetary data, such as:

(a) value added per employee;
(b) wages per employee;
(c) sales per cubic metre of shelf space;
(d) sales per square metre of floor space;
(e) sales per £1 of advertising;
(f) sales per employee in the sales force;
(g) contribution per cubic metre of shelf space, per square metre of floor space or per employee;
(h) net profit per cubic metre of shelf space, square metre of floor space or per employee;
(i) occupancy costs per square metre of floor space;
(j) cost per call of a salesperson;
(k) value of sales per call;
(l) cost per ton/mile of delivering goods.

11.10 Non-monetary data may be useful to middle or senior management, but they may also provide junior managers and supervisors with control information which is more helpful than traditional financial accounting ratios, because they are more specific to their work.

11.11 Another ratio which you might find useful is a *machine utilisation ratio* (ie the ratio of actual machine hours in operation to the total machine hours available) or a machine availability ratio (ie the ratio of total machine hours available for operations to the total machine hours capacity).

12. CONCLUSION

12.1 If plans are to be realistic and achievable they have to be developed in conjunction with a thorough analysis of the external and uncontrollable elements of the business environment.

12.2 The process and approach to planning and analysis is the same at marketing level as it is at corporate level - only the focus is different.

12.3 It is important for marketing students to clarify the level at which they are working in a given question or case scenario.

12.4 SWOT is a management tool used to provide a framework for clarifying a picture or situation.

12.5 Marketing professionals cannot abdicate all financial responsibility to accountants. Diploma students need to be competent to handle ratio analysis and interpret any financial information which they are given.

12.6 The more detailed productivity analysis can be useful particularly at departmental or branch level when you need to consider the contribution of individual sales staff or products.

TEST YOUR KNOWLEDGE

The numbers in brackets refer to paragraphs of this chapter

1. What is meant by a 'limiting factor?' Give four examples of a limiting factor. (1.8-1.11)
2. What is a marketing audit? (2.2-2.4)
3. What is a SWOT analysis? (3.2-3.4)
4. How would a marketing SWOT differ from a corporate SWOT? (3.8, 3.30)
5. What does ratio analysis involve? (4.1)
6. What are the main financial ratios which you would use to interpret a company's accounts? (4.6)
7. Is a high profit margin always a good thing? (5.13)
8. What are the implications of a company being highly geared? (6.10, 6.14)
9. How might a sales negotiation which agrees to extending the period of credit offered to the purchaser affect the financial health of the business? (7.8)
10. What is the value of productivity analysis? (11.2, 11.9)

Now try illustrative question 5

Chapter 5

MANAGING AND USING INFORMATION

This chapter covers the following topics.

1. Management information systems and databases
2. The role of marketing research

1. MANAGEMENT INFORMATION SYSTEMS AND DATABASES

1.1 Managers need easy access to good quality, relevant and up to date information if their 'where are we now' assessment is going to be a meaningful basis for planning.

1.2 As we have already seen this information needs to cover both internal performance and external variables. It must indicate not only historical results and trends, but, where feasible, must provide a forecast of future changes. The wide spectrum of issues and factors which managers need to complete their picture of the current operation means it is easy for them to suffer from information overload, possibly a worse situation than planning with no information at all.

1.3 Investment in a management information system or database is made to provide managers with a useful flow of relevant information which is easy to use and easy to access. Information is an important corporate resource. Managed and used effectively it can provide considerable competitive advantage and so it is a worthwhile investment.

1.4 The complexity of the planning process, and the systematic approach that is essential in what rapidly becomes a multi-aspect and multi-dimensional planning model, lends itself readily to the use of computers and computer databases. The diagram which follows suggests the position of the database within the planning and control system.

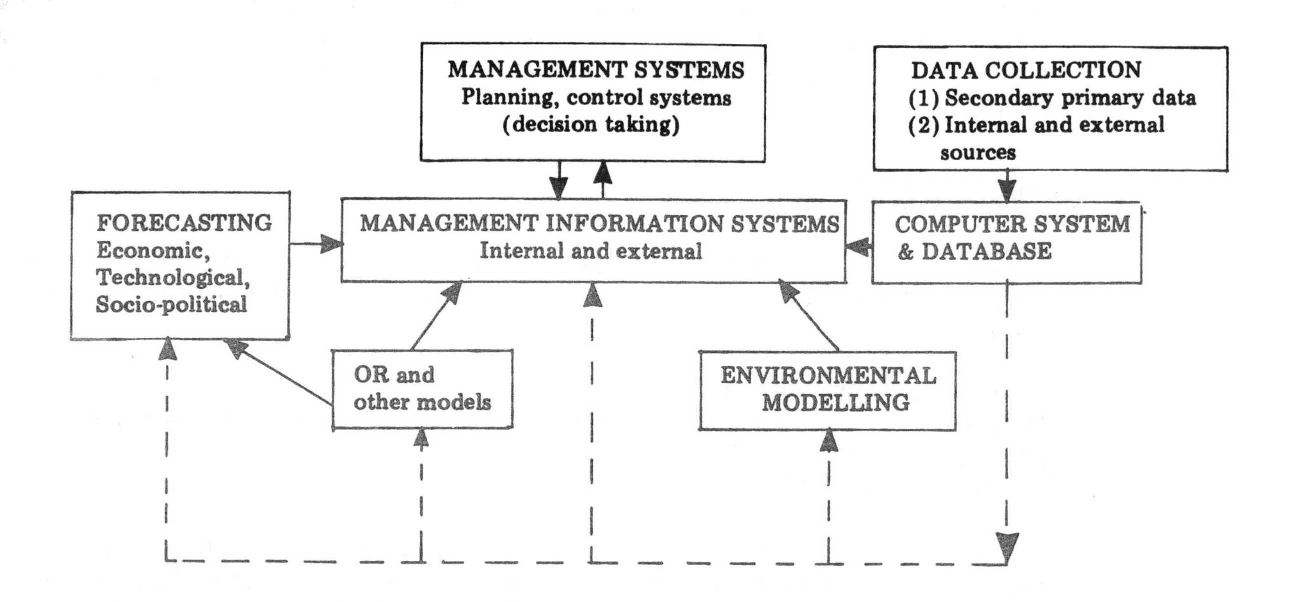

1.5 You will already be familiar with the concept of a 'database'. In simple terms, a database is a large file or files of data, with the file structured in such a way that the data can be processed by different users in a large number of different ways. A database is, by implication, a computer file, and the collection of programs that are written to process data on the file in the many different ways is referred to as a database management system (DBMS).

1.6 These definitions of database and DBMS, taken from *Computing terminology* published by the Chartered Institute of Management Accountants, may help you to distinguish between the two.

(a) *Database*. Frequently a much-abused term - in its strict sense a database is a file of data structured in such a way that it may serve a number of applications without its structure being dictated by any one of these applications, the concept being that programs are written around the database rather than files being structured to meet the needs of specific programs. The term is also rather loosely applied to simple file management software.

(b) *Database management systems*. Technically a system which uses a database philosophy for the storage of information. In practice this term is often used to describe any system which enables the definition, storage and retrieval of information from discrete files within a system. Thus many simple file-handling systems are frequently referred to as 'database systems'.

1.7 Our interest in databases is a user interest, because databases can provide valuable information to strategic planners and marketing management.

(a) Computer databases make it easier to collect and store more data/information.

(b) Computer software allows the data to be extracted from the file and processed to provide whatever information management needs.

(c) Developments in information technology allow businesses to have access to the databases of external organisations. Reuters, for example, provide an on-line information system about money market interest rates and foreign exchange rates to firms involved in money market and foreign exchange dealings, and to the treasury departments of a large number of companies.

What data should a database contain?

1.8 Ackoff suggests that a database is an integral part of the management system, since data is essential raw material for the planning process. Data is a vital resource which is needed for three purposes.

(a) For processing into information.
(b) To prompt management into wanting further information, or more details about the existing information that is available.
(c) To generate new data.

It must obviously be easily retrievable from file when it is needed, and it must be re-usable. In other words, data that is put on to file and then lost or forgotten about is useless. Management must know that the data is there, and how to retrieve it from file, and they must want to use it at some time in the future.

1.9 For a database to be useful to strategic planners or marketing management, it must contain certain items of data about the business itself and also about the environment of the business.

Environmental data

1.10 McNamee lists nine areas of environmental information that ought to be included in a database for strategic planners. These are as follows.

(a) *Competitive data*: data on:
 (i) the threat of new entrants;
 (ii) the threat from substitutes;
 (iii) the power of buyers;
 (iv) the power of suppliers;
 (v) the nature and intensity of competition;
 (vi) the strategies or likely strategies of competitors (for example their prices, marketing policies, product quality etc).

(b) *Economic data*: details of past growth and predictions of future growth in GDP and disposable income, the pattern of interest rates, predictions of the rate of inflation, unemployment levels and tax rates, developments in international trade etc.

(c) *Political data*: what influence the government is having on the industry.

(d) *Legal data*: what are the likely implications of recent legislation, what legislation is likely to be introduced in the future, and what implications would this have?

(e) *Social data*: what are the changing habits, attitudes, cultures and educational standards of the population as a whole, and customers in particular?

(f) *Technological data*: what technological changes have occurred or will occur, and what implications will these have for the organisation?

(g) *Geographical data*: data should be built up about individual regions or countries, each of them potentially segments of the market with their own unique characteristics.

(h) *Energy data*: what energy sources are going to be available, and at what price?

(i) *Data about stakeholders in the business*: including employees and management, as well as shareholders. What influence does each group have, and what is each group likely to want from the organisation?

These are the environmental factors we discussed earlier.

Internal and external databases

1.11 Data about the environment can be generated in two ways.

(a) It can be built up by the business itself in its own internal database system.
(b) It can be obtained from an external database that is operated by another organisation.

1.12 External databases are becoming increasingly specialised. One example is found in the motor car components supply industry. Manufacturers of motor car components supply their products to the car manufacturers, and they need to be able to spot trends in the use of components by car manufacturers throughout the world. A few years ago, a number of databases became available for the component suppliers.

(a) PRS, the consultancy group, has built up a database which can provide a detailed breakdown of the constituent parts of motor vehicles produced worldwide, making it possible for component suppliers to identify trends in their market.

'For example, it is easily possible, by examining four years' statistics, to track how fuel-injection systems have grown at the expense of carburettors, or the increasing market penetration of vehicles fitted with turbochargers or multi-valve engines.'
(*Financial Times*, 4 April 1986)

(b) Another PRS database holds data about new car registrations in Europe for at least the last ten years. This should be of interest to component suppliers who supply replacement parts to the 'aftermarket'.

(c) A database available from James McArdle and Associates, another consultancy firm, provides data about commercial vehicle production.

'It is possible, as just one example, to ask the database to show, over a five-year rolling period, manufacturers and their country of origin of commercial vehicles defined by the number of axles, vehicle weight, torque or power output, or cubic capacity - or a combination of these.' (*Financial Times*)

1.13 Such databases could be used by component suppliers to take much of the guesswork or number-crunching out of their planning, and to assess the likely future demand both for replacement parts and for original equipment.

Collecting external data

1.14 Much environmental data is likely to be secondary data, ie data not collected for the specific purposes of a particular data user. Sources of secondary data are published government statistics, economic forecasts by economic forecasting groups, the published reports and accounts of competitors, and information obtained from the financial press, national newspapers or professional magazines etc.

1.15 Secondary data does have its limitations, it is not always possible to ascertain why it was produced. Politically influenced data, for example the level of unemployment may be misleading. It is equally difficult sometimes to be sure of the way terms used in data collections have been defined. Again using the example of unemployment, your definition may differ from the one used as the basis for the data collection.

1.16 But secondary data is relatively cheap, usually easily available and it can cover sample sizes and geographic areas which it would not be possible for a single firm to do for itself. For example the census of population is a vast research exercise and is now used extensively as a basis for much market segmentation analysis.

1.17 However, secondary data can never be as relevant and focused as primary data, ie information collected by the organisation for a specific purpose. Therefore secondary information sources will be supplemented through marketing research activities which we will consider later in this chapter.

Using internal databases

1.18 A database can be built up of internal data about the business itself. The data can be used in the initial stages of strategic planning as follows.

(a) To carry out a *resource audit*.
(b) To assess and plan *resource utilisation* .
(c) To *control* the use of resources.

1.19 A resource audit is a survey of what resources the business has in each of its functions or divisions. There are four groups of resources.

(a) Physical resources.
(b) Human resources.
(c) Systems.
(d) Intangibles (for example company image).

1.20 Resource utilisation is concerned with the efficiency with which resources are used, and the effectiveness of their use in achieving the planning objectives of the business.

1.21 The two key words here are *efficiency* and *effectiveness*, and to ensure that there is no confusion, both terms are defined here in the context of strategic planning.

Johnson and Scholes define *efficiency* as 'how well the resources have been utilised irrespective of the purpose for which they have been employed'.

Similarly, they define *effectiveness* as: 'whether the resources have been deployed in the best possible way'.

Efficiency and effectiveness are not the same thing. It is possible to be efficient doing things that have little or no value, and it is possible to be effective in getting a job done, but use resources inefficiently in doing so.

Efficiency

1.22 Efficiency can be measured and recorded in a database in a number of ways.

(a) *Profitability*. Commercial organisations must, at the end of the day, make a profit. The efficiency of the use of resources in achieving profit can be measured in the context of cost of capital, return on finance, and how the competition is doing. The PIMS approach (Profit Impact of Market Strategy) identifies in this context company size, return on investment (ROI), profit ratios, earnings per share (EPS), dividend rates, market price of equities, liquidity ratios, size of monetary assets balances, use of assets, leverage ratios, and the intensity of investment. This latter measure identifies the amount of investment being put in by a company. There are two ratios to measure the intensity of investment: investment/sales and investment/value added. Capital intensive organisations, with a strong commitment to more investment, often have poor ROI ratios, and it is argued that capital investment is not necessarily a sign of company health, but rather a situation where hardware has become an end in itself.

For the public sector, such as a local authority, the ratios must hinge upon the efficient stewardship of resources, since there is no profit motive.

(b) *Labour productivity* and the use of human resources. Efficiency records will cover the cost of labour (white as well as blue collar workers), levels of absenteeism, labour turnover, days lost through stoppages and strikes, the balance of functional expertise in the workforce, the equality of employees and the degree of unionisation and the attitude of the unions.

(c) *Production and marketing performance*. In a production context, this refers to yield and productivity ratios, while in the marketing context, product sales analysis, sales growth, market share, width of product line, sales per employee, number of customers, rate of new product development and quality of production will be important items of data.

(d) Other measures that can be recorded are as follows.

(i) *Capacity-fill,* ie actual volume as a percentage of full capacity. This is vitally important in a capital-intensive service industry, such as hotels and restaurants.

(ii) *Working capital utilisation*. It may be that the competition is controlling working capital better and in consequence has lower financing charges.

(iii) *Operating systems*. As an example, does the company move goods in the most efficient way, minimising excessive handling, and taking advantage of any new methods of goods handling that may become available.

Effectiveness

1.23 Effectiveness may well be less easy to measure and obtain data for than efficiency. Nonetheless, it embraces such areas as the following.

(a) *The use of people*. The question must be 'are you getting out of the people what is wanted?'

(b) *Use of capital*. Is capital being raised and used to achieve its purpose? For example a hotel represents a considerable capital investment, which requires a high level of occupancy. Thus, its performance in the business market in the week, its share of the holiday market, however defined, and if appropriate, its share of the conference market will all be measures in this context.

(c) *Use of research knowledge*. Again this is an area that borders on the intangible, but the extent to which R & D is creating new products should be assessed.

(d) *Use of operating systems or logistics*. Is the organisation using its systems of operating to a good purpose or could they be used better to do other things?

(e) *Use of intangibles*. Is the company making use of its intangible assets, such as brand image, trademarks and patents, to develop its products and markets?

The database and control of resources

1.24 Johnson and Scholes suggest that once a database has been built up which recognises what resources the organisation has at its disposal and how efficiently and effectively they are being used, management can draw on information from the database to control the use of the resources.

They recognise that there could be situations where good resources are well deployed, but the actual performance is poor because of poor control. Areas that will come under review are as follows.

(a) *Control of physical resources.* For example ensuring that buildings are adequately maintained and held secure, that production control systems are adequate, and that plant is adequately maintained. In addition, in a manufacturing environment, control should be kept over suppliers in terms of quantities purchased, quality and cost. Inventory levels, stores security and operational quality control should be rigorously enforced.

(b) *Control of key personnel.* This means not just the effective handling of industrial relations problems, nor is it confined to the shop floor. Management need to ensure that subordinates continue to be aware of what is expected of them, and keep to their task to the best of their abilities.

(c) *Costing.* Fundamental to control and decision making is the awareness of how costs are affected by decisions or events. This requires that the costing system be highly effective in its operation, an area where many small companies still fall down.

(d) *Quality of materials*. Materials and components must meet the required specifications and product specifications must be suitably defined. There is the risk of over-engineering a product as well as a risk of making specifications that would be insufficient to bring a product up to its required quality standard.

(e) *Market outlets*. Control over this area is vital. Any organisation must 'sell' its output to its customers, and so it is essential that there should be adequate control over the place and method by which the organisation's products or services are put on offer to the customer.

(f) *Stock control and production control*.

Marketing information systems

1.25 All information systems are designed to provide continuous flows of information, allowing the manager to identify trends and changes in the market place and business environment.

1.26 Marketing managers, like all other managers, need information for planning and control. The marketing information system (MKIS) is a part of an organisation's overall management information system (MIS).

1.27 A typical computerised MKIS could be described as having four components.

(a) A data bank will store raw marketing data, such as data about historical sales and data from market research findings.

(b) A statistical bank will store programs for carrying out computations for sales forecasts, making advertising spending projections and calculating sales force productivity etc.

(c) A model bank will store marketing models for planning and analysis.

(d) A display unit. A marketing manager will often communicate with a MKIS via VDU screen and keyboard. Alternatively, marketing reports can be printed out in hard copy form.

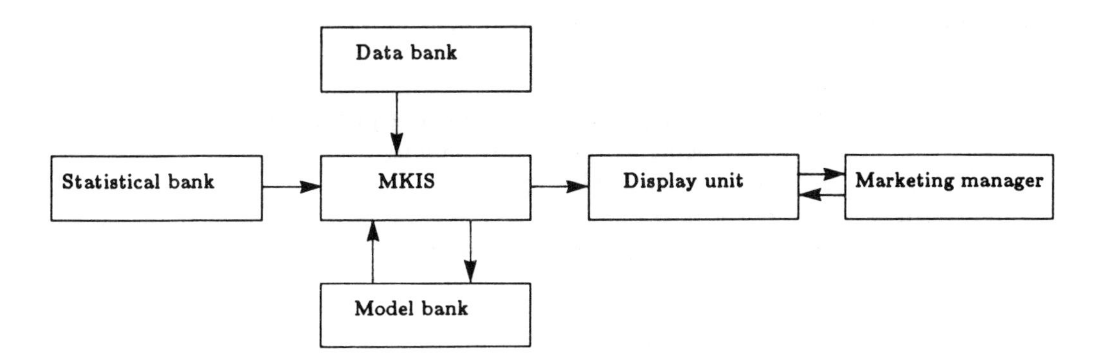

1.28 The sources of marketing data will vary from organisation to organisation, but are both internal and external, including information provided by marketing research.

1.29 A well-structured database can provide managers with information which will help them carry out their functions more thoroughly at either corporate or functional level. It must be recognised that information is not a substitute for decision making, but information does reduce the risk of making the wrong decision. Neither does using information as an aid to decision making indicate a weakness in management skills.

1.30 As a rough indication the more important the decision and the greater the cost involved if the wrong decision is made, the more information you need to help make an informed decision. The more likely it is you will then seek out additional information in the form of marketing research.

2. THE ROLE OF MARKETING RESEARCH

Definitions

2.1 'Market research' and 'marketing research' are often used interchangeably although there is a difference of scope. Market research refers to finding out information about the market for a particular product or service; marketing research was defined more broadly by the American Marketing Association as 'the systematic gathering, recording and analysing of data about problems relating to the marketing of goods and services'. This marketing research includes research on the effects of pricing, advertising and other marketing decision variables.

2.2 Alternative definitions of marketing research you may already be familiar with include the following.

- 'The objective gathering, recording and analysing of all facts about problems relating to the transfer and sales of goods and services from producer to consumer or user.'
  (Chartered Institute of Marketing)

- 'Systematic problem analysis, model-building and fact-finding for the purposes of improved decision making and control in the marketing of goods and services.'
  (Kotler)

2.3 The scope of marketing research may be listed as follows.

(a) *Market research*, which includes:
  (i) analysis of the market potential for existing products;
  (ii) forecasting likely demand for new products;
  (iii) sales forecasting for all products;
  (iv) study of market trends;
  (v) study of the characteristics of the market;
  (vi) analysis of market shares.

(b) *Product research*, which includes:
  (i) customer acceptance of proposed new products;
  (ii) comparative studies between competitive products;
  (iii) studies into packaging and design;
  (iv) forecasting new uses for existing products;
  (v) test marketing;
  (vi) research into the development of a product line (range).

(c) *Price research,* which includes:
  (i) analysis of elasticities of demand;
  (ii) analysis of costs and contribution or profit margins;
  (iii) the effect of changes in credit policy on demand;
  (iv) customer perceptions of price (and quality).

(d) *Sales promotion research,* which includes:
  (i) motivation research for advertising and sales promotion effectiveness;
  (ii) analysing the effectiveness of advertising on sales demand;
  (iii) analysing the effectiveness of individual aspects of advertising (copy, use of media etc);
  (iv) establishing sales territories;
  (v) analysing the effectiveness of salespeople;
  (vi) analysing the effectiveness of other sales promotion methods.

(e) *Distribution research,* which includes:
  (i) the location and design of distribution centres;
  (ii) the analysis of packaging for transportation and shelving;
  (iii) dealer supply requirements;
  (iv) dealer advertising requirements;
  (v) the cost of different methods of transportation and warehousing.

2.4 Marketing research also extends into other areas, such as the following.

(a) The study of corporate responsibility (for example towards the environment).
(b) Economic forecasting.
(c) International and export studies.
(d) Long term business forecasting.

2.5 By focusing on the specific information needed for an identified decision to be made, marketing research helps managers to make the correct decision, reducing the chance of 'getting it wrong'. But the quantity and quality of information provided by market research has an associated cost and the trade-off between cost and accuracy is important, particularly because risk cannot be eliminated. There is no such thing as perfect information when dealing with decision making in an uncertain world.

The use of marketing research consultants

2.6 Marketing research has been a growing source of organisation expenditure in recent years. Very few organisations believe that they can shoulder the cost of a large full-time staff of marketing research workers, especially a 'field force' of researchers spread around the country. It is quite probable, therefore, that the organisation will have a small full-time marketing research department, and will also use the services of external marketing research consultants for specific projects. In addition to market research agencies, there are market research departments in many of the large UK advertising agencies.

2.7 An external agency would bring expertise in marketing research which an organisation might not be able to supply in-house, although it would need to liaise with the organisation through its marketing research department.

2.8 Marketing research involves the following five stages of work.

(a) *Definition of the problem.* An individual marketing research project cannot be undertaken successfully until the marketing problem which management wishes to resolve has been properly defined. This stage is even more crucial when working with an external consultant.

(b) *Design of the research.* Once the research team knows what problem it must help to resolve, it will establish the type of data (secondary or primary), the collection method to be used (postal questionnaire, personal interview), the selection of a research agency (if appropriate) and if a sample is to be taken, the design of the sample. Any questions put to respondents must be carefully designed.

(c) *Collection of the data.*

(d) *Analysis of the data.*

(e) *Presentation of a report* which should then lead to a management marketing decision.

The sources of marketing research information

2.9 Marketing research data can be either *primary* data or *secondary* data. Primary data is information collected specifically for the study under consideration. Secondary data is 'data neither collected directly by the user nor specifically for the user, often under conditions that are not well known to the user'. (American Marketing Association). The collection of secondary data for marketing research is sometimes known as *desk research.*

2.10 Desk research involves collecting data from the information database already discussed. Examples are as follows.

(a) Records inside the firm, gathered by another department or section for a different purpose to the research task in hand. Internal data would include:

(i) production data about quantities produced, materials and labour resources used etc;
(ii) data about inventory;
(iii) data about sales volumes, analysed by sales area, salesperson, quantity, price, profitability, distribution outlet, customer etc;
(iv) data about marketing itself, ie promotion and brand data etc;
(v) all cost and management accounting data;
(vi) financial management data relating to the capital structure of the firm, capital tied up in stocks and debtors, etc.

(b) Published information from external sources, such as:

(i) publications of market research agencies, such as the Nielsen Index;
(ii) government statistics;
(iii) publications of trade associations;
(iv) professional journals.

2.11 Sources of secondary data for marketing vary according to the needs of the organisation.

2.12 The government is a major source of economic information and information about industry and population trends. Examples of government publications are as follows.

(a) The Annual Abstract of Statistics and its monthly equivalent, the Monthly Digest of Statistics. These contain data about manufacturing output, housing, population etc.
(b) The Digest of UK Energy Statistics (published annually).
(c) Housing and Construction Statistics (published quarterly).
(d) Financial Statistics (monthly).
(e) Economic Trends (monthly).
(f) Census of Population.
(g) Census of Production (annual). This has been described as 'one of the most important sources of desk research for industrial marketers'. It provides data about production by firms in each industry in the UK.
(h) Department of Employment Gazette (monthly) giving details of employment in the UK.
(i) British Business, published weekly by the Department of Trade and Industry, giving data on industrial and commercial trends at home and overseas.
(j) Business Monitors, giving detailed information about various industries.

2.13 Non-government sources of information include the following.

(a) The national press (Financial Times etc) and financial and professional magazines and journals.
(b) Companies and other organisations specialising in the provision of economic and financial data (for example the Financial Times Business Information Service, the Data Research Institute, Reuters and the Extel Group).
(c) Directories and yearbooks.
(d) Professional institutions (for example Chartered Institute of Marketing, Industrial Marketing Research Association, British Institute of Management, Institute of Practitioners in Advertising).
(e) Specialist libraries, such as the City Business Library in London, collect published information from a wide variety of sources.

2.14 Secondary data sources should always be scanned as a first step in a research activity. Existing information may provide enough data to reduce the risk in decision making to an acceptable level, or may provide insights which help to focus any primary research more tightly.

Field research and primary data

2.15 If further information is still required the only option is to undertake the research directly. Often referred to as field research this results in the collection of primary data, data which will be used for the first time to make this particular management decision.

2.16 Primary data can be collected in any of three ways.

(a) Experimentation.
(b) Survey.
(c) Observation.

2.17 The most well known of these is probably the survey, with the stereotype image of a lady with a clipboard. Each of the techniques has its particular strengths and choice of approach is determined by the nature of the problem and the business.

Experimentation

2.18 In a *controlled experiment* a controlled research environment is established and selected stimuli are then introduced. To the extent that 'outside' factors can be eliminated from the environment (ie depending on the degree to which a controlled environment is established) the observed effects can be measured and related to each stimulus. Controlled experiments have been used to find the best advertising campaign, the best price level, the best incentive scheme, the best sales training method etc.

2.19 When experiments are conducted in more realistic market settings, results are less reliable because of the inability to control outside factors. Nevertheless the genuine market reaction to, for example, a new product is often a prerequisite to a national launch. This is known as a test market.

Survey

2.20 The survey approach involves questioning the target market or population. In marketing research for consumer goods, it will be impossible to obtain data from every consumer in the market, because not only would this take too much time and cost too much money, but it would also be impracticable in any case. (In a small market however, such as an industrial market or government market, a census might be practicable and preferable to a sample survey). To obtain data, it is therefore usually necessary to obtain a sample to provide an estimate of the characteristics of the entire 'population' and the accuracy of the sample will depend on the following.

(a) How the sample is taken.
(b) The amount of variability in the population.
(c) The size of the sample.

The larger the sample, the greater the likelihood that the sample will provide an accurate reflection of the population as a whole.

2.21 The survey method will influence costs and response rates. Questioning can be in great depth to a relatively small sample. This is qualitative or motivational research and provides information on behaviour and attitudes. Alternatively questions can be limited and highly structured, in the form of questionnaires delivered by post, telephone or in person. This generates quantitative data providing factual responses such as how much, how many, when and where purchases were made.

Observation

2.22 Observation involves just that. It is frequently used when managers want to evaluate the impact of a new store layout or the response to a proposed new pack design. In these situations questioning may produce limited responses, but putting the change into effect in a limited way and then monitoring the effects is much more useful. It is unfortunately very labour intensive and information is limited to what customers actually did.

Strategic aspects of marketing research

2.23 You will recognise that the above review of the basic marketing research approaches is very limited. We have not considered variations such as consumer panels or alternative qualitative techniques. The Diploma examiners will expect you to have a fairly detailed tactical knowledge of marketing research techniques gained from your earlier studies or business experience. Planning and Control and the Analysis and Decision paper are likely to require you to demonstrate a more strategic appreciation of marketing research, addressing issues such as when should we undertake research, and the briefing of the researcher and managing the process.

2.24 Management issues when undertaking research projects can be summarised with the mnemonic CATS.

- Cost
- Accuracy
- Timing
- Security

2.25 We have already mentioned the cost/accuracy trade off, but managers must also stop and think about the costs against the benefits of additional information, before briefing research projects.

2.26 It can take a considerable time to conduct primary research. In the rapidly changing business world it is not always feasible to delay decisions until information is available. Managers must not use research as an excuse for not making decisions when they need to be made. An assessment of the timeframe for decision making must be made and communicated within the brief to the researcher.

2.27 The final management consideration is security. Research can sometimes give competitors an insight into a company's proposed strategy and so allow them to react quickly to it. This is most obvious in the circumstances of a test market and security issues have tended to dissuade many managers from using a test market in new product development.

2.28 The manager's role in the research process once the decision has been made to undertake research is:

(a) to identify and assess the information gap;
(b) to define the problem and put the research brief together;
(c) to identify and brief an appropriate researcher.

Note: this process is the same if using an internal research facility.

2.29 The key to ensuring that marketing research provides information which is good value for money and which will make a positive contribution to the decision making process lies in the research brief. The elements in the brief should include the following.

(a) A clear statement of the marketing problem being examined.
(b) A full statement of the relevant background and any secondary data already available.
(c) A negotiated statement of what the research outcomes are expected to be, ie the research objectives.
(d) Specified requirements in terms of cost, accuracy, timing and security.

2.30 Diploma students must be prepared to support any recommendations for marketing research with a specific research brief.

3. CONCLUSION

3.1 Successful planning is dependent on the availability of reliable databases and the facility for additional marketing research.

3.2 Information is a valuable business resource. Its quantity and quality can be improved with investment. Although it is not a substitute for decision making, it can reduce the risks involved.

3.3 Information available to managers through an information system must encompass both internal and external data. Existing information has its limitations and so marketing research is necessary to provide specific information.

3.4 Managers should concern themselves with the cost, accuracy, timing and security of their research activities. Research should only be undertaken when the benefits of further information outweigh any of these costs.

3.5 Writing a research brief is critical to the success of the research activity and it is a competence which practising managers need to develop.

TEST YOUR KNOWLEDGE

The numbers in brackets refer to paragraphs of this chapter

1. What is a database management system? (1.6)
2. What is the difference between efficiency and effectiveness? (1.21)
3. What are the four components you would expect in a marketing information system? (1.27)
4. What is the distinction between market research and marketing research? (2.1)
5. Why might a company use a research consultant? (2.6, 2.7)
6. What are the five stages in a research project? (2.8)
7. What are the three broad approaches for collecting primary data? (2.16)
8. What are the four issues management need to consider when proposing any research activity? (2.24)
9. What should be included in the research brief? (2.29)

Now try illustrative question 6

PART C
STRATEGIC DIRECTION AND STRATEGY FORMULATION, CHOICE AND EVALUATION

Chapter 6

MISSION AND OBJECTIVES: WHERE ARE WE GOING?

This chapter covers the following topics.

1. Mission statements and policy
2. Setting objectives
3. Non-financial objectives
4. Unit objectives

1. MISSION STATEMENTS AND POLICY

1.1 A common cause of confusion amongst students is the distinction between mission statements, policy, objectives and sometimes strategy. In this part of the study text we will examine each of these planning elements and clarify their role and significance. It is important that you appreciate these distinctions because the examiners will expect you to demonstrate your understanding of them and ability to produce them for any given case scenario.

Mission statements

1.2 A mission statement is very important to any operation. It sets the scene and provides the broad parameters within which management is expected to operate. The firm's mission is a clear statement of the business it identifies itself as being in or intending to be in.

1.3 A mission statement that... 'we are in the business of making profits', is not really adequate. It gives little guidance to managers who could presumably within such a remit embark on any project from drug dealing to gun running.

1.4 How the business sees itself reflects to some extent its culture and is likely to strongly influence the future strategic position of the organisation.

1.5 Mission statements which are too narrow tend to blinker management thinking, closing their eyes to emerging threats and new competitors as well as to opportunities for developing the business. The classic example of getting the mission statement wrong is often attributed to British Rail, who for decades saw themselves in the railway business. Protected by their monopoly position and narrow image of their business, they failed to respond strategically to the development of motorways, the growth of car ownership and the developing domestic airline network.

1.6 If British Rail had seen themselves as being in the business of 'transporting people and freight throughout Britain', the competitive threats would have been identified and the system of transport within this country may have evolved very differently.

1.7 Without being so wide as to provide no clear focus, the mission should encompass the opportunities for diversification and development which will encourage synergy within the total operation. The 'Britain' tag in our revised BR mission may in fact be too narrow. It would preclude investment in overseas networks and with the opening of the Channel Tunnel would certainly require reconsidering.

1.8 Mission statements do not remain unchanged forever. They can be changed and should be challenged if there is a good case for doing so. They should not however be changed weekly, because they act as a broad umbrella statement under which managers can plan medium term strategy. They represent an important anchor for the business ensuring that it does not attempt to be all things to all people.

1.9 A good mission statement should not be long, only a few lines, perhaps up to five or six. It should clearly answer the question, 'what business are we in'. It is not normally necessary to add financial or profit dimensions as these are contained much more specifically in the corporate objectives. However if there is a strong commitment to quality, environmental issues or charitable activities then these would be legitimately communicated through the mission statement.

Example: mission statement

1.10 'We are in the business of manufacturing and distributing environmentally friendly packaging and paper products to generate funds for rain forest protection projects.'

1.11 Such a mission clearly tells managers where their main activities should be focused. They could do the following.

(a) Spend on R & D to develop a more environmentally friendly plastic packaging.
(b) Launch an own brand range of writing papers and gift wrap papers to be distributed through 'party' selling agents.

They cannot do the following.

(a) Develop their own brand of soap powder.
(b) Support a clean water project in India.
(c) Distribute a highly profitable but environmentally unfriendly range of plastic packaging.

In this way you can see how the mission provides a framework within which managers know they can operate.

Exercise 1

Spend a little time producing a short mission statement for each of the following organisations. Make clear any differences between what you think their current mission statement is and what you think it should be.

(a) The local library.
(b) Your local college.
(c) Your GP's practice.
(d) A local sports club or centre you are familiar with.

1.12 You may be surprised at how difficult this task actually is and the important choices included in writing a mission statement.

(a) Is the library in the business of lending books? Then what about other media, videos, software and records etc? Is the library in the business of leisure - providing popular materials, or the business of education - giving priority to the purchase of classics and reference materials?

(b) Many colleges have had long debates as to whether they are in the business of training (giving skills) or education (providing knowledge). If you are attending college, should your tutors be in the business of teaching you about marketing or helping you to pass an examination? Unfortunately the two are not always the same.

(c) The current changes to the funding of general practices have been centred very much on the 'what business are we in' debate. Should your GP be in the business of making you well, or preventing you from getting ill? The targets, organisation and services provided will be very different according to which you have selected.

(d) This last one will vary dramatically according to the nature of the centre you chose. It may be in anything from the leisure and recreation business to the fitness and health business but many other decisions will depend on the position selected. For example a club in the leisure business may pay equal attention to the social side of its activities, with a bar, social events and members. At the fitness and health end of the spectrum, the facility may be no smoking, offer healthy drinks and snacks and main events are likely to be linked to sporting activities such as major competitions.

Exercise 2

Practise writing mission statements and then thinking through their implications. Find out what your organisation's mission is. If there isn't one then write one. If there is but it needs improving, modify it.

Policy

1.13 Policy statements have a similar function to mission statements in that they lay down guidelines and rules about how business and activities are to be conducted.

1.14 Policy can be inspired by legislation, economics or the culture of the organisation. It can be focused at any level in the organisation from strategic to tactical. In essence policy represents operating decisions which individual managers are not free to make, because they have been made for the organisation as a whole.

1.15 You will probably be very familiar with the policies of your own organisation. They may include the following.

(a) It is our policy to be equal opportunity employers.
(b) It is our policy to prosecute shoplifters.
(c) It is our policy to give credit.
(d) It is our policy for staff to travel second class on journeys of less than 100 miles.

1.16 Policy exists to ensure consistency of decision making on important issues such as employment terms and conditions, health and safety and customer relations. Any strategy you develop must obviously be consistent with any stated policy, but where appropriate, policy can be challenged. Sometimes policies have been laid down for a number of years and changed circumstances do warrant their review.

2. SETTING OBJECTIVES

2.1 Objectives are clear statements of what the business or department intends to achieve. They are created in hierarchies with the objectives lower down in the hierarchy contributing to those higher up.

2.2 *Corporate objectives.* Corporate objectives are those which are concerned with the firm as a whole. Objectives should be explicit, quantifiable and capable of being achieved. The corporate objectives outline the expectations of the firm and the strategic planning process is concerned with the means of achieving the objectives.

2.3 Corporate objectives should relate to the key financial factors for business success, which are typically:

- profitability (return on investment)
- market share
- growth
- cash flow

2.4 *Unit objectives.* Unit objectives are objectives that are specific to individual units of an organisation, and are often 'operational' objectives, ie marketing or production. Examples are as follows.

(a) *From the commercial world*

(i) Increasing the number of customers by x% (an objective of a sales department).
(ii) Reducing the number of rejects by 50% (an objective of a production department).
(iii) Producing monthly reports more quickly, within five working days of the end of each month (an objective of the management accounting department).

(b) *From the public sector*

(i) To reduce the cost of travel by introducing an X% subsidy on bus travel (an objective of a local authority transport department).
(ii) To introduce 1,000 more nursery education places (an objective of a borough education department).
(iii) To reduce the response times to emergency calls by two minutes (an objective of a local police station, fire department or hospital ambulance service).

Primary and secondary objectives

2.5 Some objectives are more important than others, and it could be argued that in the hierarchy of objectives, there is a *primary corporate objective* (restricted by certain constraints on corporate activity) and other *secondary objectives* which are strategic objectives which should combine to ensure the achievement of the overall corporate objective.

2.6 For example if a company sets itself an objective of growth in profits as its primary aim, it will then have to develop strategies by which this primary objective can be achieved. An objective must then be set for each individual strategy, and so many secondary objectives may simply be targets by which the success of a strategy can be measured. Secondary objectives might then be concerned with sales growth, continual technological innovation, customer service, product quality, efficient resource management (for example labour productivity) or reducing the company's reliance on debt capital etc.

2.7 Many writers accept that profitability must be the primary objective for a profit-making commercial organisation, but there are different ways of measuring profitability, in one form or another. It is not clear, however, whether there should be a single primary objective or several objectives, nor how different aims and objectives inter-relate. Argenti cited the creation of customers, servicing society, providing employment and maximising profits as various objectives, and concluded that an objective must be expressed as follows.

(a) It must identify the beneficiaries.
(b) It must state what the nature of the benefit is to be.
(c) It must state the size of the benefit.

More will be said about this later.

Trade-off between objectives

2.8 When there are several key objectives, some might be achieved only at the expense of others. For example, a company's objective of achieving good profits and profit growth might have adverse consequences for the cash flow of the business, or the quality of the firm's product. Attempts to achieve a good cash flow or good product quality, or to improve market share, might call for some sacrifice of profits.

2.9 There will be a trade-off between objectives when strategies are formulated, and a choice will have to be made. For example there might be a choice between the following two options.

Option A 15% sales growth, 10% profit growth, a £2 million negative cash flow and reduced product quality and customer satisfaction.

Option B 8% sales growth, 5% profit growth, a £500,000 surplus cash flow, and maintenance of high product quality/customer satisfaction.

If the firm chose option B in preference to option A, it would be trading off sales growth and profit growth for better cash flow, product quality and customer satisfaction.

Long-term and short-term objectives

2.10 Objectives may be long-term and short-term. A company that is suffering from a recession in its core industries and making losses in the short term might continue to have a primary objective in the long term of achieving a steady growth in earnings or profits, but in the short term, its primary objective might switch to survival.

2.11 Secondary objectives will range from short-term to long-term. Planners will formulate secondary objectives within the guidelines set by the primary objective, after selecting strategies for achieving the primary objective.

2.12 For example a company's primary objective might be to increase its earnings per share from 30p to 50p in the next five years. Strategies for achieving the objective might be selected to include the following.

- Increasing profitability in the next 12 months by cutting expenditure.
- Increasing export sales over the next three years.
- Developing a successful new product for the domestic market within five years.

Secondary objectives might then be re-assessed to include the following.

- The objective of improving manpower productivity by 10% within 12 months.
- Improving customer service in export markets with the objective of doubling the number of overseas sales outlets in selected countries within the next three years.
- Investing more in product-market research and development, with the objective of bringing at least three new products to the market within five years.

2.13 Objectives, targets and plans are inter-related aspects of the strategic planning process. Targets cannot be set without an awareness of what is realistic. For example setting an objective of doubling profits within the next three years might seem fine on paper, but if it is not a realistic aim, it will not be worth the paper it is written on. Quantified targets for achieving the primary objective, and targets for secondary objectives, must therefore emerge from a realistic 'situation audit' of the organisation's position and resources, and from the planning process. P M Chisnall *Strategic industrial marketing* has written about marketing objectives: 'Organisations should set realistic objectives; these should be related both to short-term and long-term goals. Since marketing is concerned with the efficient use of corporate resources to meet specific market needs, these targets, short- or long-term, should be based on budgets which are tied in with levels of forecasted demand.'

Trade offs between short-term and long-term objectives

2.14 Just as there may have to be a trade-off between different objectives, so too might there be a need to make trade offs between short-term and long-term objectives. This is referred to as S/L trade-off.

2.15 In practice, managers' performance is usually judged by short-term achievements.

(a) Middle and senior management are expected to achieve budget targets, and are criticised if they do not.

(b) The board of directors of a public company are expected by City analysts to achieve a certain growth in profits and EPS each year. If they do not, the share price will be marked down, and the board will be criticised for poor corporate results.

2.16 Since performance is judged by short-term achievements, it is hardly surprising that the natural tendency for managers is to sacrifice longer term aims in order to achieve short-term targets. In some situations, this might be the 'right' thing to do; in others, it might be short-sighted and ultimately a bad decision. Ideally, an organisation should try to control S/L trade-offs, to ensure that the most suitable decisions are taken in each situation, whenever some trade-off is unavoidable.

2.17 Decisions which involve the sacrifice of longer term objectives include the following.

(a) Postponing or abandoning capital expenditure projects, which would eventually contribute to (longer term) growth and profits, in order to protect short term cash flow and profits.

(b) Cutting R&D expenditure to save operating costs, and so reducing the prospects for future product development.

(c) Reducing quality control, to save operating costs.

(d) Reducing the level of customer service, to save operating costs.

2.18 Steps that could be taken to control S/L trade-offs, so that the 'ideal' decisions are taken, include the following.

(a) Making short term targets realistic. If budget targets are unrealistically tough, a manager will be forced into a situation where he must make S/L trade-offs.

(b) Providing sufficient management information to allow managers to see what trade-offs they are making. Managers must be kept aware of long term aims as well as shorter term (budget) targets.

(c) Evaluating managers' performance in terms of contribution to long term as well as short term objectives. A corporate culture that recognises long term aims would be essential.

Open objectives and closed objectives

2.19 An objective might be quantified, and given a specific timescale. For example, a company might set an objective of achieving a return on capital employed of 25% per annum, or an objective of achieving growth in earnings per share (EPS) of 15% in 1991, 20% in 1992 and 25% in 1993. These quantified objectives are sometimes called *closed objectives.*

2.20 In contrast, an objective might be stated in non-quantified terms, such as the following.

(a) Providing high quality products that satisfy customer needs.
(b) Providing sound investment opportunities for shareholders and worthwhile job prospects for employees.
(c) Achieving customer satisfaction and real growth in EPS.

These non-quantified objectives are sometimes called *open objectives* or *aims.*

2.21 Vencil distinguished between objectives (open objectives) and goals or targets (closed objectives) by referring to one of John F Kennedy's declared objectives in 1960, which was to re-establish and maintain America's role as a leader in the fields of science and technology, whereas one of his goals was to land a man on the moon and return him safely before the end of the decade. Thus a goal had a time constraint attached to it and had a specific end in view.

Both corporate and unit objectives may be open or closed.

Must objectives be quantified?

2.22 There is a view that an *objective* must be expressed as a *target*, ie in quantitative terms, if it is to have any practical value for planning. The only practical objective is therefore a closed one. For example a corporate objective cannot be to earn a 'satisfactory' return on capital employed; it must be to earn a ROCE of at least x% for a given number of years, otherwise 'satisfactory' has no concrete meaning.

2.23 Although there may be some academic debate about the need to quantify objectives, for all practical purposes you should take it as essential. Once objectives have been quantified, control criteria can easily be established and resources allocated. Examiners will expect you to include objectives which are quantified over time.

A primary corporate objective

2.24 It can be argued that all subsidiary objectives should stem from the primary objective and should not be formulated until the primary objective has been agreed. For companies, this primary objective should be concerned with the benefits to their owners, ie the ordinary shareholders.

2.25 It is a well-accepted maxim that risk should be rewarded. Ordinary shareholders, as the owners of a company and so its 'entrepreneurs' bear the greatest risks and so ought to stand to gain more. A satisfactory return for a company must be sufficient to *reward shareholders* adequately in the long run for the risks they take. The reward will take the form of profits, which can lead to dividends or to increases in the market value of the shares.

2.26 The size of return which is 'adequate' for ordinary shareholders will vary according to the risk involved. Shareholders must accept the risk of a down-turn in the stock market, or a slump in their company's profits, and so when times are good, they should expect to be rewarded accordingly. (Shareholders in private companies, without the benefit of a stock exchange for trading their shares, and so with no prospect of capital growth, must look to dividends for their return, and so it is quite common for private companies to pay out a large proportion of their profits as dividends.)

Alternative primary financial objectives

2.27 The primary objective for a company must be a financial objective based on earning profits, but there are different ways of expressing such an objective in quantitative terms. Various financial objectives would include the following.

(a) Profitability.
(b) Return on capital employed (ROCE) or return on investment (ROI).
(c) Survival.
(d) Growth in earnings per share and a target PE ratio.
(e) Growth in dividends to shareholders.
(f) Various management ratios.
(g) Return on shareholders' capital with an allowance for the element of risk.
(h) Several of these objectives simultaneously, so that there are multiple targets of 'equal' importance.

2.28 *Profitability*
It is widely agreed that a company must make profits, but profitability on its own is not satisfactory as an overall long-term corporate objective because it fails to allow for the size of the capital investment required to make the profit. For example suppose that a company makes a profit after tax in 19X0/X1 of £1 million, with capital employed of £10 million. If the corporate objective is to raise profits to £2 million by 19X5/X6, but to do so would require the injection of an additional £30 million of shareholders' capital (supposing that the new sources of share finance are freely available) the objective would be unsatisfactory because the return on capital employed and probably the earnings per share would both be worse. Profitability on its own is not a measure of the stewardship and good use of assets employed.

2.29 Further drawbacks to the use of profitability as a primary overall objective are as follows.

(a) Since capital is often in restricted supply profitability must be measured in terms of the limiting factor, ie in terms of the scarce financial resources that a company will have at its disposal, therefore ROI or return on shareholders' capital would be a more appropriate objective.

(b) Shareholders, as a group, should be interested in maximising profits over time, not short-term current year profits. In order to maximise profits over time, costs will have to be incurred today in order to generate returns in the future, and so a profit-maximising firm will seek to make investments - in physical capital, human capital, advertising and so on.

Since *long term* profitability would be the central objective, there would inevitably be confusion due to the conflict between expenditure for long term benefits (for example R & D) and short term demands on the limited resources available.

2.30 Profitability, despite its shortcomings, must remain a yardstick for managerial performance, provided that profit targets are stated in acceptable and consistent terms. But profitability per se should be a financial objective which is subsidiary to the prime corporate objective, principally because it does not take into consideration the amount of capital employed.

2.31 *Return on capital employed (ROCE) or return on investment (ROI)*
Alfred P Sloane Jr. wrote that '...the strategic aim of a business is to earn a return on capital and if in any particular case, the return in the long run is not satisfactory, then the deficiency should be corrected or the activity abandoned for a more favourable one'. Although some companies use an accounting ROCE as a prime objective there are drawbacks to its use.

(a) Capital employed is notoriously suspect as a financial measure, since a book value in the balance sheet will probably bear little or no comparison with the 'true' value - net replacement cost, gross replacement cost, net realisable value or economic value of the asset. (It should be noted that there is a slightly better argument for using a current cost ROCE as the primary objective, but many of the drawbacks to the use of ROCE would remain.)

Considerable dissatisfaction has been expressed with the balance sheets of public companies, which are criticised for failing to show the true value of the company's assets. Rowntree, in its unsuccessful takeover defence against Nestle in 1988, argued that its branded goods had a market value which the balance sheet simply didn't show. Since then, many companies have included brands on their balance sheets, including Guinness and Grand Metropolitan with capitalised brands amounting to £588m and £1,375m respectively.

(b) If ROCE were used, there would be some difficulty in balancing short term results against long-term requirements. ROCE would be improved if a company continues to use old assets which are fully depreciated and worsened in the short term by buying new assets to replace worn-out equipment (because new equipment reduces profit through higher depreciation charges and increases the value of capital employed). Similarly, there are long term needs to spend money on research and development which would reduce profits in the short term.

(c) The choice of ROCE as an objective also ignores the *risk* of investments. High risk projects might promise a high return if they succeed, but it may be safer to opt for a project with a lower return but a greater guarantee of success.

2.32 *ROCE example: Black and Decker in the 1960s and 1970s*
Robert Appleby was the architect of the success of Black and Decker, the power tool company, in the 1960s. Appleby's aim was to sell the highest quality power tools at the lowest possible cost. The plant at Spennymoor, County Durham, was geared up for very high production capacity. Appleby also aimed to achieve a high ROCE, and he considered the acceptable 'norm' of British industry - then about 15 to 20% - to be ridiculously low. Through high volume selling of low-cost goods, Black and Decker earned a return of 40.6% on its capital investment in 1967. It is

interesting to note, in the context of this example, that the success in setting and achieving a high target ROCE was not gained by exploiting consumers in the market or coercing the workforce. High profits and ROCE can be consistent with a strong sense of social service and good labour relations. In social terms, Black and Decker provided the market with high quality power tools at a price within the reach of every wage earner's income, and which were easy to use. A consequence of this over time has been a marked improvement in the quality and range of domestic repairs and amenities, by do-it-yourself enthusiasts.

2.33 *Survival*

Drucker *(Theory of business behaviour 1958)* suggested that the prime objective of a company is not simply financial, but is one of survival.

He argued that there are five major areas in which to decide objectives for survival.

(a) There is a need to anticipate the social climate and economic policy in those areas where the company operates and sells. A business must organise its behaviour in such a way as to survive in respect to both.
(b) A business is a human organisation and must be designed for joint performance by everyone in it.
(c) Survival also depends on the supply of an economic product or service.
(d) A business must *innovate*, because the economy and markets are continually changing.
(e) Inevitably, a business must be *profitable* to survive.

2.34 The needs and opportunities in each of these five areas in turn affect performance and results in the others. 'Success, like failure, is multi-dimensional.'

(Note: survival is not widely accepted as a corporate objective. Argenti, for example, has argued that the owners of a company might choose, in some circumstances, to wind up their business or sell out to another company in a takeover bid, and so their objectives would obviously be better served by *not* surviving.)

2.35 *EPS and dividends*

Earnings per share or dividend payments may be used as a basis of re-establishing corporate objectives. They are both measures which recognise that a company is owned by its shareholders and the ultimate purpose of a company must be to provide a satisfactory return for its owners. Failure to provide a satisfactory EPS or dividend would presumably lead the shareholders to sell their shares and perhaps eventually to sell off the company's assets. When earnings and dividends are low, the market value of shares will also be depressed unless there is a strong prospect of dividend growth in the future.

2.36 The main disadvantage of using EPS or dividend per share as an objective is that earnings and dividends (in pounds or pence) do not relate shareholder profit or revenue of the amount of money invested by the shareholders. Suppose, for example, that a company has current earnings of £50,000 and 100,000 shares in issue, each with a market value of £4. If the company proposes a rights issue of 1 share for every 4 held, at a price of £3 each, with the intention of raising annual earnings to £60,000, the EPS would fall, but the size of earnings as a proportion of the shareholder's investment (at market value) would improve.

	Before		*After*
Shares	100,000		125,000
Market value	£400,000	(theoretical)	£475,000
Earnings	£50,000		£60,000
EPS	50p		44p
Earnings/market value	12.5%		12.7%

2.37 A similar argument would apply to dividends, ie the shareholder is concerned with the size of the return he gets, but also with the size of the investment he must make to achieve the return. To overcome this problem, earnings and dividend growth could be expressed as:

(a) dividends received; plus
(b) capital growth in market value expressed as a percentage of market value at the start of the period under review.

2.38 *Growth*
It is arguable that a company should make growth its prime objective - growth in EPS, growth in profits, growth in ROCE or growth in dividends per share. There are some difficulties however, in accepting growth as an overall objective.

(a) Growth of what? If we suppose that the aim is 'balanced growth', ie a commensurate growth in profits, sales, assets, number of employees etc, such a policy might be applicable in the short term, but in the long run, some elements must be expected to grow faster than others because of the dynamics of the business environment.

(b) In the long run, growth might lead to diseconomies of scale so that inefficiencies will occur and the growth pattern will inevitably stagnate. The idea that a company must grow to survive is no longer widely accepted.

(c) There is no reason why companies should not pay all their earnings as dividends and have no growth.

2.39 However, growth must be high among the priorities for many companies, and expressed in financial terms. Growth in volume of assets, number of employees or even turnover would be inadequate. Growth should be expressed, more suitably, as growth in profits, returns, earnings, dividends or capital value etc.

2.40 Growth is likely to be a prime objective for the following types of company.

(a) Smaller companies since these will usually have a greater potential for significant rates of growth.

(b) Larger companies which are seeking to achieve a size which will enable them to compete with other multinationals in world markets. Very big companies will probably only achieve significant growth through takeovers or mergers, rather than through internal growth.

Public companies have been able to use their 'paper', ie to issue more of their own shares, to acquire other companies in a share exchange deal. If the acquired company is bought on a price/earnings ratio which is lower than the P/E ratio of the 'predator' company, the predator company's EPS will go up as a result of the takeover. The Hanson Trust, like some other conglomerate companies, has had notable success in a strategy of EPS growth through acquisitions in recent years.

2.41 *Return on shareholders' capital (ROSC)*
Ansoff suggested that return on equity should be the overall corporate objective. This should be a measurable target over the 'proximate' period, ie for the next three to ten years, when forecasts can be made with reasonable accuracy. Beyond this period, however, when accurate forecasts are impossible, Ansoff suggested that a variety of long-term subsidiary objectives should be substituted for return on equity because they are more easily measurable and contribute towards the overall return. These subsidiary objectives used include the following.

(a) Growth in sales to keep a share of the market.
(b) Increase in market share.
(c) Growth in EPS.
(d) Product innovation and finding new markets.
(e) Stability of sales patterns (ie avoiding cyclical trends).
(f) Full use of production capacity.

2.42 Argenti also suggested that return on shareholders' capital (ROSC) should be the prime corporate objective and he specified the method whereby a target ROSC could be derived. Although the detailed calculations are not appropriate to this text, it is possible to calculate a historical ROSC (using discounted cash flow techniques) by relating dividends paid to shareholders over a number of years to the market value of the shares. By making allowance for expectations in the future, it should be possible to estimate an ROSC target for the company.

2.43 *ROSC and risk*
Both Ansoff and Argenti acknowledged the need to allow for risk in deciding the size of return as the target for the corporate objective.

2.44 Ansoff suggested that the required return on equity should depend on the risk of the business as an investment and that there is an 'acceptable threshold' depending on opportunities available, past and future prospects and the need for not only long-term profits but also short-term profits in order to safeguard liquidity.

2.45 For example a company in a low-risk business might be satisfied with a return of, say, 15%, whereas in a comparable high-risk business the required return might be a minimum of 25%. Similarly, a company which needs a short payback period for its investments might accept a minimum return of 10%, whereas longer projects may be expected to offer a higher return of, say, at least 20%, to compensate for the slower payback of cash into the organisation.

2.46 Argenti approaches risk from a slightly different angle. He suggests that return on shareholders' capital (ROSC) is the prime corporate objective, but adds the following.

(a) There is a minimum return that shareholders will accept, allowing for the risk of the investment.

(b) The target return must exceed the minimum, but may be satisfactory or even excellent. 'It seems probable that what shareholders really have in mind when they invest capital is a performance-risk curve. They are seeking an investment which stands a good chance of yielding a high rate of return and at the same time a very low risk of achieving a poor rate of return.... It follows that a company should not seek to make a satisfactory profit, nor required profits, nor to aim at spectacular success, nor to avoid an unsatisfactory return; it should aim at all these - but each associated with a different level of work.'

2.47 Argenti's performance-risk curve for ROSC would be as follows.

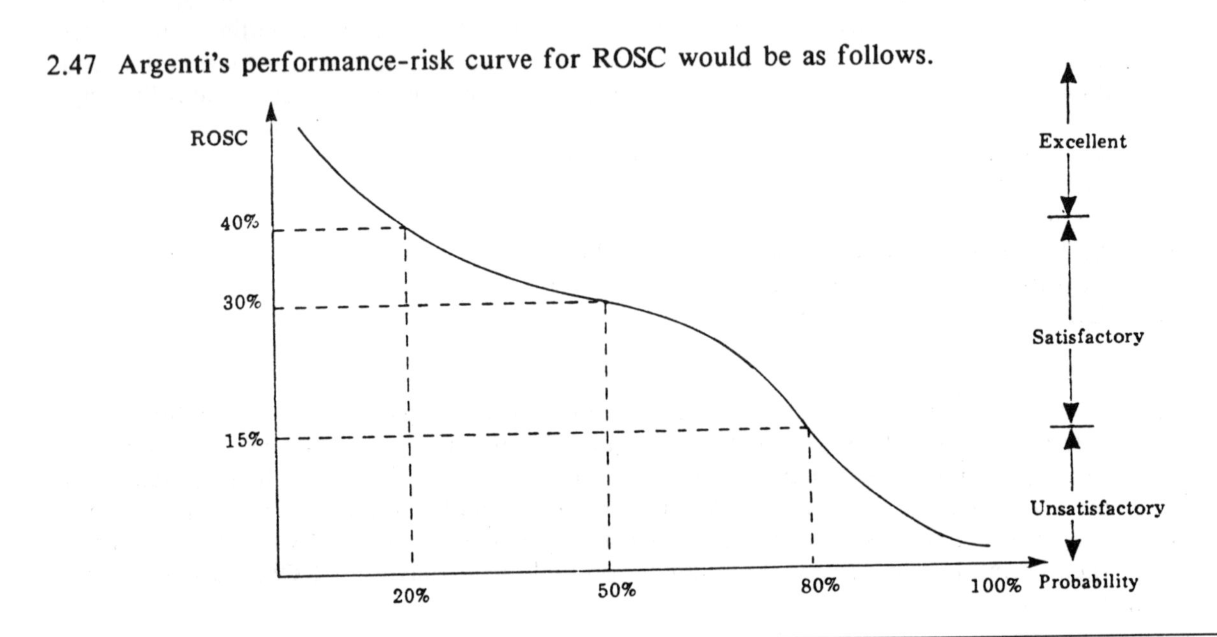

In this example, the target ROSC would be as follows.

(a) To have a 20% chance of achieving an ROSC of 40% or more.
(b) To have a 50% chance of achieving an ROSC of 30% or more.
(c) To have an 80% chance of achieving an ROSC of 15% or more.

2.48 *Multiple objectives*
A firm can identify several objectives. For example, Linneman argues that a firm should be concerned with its risk posture, and that its objectives should therefore have regard to its financial risk, expressed as its debt/equity ratio. He suggests that there is a 'golden mean' or optimum combination of the following.

(a) Scope for *growth* and enhanced *corporate wealth*, through a suitable balance between equity and debt finance.

(b) Maintaining a policy of paying attractive but not over-generous *dividends*.

(c) Maintaining an acceptable, but flexible, *gearing ratio*. The acceptable norm will vary from industry to industry.

2.49 Linneman also discusses *relative* ranking in the market. This is really a subsidiary marketing objective, concerned with market position and market share. Most top executives of a company are interested in maintaining or achieving a certain rank relative to other competitors in their market. Obviously, their interest will be partly stimulated by the urge for 'self-preservation' but relative ranking is also an expression of marketing strategy. For example both Wiggins Teape (paper) and Avis (car hire) recognised that they could never be number one in their field; instead, they aimed to be excellent seconds.

2.50 It is interesting to note the stated objectives of the American Mead Corporation, some years ago. Recognising that no one ratio or financial target is a unique target, Mead stated the following.

'Our long term goal is to be in the upper quartile of those companies against which we are compared. While we recognise that as markets, competitors and external factors such as the rate of inflation change, the quantified objectives may change. However, as things stand, we are aiming for:

Financial goals

Return on net assets	12%
Sustained growth rate	10%
Debt/equity ratio	50%
Dividend payout	± 30%'

Example: evaluating a proposed strategy

2.51 ABCD plc's financial performance for the past 12 months has been reported to its board of directors as follows.

Sales turnover	£20 million per annum
Market share	16%
Contribution/sales ratio	50%
Operating profit/sales ratio	10%
Sales/capital employed ratio	1.2 times
P/E ratio	11.4
Average P/E ratio for the industry	16.7

The directors are considering a new strategy of spending an extra £500,000 per annum on advertising and sales promotions, to try to boost sales, combined with more liberal price discounts to regular customers.

Required

(a) Evaluate the possible financial implications of the proposed new strategy.

(b) What does the P/E ratio of 11.4 imply when compared with the average P/E for the industry as a whole?

Solution

2.52

Turnover per annum	£20,000,000
Operating profit (10% x £20 million)	£2,000,000
ROCE (10% x 1.2)	12%
Capital employed (£2,000,000 ÷ 12%)	£16,666,667
Market capitalisation*	£22,800,000

*Earnings x P/E ratio, here assumed to be operating profit x P/E

2.53 Extra advertising expenditure will reduce profit by £500,000 per annum (tax is ignored here, for simplicity). Higher price discounts to regular customers will reduce the C/S ratio and so will reduce profitability too. If we suppose that 25% of customers are given a further 5% price discount, the cost of this would be 25% x £20,000,000 x 5% = £250,000 per annum.

2.54 To justify this strategy, the extra sales from greater advertising and higher price discounts must yield extra contribution of at least £750,000 per annum which, given a C/S ratio of 50%, implies extra sales of £1.5 million per annum, which is 1.2% of the market. (Total market = £20 million ÷ 16%.) This might be a reasonable target which the company could hope to achieve.

2.55 If higher sales and higher profits can be achieved, the sales/capital employed ratio would improve and the profit on sales ratio *might* also improve. The end result will be a higher ROCE. If there is no change in the P/E ratio, the market capitalisation of the company will improve by £11,400 for each £1,000 increase in the annual profit.

2.56 The current P/E ratio is substantially lower than the industry average, which suggests that the market has made the following judgements about ABCD.

(a) ABCD is 'under-performing' when compared with its rivals.

(b) ABCD's earnings growth potential is less than the growth potential of other firms in the industry.

(c) The 'quality' of ABCD's earnings are not as good, ie there is some risk that profits might decline in the future.

Subsidiary objectives

2.57 Whatever primary objective or objectives are set, subsidiary objectives will then be developed beneath them. The diagram below illustrates this process in outline.

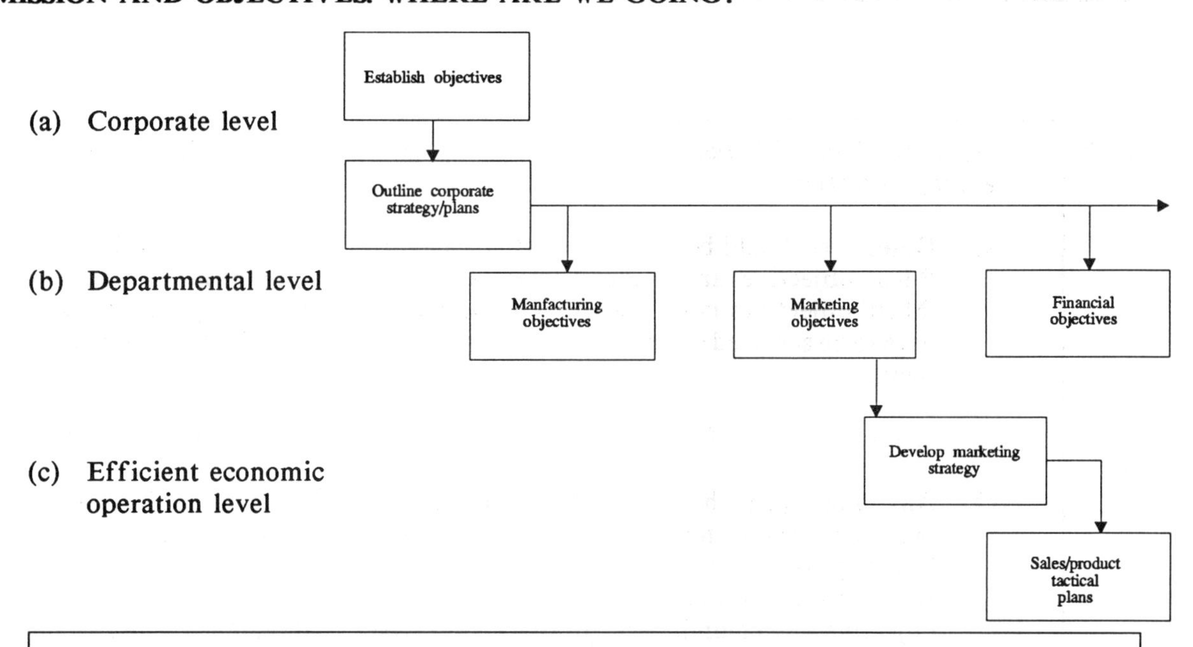

2.58 This diagram might suggest a further important point. Unless an organisation is so small that it is a single unit, without functional departments, the overall objectives of the organisation will indicate different requirements for different functions. It is essential to identify those elements within the overall objectives which give rise to subsidiary objectives for each individual function.

2.59 These functional objectives, which are subsidiary to the primary objectives, must be specific and clear cut. Returning to the example of Black and Decker (paragraph 2.32), production at Spennymoor was geared to a high volume of output. However, to achieve its objectives, the company also had to produce at low cost. Already closely controlled, the company aimed at further cost reductions through improvements in productivity. Black and Decker applied a philosophy, commonly found in Japanese companies, that products must achieve a targeted cost reduction every year without any sacrifice in quality or performance.

2.60 Furthermore, it was also implicit within the company objective to produce in large volumes that all output should be sold, and so inventory had to be kept to a minimum. The overall objectives of the company thus gave rise to subsidiary objectives for the production and marketing departments, and also for working capital (finance objective).

Ranking objectives in order of importance

2.61 Some objectives are clearly subordinate to others. For example departmental objectives are subsidiary to corporate objectives. However, where there are multiple corporate objectives, and multiple departmental objectives, a problem of ranking can arise.

(a) *There is never enough time or resources to achieve all of the desired objectives,* even if, when taken individually, it would be possible to achieve them.

(b) *There are degrees of accomplishment.* For example, if there is an objective to achieve a 10% annual growth in earnings per share, an achievement of 9% could be described as a near-success. Even annual growth rates of 8% or 7% would not be described as a total failure. When it comes to ranking objectives, a target ROCE of, say, 25% might be given greater priority than an EPS growth of 10%, but a lower priority than an EPS growth of, say, 9% etc.

2.62 Kepner and Tregoe *The rational manager 1965* recommended the following approach to ranking objectives.

(a) Objectives should be divided into two categories: *must* and *want* objectives. 'Must' objectives are absolutely essential, whereas 'want' objectives are not. 'Must' objectives rank equally, with no hierarchy or ranking since they all have to be achieved and so resources must somehow be committed to achieving them.

(b) A minimum level of achievement should be specified for each 'must' objective.

(c) Anything beyond the minimum level of achievement for 'must' objectives are 'want' objectives, and should be ranked in order of preference. There may not be enough resources to achieve all the 'want' objectives, and management must ensure that resources are not diverted away from achieving the 'must' objectives. If commitment to 'must' objectives is threatened, then 'want' objectives are best forgotten.

The monitoring and revision of objectives

2.63 Successful planning requires a commitment to objectives, and so objectives should not be subject to too frequent change. It is hard to be committed to something which never seems to remain the same! At the same time, there must also be some flexibility. In a world of rapid change, objectives and plans must be subject to review.

Strategic planning should not be a rare event. Rather, a planning review should take place regularly, perhaps once a year, in which objectives should be reassessed, and planning horizons reviewed. In some companies, this annual exercise only just precedes the budgetary process, with the deliberate intention of linking the budget to the latest review of the long-term strategic plan.

2.64 You will be required to demonstrate an awareness of the need to review objectives in a changing environment, with environmental influences persuading or forcing organisations to change their objectives, or to add new constraints on the ways in which objectives can be pursued.

3. NON-FINANCIAL OBJECTIVES

3.1 The primary and subsidiary corporate objectives so far discussed have been financial or commercial. A commercial organisation might also identify other objectives which are non-financial, and although they are not the primary objective of the organisation, they can act as a brake or constraint on the organisation's pursuit of its primary targets.

Social and ethical obligations: social responsibility

3.2 Although many writers agree that there should be an overall financial objective, expressed as a quantifiable target, they acknowledge that there are certain social or ethical obligations which a company must fulfil.

3.3 A company supplies goods and services to customers and employs people. Therefore, it is an integral part of society and is subject to the pressures of that society. Most companies seek a good public image and take account of the following points in pursuing their activities.

(a) They are increasingly conscious of the need to conserve energy, and to protect the environment from the pollution of industrial waste and spillages.

(b) They attempt to be good employers.

(c) They try to provide facilities for welfare to the local communities or the country as a whole (for example the sponsorship of sports, which is not always associated with a blaze of advertising and publicity, donations to charity etc).

3.4 Ansoff suggested that a company has the following objectives.

(a) A primary objective, which is economic, aimed at optimising the efficiency and effectiveness of the firm's 'total resource-conversion process'.

(b) Social or non-economic objectives, which are secondary and modify management behaviour. These social objectives are the result of the inter-action among the individual objectives of the differing groups of 'stakeholders'.

(c) In addition to economic and non-economic objectives, there are two other factors exerting influence on management behaviour.

(i) *Responsibilities:* these are obligations which a company undertakes, but which do not form a part of its 'internal guidance or control mechanism'. Responsibilities would include charitable donations, contributions to the life of local communities etc.

(ii) *Constraints:* these are rules which restrict management's freedom of action, and would include government legislation (on pollution levels, health and safety at work, employment protection, redundancy, monopolies, illegal business practices etc) and agreements with trade unions.

3.5 The stakeholder view or the consensus view of corporate objectives would suggest that an organisation will sometimes make decisions which are not purely in the interests of shareholders and which mean that an objective of achieving growth or maximising profits will sometimes be compromised. Examples are as follows.

(a) If profit growth can be achieved through a merger with another company, the jobs of many employees and managers might be threatened by the 'rationalisation' measures taken after the merger. Management and employees might therefore resist a merger, and the corporate decision by the board of directors might be to organise defensive tactics to defeat the merger/takeover bid.

(b) Profit growth might also be reduced by a willingness of managers to award employees (and themselves!) good annual pay rises.

(c) Dividend growth might be thwarted by a management decision (at board level) to retain more profits in the business, to finance growth and so provide greater job security. (Shareholders cannot increase the size of the final dividend proposed by the board of directors at the AGM!).

(d) A company's profitability might benefit from relocation, for example a move out of the UK to Holland, say, or France, but employee interests might prevent such a move from taking place.

4. UNIT OBJECTIVES

Marketing

4.1 Once the corporate objectives have been established and management have indicated broadly how these should be achieved, by giving an indication of corporate strategy, the various units within the organisation can develop their own objectives.

4.2 Corporate strategy has to be clarified to ensure that all the functions are working together. Not just aiming towards the same end goal, but approaching it along the same path. The corporate objectives and strategy ensure a synergy of effort between the departments and functions.

4.3 Without a lead on strategy from senior management, middle managers could be faced with a corporate objective of increasing profitability by x% over three years. In pursuit of this, operations could cut costs, reduce stockholdings and trim back production levels. Marketing could be implementing strategies to increase revenue, through higher sales. These two departments would clearly be working against each other, although both aiming to contribute to the stated corporate goal.

4.4 Armed with clear, quantified corporate objectives and the co-ordinating influence of a corporate strategy, the unit managers can develop their own functional plans.

4.5 The first step is to generate unit objectives. In essence this requires translating the corporate objectives and strategy into terms that have a meaning to those working within the department, in our case marketing.

4.6 Marketing objectives are usually expressed in sales terms, ie market share or revenue or sales volume, for example to increase market share to 43% by 1995.

4.7 This objective can then be further developed by the sales manager who can forecast that 43% in 1995 will equal 1million cases. In turn the sales manager can then develop the next level of objectives into terms which mean something to those in the sales team: to sell 1,000 more cases per month by 1995.

4.8 Note that the individual sales targets or objectives can be set from this. With a salesforce of 20, each salesperson needs to be selling 50 extra cases per month by 1995.

4.9 If each level in the organisation achieves the set objectives in combination then the corporate objective will be achieved. Setting up controls to monitor performance against these quantified objectives and targets allows management to identify any problem areas and either take corrective measures or modify the plan.

5. CONCLUSION

5.1 The mission and policy statements are important starting points for the planning process. They provide the umbrella framework within which management should operate and provide a structure of consistent key decisions which guide the decision making in important areas.

5.2 Mission and policy statements are not written in tablets of stone. When and where necessary they should be challenged and modified, but they should not be changed too frequently or they lose their value as a consistent point of reference for managers.

5.3 Planning is a hierarchical process, each level's objectives and strategies influencing the level below. Each levels performance contributes to the attainment of the primary corporate objective.

5.4 Objectives must be written in terms that mean something to their audience. Corporate objectives are therefore expressed in financial terms for a commercial organisation, in market share and sales terms at marketing level and in sales target terms at sales department level.

5.5 To be of value at any level, objectives must have three essential characteristics.

(a) They must be quantified over time.
(b) They must be realistic.
(c) They must be perceived to be achievable.

5.6 Strategies will be developed to achieve the stated objectives. However it should be recognised that there will be other influences affecting the final choice of those strategies, besides economic considerations, such as the interests of various stakeholder groups and the acknowledgement of social responsibilities.

TEST YOUR KNOWLEDGE

The numbers in brackets refer to paragraphs of this chapter

1. What is a mission statement? (1.2)

2. What is the danger of a very narrow mission statement? (1.5)

3. Can mission statements be changed? (1.8)

4. What is the function of corporate policy? (1.13, 1.14, 1.16)

5. What are the essential characteristics of a good corporate objective? (2.2)

6. What is the distinction between:
   - primary and secondary objectives; (2.5)
   - short and long term objectives? (2.14)

7. What are the drawbacks of using profitability as an overall primary objective? (2.29)

8. In what type of company is growth likely to be a primary objective? (2.40)

9. Why do unit objectives have to be agreed after corporate strategy has been clarified? (4.2)

10. How are marketing objectives established? (4.5)

Now try illustrative question 7

Chapter 7

STRATEGY FORMULATION AND EVALUATION

This chapter covers the following topics.

1. GAP ANALYSIS AND FORECASTING

1.1 Having established *where we are now* through the position audit, and *where we are going* via the statement of corporate objectives, the next step in the planning process is deciding *how we get there*.

Strategic planners must think about the extent to which new strategies are needed to enable the organisation to achieve its objectives. One technique whereby this can be done is gap analysis.

Gap analysis is based on establishing the following.

(a) What are the organisation's targets for achievement over the planning period?

(b) What would the organisation be expected to achieve if it 'did nothing' and did not develop any new strategies, but simply carried on in the current way with the same products and selling to the same markets?

There will be a difference between the targets in (a) and expected achievements in (b).

This difference is the 'gap'. New strategies will then have to be developed which will close this gap, so that the organisation can expect to achieve its targets over the planning period.

Definitions

1.2 Some definitions produced by the Chartered Institute of Management Accountants can usefully be introduced at this stage.

(a) *Forecasting* is 'the identification of factors and quantifications of their effect on an entity, as a basis for planning.'

(b) *Projection.* A projection is 'an expected future trend pattern obtained by extrapolation. It is principally concerned with quantitative factors whereas a forecast includes judgements.'

(c) *Extrapolation* is 'the technique of determining a projection by statistical means'.

(d) *Gap analysis* is 'the comparison of an entity's ultimate objective with the sum of projections and already planned projects, identifying how the consequent gap might be filled.'

A forecast or projection based on existing performance: F_0 forecasts

1.3 This is a forecast of the company's future results assuming that it does nothing new. The company is expected to continues to operate as at present without any changes in its products, markets, organisation, assets, manpower, research spending, financial structure, purchasing and so forth.

1.4 If the company employs 100 workers and sells ten products in eight markets, produces them on a certain quantity and type of machinery in one factory, has a gearing structure of 30%, a forecast will be prepared, covering the corporate planning period, on the assumption that none of these items is changed. Argenti calls these forecasts 'F_0 forecasts'.

1.5 Argenti identified four stages in the preparation of an F_0 forecast.

(a) The analysis of revenues, costs and volumes.
(b) Projections into the future based on past trends.
(c) Other factors affecting profits and return.
(d) Finalising the forecast.

1.6 The first step is to *review past results and analyse* the following for each *significant* item.

(a) Revenues is analysed by units of sale and price.
(b) Costs are analysed into variable, fixed, and semi-variable costs.

1.7 A projection into the future for each major item of revenue and cost should be made up to the end of the planning period. Forecasting techniques should be selected with care and although it is impossible to guarantee accurate forecasts, unnecessary inaccuracies should be avoided, so that some degree of confidence can be achieved in the prepared estimates. Sales volumes and revenues should be assessed with reference to the expected product life-cycle of each item (to be discussed in the next chapter).

1.8 Having prepared projections for revenues from each product or service item, and the costs of materials, direct labour, research and development, administration, distribution costs etc, *tests for absurdity* should be carried out. For example if the ratio of administration costs to manufacturing costs in the period 1978/88 was about 20% each year, a forecast would be suspect if the administration/manufacturing cost ratio in 1993 or 1998 is expected to be 50%.

1.9 The third stage in preparing the F_0 forecast is to *consider any other internal or environmental factors* which might significantly affect the projections. This will involve the use of judgement. Examples are as follows.

(a) What is the likelihood of strikes and what might they cost the company in lost profits or higher wages?

(b) What is the likelihood that machinery will break down more in future than in the past, and what would it cost in lost production, sales and profit?

(c) What is the likelihood that raw materials will be difficult to obtain, that their prices might rise dramatically, or that new materials or new sources of supply will become available?

(d) What are the likely changes in competition, and what effect might this have?

(e) What are the likely changes in the pattern and loyalty of customers, and how might this affect sales forecasts?

(f) What is the likelihood that new technology will transform products and market demand? For example organs became popular with the development of electronic keyboards, but now they have been superseded by other types of keyboards such as synthesisers.

(g) What is the likelihood of action by governments to aid or restrain sales and profits? For example legislation against certain ingredients in foods or medicine might force companies to increase their costs to keep product quality within permitted limits.

1.10 The strategic planners should consult with executive managers to assess the possible impact of these factors and to revise the projections into F_0 forecasts for revenues, costs and profits.

1.11 It may be argued that the F_0 forecast is unrealistic because it allows the company no new products or markets and no other new strategies and is therefore of little value. But the purpose of the F_0 forecast and gap analysis is to determine the size of the task facing the company if it wishes to achieve its target profits. The gap must be filled by new strategies and since the gap is quantifiable in money terms, an attempt can be made to estimate the extent to which any individual strategy or group of strategies might close the gap.

Errors in the forecast

1.12 A forecast cannot be expected to guarantee accuracy and there must inevitably be some latitude for error. If possible, the error should be quantified in either of the following two ways.

(a) By predicting the profit and estimating likely variations. For example 'in 1995 the forecast profit is £5 million with possible variations of plus or minus £2 million'.

(b) By providing a probability distribution for profits. For example 'in 1995 there is a 20% chance that profits will exceed £7 million, a 50% chance that they will exceed £5 million and an 80% chance that they will exceed £2½ million. Minimum profits in 1995 will be £2 million.'

The profit gap

1.13 The profit gap is the difference between the target profits (according to the overall corporate objectives of the company) and the profits on the F_0 forecast.

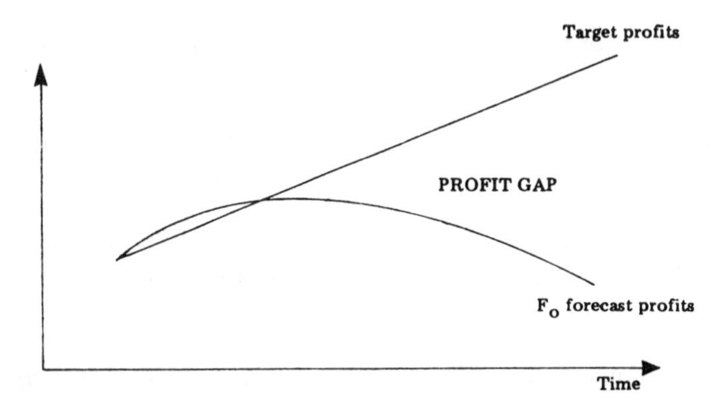

1.14 It is now that the company must decide what the options are for bridging the gap.

This gap represents the extra task facing the company, in addition to just continuing the existing business. It indicates how much extra profit *has to be* generated by the decisions and the commitments to be made over the next few years.

In deciding the size of the gap that must be closed, allowance must be made for errors in the forecast.

The sales gap

1.15 Sizer (1968) described a *sales gap* that could be filled by new product-market growth strategies as follows.

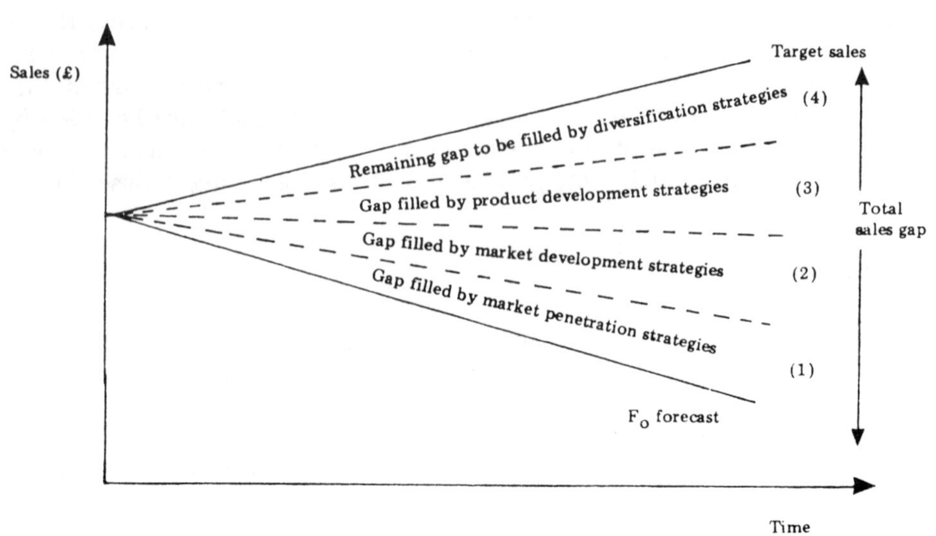

Other forms of gap analysis

1.16 Gap analysis has been described here in the context of achieving the overall objective of the organisation, whether it be quantified in terms of return on shareholders' capital, or even simply sales growth (sales gap analysis).

1.17 The same basic technique can be used as a starting point for formulating any particular strategy.

(a) In planning for manpower, gap analysis would be used to assess the difference over time between the following.

(i) What the organisation *needs to have* in terms of manpower, of differing skills and seniority.

(ii) What the organisation is *likely to have*, allowing for 'natural wastage' of staff, assuming that it does nothing to train staff or appoint new staff as vacancies arise.

Gap analysis would then be used to estimate how the gap between target and current forecasts could be closed. For example how many appointments at each level of seniority and in each functional skill should be filled by promotion (with or without training), transfers of staff, part time workers or recruitment from outside etc?

(b) In planning facilities, a similar analysis can be made of the gap between the facilities which the organisation needs to have, and what it is likely to have if nothing is done about the situation.

1.18 Gap analysis quantifies the size of the profit gap, or the sales gap, the EPS gap, the return on capital gap, the performance-risk gap, or whatever gap is being measured between the objective/targets for the planning period and the forecast based on the extrapolation of the current situation.

1.19 We can now summarise the stages in the strategic planning process as follows.

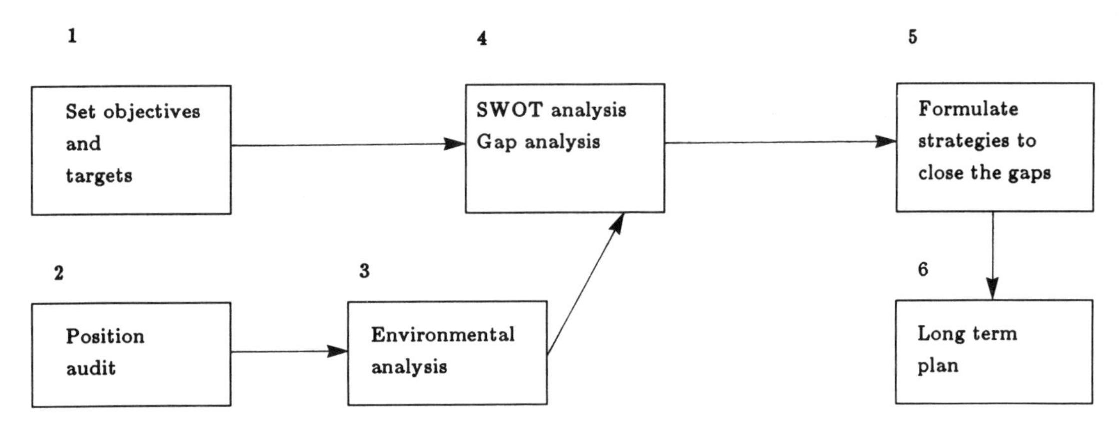

Demand, market and sales forecasts

1.20 Forecasting is far from an exact science, but planning is dependent on forecasts of future demand, what is likely to happen to the generic market and how will sales of our product change, with and without strategic action.

1.21 A demand function is simply an expression which shows how sales demand for a product is dependent on several factors.

These demand variables can be grouped into two broad categories.

(a) *Controllable variables or strategic variables*
These are factors over which the firm's management should have some degree of control, and which they can change if they wish. Controllable variables include:

- (i) the product's price. Also size of discounts, credit allowed etc;
- (ii) the amount spent on advertising and sales promotion;
- (iii) the amount spent on direct selling by a sales force;
- (iv) the design or quality of the product;
- (v) the distribution of the product, for example the number and geographical extent of sales outlets, such as shops which sell the product.

(b) *Uncontrollable variables*
These are factors over which the firm's management has no control. Uncontrollable variables can be sub-divided into three categories.

(i) *Consumer variables.* These are variables which are dependent on decisions by consumers, or the circumstances of consumers (for example their wealth). They include:

- (1) their income;
- (2) their tastes, preferences and attitudes;
- (3) their expectations about future price changes, which will affect their decisions about whether to buy now or later.

(ii) *Competitor variables.* These are variables which are dependent on decisions and actions by other firms, particularly competitors. They include:

- (1) the price of other goods which are either substitutes or complements;
- (2) advertising of these goods by other firms;
- (3) the quality and design of these goods.

(iii) *Other variables.* These are variables which are dependent on other factors, such as decisions by other organisations (for example the government) or factors which are outside the control of anyone (for example weather conditions, or the total size of the population).

1.22 A demand function can be set out as follows.

The determinants of demand for a product

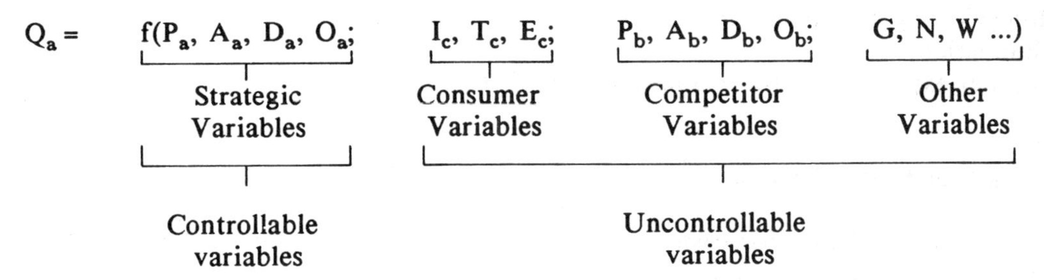

where

Q_a is quantity demanded of a product A per period
P_a is price of product A
A_a is advertising and sales promotion for product A
D_a is the design or quality of product A
O_a is the number of retail outlets or other outlets for distribution of product A

I_c is incomes of consumers/customers
T_c is the tastes and preferences of consumers
E_c is the expectation of consumers about future prices etc
P_b is the prices of related goods (substitutes, complements)
A_b is advertising/promotion for related goods
D_b is design and quality of related goods
O_b is the number of outlets for distribution of related goods

G is government policy
N is the number of people in the economy/potential market
W represents the weather conditions

1.23 The demand function set out above is little more than common sense. But what firms should want to estimate or forecast is what future demand is likely to be. To do this, an attempt should be made to quantify the relationship between demand for a product and the significant demand variables.

1.24 For example a demand function might be measurable as

$$Q_a = 3{,}000 - 0.032\ P_a + 240\ A_a + 0.05\ O_a + 0.35\ P_b - 320\ A_b - 0.02\ O_b + 36\ I_c$$

1.25 There are two problems with measuring a demand function in this way.

(a) There is the problem of deciding how to measure variables, especially qualitative variables such as product design, and consumer tastes.

(b) Then there is the mathematical problem of putting values to the 'constants' or coefficients for each variable. This might be done using *regression analysis*.

1.26 There are alternatives to mathematical techniques of demand forecasting like regression analysis. These include the following.

(a) Interviewing consumers or experts.
(b) Simulations.
(c) Market experiments (for example test marketing).

Market forecasts and sales forecasts

1.27 Market forecasts and sales forecasts complement each other. They should not be undertaken separately and the market forecast should be carried out first of all and should cover a longer period of time.

(a) *Market forecast*
This is a forecast for the market as a whole. It is mainly involved in the assessment of environmental factors, outside the organisation's control, which will affect the demand for its products/services. Often it consists of three components:
   (i) the economic review (national economy, government policy, covering forecasts on investment, population, gross national product, etc);
   (ii) specific market research (to obtain data about specific markets and forecasts concerning total market demand);
   (iii) evaluation of total market demand for the firm's and similar products, for example profitability, market potential etc.

(b) *Sales forecasts*
These are estimates of sales of a product in a future period:
   (i) at a given price;
   (ii) using a stated method(s) of sales promotion which will cost a given amount of money.

Unlike the market forecast, a sales forecast concerns the firm's activity directly. It takes into account such aspects as sales to certain categories of customer, sales promotion activities, the extent of competition, product life cycle, performance of major products.

Sales forecasts are expressed in volume, value and profit, and in the case of national and international organisations regional forecasts are usual, by product.

Research into potential sales

1.28 Sales potential is an estimate of the part of the market which is within the possible reach of a product. The potential will vary according to the price of the product and the amount of money spent on sales promotion, and market research should attempt to quantify these variations. Sales potential also depends on the following.

(a) How essential the product is to consumers.
(b) Whether it is a durable commodity whose purchase is postponable.
(c) The overall size of the possible market.
(d) Competition.

1.29 Whether sales potential is worth exploiting will depend on the cost of sales promotion and selling which must be incurred to realise the potential.

Example
Market research has led a company to the opinion that the sales potential of product X is as follows.

	Sales value	*Contribution earned before selling costs deducted*	*Cost of selling*
either	£100,000	£40,000	£10,000
or	£110,000	£44,000	£15,000

In this example, it would not be worth spending an extra £5,000 on selling in order to realise an extra sales potential of £10,000, because the net effect would be a loss of £(5,000 - 4,000) = £1,000.

1.30 Sales potential will influence the decisions by a company on how much of each product to make its *production mix*. The market situation is dynamic, and market research should reveal changing situations. A company might decide, for example, that maximum profits will be earned by concentrating all its production and sales promotion efforts on one segment of a market. Action by competitors might then adversely affect sales and market research might reveal that another market segment has become relatively more profitable. The company might therefore decide to divert some production capacity and sales promotion spending to the new segment in order to revive its profits.

1.31 Estimates of sales potential are required in deciding whether to invest money in the development of a new or improved product.

1.32 Market research, to be comprehensive, must show an awareness of the economic, fiscal, political and social influences which may affect supply and demand for a product. The influence of the environmental framework of marketing has already been described. Changes within this framework should wherever possible be anticipated.

2. IDENTIFYING ALTERNATIVE STRATEGIES

> *Note:* in some instances you might find it difficult to distinguish between corporate strategy and marketing strategy. The important thing to remember is that:
>
> - corporate strategy will involve decisions and direction for all functions of the operation;
> - marketing strategy incorporates decisions relating to the positioning of the marketing mix.

2.1 Having determined the extent of the gap which needs to be filled, we can now turn our attention to the strategies needed to fill it. The important point to recognise is that there will amost always be alternatives. Identifying these alternatives and carefully evaluating the options is an essential part of the planning process.

2.2 If a company recognises that it is in a declining business, or one where future growth will be restricted, it should seek to expand in other areas. Since decisions of this nature cannot be implemented quickly, or without careful thought, they should be formulated as strategies within the corporate plan. Tobacco companies, for example, recognising that their markets in the West are declining because of the trend away from smoking, have opened up new markets for tobacco products in the Third World and also diversified into paper, retailing, hotels etc.

Competitive advantage

2.3 Competitive advantage is anything which gives one organisation an edge over its rivals in the products it sells or the services it offers. One form of competitive advantage would be a large network of distributors or outlets, when competitors have smaller distribution networks or fewer sales outlets. Much of the competitive advantage which an organisation might hope to achieve, however, is provided by the nature/quality/price of its products. One company's products might have a definite edge over its rivals because it is better in quality, or cheaper in price. Where rival products are much alike (for example petrol, many processed foods etc) competitive advantage may be sought by creating a superior brand image and making the product *seem* different and more desirable than a rival producer's similar product. This advantage will have been identified as a corporate strength.

2.4 The environment within which many firms operate is characterised by the need to achieve competitive advantage. However, having gained a particular advantage, the firm will find it being eroded as competitors seek to share in the obvious benefits, unless the competitive advantage can be protected. This means that a continuous search for new product-market opportunities must be an indispensable part of a firm's strategy to maintain sales and profits in the face of competition.

Competitive strategies

2.5 Michael Porter *(Competitive strategy* and *Competitive advantage)* argues that a firm should adopt a competitive strategy which is intended to achieve some form of competitive advantage for the firm.

2.6 Competitive strategy means 'taking offensive or defensive actions to create a defendable position in an industry, to cope successfully with... competitive forces and thereby yield a superior return on investment for the firm. Firms have discovered many different approaches to this end, and the best strategy for a given firm is ultimately a unique construction reflecting its particular circumstances.' (Porter *Competitive strategy)*

2.7 Obviously, a competitive strategy is only required for organisations which face competition. Commercial organisations are the obvious example, whereas it might be difficult to think of government departments as operating in a competitive environment. Even so, some government departments need to plan competitively. Examples are as follows.

(a) A transport department in national or local government must plan for public transport to compete with private forms of transport (for example the railways versus road haulage firms; buses versus cars etc).

(b) Public health services must be aware of the effects of competition from private medicine.

2.8 Firms with a monopoly must also compete to retain their monopoly position, and prevent encroachments from competitors. Some monopolies compete with each other (for example solid fuel, gas or electricity as sources of power).

The choice of competitive strategy

2.9 Competitive strategy is largely based on product-market strategies, but manufacturing strategy could be important too. These are considered in detail in the next chapter. Porter suggests that there are three broad competitive strategies as follows. One of them is a manufacturing strategy, two of them are product-market strategies.

(a) Overall cost leadership.
(b) Differentiation.
(c) Focus, ie segmentation.

2.10 The type of competitive strategy which a firm adopts will depend on the competitive strategies adopted by rivals and will have implications for product design and quality, pricing and marketing.

2.11 The most appropriate form of competitive strategy will also depend on the type of product or service that the firm is producing. A distinction can be made into three categories of product.

(a) *Search products*. These are products whose attributes the consumer can discern, evaluate and compare fairly easily, for example size and colour, as with a style of dress, and these easily-assessed 'searched attributes' form the major factors in the consumer's purchase decision.

(b) *Experience products*. These are products whose important attributes cannot be discerned by the consumer until the consumer has had some experience of using the product, for example taste in the case of food, and product durability.

(c) *Credence products*. These are products whose important attributes cannot be evaluated by the consumer, even if the consumer has purchased it before, either because the product's attributes might vary the next time (for example quality of service in a restaurant) or because the product's attributes cannot easily be evaluated (for example pet food, the competence of professional advice from a solicitor or insurance broker etc). The consumer must therefore show 'faith' or 'credence' in the product.

2.12 *Cost leadership strategy*
A cost leadership strategy seeks to achieve the position of lowest-cost producer in the industry. By producing at the lowest cost, the manufacturer can compete on price with every other producer in the industry, and earn the highest unit profits.

2.13 Achieving overall cost leadership depends on the following.

(a) Setting up production facilities for mass production, so as to obtain economies of scale.

(b) Using the latest technology.

(c) In high-technology industries, and in industries depending on labour skills for product design and production methods, there will be a *learning curve effect* (also called a *cost experience curve)*. By producing more items than any other competitor, a firm can benefit more from the learning curve, and achieve lower average costs.

(d) Concentrating on productivity objectives, and seeking productivity improvements and cost reductions in various ways (for example zero base budgeting, value analysis programmes etc).

(e) Cost minimisation in areas of overhead costs - such as R & D, the sales force, advertising costs etc.

(f) Favourable access to sources of raw materials supply would also contribute towards overall cost leadership.

2.14 In some industries, there might be a low *critical mass* of production output where maximum economies of scale are achievable. In these industries, cost leadership would be difficult to achieve, because many rival firms should be able to achieve similar low costs too. It is only when the critical mass of production is high that a cost leadership strategy is likely to be effective. For example suppose that in the industry for manufacturing widgets, unit costs are 10% lower if a firm can obtain a 15% market share, costs are 25% lower if a firm can obtain a 30% market share and 60% lower if the firm can capture half the market. The strategic advantage of capturing half the market by becoming the least-cost (and so least-priced) producer might seem obvious!

2.15 Since overall cost leadership depends on large-scale production economies of scale and the learning curve etc, it is a necessary feature of this strategy that the organisation should aim for market leadership, or other significant advantages, such as a unique low-cost system of production, or marketing and distribution advantages (for example a cheap distribution system).

2.16 This strategy therefore has implications for pricing, product quality, and marketing, especially in the case of *search products*.

(a) *Pricing*. To achieve high volumes of sales, the firm may need to keep prices low, if the price elasticity of demand for a product is high. (This means that demand for a product is sensitive to its price.) The firm might also use promotional pricing. The importance of low prices suggests the need for low-cost production.

(b) *Product quality*. A cost leadership strategy is well suited to search products, where consumers can readily compare the attributes of competing products from rival firms. With such products, firms must be able to match the product quality of rivals, otherwise they will lose customers to these rivals. On the other hand, firms should not incur costs to improve quality attributes which have little, if any, impact on the consumer's purchasing decision.

(c) *Marketing*. Advertising may be used to boost sales volume, especially where advertising emphasises price discounts, or 'unbeatable prices'. In the case of search products, advertising should be *informative* about the key attributes of the product (for example price) and persuasive advertising is unlikely to have much effect on demand.

2.17 The implementation of a strategy for overall cost leadership would call for the following.

(a) A large amount of 'up-front' capital expenditure on top quality and up to date equipment.
(b) Aggressive pricing and a willingness to bear large losses initially in order to build up market share.

2.18 The drawbacks to this strategy are as follows.

(a) The risk that technological change will mean even more capital investment to keep up to date, and which may nullify all the cost advantages so far achieved by experience and the learning curve process.

(b) The need to stay up to date in technology.

(c) The threat of competition from other countries where certain costs are even lower, such as Taiwan and South Korea, where labour costs are very low compared with Europe and the USA. Selling on price always means that the organisation is in danger of being undercut.

(d) The threat by competitors to fragment the market, or build up a high-price high-quality brand image. An overall low cost producer would then have to compete on cost in each market segment it operated in and hope that cheaper prices can compete successfully against brand image.

(e) Cost inflation is always a danger, especially when competitors in other countries do not have the same problems (for example rising labour costs). Fluctuations in foreign exchange rates do not necessarily nullify inflation differences between countries, as UK manufacturers have learned all too well in recent years.

2.19 *Differentiation strategy: product differentiation*
Whereas a cost leadership strategy seeks to achieve value for the customer by providing a good basic product at a low price, differentiation strategy seeks to raise the quality of the product, and in doing so, to raise the product's cost and sales price. The improvements in quality should be of more value to the customer than the price increase, so that the customer is willing to pay more for the superior quality: there must be perceived added value.

2.20 A differentiation strategy is therefore aimed at achieving an optimal balance for the customer between quality and price. ('Quality' is a term used to refer to desirable attributes, including customer service.) Firms try to provide greater quality relative to price than rival firms are offering. There is a limit to what a consumer will pay for a product, and so there will be a trade-off by the consumer between quality and price which firms must incorporate into their differentiation strategy.

2.21 A differentiation strategy is based on the assumption that competitive advantage can be gained through particular characteristics of a firm's products. Products may be categorised as follows.

(a) *Breakthrough products* which offer either a radical performance advantage over competition, a drastically lower price, or ideally, it may offer both. An example of a breakthrough product in the past was float glass, developed by Pilkington. Another example, but one which failed to gain commercial success and acceptance, was the Concorde supersonic airliner.

(b) *Improved products* which are not radically different to their competition but are obviously superior in terms of better performance at competitive price. It will usually be the result of incorporation of recent advances in technology, applied to a particular product. An example would be the much-improved capabilities of pocket calculators in the 1980s and colour televisions in the 1970s. A problem for producers is that product improvements are quickly copied by competitors.

(c) *Competitive products* which show no obvious advantage over others, but which derive their appeal from a particular compromise of cost and performance. The car industry provides excellent examples of competitive products. Cars are not all sold at rock-bottom prices, nor do they all provide immaculate comfort and performance. Nearly all makes of car are a compromise between price, comfort and performance, and they compete with each other by trying to offer a more attractive compromise than rival models.

2.22 With a successful differentiation strategy, loyalty to the firm's products will build up, and because customers are not always sensitive to price the firm can sell its products at prices that are higher than the least-cost producer in the market. It is probable that a firm which uses a strategy of differentiation will not be the market leader in terms of market share.

2.23 The main risk with a differentiation strategy is that customers will not want to pay higher prices for the different product: although differentiation exists, it is not worth paying more than the cheapest product on the market. The quality of the marketing strategy will be a critical success factor.

> A *critical success factor* is any factor which is essential to the success of the strategy, plan or organisation. Organisations which identify these critical factors are able to concentrate management attention on these essential factors, ensuring their performance is on target. Where control information indicates a failure in one of these areas, corrective management action can be taken immediately.

2.24 Some implications for differentiation strategy are as follows.

(a) The firm must seek to provide superior quality and superior service, relative to price, in the eyes of consumers.

(b) The firm must continually seek to innovate, in order to stay ahead of rivals in quality. If rivals innovate, the firm should try to emulate them quickly. Consequently, a differentiating firm will probably have a large research and development budget, or a large promotional budget.

2.25 *Example: product differentiation*
Consider a company that specialises in making cheap novelty toys for children's parties and other celebrations. These products will often have the following characteristics.

(a) They need to be cheap, because consumers will not pay a lot of money for toys that are not intended to have long use.

(b) They will not have a long life cycle, because their novelty wears off.

(c) There must be enough different products to persuade the customer that he or she is not buying a lot of the same thing.

2.26 Product differentiation and innovation has to be achieved at a low cost, which probably means using the same sort of equipment and machinery to make many of the items. Differentiation can be achieved as follows.

(a) Colour differences.
(b) Size differences.
(c) Different wrappings or containers.
(d) Variants of the product for different market segments (for example children, adults, senior citizens).
(e) Small changes in the products' formulations to maintain their novelty value.

2.27 *Focus strategy*
The third type of competitive strategy identified by Porter is a focus strategy, whereby a firm concentrates its attention on one or more particular segments or niches of the market, and does not try to serve the entire market with a single product.

2.28 A *focus* strategy is a strategy based on fragmenting (ie segmenting) the market and focusing on particular market segments. The firm will not sell its products industry-wide (in contrast to a differentiation strategy) but will focus on a particular type of buyer or geographical area. 'The strategy rests on the premise that the firm is thus able to serve its narrow strategic target more effectively or efficiently than competitors who are competing more broadly. As a result, the firm achieves either differentiation from better meeting the needs of the particular target, or lower costs in serving this target, or both.' *(Porter)*

(a) A *cost-focus* strategy involves selecting a segment of the market and specialising in a product (or products) for that segment. The firm, by specialising in a limited number of products, or by concentrating on a small geographical area, can keep costs to a minimum within that market segment. This type of strategy is often found in the printing, clothes manufacture and car repairs industries, as just three examples.

(b) A *quality-focus* strategy involves selecting a segment of the market and competing on the basis of quality (through product differentiation) for that segment. Luxury goods are the prime example of such a strategy.

2.29 A focus strategy is often best-suited to a firm that is trying to enter a market for the first time. The implications of a focus strategy for product quality, price and advertising will be:

(a) for a cost-focus strategy, similar to a cost leadership strategy;
(b) for a quality-focus strategy, similar to a differentiation strategy.

2.30 The risk in a focus strategy is that the market segment might not be big enough to provide the firm with a profitable basis for its operations.

2.31 The niche marketing of the 1980s (eg Sock Shop, Tie Rack) is an example of focus strategy, but few of the niche retailers have survived the recent recession indicating that their market segments may have been too narrow to cover a burgeoning cost base. One exception to this has been Body Shop, reflecting the growing appeal of its positioning as a 'caring' company as far as the environment is concerned, and its exploitation of the widespread belief that 'natural' equals 'healthy'.

2.32 Although there is a risk with any of the three broad competitive strategies he identified, Porter argues that a firm must pursue one of them. A 'stuck-in-the-middle' strategy is almost certain to make only low profits. 'This firm lacks the market share, capital investment and resolve to play the low-cost game, the industry-wide differentiation necessary to obviate the need for a low-cost position, or the focus to create differentiation or a low-cost position in a more limited sphere.'

3. EVALUATING ALTERNATIVE STRATEGIES

3.1 This overview of the stratgic choices facing the firm makes clear that organisations face a number of options. The next chapter breaks these down even further, considering the product-market and manufacturing strategies open to the operation. Careful evaluation of all the alternative strategies identified is important at both the corporate and marketing levels of planning.

As we have seen organisations can be faced with a number of strategic options. Individual strategies should be tested against a list of criteria for acceptance as follows.

(a) To what extent will the strategy contribute towards company financial objectives in both the short and long term?

(b) Is the strategy consistent with the social responsibilities of the company?

(c) Does the strategy conform to other strategies pursued by the company, or is it a completely new direction? (for example conglomerate diversification, or investment in pure research might be proposed strategies which are currently not pursued by the company).

(d) The element of risk attached to a proposed strategy should not be too high compared with the potential rewards. If the strategy can only be successful under the most favourable conditions, then the risk is probably too great.

(e) Is the strategy capable of succeeding in spite of the likely reaction by competitors?

(f) Will there be adequate control techniques? A new strategy needs a careful check on performance to put any necessary remedial steps into effect, particularly in the early stages. The lack of an adequate control system may be serious hindrance to effective decision making.

(g) Is the strategy preferable to other, mutually exclusive strategies? Is there an option to combine two separate strategies into one action? 'While it is often sufficient to solve problem A by taking action A, and to solve problem B by taking action B, greater economy in effort and in cost would be achieved if one could take action C to solve both problem A and problem B at the same time - two birds with one stone, as it were.' *(Argenti)* Argenti used the example of one department buying a computer for £50,000 for accounting work, a second department buying a £30,000 computer for scientific work, when a £60,000 computer would have been capable of handling the workload of both departments.

(h) Are the technology and resources available to carry out the strategy? The time span within which a strategy is expected to achieve its purpose must not be so short that the company suffers from severe 'indigestion' during this period. Time must be allowed for new organisational and communication patterns to develop and operate freely, and for personal abilities and relationships to mature.

(i) Is the new strategy flexible and capable of adjusting to change in the business environment?

3.2 Argenti simplifies this list of criteria for testing strategy into six items.

(a) Can it be shown that the strategy gives the company an expected return with a given business risk attached, similar to the one expected by its shareholders?

(b) Does the company have the necessary competence to carry out the strategy?

(c) Does the strategy eliminate all the significant weaknesses of the company, as identified by the internal appraisal?

(d) Does the strategy exploit any opportunities which have been identified as possibly arising in the future?

(e) Does the strategy reduce the impact of any significant external threats?

(f) Does the strategy call for action by the company which is objectionable on social or moral grounds?

3.3 *Evaluating strategy: financial considerations*
Economic and financial considerations are closely related to the financial objectives of the firm and so strategies will be evaluated by considering how far they contribute to meeting the dominant objectives, for return on investment, profits, growth, EPS and cash flow.

3.4 *Evaluating strategy: synergy*
A strategy for product or market development, or for diversification, should be evaluated in terms of whether it is likely to result in synergy and if so, what kind of synergy would be expected and what the value of the synergy would be.

3.5 *Evaluating strategy: company image*
In recent years, there has been an increase in the number of large multinational companies taking steps to build up their company image. Investment decisions might be taken with due regard being given to their effect on public opinion. Multinational companies in particular appear to be conscious of their image, perhaps because of their size or perhaps because they feel vulnerable to accusations that they trample roughshod over national interests for the gain of shareholders abroad. You might well have seen television advertisements publicising the size of a company's investment in Britain's economy or how the company is safeguarding or promoting the general welfare of the nation.

3.6 A good company image might be considered essential to continued commercial success, especially for companies manufacturing consumer goods and in view of the continually growing public concern about conservation of natural resources and the environment.

3.7 *Evaluating strategy: customer satisfaction*
In some cases, companies give consideration to customer satisfaction, not just for the sake of making more sales through the goodwill it creates, but out of a genuine wish to be socially or ethically conscientious. Nationalised industries in particular have a tradition of providing a high quality of service as well as a wish to make profits or cut losses.

3.8 *Evaluating strategies: resource utilisation*
Strategies which do not make use of the existing manpower skills and technical expertise of the company, and which therefore call for new skills to be acquired, might be unacceptable to the corporate planners for the following reasons.

(a) Acquiring expertise and experience through organic growth of the company would be a long process.
(b) If a takeover of another company is therefore necessary for faster entry into a new product-market area, the disadvantages of an acquisition policy might outweigh the advantages.

3.9 *Evaluating strategies: a summary*
Strategies are evaluated to decide whether they will help to achieve the organisation's objectives and so whether they are desirable. The final list of desirable strategic opportunities, if it is not empty, will be a list for ranking in order of priority.

3.10 To provide the firm with an attractive overall product-market mix, it will be necessary to group together various combinations of opportunities that seem to achieve best the firm's mix of objectives.

3.11 Whenever a portfolio of strategies is considered, it is necessary to prepare a revised forecast to decide whether the profit gap will be closed. Argenti calls these revised forecasts F_p forecasts.

3.12 Only when the gap has been closed (or closed sufficiently) will an acceptable portfolio of strategies have been found.

The strategic programme

3.13 We can now summarise the stage that we have reached in strategy selection.

(a) We have evaluated the likely costs, benefits and financial return of each strategy and expressed the likelihood of its accuracy.

(b) We have identified the profit gap between planned target profit and projected profit based on the existing situation. From this we have developed various combinations of strategies which will enable this gap to be filled.

(c) The next stage is to check each combination against the financial resources and other resources of the company. At this stage, various combinations can be discarded as being unsuitable, having regard to the company's resources.

(d) Finally, the optimum combination of strategies will be selected to form a strategy which will become a strategic budget when the policy statement has been approved.

3.14 The *policy statement* describes the planned long-term strategy of the company, identifying the objectives, constraints and strategies to be pursued over the corporate planning period. Argenti believes that this statement should be short, and restricted to identifying a few key strategies. However, to 'sell' the plan to junior managers and employees, the ideas in the statement might need to be 'packaged' with explanations for presentation and communication to staff. We will be considering the issue of internal marketing later in this text.

3.15 The *strategic budget* is a working document for implementing the whole process of business planning. It allocates the responsibility for carrying out the declared intentions of the company, as expressed in the policy statement.

3.16 Drucker defines business planning as follows.

> '. . . a continuous process of making present entrepreneural decisions systematically and with best possible knowledge of their futurity, organising systematically the effort needed to carry out these decisions, and measuring the results of these decisions against expectations through organised feedbacks . . .'

The strategic budget is the key planning document which will 'organise systematically the effort needed to carry out these decisions'. There are three main sections.

(a) A performance budget: who takes what action, what targets should be reached.

(b) A resource budget: a time schedule of resources committed to the strategy.

(c) A profit budget: a forecast of the results expected, usually shown in the form of a forecast profit and loss account and balance sheet.

3.17 The purpose of a strategic budget is therefore as follows.

(a) To specify organisational responsibility for the achievement of the plan.

(b) To outline the sources and uses of finance.

(c) To state the resources to be used in implementing the plan.

(d) To establish feedback by means of performance indicators to monitor the achievement of the plan.

3.18 Once the corporate plan has been developed, operations planning will take place to ensure that the corporate target is achieved. This is the stage at which the marketing plan needs to be developed.

3.19 The diagram which follows summarises the stages in developing a corporate strategy, showing how a company might progress through a sequence of defining its business, assessing external factors, analysing its strengths and assessing weaknesses and formulating objectives through to the evaluation of alternative courses of action.

Developing the strategic plan

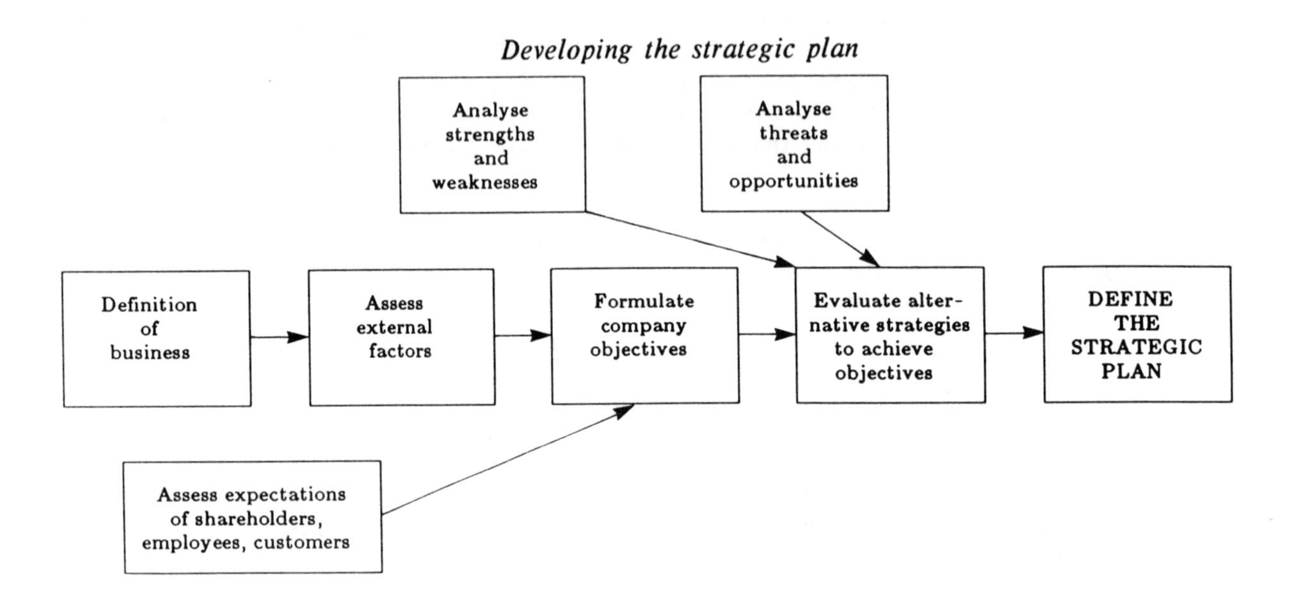

4. MODELS FOR STRATEGIC EVALUATION

4.1 A number of models, tools and techniques exist which can help the manager make strategic choices. Some of these, such as breakeven analysis and DCF analysis you will be familiar with from your financial studies. Others such as experimentation and test marketing you will have met in other marketing subjects.

CVP analysis

4.2 CVP analysis (cost-volume-profit or breakeven analysis) can be very useful in strategic planning in order to assess what share of the market a company would need to break even or to achieve a target return with a particular strategy.

4.3 For example if a company is planning to make a new product for a particular market and estimates of fixed and variable costs were fairly reliable, the company could assess the following for a number of different sales prices.

(a) What level of sales would be needed to break even each year and so what market share would be needed?

(b) What is the margin of safety? ie the difference between the forecast level of sales and the level needed to break even.

4.4 Johnson and Scholes advocate that cash flow planning, funds flow planning and CVP analysis as useful techniques to assess whether a strategy is realistic and feasible from a financial viewpoint.

Example: cost-volume-profit analysis

4.5 Snapper Flatt Ltd makes and sells a single product. The variable cost of production is £3 per unit, and the variable cost of selling is £1 per unit. Fixed costs total £6,000 and the unit sales price is £6.

The company budgets to make and sell 3,600 units in the next year.

Required: a breakeven chart showing the expected amount of output and sales required to break even, and the safety margin in the budget.

4.6 A breakeven chart records the amount of fixed costs, variable costs, total costs and total revenue at all volumes of sales, and at a *given sales price* as follows.

(a)

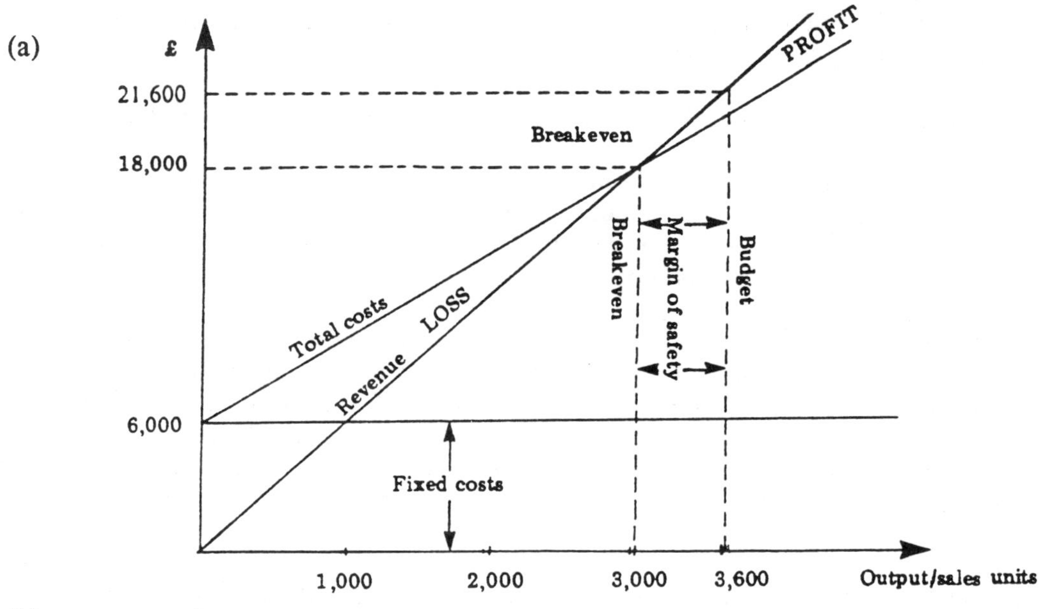

(b)

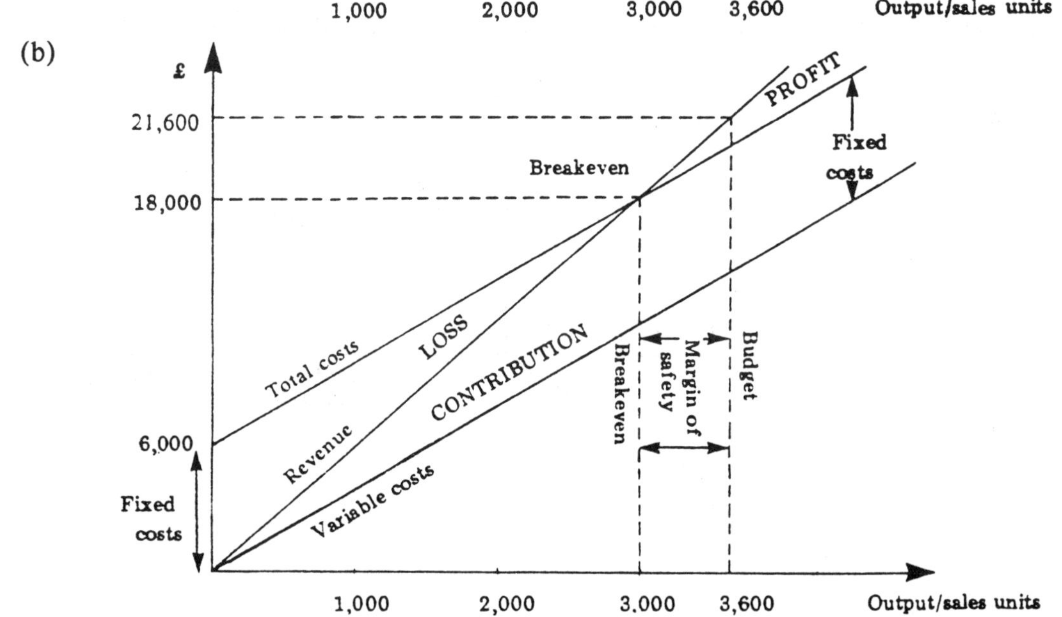

4.7 The difference between the two breakeven graphs is simply that in (a), total costs are analysed into fixed and variable costs with variable costs built on top of a fixed cost base, whereas in (b) variable costs appear below fixed costs in the total cost analysis. Graph (a) is perhaps more commonly used but (b) portrays how the contribution margin increases with extra sales volume, until at the breakeven point, the total contribution equals the amount of fixed costs.

4.8 The breakeven point can also be calculated arithmetically as follows.

$$\frac{\text{Fixed costs (required contribution)}}{\text{Contribution per unit}} = \frac{£6{,}000}{£(6-3-1)}$$

$$= £6{,}000 \div £2 \text{ per unit}$$

$$= 3{,}000 \text{ units}$$

The P/V chart

4.9 The P/V (profit-volume) chart is a variation of the breakeven chart which provides a simple illustration of the relationship of costs and profit to sales, and of the margin of safety. A P/V chart is constructed as follows.

(a) The horizontal axis comprises either sales volume in units, or sales value.

(b) The vertical axis comprises profit in value, extending above and below the horizontal axis with a zero point at the intersection of the two axes, and the negative section below the horizontal axis representing fixed costs. This means that at zero production, the firm is incurring a loss equal to the fixed costs.

(c) The profit-volume line is a straight line drawn with its starting point (at zero production) at the intercept on the vertical axis representing the level of fixed costs, and with a gradient of contribution/unit (or the C/S ratio if sales value is used rather than units). The P/V line will cut the horizontal axis at the breakeven point of sales volume. Any point on the P/V line above the horizontal axis represents the profit to the firm (as measured on the vertical axis) for that particular level of sales.

4.10 Returning to the example in paragraph 4.5, a P/V chart could be constructed as follows.

P/V chart

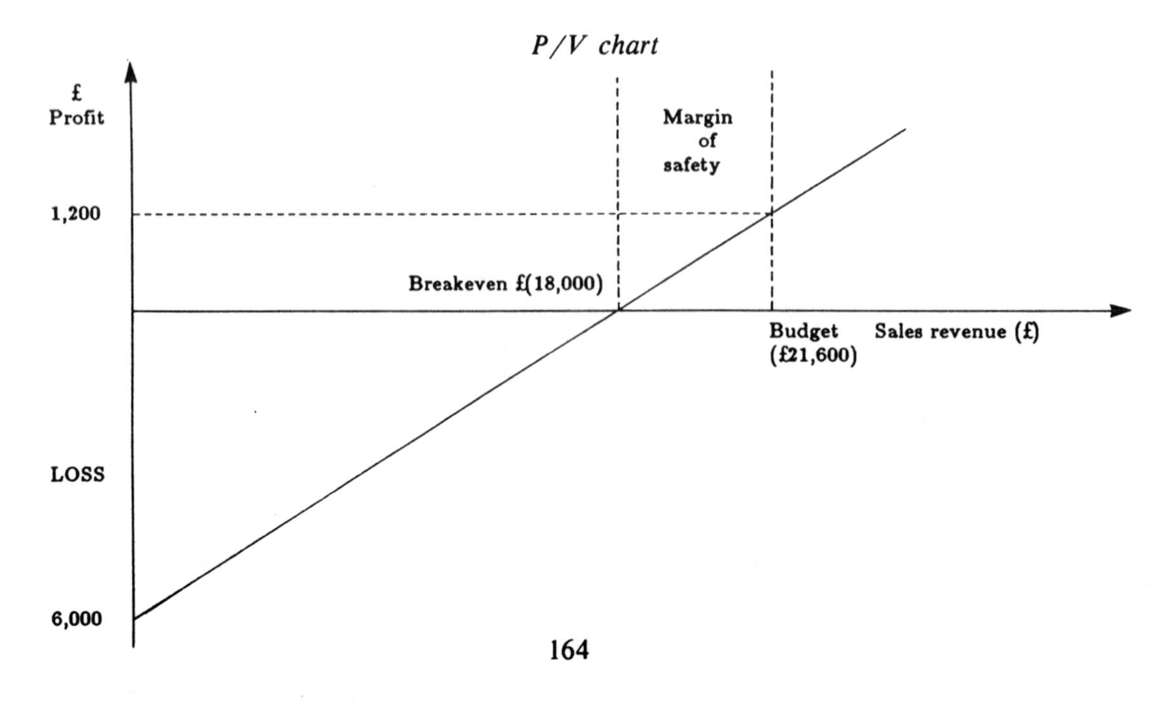

The breakeven point may be read from the graph as £18,000 in sales revenue, and the margin of safety is £3,600 in sales revenue or 16.67% budgeted sales revenue.

The multi-product P/V chart

4.11 If a firm sells more than one product, a P/V chart can be used to show the relative contribution earned by each product towards the total budgeted profit. To a limited extent, this may help management to decide whether the optimum mix has been selected, or whether some products should be sold in greater proportions, or some products discontinued.

Example: multi-product P/V chart

4.12 A company sells three products, X, Y and Z. Cost and sales data for one period are as follows.

	X	*Y*	*Z*
Sales volume	2,000 units	2,000 units	5,000 units
Sales price per unit	£3	£4	£2
Variable cost per unit	£2.25	£3.50	£1.25
Total fixed costs	£3,250		

4.13 A P/V chart may be constructed in the normal way.

	X	*Y*	*Z*	*Total*
	£	£	£	£
Contribution per unit	0.75	0.50	0.75	
Budgeted contribution (total)	1,500	1,000	3,750	6,250
Fixed costs				3,250
Budgeted profit				3,000

4.14 The contribution earned by each individual product is shown separately, in order (left to right on the graph) of the size of their C/S ratio.

	C/S ratio	*Sales*	*Contribution*
		£'000	£'000
X	25%	6,000	1,500
Y	12.5%	8,000	1,000
Z	37.5%	10,000	3,750
		24,000	6,250

Multi-product P/V chart

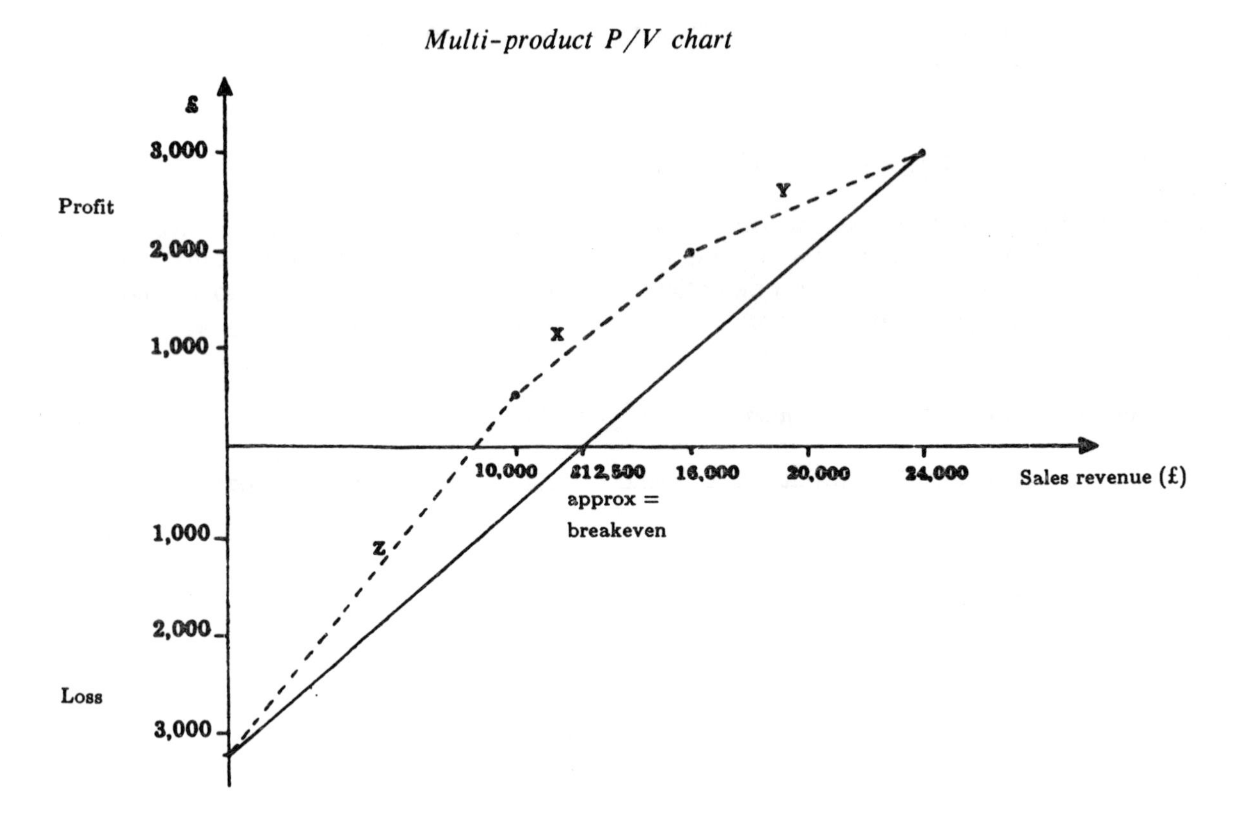

4.15 The bold line on the completed graph shows the profit which will be earned from the sales of these products *in the given mix.*

Assumptions and criticisms of CVP analysis

4.16 There are several assumptions normally applied in CVP analysis, in addition to those of constant unit variable cost, constant total fixed costs and the divisibility of mixed costs into fixed and variable elements. These assumptions are as follows.

(a) The sale price per unit is constant over the entire relevant range of output.

(b) Stock levels do not vary significantly, so that production output and sales volumes are the same.

(c) The activity (usually sales volume and production output) has been chosen correctly as the factor which most influences cost behaviour.

(d) The sales mix is constant at all levels of activity, where more than one product is included in the analysis.

The relevant range of activity and assumptions of cost behaviour

4.17 Cost-volume-profit analysis can only be made within the *relevant range* of activity of the business, ie within the normal range of output levels where the linear assumptions about cost behaviour are considered to be relatively accurate.

The breakeven chart and P/V graph both start at nil output and sales, but this is merely for convenience and simplicity of illustration.

The graphs also show that fixed costs are constant at all levels of output, so that if there is no output at all, there will be a loss equal to the amount of fixed costs. It might be tempting to assume that this is true, but it could be a seriously misleading assumption because many 'fixed cost' items are step cost in nature over a wide range of activity. Fixed costs estimates should therefore apply within the relevant range of activity only.

Criticisms of CVP analysis

4.18 The accountant's approach to CVP analysis has been criticised in the past for a number of different reasons. The main criticisms are as follows.

(a) It assumes that sales volume and production volume are the same.

(b) It assumes that in a multi-product firm, the sales mix is constant.

(c) It assumes linearity of the sales revenue function and total cost function.

(d) It is often used as a simple 'deterministic' model, ie risk and uncertainty analysis is not always applied to the calculations, and estimates of unit sales price, unit variable costs and total fixed costs are assumed to be accurate.

(e) It generally assumes that there are no 'constraints' or limiting factors on production.

The problem of the sales mix for CVP analysis

4.19 Perhaps the most serious drawback to CVP analysis is that in a multi-product business, the sales mix is assumed to be constant. Consider the following example.

4.20 Tredgett Ltd sells two products, Widgets and Splodgets, for which the following budgeted information is available.

	Widgets		*Splodgets*		*Both products*
Sales	2,000 units		6,000 units		8,000 units
	Per unit	Total	Per unit	Total	
	£	£	£	£	£
Revenue	8	16,000	9	54,000	70,000
Variable costs	4	8,000	8	48,000	56,000
Contribution	4	8,000	1	6,000	14,000

Total fixed costs are expected to be £7,000. What is the breakeven point?

4.21 One solution might be that by selling 7,000 Splodgets but no Widgets, the company would earn contribution of £1 x 7,000 = £7,000 and so break even. However, in CVP analysis, the sales mix is assumed to be constant, in the budgeted proportions.

Budgeted total contribution	£14,000
Budgeted sales	8,000 units for £70,000 revenue
Budgeted (joint) C/S ratio (£14,000 ÷ £70,000)	20%
Budgeted contribution per unit (average per unit)	£1.75

Breakeven:	Required contribution / Contribution per unit	or	Required contribution / C/S ratio
	£7,000 / £1.75		£7,000 / 20%
	4,000 units	or	£35,000

Since there are two different products, the breakeven position would be better expressed in revenue than in units. But the breakeven point of 4,000 units means in this case 1,000 Widgets and 3,000 Splodgets, given a budgeted sales mix ratio of 1:3

Risk appraisal in strategy evaluation

4.22 Risk has been mentioned before. It is clearly important, in view of the uncertainty about the future. Some strategies will be more risky than others.

One of the problems arising when evaluating alternative strategies is the reliability of the data used. Since the figures are compiled on estimates of the future, there must be considerable uncertainty about the final accuracy of the figures. Business planners frequently use various operational research techniques to measure the degree of uncertainty involved. These include the simple 'rule of thumb' methods of expressing a range of values from worst possible result to best possible result with a best estimate lying between these two extremes. Also, there is the use of basic probability theory to express the likelihood of a forecast result occurring. This would evaluate the data given by informing the decision maker that there is, for example, a 50% probability that the best estimate will be achieved, a 25% chance that the worst result will occur and a 25% chance that the best possible result will occur. This evaluation of risk might help the executive to decide between alternative strategies, each with its own risk profile.

4.23 Ansoff suggests that decision theory is of limited relevance in measuring risk, and *sensitivity analysis* should be used in preference. This involves identifying each variable factor in the calculation and assessing what would be the effect on the final result if the variable was amended by x% up or down. This will highlight those variables which are most likely to have a significant effect on the final result.

4.24 When evaluating a strategy, management should consider the following.

(a) Whether an individual strategy involves an unacceptable amount of risk. If it does, it should be eliminated from further consideration in the planning process.

(b) However, the risk of an individual strategy should also be considered in the context of the overall 'portfolio' of investment strategies adopted by the company. If you have already studied portfolio theory you will be aware of the following.

(i) If a strategy is risky, but its outcome is not related to ('correlated with') the outcome of other strategies, then adopting that strategy will help the company to spread its risks. (Diversification, after all, is intended to 'put more eggs into different baskets').

(ii) If a strategy is risky, but is negatively correlated with other adopted strategies, so that if strategy A does well, other adopted strategies will do badly and vice versa, then adopting strategy A would actually reduce the overall risk of the company's strategy portfolio.

NPV analysis

4.25 The principles of relevant costs for decision making and the techniques of discounted cash flow (DCF), particularly using net present value (NPV), should be familiar to you already. However, for planning purposes you must be able to apply these principles and techniques to situations where the data is either subject to uncertainty in the estimates, or else is incomplete.

4.26 As a general guideline, you should try to the following.

(a) Recognise the management decision for which the information is needed, ie what are we trying to do?

(b) Assess whether the data is incomplete. If so, make any suitable assumptions that might be necessary. In answering an examination question, state your assumptions clearly.

(c) Recognise whether any estimated data is uncertain, and of dubious reliability. If possible, assess how variations in the estimates would affect your financial analysis and recommendation.

4.27 It will probably be helpful to relate these general guidelines to a specific example. You will find a table of present value factors in the appendix to this text.

First example: DCF analysis

4.28 Booters plc is a company which specialises in purchasing and re-selling land with development potential. The following data is available.

Market value of agricultural land	£20,000 per acre
Market value of land that can be developed	£200,000 per acre
Maintenance cost of land, per acre	£2,500 pa
Booters plc's cost of capital	19%

Agricultural land that is held by Booters plc can be let to farmers on short term leases for £300 per acre per annum, but maintenance costs would be payable by Booters.

The company has now received invitations to bid for two properties.

Property 1. $1\frac{1}{2}$ acres of land near a planned major road. Some of the land is about to be made subject to a compulsory purchase order, for sale to the local authority for £25,000. The remaining land (0.8 of an acre) can be re-sold to a property developer for £190,000, but not until about five years' time.

Property 2. A country estate of 160 acres, of which 15 acres might be released for residential housing development at any time in the next four years. Development of the remaining 145 acres will not be allowed.

This land will be put up for auction, unless Booters plc agrees now to pay a price of £1,400,000 beforehand. If the land goes up for auction, it is believed that a local businessman might offer £1,600,000, but the reserve price will be only £900,000.

Required: in the case of each property, what should Booters bid for the property, if anything?

Discussion

4.29 In this example, the data is incomplete. Some of the missing items would be readily available in a real-life situation, but other data would be unobtainable, except as guesswork.

4.30 *Property 1.* Most of the data we need for a simple financial analysis exists, but the data does not state whether the land is *agricultural* land or not, and so whether it can be let out to a farmer.

Otherwise, we have a straightforward DCF analysis.

	Year	*Value/ cost* £	*Discount factor at 19%*	*Present value* £
Sale value of land, subject to compulsory purchase order	0	25,000	1.00	25,000
Sale value of remaining land	5	190,000	0.42	79,800
Maintenance cost of land, assumed to be £2,500 x 0.8 pa	1-5	(2,000)	3.06	(6,120)
Maximum purchase price				98,680

4.31 If the land sold under the compulsory purchase order takes time to sell, say one year, the value of the land would be lower, with the £25,000 sale value having to be discounted by a factor of 0.84 and a maintenance cost of land to be included (0.7 acres x £2,500, as a year 1 cost).

A maximum price of £98,000 might be indicated.

4.32 *Property 2*
Here the data is incomplete and uncertain.

(a) How likely is it that the 15 acres will be released for housing development?

(b) When is it most likely to be released?

(c) Is it agricultural land, and so could it be leased out to tenant farmers?

(d) Would the unwanted 145 acres be saleable at agricultural land prices, and if so, when would Booters plc know which land it did not want? Have the 15 acres for re-development been specifically identified?

(e) If the land goes for auction, would a bid above the reserve price be likely?

It is only by recognising what data is missing or uncertain that we can begin to carry out a sensible financial analysis.

4.33 Here the following assumptions are made. *In an examination, you should state your own assumptions clearly!*

(a) The land is agricultural land.
(b) The 15 acres for redevelopment have not been identified specifically. The remaining 145 acres cannot be re-sold until the planning permission has been obtained on the other 15 acres.
(c) The 145 acres could then be resold at agricultural land prices.

4.34 Two further assumptions call for business judgment.

(a) The 15 acres *will* be released for residential housing. There is a risk, of course, that it won't be.

(b) The land will not be released for four more years. It could, of course, be sooner.

4.35 Now we can carry out a DCF analysis.

	Year	*Value/ cost* £	*Discount factor at 19%*	*Present value* £
Sales value of 15 acres (15 x £200,000)	4	3,000,000	0.50	1,500,000
Sales value of 145 acres (145 x £20,000)	4	2,900,000	0.50	1,450,000
Sub-letting of 160 acres at £300 per acre	1-4	48,000	2.64	126,720
Maintenance cost of 160 acres at £2,500 pa	1-4	(400,000)	2.64	(1,056,000)
Maximum value of the land				2,020,720

4.36 Since Booters plc has been offered the chance to buy the property prior to auction for £1,400,000, the key questions are as follows.

(a) Is buying the land too much of a risk? If the land is *not* released for development, the 15 acres would be sold for only £300,000, and the PV of this would be only £150,000, not the £1,500,000 in the table above. The maximum value of the land would now be £1,350,000 less, at just £670,720!

(b) If the risk is considered to be worth accepting, should a price of £1,400,000 be accepted, or is it worth trying to get the land for something near the reserve price of £900,000 and running the risk of having to outbid a rival, by offering as much as £1,600,000 or even more?

4.37 There is no clear answer to either question, but a decision has to be taken. This is what strategic management is about!

5. CONCLUSION

5.1 To develop a strategic plan, an organisation's management must be aware of the current position of the organisation, the threats and opportunities it faces, and the weaknesses or 'gaps' in its position. Strategies should be developed which fill gaps in any area, ie remove weaknesses or develop strengths and exploit opportunities and counter threats.

5.2 Gap analysis quantifies the size of the profit gap, or the sales gap, the EPS gap, the return on capital gap, the performance-risk gap, or whatever gap is being measured between the objective/targets for the planning period and the forecast based on the extrapolation of the current situation.

5.3 The organisation must then identify different actions or strategies which would help to fill the identified gap.

5.4 A number of alternative approaches to competitive strategy exist, but Porter suggest three basic types:

- overall cost leadership
- differentation
- segmentation

The purpose of competitive strategy is to provide the organisation with a competitive advantage.

5.5 Strategies need to be annually evaluated against a list of carefully considered criteria.

5.6 Potential strategies need to be carefully evaluated to identify those which will fill the identified planning gap within the limits of the resources and strengths of the organisation. A number of financial and marketing tools are available to help managers make their strategic evaluations.

TEST YOUR KNOWLEDGE

The numbers in brackets refer to paragraphs of this chapter

1. What is the purpose of gap analysis? (1.2)
2. What is meant by competitive advantage? (2.3)
3. What are the three broad competitive strategies identified by Porter? (2.6)
4. What are the disadvantages of following a cost leadership strategy? (2.18)
5. How would you describe a focus strategy? (2.28)
6. How would you explain the difference between credence products and experience products? (2.11)
7. What sort of products are most likely to benefit from a differentation strategy? (2.21)
8. What is a critical success factor? (2.29)
9. What are the criteria against which any new strategy proposal should be evaluated? (5.1,5.2)
10. What is the strategic budget? (5.15)

Now try illustrative question 8

Chapter 8

DEVELOPING PRODUCT-MARKET AND MANUFACTURING STRATEGIES

This chapter covers the following topics.

1. Market segmentation and product-market development
2. The contribution of the product life cycle concept
3. The importance of market share and the need for market positioning
4. The product-market mix
5. Portfolio planning
6. The manufacturing development strategy

1. MARKET SEGMENTATION AND PRODUCT-MARKET DEVELOPMENT

1.1 The last chapter gave an overview of the process of identifying the options for competitive strategy and techniques for evaluating those options. In this chapter we are going to consider in more detail the problems of developing product-market strategies and the key elements of manufacturing strategy. Product-market strategy is the corner stone of marketing strategy and only when decisions on the products and markets have been made is it possible to develop detailed marketing plans.

1.2 Although you would expect the marketing team to play an important role in informing and advising senior management on product-market opportunities, it is still a key element of corporate strategy and so is likely to be decided at the most senior level.

1.3 In essence developing product-market strategy is a more detailed consideration of the differentation and focus strategies identified by Porter and discussed in the last chapter, whilst manufacturing strategy is based on his cost leadership appraoch.

Market segmentation

1.4 An organisation can only sell its products or services if there are customers who want to buy them at the price offered. It therefore follows that success in marketing depends heavily on providing goods or services that satisfy the identified needs of customers.

1.5 A single standard product might satisfy the needs of all customers in the market. On the other hand, variations in a product's design might appeal more strongly to some prospective customers than to others. As we have seen, organisations are therefore faced with the following decisions.

(a) Whether to manufacture several variations of a basic product, with each product variation designed to satisfy the needs of a particular 'segment' of customers in the market. Each variation of the product could be priced differently, according to the strength of demand in each market segment (differentation strategy).

(b) Whether to concentrate on making a product for just one or two particular market segments, leaving the rest of the market to other firms (focus strategy).

1.6 'Market segmentation is the sub-dividing of a market into distinct subsets of customers, where any subset may conceivably be selected as a target market to be reached with a distinct marketing mix.' *(Kotler)*

Customers differ in various respects - according to age, sex, income, geographical area, buying attitudes, buying habits etc. Each of these differences can be used as a basis for segmenting a market.

1.7 The strategic significance of market segmentation is that a firm can expect to stimulate demand from a particular type of customer by developing a differentiated product for a new or growing market segment. The fairly recent rapid growth of the home computer industry is an example of the potential for developing new market segments - in this case, a segment of the microcomputer industry.

1.8 You should be able to recognise different market segments for any major product. As just one example, think of milk. Milk might seem to be a standard product with a mass market, but we have the following variations.

(a) Skimmed, semi-skimmed and non-skimmed milk.
(b) Long life milk.
(c) Powdered milk.
(d) Milk in bottles and milk in cartons. Milk in small bottles for schools.
(e) Milk delivered to doorsteps and milk sold through shops.

Each variation of the product has a certain appeal to a group of customers, which is why they buy it. Total sales of milk are almost certainly higher through segmentation than if a standard product were sold in a standard-sized bottle.

1.9 Market segmentation is the basis for successful strategic marketing planning. By identifying or creating a new market segment or entering a growing market segment a company can hope to achieve the following.

(a) Increase sales and profits.
(b) Extend the life cycle of the product.
(c) Capture some of the overall market share from competitors.
(d) Survive against competition from the mass-producing, low-cost, low-price, market leaders. This is usually how small firms survive against competition from large firms.

1.10 Dominant firms in a market might have to be aware of the threat that competitors will seek to segment the market, and so eat into their market share. This means that even market leaders in a mass production industry would ignore at their peril the option to segment the market. We will return to segmentation later when we examine the development of marketing strategy in more detail.

1.11 Marketing professionals should remember that the tools and techniques of segmentation are amongst the most important they use as managers. Accurate segmentation represents the key to both business success and ensuring the most effective use of marketing resources.

1.12 It is equally essential to bear in mind that market segments continually require reviewing to identify if (and how) customers are changing, and whether there are new and better ways of profiling consumer groups.

Product-market development

1.13 Products, markets and manufacturing systems should be continually developed, to keep pace with the changing needs of customers and changing technologies.

An illustration is the virtual extinction of the British motor cycle industry in the face of competition from Japan. From a position of market dominance with a well-engineered product, the British motor cycle industry collapsed because of obsolete engine design, old fashioned styling, restricted product range, lower performance and higher prices. The UK industry failed to recognise the changes taking place in the market, (ie the changes in the type of people wishing to own motorcycles, privately and commercially) and the concomitant changes in demand specifications which were so ably exploited by the wide range of more attractive two-stroke and four-stroke machines from Japan.

1.14 A successful business must therefore continue to develop its products and markets, and manufacturing methods, if it is to avoid eventual extinction. It was suggested earlier that strategic choice involves the matching of an organisation's resources and investment plans with the activities that it intends to pursue. This calls for strategic decisions about product-market development and manufacturing (or the process of providing services in the case of service companies).

(a) *Product-market strategy*
This is simply a term used to describe the strategy or strategies for developing products and markets. (Products are the product items or services that are sold and markets are where they are sold and the customers to whom they are sold.)

(b) *Manufacturing strategy* (for a manufacturing organisation) which is concerned with how the products should be made and how production systems should develop.

1.15 The factors to be considered in product-market development are as follows.

(a) The appeal of each product to the customer and markets at which it is aimed; it may be necessary to undertake *market research* to establish what characteristics or features are needed.

(b) *Market segmentation*. This was discussed earlier.

(c) *Sphere of influence.* This refers to the type of product in which the company has particular expertise and where customers acknowledge the high standing of the company's products. Thus Hotpoint have a sphere of influence in domestic electrical equipment, but not in motor cars.

(d) *Price elasticity of demand* for products. The size of the total market depends both on price and the demand curve for the product. If demand is elastic, the market size will be more susceptible to changes in the price level.

(e) *Product positioning.* Should the product be expensive or relatively cheap, and what are its characteristics in relation to competitive and substitute goods on the market?

(f) *Product life cycle.* A company should plan to have a range of products which are at differing stages of their life cycle. There could be a combination of:

(i) tomorrow's breadwinners;
(ii) today's breadwinners;
(iii) products capable of profits if something drastic is done;
(iv) yesterday's breadwinners;
(v) 'also-rans' - products which have only ever made modest profits;
(vi) failures - these are inevitable in the essential search for new products.

(g) *Product range.* A company should be aware of its range of products, which should be sufficiently wide to win customers. A manufacturer of eating forks will not sell its product unless it also makes knives and spoons. An awareness of product range might also suggest new product ideas. For example, a cutlery manufacturer might extend its product range to include kitchen utensils.

2. THE CONTRIBUTION OF THE PRODUCT LIFE CYCLE CONCEPT

2.1 The profitability and sales of a product can be expected to change over time. The 'product life cycle' is an attempt to recognise distinct stages in a product's sales history.

2.2 Marketing managers distinguish between the following.

(a) *Product class:* this is a broad category of product, such as cars, washing machines, newspapers, also referred to as the generic product.

(b) *Product form:* within a product class there are different forms that the product can take, for example five-door hatchback cars or two-seater sports cars; twin tub or front loading automatic washing machines; national daily newspapers or weekly local papers etc.

(c) *The particular brand or make* of the product form (for example Ford Escort, Vauxhall Astra; Financial Times, Daily Mail, Sun etc).

2.3 The product life cycle applies to differing degrees in each of the three cases. A product-class may have a long maturity stage, and a particular make or brand might have an erratic life cycle. Product forms however tend to conform to the 'classic' life cycle pattern, commonly described by a curve as follows.

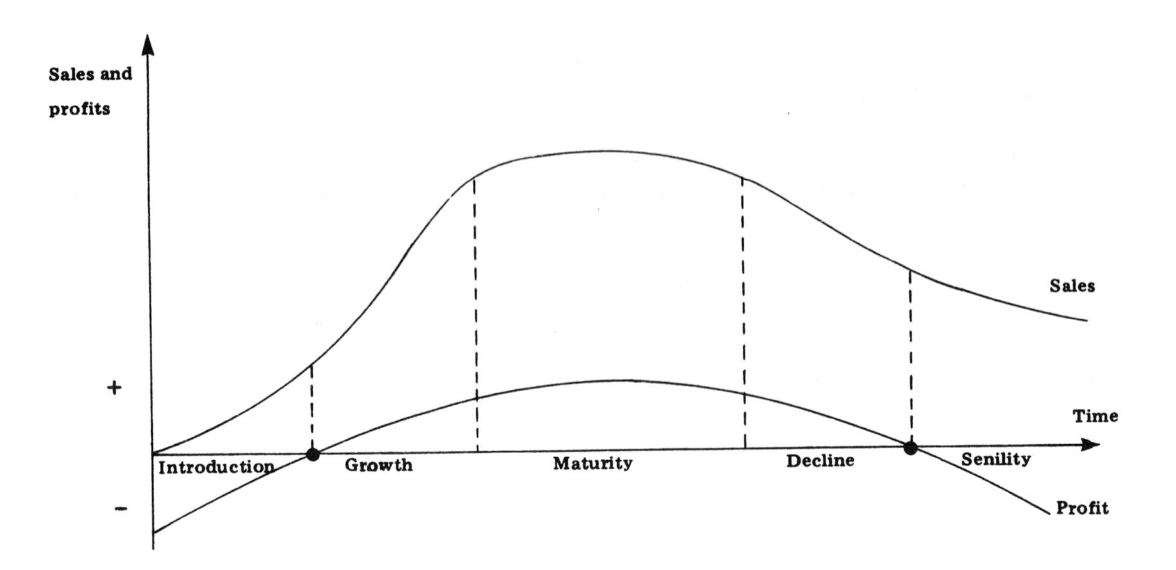

2.4 (a) *Introduction:* a new product takes time to find acceptance by would-be purchasers and there is a slow growth in sales. Only a few firms sell the product, unit costs are high because of low output and expensive sales promotion; there may be early teething troubles with production technology and prices may be high to cover costs as much as possible (for example pocket calculators, colour televisions and video cassette recorders were all very expensive when first launched). The product for the time being is a *loss-maker.*

(b) *Growth:* if the new product gains market acceptance, sales will eventually rise more sharply and the product will *start to make profits.* As sales and production rise, unit costs fall. Since demand is strong, prices tend to remain fairly stable for a time. However, the prospect of cheap mass-production and a strong market will attract competitors so that the number of producers is increasing. With the increase of competition, manufacturers must spend money on product improvement, sales promotion and distribution to obtain a dominant or strong position in the market.

(c) *Maturity:* the rate of sales growth slows down and the product reaches a period of maturity which is probably the longest period of a successful product's life. Most products on the market will be at the mature stage of their life.

(d) *Decline:* most products reach a stage of decline which may be slow or fast. Eventually, sales will begin to decline so that there is over-capacity of production in the industry. Severe competition occurs, profits fall and some producers leave the market. The remaining producers seek means of prolonging the product life by modifying it and searching for new market segments. Many producers are reluctant to leave the market, although some inevitably do because of falling profits. If a product remains on the market too long, it will become unprofitable.

2.5 Brands or individual makes of a product have a shorter life cycle than product forms, although the same 'pattern' applies to many of these too. For example there are many different makes or brands of radial tyre. Some of these have a long life and others will have a much shorter life; however, all of them (or nearly all, at least) will have a shorter life cycle than the overall product form, 'radial tyres'.

2.6 *The relevance of the product life cycle to strategic planning*
A company selling a range of products must try to look into the longer term, beyond the immediate budget period, and estimate how much each of its products is likely to contribute towards sales revenue and profitability. It is therefore necessary to make an assessment of the following.

(a) The stage of its life cycle that any product has reached.

(b) Allowing for the price changes, other marketing strategies, cost control and product modifications, for how much longer the product will be able to contribute significantly to profits and sales.

2.7 Another aspect of product life cycle analysis is *new product development*, and strategic planners must consider the following.

(a) How urgent is the need to *innovate*, and how much will have to be spent on R & D to develop new products in time?

(b) *Capital expenditure and cash flow*. New products cost money to introduce. Not only are there R & D costs, but there is also capital expenditure on plant and equipment, and probably heavy expenditure on advertising and sales promotion. A new product will use up substantial amounts of cash in its early life, and it will not be until its growth phase is well under way, or even the maturity phase reached, that a product will pay back the initial outlays of capital and marketing expenditure.

2.8 It is perhaps easy enough to accept that products have a life cycle, but it is not so easy to sort out how far through its life a product is, and what its expected future life might be.

(a) There ought to be a regular review of existing products, as a part of marketing management responsibilities.

(b) Information should be obtained about the likely future of each product and sources of such information might be as follows.
(i) An analysis of past sales and profit trends.
(ii) The history of other products.
(iii) Market research.
(iv) If possible, an analysis of competitors.

The future of each product should be estimated in terms of both sales revenue and profits.

(c) Estimates of future life and profitability should be discussed with any experts available to give advice, for example R & D staff about product life, management accountants about costs and marketing staff about prices and demand.

2.9 Once the assessments have been made, decisions must be taken about what to do with each product. The choices are as follows.

(a) To continue selling the product, with no foreseeable intention yet of stopping production.

(b) To initiate action to prolong a product's life, perhaps by advertising more, by trying to cut costs or raise prices, by improving distribution, or packaging or sales promotion methods, or by putting in more direct selling effort etc.

(c) To plan to stop producing the product and either to replace it with new ones in the same line or to diversify into new product-market areas.

Costs might be cut by improving the productivity of the workforce, or by re-designing the product slightly, perhaps as a result of a value analysis study.

2.10 *Criticisms of the product life cycle concept*
There are some legitimate criticisms of the product life cycle concept as a practical tool in strategic planning.

(a) How can marketing managers, or other managers, recognise just where a product stands in its life cycle? An extrapolation of past sales into the future together with experience of other product life cycles in the past might be an insufficient basis for forecasting a product's future life with any reliable accuracy.

(b) The traditional S-shaped curve of a product life cycle does not always occur in practice. Some products have no maturity phase, and go straight from growth to decline. Others have a second growth period after an initial decline. Some have virtually no introductory period and go straight into a rapid growth phase.

(c) Strategic decisions can change a product's life cycle, for example by re-positioning a product in the market, its life can be extended. If strategic planners 'decide' what a product's life is going to be, opportunities to extend the life cycle might be ignored.

(d) Competition varies in different industries, and the strategic implications of the product life cycle will vary according to the nature of the competition. The 'traditional' life cycle presupposes increasing competition and falling prices during the growth phase of the market and also the gradual elimination of competitors in the decline phase and strategic planning would be based on these presuppositions. But in practice, this pattern of events is not always found. The financial markets are an example of markets where there is a tendency for competitors to follow-my-leader very quickly, so that competition has built up well ahead of demand. The rapid development of various banking services in an example of this, for example with cash dispenser cards, when one bank developed the product all the other major banks followed immediately.

New products and the diffusion process

2.11 An important issue to planners is how quickly a new product will be adopted by the market, in otherwords what sort of time scale is expected along the horizontal axis of the PLC.

2.12 A number of factors influence the speed at which new ideas and product innovations will spread or be diffused through the marketplace:

- the complexity of the new product
- the relative advantages it offers
- the degree to which the innovation fits into existing patterns of behaviour/needs etc
- the ability to try the new product, samples, test drives or low value purchases entailing little risk
- the ease with which the products benefits can be communicated to the potential customer.

2.13 The market segments attitude to change, accessibility to channels of communication and the time frame involved in the *adoption process* are all critical factors in assessing the diffusion process.

2.14 The *adoption process*, sometimes referred to as the decision making process refers to the stages a customer goes through before making a purchase decision, or a decision not to purchase or repurchase. The five stages identifiable in most models of this process are:

awareness → interest → evaluation → trial → adoption

There can be a considerable time lag between awareness and adoption.

2.15 In *Consumer behaviour* Schiffmann and Kanuk offer a modified analysis of Everett Rogers' earlier *Sequence and proportion of adopter categories.*

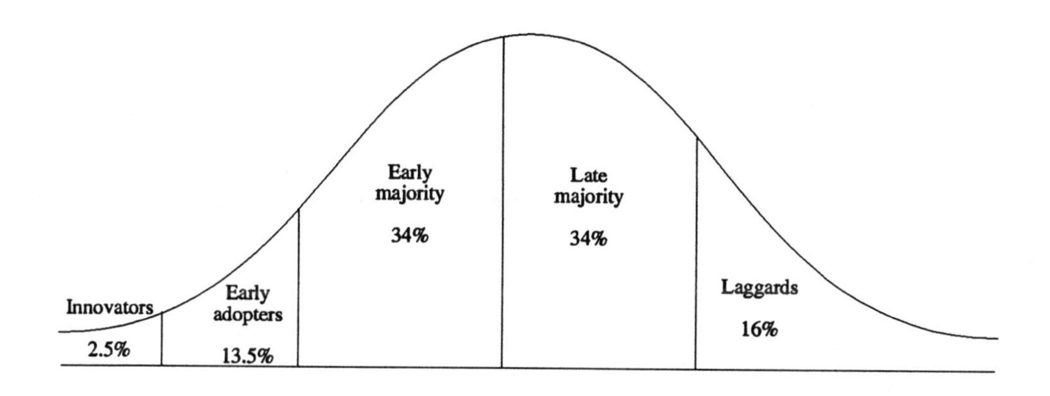

Percentages of adopters by category sequence

2.16 The characteristics of consumers in these adopter categories varies and so the marketing planner wishing to get the best from a new product, encourage its diffusion and avoid wasting budget, will focus market attention on these different segments, as the product passes through the life cycle.

Innovators These are eager to try new ideas and products and often in close contact with change agents like sales staff and other opinion leaders. Often perceived to be risk takers, prepared to try and willing to pay often premium prices for 'being the first'.

Early adopters	They too are willing to change and are often opinion leaders themselves. They are likely to have greater exposure to the mass media than later adopters and certainly more willing to change. They are likely to seek out information actively about new products in specialist journals etc.
Early majority	A more conservative segment who tend to purchase a new product just ahead of the average time, but who will have given it some thought before the purchase.
Late majority	These are slower than the average and sceptical about new products. They are very cautious purchasers likely to need some persuading.
Laggards	These are the smaller group of traditionalists actually unwilling to change. They may actually be forced to change only when their previous choice is obsolete and no longer available.

2.17 *Diffusion and marketing strategy*

Marketers usually want to ensure a rapid diffusion or rate of adoption for a new product. This allows them to gain a large share of the market prior to competitors responding. A *penetration* policy associated with low introductory pricing and promotions designed to facilitate trial are associated with such a strategy. However in some markets, particularly where R & D cost has been high, where the product involves 'new' technology or where it is protected from competition perhaps by patent, a *skimming* policy may be adopted.

Here price is high initially usually representing very high unit profits and sales can be increased in steps with price reductions, in line with available capacity or competitors responses.

2.18 *The strategic implications of the product life cycle*
Having made these reservations about product life cycle planning, the strategic implications of the product life cycle might be as follows.

	Phase			
	Introduction	*Growth*	*Maturity*	*Decline*
1. *Products*	Initially, poor quality. Product design and development are a key to success.	Competitors' products have marked quality differences and technical differences.	Products become more standardised and differences between competing products less distinct.	Products even less differentiated. Quality becomes more variable.

		Phase			
		Introduction	*Growth*	*Maturity*	*Decline*
		No standard product and frequent design changes (eg. microcomputers in the early 1980's)	Quality improves. Product reliability may be important.		
2.	*Customers*	Initial customers willing to pay high prices. Customers need to be convinced about buying.	Customers increase in number.	Mass market. Market saturation. Repeat-buying of products becomes significant. Brand image also important.	Customers are 'sophisticated' buyers of a product they understand well.
3.	*Marketing*	High advertising and sales promotion costs. Emphasis on awareness High prices possible	High advertising costs still, but as a % of sales, costs are falling. Emphasis on repeat purchase Prices falling	Markets become segmented. Segmentation and extending the maturity phase of the life cycle can be key strategies.	Less money spent on advertising and sales promotion.
4.	*Competition*	Few or no competitors.	More competitors enter the market. Barriers to entry can be important.	Competition at its keenest: on prices, branding, servicing customers, packaging etc.	Competitors gradually exit from the market. Exit barriers can be important.
5.	*Profit margins*	High prices but losses due to high fixed costs.	High prices. High contribution margins, and increasing profit margins. High P/E ratios for quoted companies in the growth market.	Falling prices but good profit margins due to high sales volume. Higher prices in in some market segments.	Still low prices but falling profits as sales volume falls, since total contribution falls towards the level of fixed costs. Some increase in prices may occur in the late decline stage.

	Phase			
	Introduction	*Growth*	*Maturity*	*Decline*
6. *Manufacturing and distribution*	Over-capacity. High production costs. Few distribution channels. High labour skill content in manufacture.	Under-capacity. Move towards mass production and less reliance on skilled labour. Distribution channels flourish and getting adequate distribution channels is a key to marketing success.	Optimimum capacity. Low labour skills. Distribution channels fully developed, but less successful channels might be cut.	Over-capacity because mass production techniques still used. Distribution channels dwindling

2.19 The product life cycle concept probably has more value as a *control tool* than as a method of *forecasting* a product's life. Control can be applied to speeding up the growth phase, extending the maturity phase and recognising when to cease making a product altogether. 'The value of the product life cycle depends on its use; ie it has greater value as one goes down the scale from a predictive or forecasting tool, through a planning tool to a control tool.' (Robin Wensley)

3. THE IMPORTANCE OF MARKET SHARE AND THE NEED FOR MARKET POSITIONING

3.1 *Market share* is 'one entity's sales of a product or service in a specified market expressed as a percentage of total sales by all entities offering that product or service'. (CIMA) Thus, a company may have a 30% share of a total market, meaning that 30% of all sales in the market are made by that company.

3.2 McNamee has defined *relative market share* as the share of the market relative to that of the manufacturer's largest competitor.

An evaluation of market shares helps to identify who the true competitor really is, and avoids trying to outdo the wrong competitor, like Ford trying to outdo GM in Europe, when the real competitor was Fiat! Secondly, the approach serves as a basis for marketing strategy, with a firm seeking as a target to build up an x% share of a particular market.

3.3 *Profit Impact of Marketing Strategies (PIMS)*
PIMS analysis attempts to establish the profitability (ie. return on capital) of various marketing strategies, and identifies a link between the size of return on capital and market share.

3.4 A 1973 research study in the USA found that there was a positive correlation between *market share* and return on capital, so that companies in a strong competitive position in the markets for their base products would be earning high returns. Three possible reasons were put forward for this correlation.

(a) *Economies of scale* enable a market leader to produce at lower unit costs than competitors, and so make bigger profits.

(b) *Bargaining power*. A strong position in the market gives a firm greater strength in its dealings with both buyers and suppliers.

(c) *Quality of management*. Market leaders often seem to be run by managers of a high calibre.

3.5 PIMS researchers would argue that since profitability is a key objective, and since profitability depends on market share, companies should formulate market share objectives. There are four broad groups of market share strategies.

(a) *Building:* an aggressive strategy to build up market share.
(b) *Holding:* a defensive strategy to hold on to market share.
(c) *Harvesting:* allowing market share to fall to earn better short-run profits.
(d) *Divesting:* pulling out of the market.

3.6 Market share strategies for *declining industries* would include harvesting or divestment options, in addition to the following.

(a) *Leadership strategy:* aim to be a market leader in a declining market, and so achieve above-average returns for the industry.

(b) *A niche strategy:* identify a market segment in the declining industry where demand will remain stable or decline only very slowly, and where the scope for high returns still exists. The firm will pull out of the other segments of the market and concentrate on its profitable 'niche'.

3.7 It would be wrong to suggest that a low market share will inevitably mean poor returns. If this were so, small firms would always make low returns, and this is simply not true. However, certain conditions must exist for a low market share to be compatible with high returns.

3.8 A company can prosper with a low market share in the following ways.

(a) Market segmentation, and creating new market segments which are a small proportion of the total market, but profitable.

(b) Emphasising product quality, and charging higher prices. (Efficient use would have to be made of R & D in manufacturing industries).

(c) Wanting to stay small, and consciously avoiding growth.

(d) Strong management.

3.9 Alternatively, if there is a large, stable market, where product innovations and developments are uncommon, and where repeat-buying by customers is frequent, a company can earn good profits with only a low market share. Research by Woo and Cooper (1982) has suggested that businesses can earn good profits with a low market share in a low-growth market in the following circumstances.

(a) Their products do not change often.
(b) Most products are standardised.
(c) Companies produce supplies or components for industrial customers, and have built up a close working relationship with these customers.
(d) Repeat-buying is frequent.
(e) The *value added* to sales ratio of the products is high (so that a bigger share of the sales revenue can be kept by the shareholders).

3.10 There are practical difficulties with PIMS research, which might raise questions about its usefulness. These are as follows.

(a) Identifying each market segment properly. An up-market producer is in a different market segment to a down-market cheap-goods producer, and it would be wrong to classify them as competitors in the same market.

(b) Measuring the actual size of the market, and so the company's own market share in proportional terms.

(c) Establishing what returns are available from a particular market share.

It has also been argued that PIMS analysis is more relevant to industrial goods markets than to consumer goods markets, where the correlation between high market share and high returns is not as strong.

3.11 *Strategic implications of market share*
Two important implications of market share should be considered in product-market development planning.

(a) *How easy will it be to build up a market share?* This will depend on the rate of sales growth in the market. Obviously, it is easier to penetrate a growing market than a static one. This has been seen in the comparative success of Virgin Atlantic Airlines in a market where only recently Laker and Air Florida had failed.

(b) *What share of the market will be needed to earn a reasonable profit and return on capital?* Depending on costs, sales prices and total sales volume in the market, the size of market share needed to make a profit will vary.

3.12 *Developing a strategy for market share*
The four strategic options for market share which were referred to earlier warrant a more detailed analysis.

(a) *Building a market share.* This is usually easiest when the product is in the early stages of its life, and the market is growing. There are a variety of tactics that can be used, even in a competitive market: simple price cutting, improved quality or technical content, better delivery, service, distribution and advertising, narrowing the range of products offered or concentrating on small segments of the market. However, entry into a market with a low-price strategy is fraught with risks mainly because of the high cost of entry. As long ago as 1972, W E Fruhan noted that in the United States, major efforts by large competitors to break into the computer industry, retail grocery business and domestic airlines proved costly, inappropriate and unsuccessful. Fruhan advocated that if a large market share is the strategic objective, three questions need to be considered.

(i) Is the industry one that requires extremely heavy financial resources? For example, the breakeven position in the UK paint industry is thought to be about 15% of a market segment, and not all manufacturers are achieving this.

(ii) Is an expansionist strategy likely to be the victim of any form of regulation? A takeover bid for a company that if successful would give the bidding company a significant market share might create a monopoly. In the UK, such bids might be referred to the Monopolies and Mergers Commission, and prohibited if they are against the public interest.

(iii) Are new regulatory hurdles being planned? There is mounting pressure for greater control on the distribution of tobacco and alcohol products. Plans to increase market share in these industries should give recognition to these threats. In the UK, for example, brewery companies have tried to promote low-alcohol and alcohol-free beers and lagers.

(b) *Holding a market share*. This strategy is appropriate in a situation where the products are mature, and in a mature market, and so it is considered desirable to maintain the status quo.

Holding market share is not easy. Competition will come from innovators, and competitive promotions. Where a firm is dominant in its market, it needs to avoid complacency, and its strategy should be to avoid being 'caught out' in a sector it had ignored. Xerox lost out, for example, by ignoring the lower end of the photocopier market, as Japanese competitors entered this part of the market and took most of Xerox's market share and, more importantly, share of income. In contrast, Black and Decker protected its market in power tools by filling all the related product niches to prevent competitors from establishing a strategic 'base camp' in the market place.

(c) *Harvesting*. Harvesting means aiming for a lower market share which gives the company its best short-run returns, with a longer-term view of eventually pulling out of the market. This strategy is appropriate in the following situations.

(i) Where the product has a poor market share in a declining market.
(ii) Where the product has a poor share of a growing market. A classic example of this is the Philips VCR which has largely failed to make inroads into the Japanese domination of the European VCR market.

The term 'harvesting' indicates that such a strategy can be used to gather in funds which can then be diverted into other investments.

(d) *Withdrawal*. Here, there is no cash advantage to the company, other than perhaps stopping a running sore. In such circumstances, the market share is so low that the product is no longer viable, as demonstrated by the current state of the UK commercial vehicle industry, which is very competitive, but where most competitors are making heavy losses. Already, there have been some bankruptcies (Foden) and mergers, but the problems of the industry are still far from over.

3.13 *Example: market share and Kodak*
At the beginning of the 1980s, Kodak dominated the UK market for camera film, with about 75% of the market. In the early 1980s, there was a resurgence of demand for 35mm film, which had been unpopular with amateur camera users until then, because it was difficult to load into cameras.

The unforeseen surge in market demand created an opportunity for Kodak's competitors, such as 3M and Fuji, to attack Kodak's dominance of the market. Another important development in the market was own-label films, sold by high-street film developers and retailers (such as Boots).

Kodak's market share fell, perhaps to about 40%. The company's response was as follows.

(a) To challenge the own-label brands with a new low-priced Value Range film.
(b) To offer a higher-priced quality Gold film range, hoping to appeal to consumers on the basis of better-coloured photographs, (with an expensive advertising campaign when the product range was launched in 1987, to get the message across).
(c) To introduce specialist films (the Ektar range) offering a more varied choice of film for particular lighting conditions or definition requirements.

The need for market positioning

3.14 Market positioning is concerned with establishing a general idea about where the company stands in the market, in terms of meeting customer needs in that market and *in relation to what competitors are offering*. Positioning is therefore concerned with matters such as product quality and reliability, price, distribution outlets, the type of customers (market segments) which the organisation's products are aimed at, as well as product *image* and brand image.

3.15 Market positioning is therefore a different concept from *market share* although an organisation's share of the market might well be related to its attitude to the market positioning. For example a company which cannot be market leader because the number one position is held securely by a competitor, might decide to develop high-quality 'up-market' products for the high-income customers in the market and to have a reputation for reliability and efficiency. For example The Times newspaper does not aim to be the top selling national daily in the UK.

3.16 *Example of segmentation and positioning strategy: Texas Instruments*
Texas Instruments, the US electronics manufacturer, aimed until 1985 to be the market leader in the world's semiconductor industry, competing with Japanese companies for the biggest share in the mass market for 'commodity' microchips, such as dynamic random access memory chips (ie the data storage chips used in every type of computer).

Other US chip manufacturers had long since given up competing in the mass market, and had concentrated on custom-made and original-design chips for specific customers or specific uses, which earn a higher profit margin on sales.

3.17 In 1985, prices of dynamic random access memory chips (DRAMs) fell sharply, and Texas Instruments went from record profits to record losses. The company re-assessed its marketing strategy, and made the following policy decisions.

(a) It should still remain in the DRAM business, because the technological know-how obtained in this industry would spill over into other parts of TI's business, and help to keep the company in the forefront of technological developments. However, it was no longer to be an objective to be the world's market leader in the DRAM business. Sales growth was no longer a number one priority.

(b) Some cost cutting in its DRAM business was necessary. In 1985, TI's workforce was cut by 10%, and two semiconductor factories were closed down. A strategy for re-organisation and improving productivity was therefore pursued.

(c) The company recognised the need to adopt a more marketing-oriented approach, since customers were now expecting better service from microchip manufacturers. The philosophy that superior technology will sell itself was abandoned, and instead the company began to recognise that customers didn't necessarily want the 'best' microchips; they wanted the chips that would solve their particular processing problems. The president of TI was quoted as follows.

> 'There is a new emphasis across the corporation on strengthening our customer relationships. This will be a key to our long-term success. We must and will be market-oriented. Profitability will only come as a result of identifying and satisfying the real needs of our customers.'

(d) The company began to focus more attention on four specific segments of the market.

(i) The market for microchips tailored to the needs of specific customers, ie custom-made chips.
(ii) The microprocessor market for 'application processors', ie microprocessors for special uses such as graphics and local area networks.
(iii) Developing highly-integrated standard logic chips.
(iv) The market for microchips for military uses.

Cost-cutting measures were introduced into other areas of TI's business - oil exploration and home computers.

Long-term strategy involves the development of two programmes of R & D, in artificial intelligence and factory automation, with large research and development budgets being allocated. The president of TI has again been quoted as follows.

> 'Artificial intelligence and industrial automation both have the potential of becoming important businesses to TI. But a significant, additional advantage will come from our ability to focus these skills, strengthen them and infuse them back into our core businesses.'

4. THE PRODUCT-MARKET MIX

4.1 Product-market mix means the range of products or services which an organisation provides to a range of markets or market segments. It is a short hand term for the products a firm sells (or a public sector organisation provides) and who it sells them to.

4.2 The structure of competitive advantage is determined by the firm's overall product-market mix, ie a combination of current and new products in current and new markets, described as follows.

(a) *Market penetration* in which the firm seeks to maintain or to increase its share of current markets with current products, for example through competitive pricing, advertising, sales promotion, spending more on distribution or direct selling etc.

(b) *Market development* in which the firm seeks new markets for its current products, such as exporting if the firm has previously served only the domestic market.

(c) *Product development* in which the firm seeks to create new products to replace existing ones, for current markets and through existing distribution channels.

(d) *Diversification* in which the firm seeks to develop new products in new markets.

4.3 These four options are shown in the following table, known as an Ansoff matrix.

	Present products or services	*New products or services*
Present markets	(1) Market penetration	(3) Product/service development
New markets	(2) Market development	(4) Diversification

Notes

(a) The term 'market' can also refer to market segments.

(b) It is convenient to assume that a firm will always seek profit growth and so would look for product-market growth. However, firms might choose to drop some products from its product line and pull out of certain markets - ie divest as a strategy for increasing profits.

4.4 A company, as we shall see, will probably need to adopt each of these four product-market growth strategies within its corporate plan. Taken together, they deal with a basic strategic problem for the firm, which is *'What business are we in, and what business do we want to be in?'*

4.5 The product-market matrix described above can be elaborated as follows:

<table>
<tr><td colspan="2" rowspan="2">Product
Market</td><td rowspan="2">Present</td><td colspan="2">New</td></tr>
<tr><td>Related</td><td>Unrelated</td></tr>
<tr><td colspan="2">Present</td><td>X</td><td></td><td></td></tr>
<tr><td rowspan="2">New</td><td>Related</td><td></td><td></td><td></td></tr>
<tr><td>Unrelated</td><td></td><td></td><td></td></tr>
</table>

4.6 This shows that strategies of product development and market penetration can be leaps into the unknown, with moves into product-market areas that are entirely new to the firm; on the other hand, the new products or new markets might be fairly closely related to the existing products and markets of the firm.

4.7 For example it is not such a big leap from selling banking services to customers to selling life assurance schemes to the same customers (both are financial products) nor from selling life assurance to selling pensions and other forms of insurance - and this is what the clearing banks have done in the UK.

4.8 *Current products and current markets*
Linneman suggests that good and successful product-market planning should begin with improving efficiency levels within the present area of operations. Although improvements in this area will not provide a complete answer to the organisation's need for profits, it is a valuable starting point for strategic planning.

4.9 An investigation into improving efficiencies in the production and sales of current products to existing markets might usefully consider four areas.

(a) *Manufacturing*

(i) Improving productivity, reducing manpower, improving equipment, better capacity utilisation, reductions in idle time.
(ii) Eliminating unnecessary expenditures.
(iii) Elimination of short production runs with high setting up and dismantling costs.
(iv) Energy conservation; alternative fuels (for example coal instead of oil).
(v) More preventive maintenance to reduce the incidence of breakdowns.
(vi) Better control of inventory levels.
(vii) On a more extreme scale, relocation of factories so as to be nearer distribution centres, raw material supplies or customers; shutting down uneconomic plants.

(b) *Finance*

(i) Control of debtors and cash levels, discounts and rebates.
(ii) Loan funding, gearing and debt levels.
(iii) Post-audit of capital investment programmes, to monitor the success or reasons for failure of current capital projects.
(iv) Cost control through budgetary control and variance analysis etc.

(c) *Personnel*

For many service industries or labour-intensive manufacturing industries, manpower costs are a substantial proportion of total costs and substantial reductions in cost can be achieved by improvements in productivity and the utilisation of labour effort.

(i) Where the costs of 'in-house' staff are high, it might be cheaper to sub-contract work. Already, some UK local authorities have sub-contracted refuse disposal to private companies, and the National Health Service now sub-contracts laundry work.

(ii) Savings might be obtained by either of the following steps.

(1) Cutting out a shift and replacing it with overtime so as to eliminate excessive idle time on the second shift.
(2) Cutting out overtime and introducing a second shift. It may seem odd that two shifts might be cheaper than one shift with overtime. However, it can be so. Thermos, for example, has successfully operated a twilight shift staffed by local women who are tied to their homes during the day, but who are available in the evenings for a few hours' work. Twilight workers, being fresher, are likely to be more productive and cost-effective (in unskilled work, at least) than tired day-workers on overtime.

(iii) Relocation of production in rural areas might cut costs, on the assumption that it will be easier to obtain talented staff and the pressures of life are less. However, whereas relocation to rural areas seems to have had the desired effect in the United States, experience in the UK has been more varied.

(iv) Other areas for improving labour efficiency and so costs, are training, job enrichment, (for example more delegation of authority or motivation through participation in decision making) better recruitment and selection methods etc.

(d) *Marketing*

(i) An effort might be made to increase the usage of the organisation's products by current customers. For example, British Telecom have tried to increase the number of calls made by telephone users.
(ii) It might be possible to attract new customers away from the products of competitors.
(iii) Pricing policy should be continually reviewed; indeed, the marketing mix as a whole should be planned so as to obtain greater benefits (ie greater sales) in current product-market areas.

4.10 *Present products - new markets (market development)*
Having considered how sales of current products in current markets can be improved (so as to increase profitability) the next stage in product-market planning should be to consider market development and product development.

4.11 A plan to develop new markets for existing products presupposes that the strength of the company is in its product/service technology or that the company is currently restricted in the markets it sells to.

4.12 Packaging for the consumer food market provides an interesting example of market development.

(a) The food industry developed a market segment based on larger packages for the home freezer market, recognising that home freezers had created a new type of customer, buying in large quantities and at less frequent intervals from 'car-park supermarkets'. At the same time, food companies which specialised in selling goods in bulk to hospitals and the catering industry already had large packaging, which could be adapted for selling to consumer markets through hyper-markets.

(b) At the other end of the package-size scale, some food firms have identified a growing market segment consisting of people living alone, many of them young, who, rather than risk the deterioration of food left in opened packets, prefer to pay slightly more for single portion convenience foods.

4.13 Other ways of developing markets include the following.

(a) Expansion into new geographical areas (for example a radio station building a new transmitter to reach a new audience).

(b) Expansion into export markets.

(c) The creation of new distribution channels (for example a manufacturing firm might open up its own shops).

(d) Differential pricing policies to attract different types of customer and create new market segments. Examples are as follows.

(i) Hotels offer various cut-price rates for off-season weekends and bargain breaks etc.

(ii) Travel companies have developed a market for cheap long-stay winter breaks in warmer countries for retired couples.

(iii) Concorde has been used by charter companies for champagne and caviar parties over the Bay of Biscay at Mach 2, and day trips to Cairo, Rekjavik and ballet weekends in Moscow.

4.14 *New products - present markets (product development)*
Product development is a third element in product-market planning. Two examples cited by Linneman will help to illustrate the approach.

(a) Hallmark Cards Inc have a well-recognised and respected trade name for the sale of greetings cards, with a large distribution network in the USA and to a lesser extent, in the UK. Their cards are commonly found in card shops, stationery shops and department stores. Their product line of cards was expanded, and the new products sold through existing outlets.

(i) In the UK, the company diversified into new card items, general stationery, soft toys and fancy goods.
(ii) In the USA, it diversified even further, into crystal, pewter and jewellery products.

(b) The teenagers' magazine Musicale (in the USA) started to market clothing, with some success, to its teenage readers.

4.15 Product development is not automatically successful, in spite of high sales synergy. Again, in the USA, Sears knew that they had up-market customers for their domestic electrical appliances, but found that they could not successfully up-grade the quality of the clothes they could sell.

Translating the Sears experience into a UK analogy, you might like to speculate on how successful Marks and Spencer would be if they up-graded their good quality men's clothing still further to compete with, say, Austin Reed or Simpsons of Piccadilly.

4.16 *New products - new markets (diversification).* Most firms would prefer to develop their product-market mix by keeping within their current general line of products or within their current markets. This policy is far less drastic and risky in comparison with diversification into new products for new markets.

4.17 When a firm decides to make unfamiliar products for unfamiliar markets simultaneously, it should have a clear idea about what it expects to gain from diversification. The benefits might be as follows.

(a) Attaining objectives that cannot be met by developing its product-market scope through expansion of existing product lines and markets. This may be due to product-line obsolescence, a decline in demand or market saturation in existing markets. If there are no signs of growth in the industry, the only way to achieve growth would be to fight for a bigger market share in what might become an increasingly price-competitive industry. New products and new markets should be selected which offer prospects for growth which the existing product-market mix does not.

(b) Investing surplus funds not required for other expansion needs. Diversification into new operations might be more profitable than keeping the surplus funds as liquid resources, deposited with a bank, say, but with comparatively low rates of return.

(c) Achieving greater profitability than with expansion opportunities, even though current objectives are being realised. This may occur because:

(i) outstanding new products have been developed by the firm's research and development department;
(ii) the profit opportunities from diversification are high.

(d) To provide a more comprehensive service to customers.

4.18 One way of analysing product-market strategy options for growth would be to identify four types of expansion and diversification.

(a) Horizontal integration.
(b) Vertical integration.
} related diversification

(c) Concentric diversification.
(d) Conglomerate diversification.
} unrelated diversification

4.19 The *stability* of a firm is not greatly improved by horizontal diversification because of the *lack of flexibility in the product-market mix.* The firm still relies on the same markets or the same products as before. For example, in recent years, the clearing banks have extended the range of services they sell through their branch network to their customers, but this horizontal integration has not really added to the stability of the clearing banks because their customer base has been unchanged.

4.20 *Vertical integration,* or vertical diversification, occurs when a company becomes either one of the following.

(a) Its own supplier of raw materials or components (ie *backward vertical integration)*. For example, backward integration would occur where a milk producer acquires its own dairy farms rather than buying raw milk from independent farmers.

(b) Its own distributor or sales agent (ie *forward vertical integration)*. This would occur:

(i) where a manufacturer of synthetic yarn begins to produce shirts from the yarn instead of selling it to other shirt manufacturers;

(ii) where a manufacturer sells direct to customers by acquiring a retail network, or by establishing a direct selling operation through mail order or door-to-door selling.

4.21 The purpose of vertical integration may be as follows.

(a) To provide a secure supply of components or raw materials with more control over quality, quantity and price.

(b) To strengthen relationships and contacts of the manufacturer with the 'final consumer' of the product.

(c) To win a share of the higher profits which might be obtainable in the raw materials market or end-user market.

4.22 Just in Time manufacturing methods place great reliance on one or two key suppliers for each component or raw material, and manufacturers that use JIT may wish to secure the quality and timeliness of supplies by buying up the supplier.

4.23 The disadvantages of vertical integration are as follows.

(a) Synergy is probably low or non-existent.

(b) A company places 'more eggs in the same end-market basket' (Ansoff) therefore such a policy is fairly inflexible, more sensitive to instabilities and increases the firm's dependence on a particular aspect of economic demand.

4.24 Both horizontal and vertical integration are forms of *related diversification*, which is diversification into related products or markets. This is shown by the following diagram.

Related diversification

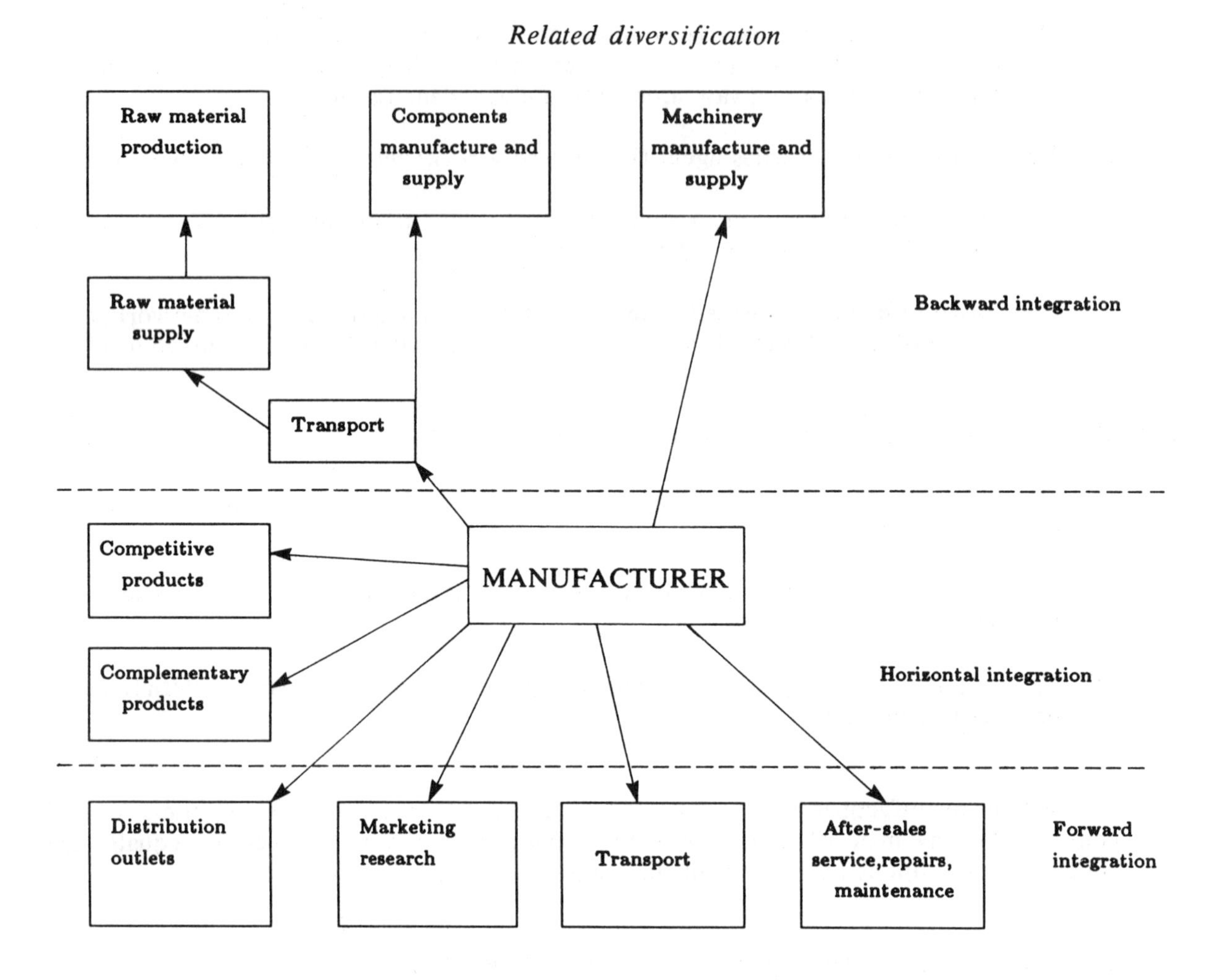

Unrelated diversification

4.25 *Concentric diversification* occurs when a company seeks to add new products that have technological and/or marketing synergies with the existing product line. These products will normally appeal to new classes of customer.

4.26 For example Ansoff refers to a motor manufacturer who decides to make farm machinery because there is a technological similarity between the two, although the class of customer will be different. Some synergy might be expected in production (technical know-how and perhaps the use of some existing plant) and possibly marketing (know-how amongst salesmen, common outlets and existing after-sales service team).

4.27 *Conglomerate diversification* consists of making entirely new products for new classes of customers. These new products have no relationship to the company's current technology, products or markets.

4.28 There may be some management synergy in conglomerate diversification where the company's managers are already experienced in running a conglomerate group of companies. An example of conglomerate diversification would be the move by a milk-producer into animal feeds.

Factors to consider when developing a diversification strategy

4.29 You might be ready enough in your own mind to accept that the advantages of diversification are to extend a company's range of profitable products and markets in a way that reduces the 'risk' in the overall span of operations. However, a decision to diversify is easy to take as a matter of general principle, but it is less easy to decide how much to diversify and what to diversify into.

4.30 A general list of matters to consider when deciding how to develop a diversification strategy is as follows.

(a) What is the purpose of diversification? It might be to build up a new range of products to replace an existing ageing product line. It might be to find more profitable investment opportunities. It might be to create growth for the company.

(b) What amount of resources can be devoted to diversification? The investment of resources will put a constraint on how far diversification can take place, and to what extent diversification can be created by developing internal resources (as distinct from pursuing a policy of mergers or takeovers).

(c) What is the required rate of return on the new investments?

(d) Are there any alternative strategies to diversification which would enable the company to achieve its objectives just as well if not better?

(e) What products or markets might provide some useful start-up synergy or operating synergy etc. if the company were to diversify into them?

(f) If there are no positive ideas yet about how a policy of diversification should be pursued (for example what products should the company diversify into?) who should be given the task of finding out what opportunities there are? Has the R & D department been working on new products?

(g) For any product under consideration as a potential area for diversification:

(i) what is the size of the product's market?
(ii) what is the market potential, and what growth can be expected in the market?
(iii) is it a competitive market? If not, can more competition be expected in due course?
(iv) how profitable is it?
(v) what resources (facilities, manpower, equipment etc.) would be needed to start up in this industry? Are there any companies within the industry 'ripe' for takeover?
(vi) what market share might the company expect to gain?
(vii) what market position might the company seek to establish (for example the low-quality cheap end of the market or the top quality end etc.)?
(viii) what government 'interference' or legislation might be expected if the company becomes involved in this market?
(ix) what is the likelihood of success, and the risk of failure in this venture?

Test marketing

4.31 Although more likely to be part of the evaluation strategy, process for a marketing for a new product, if a producer wishes to test a strategy or whether the marketing mix is 'correct', the product could be test-marketed in one or two trial areas first. Adjustments would then be made in the light of experience with the test market. The information generated can be used to modify forecasts and plans.

4.32 The purpose of test marketing is to obtain information about how consumers react to a new product - ie will they buy it, and if so, will they buy it again? Will they adopt the product as a regular feature of their buying habits, and if so, how frequently will they buy it? With this information an estimate of the total market demand for the product can be made.

4.33 A test market involves testing a new consumer product in selected areas which are thought to be 'representative' of the total market. This avoids a blind commitment to the costs of a full-scale launch while permitting the collection of market data. In the selected areas, the firm will attempt to distribute the product through the same types of sales outlets it plans to use in the full market launch, and also to use the advertising and promotion plans it intends to use in the full market. A test marketing exercise can be expensive, but it enables the company to 'test the water' before launching the product nationally. Not only does it help to make sales forecasts, it can also be used to identify flaws in the marketing mix which can then be dealt with before the product is launched nationally.

4.34 For a test market to be useful it must have the following characteristics.

(a) The test market area should be large enough to be representative of how the 'full' market might behave, but not so large as to be almost as expensive as a full national market launch.

(b) The test period should be sufficiently long to give customers time to become aware of the product, and to monitor not only initial sales demand but also 'repeat buying' habits.

(c) The test market must be as closely representative of the national market as possible.

(d) The test market should have promotional facilities available. For example, one of the television regions could be used as a test area.

4.35 The possible benefits of test marketing are as follows.

(a) The company can pre-test a planned marketing mix. For example they may be able to identify product faults not identified at the development stage, or they may discover potential distribution problems.

(b) Expensive product failure may be avoided.

(c) Results from the test market may enable the company to prepare more accurate sales forecasts.

4.36 Test marketing does have some disadvantages.

(a) Unless the test market area is typical of the market as a whole, the information obtained about potential demand will be biased and misleading.

(b) A lengthy test market will show competitors what the firm is planning to do, and give them time to prepare their own response to the new product.

(c) Only a small sample will be used, which raises statistical problems.

(d) Consumers may be aware of the test and distort their answers accordingly.

(e) Estimates for the future cannot reliably be based on results recorded today.

(f) Competitors may decide to sabotage the test, for example by flooding the area with increased advertising activity.

(g) It is difficult to translate national media plans into local equivalents.

(h) Some goods, for example consumer goods such as household furniture, have lengthy repurchase cycles which would make test marketing far too lengthy to be of any practical forecasting value.

4.37 Other forms of experimentation, which are different from test marketing, include the following.

(a) *Simulated store technique* (or laboratory test markets). In these tests, a group of shoppers are invited to watch a selection of advertisements for a number of products, including an advertisement for the new product. They are then given some money and invited to spend it in a supermarket or shopping area. Their purchases are recorded and they are asked to explain their purchase decisions (and non-purchase decisions). Some weeks later, they are contacted again and asked about their product attitudes, repurchase intentions, etc. These tests help to assess advertising effectiveness as well as to forecast sales volumes; in addition the results are made available relatively quickly.

(b) *Controlled test marketing* . In these tests, a research firm pays a panel of stores to carry the new product for a given length of time. The research firm can decide on shelf locations, point-of-sale displays and pricing, etc; the sales results are then monitored. This test (also known as 'minimarket testing') helps to provide an assessment of 'in-store' factors in achieving sales as well as to forecast sales volumes for the new product.

5. PORTFOLIO PLANNING

5.1 Portfolio planning is a term used to describe methods of analysing a product-market portfolio with the following aims.

(a) To identify the current strengths or weaknesses of an organisation's products in its markets, and the state of growth or decline in each of those markets.
(b) To identify what strategy is needed to maintain a strong position or improve a weak one.

Several matrices have been developed over the years to analyse market share, market growth and market position. Some of these will be described in the following paragraphs.

Market share, market growth and cash generation: the Boston classification

5.2 The Boston Consulting Group (BCG) have developed a matrix, based on empirical research, which classifies a company's products in terms of potential cash generation and cash expenditure requirements.

		Market share	
		High	Low
Market growth	High	Stars	Question marks ??
	Low	Cash cows	Dogs

5.3 This *growth/share matrix* for the classification of products into stars, cash cows, question marks and dogs is known as the *Boston classification* for product-market strategy.

(a) *Stars* are products with a high share of a high growth market. In the short term, these require capital expenditure, in excess of the cash they generate, in order to maintain their market position. This is the important strategic feature of stars - they promise high returns in the future, but at the moment, they need finance to fund their market development and growth.

(b) In due course, however, stars will become cash cows, with a high share of a low-growth market. *Cash cows* need very little capital expenditure and generate high levels of cash income. The important strategic feature of cash cows is that they are *already* generating high cash returns, which can be used to finance the stars. A firm with stars in its product portfolio also needs cash cows. In high technology industries, this is a special problem for small firms developing tomorrow's best-seller. Without a cash cow to fund the star's development, the small firm must link up with a big firm (for example be taken over) or sell its patents or go into liquidation.

(c) *Question marks* are products in a high-growth market, but where they have a low market share. A decision needs to be taken about whether the products justify considerable capital expenditure in the hope of increasing their market share, or whether they should be allowed to 'die' quietly as they are squeezed out of the expanding market by rival products. Because considerable expenditure would be needed to turn a question mark into a star by building up market share, question marks will usually be poor cash generators and show a negative cash flow.

(d) *Dogs* are products with a low share of a low growth market. They may be ex-cash cows that have now fallen on hard times. Dogs should be allowed to die, or should be killed off. Although they will show only a modest net cash outflow, or even a modest net cash inflow, they are 'cash traps' which tie up funds and provide a poor return on investment, and not enough to achieve the organisation's target rate of return.

There are also *infants* (ie products in an early stage of development) and *warhorses* (ie products that have been cash cows in the past, and are still making good sales and earning good profits even now).

5.4 The car industry provides interesting examples to fit the BCG matrix. Ford, with the Fiesta, Escort and to a lesser extent, the Sierra have had a range of stars, which cost a substantial amount to develop and launch, but which soon became cash cows. Vauxhall invested heavily in the Cavalier, with great success, and here we see an example of a question mark turning into a star and then a cash cow, and the Cavalier has been at the forefront of Vauxhall's return to marketing success. On the other hand, examples of dogs in the past were the axeing of the Triumph TR7 and the MGB by BL, but Ford replaced the Cortina with the Sierra when some observers felt that it still had a long prospective life as a good cash generator (ie a cash cow).

Product life cycle and market share/market growth analysis

5.5 The product life cycle concept can be added to a market share/market growth classification of products, as follows.

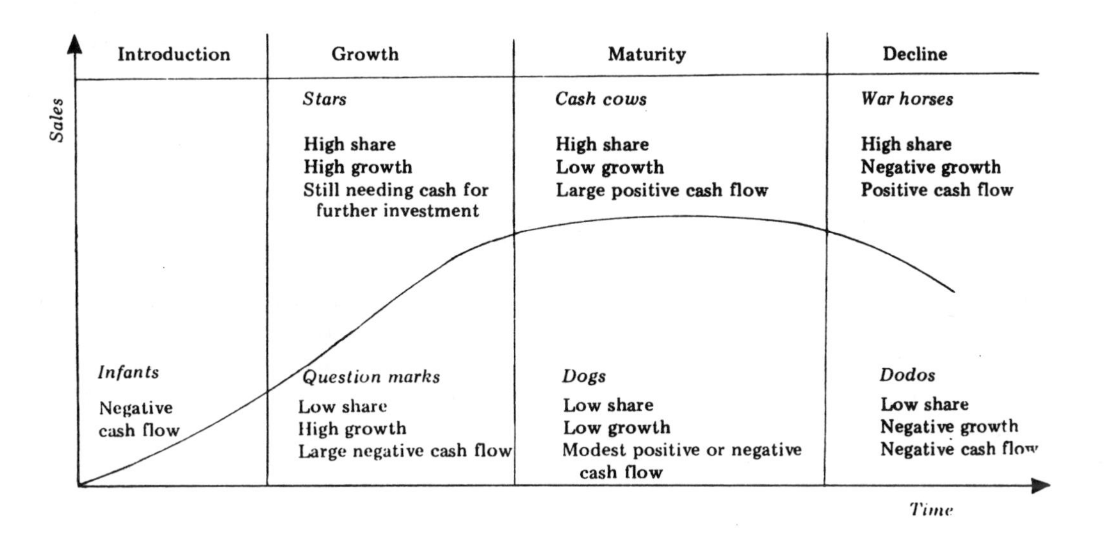

Competitiveness of products

5.6 Johnson and Scholes cite a variation on the BCG matrix. General Electric's Business Screen compares the following.

(a) The competitive position of products compared with rival products in the market.

(b) The strength of attraction that the product has in general for customers (for whatever reasons).

COMPETITIVE POSITION
- ie. business strengths of the firm

Strength of product attraction	Strong	Average	Weak
High	Invest for growth	Invest selectively for growth	?
Medium	Invest selectively for growth	?	Harvesting strategy
Low	?	Harvesting strategy	Harvesting strategy

General Electric business screen

? means that the choice of strategy is uncertain, and should be made selectively for each product and market.

The product life cycle: a product-market evolution matrix

5.7 General Electric's Business Screen can be developed further into a product-market evolution matrix. This matrix considers competitive position with the product's position in its life cycle. The position of existing products or contemplated new product developments can be plotted on the matrix and depending on where its position is, a decision can be taken about whether to pursue the product or market development.

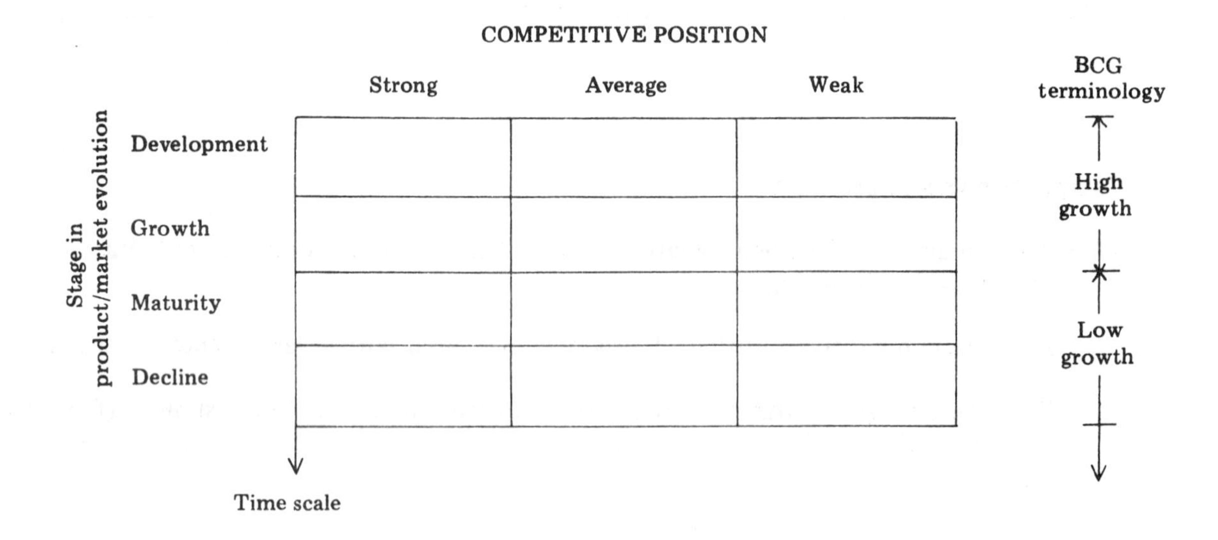

5.8 The relative attractiveness of products should be fairly easy to recognise, especially when growth *rates* are brought into consideration. Investing in a product at the development stage or growth stage of its life where the company has a strong competitive advantage for one reason or another, would clearly be an appealing and potentially profitable proposition.

Product-market decisions: a directional policy matrix

5.9 A final variation in the technique of matrix analysis has European origins. This is the directional policy matrix, developed by Shell Chemicals. The matrix, shown below, makes it possible to analyse products and product ranges, with a general indication of what the future investment policy should be, depending on where the product or product range is placed in the matrix. (Placings in the matrix would be determined by a points-scoring system for both market sector potential and the company's competitive position.)

		Prospects for market sector profitability		
		Unattractive	Average	Attractive
Company's competitive position	Weak	Disinvest	Gradual withdrawal	More selective backing
	Average	Gradual withdrawal	Cautious investment only	Invest more
	Strong	Cash generator	Largely self-financing growth	Maintain leadership

The advantages and disadvantages of portfolio planning

5.10 Portfolio planning, whether by means of market growth/market share analysis or product life cycle analysis, is something that you might be called on to apply yourself in a case study-type examination question.

It is a useful approach to the *analysis* of a firm's product-market mix. It is more difficult, however, to convert the analysis into a planning technique for making the following decisions.

(a) How the position of the company's products in its markets should be improved, ie how much extra or less market share to go for.

(b) What the mix of stars and cash cows ought to be.

(c) How a policy of developing stars into cash cows can be implemented in practice.

Nevertheless, portfolio planning provides an excellent framework for analysis, and a starting point for developing a product-market mix strategy.

Guidelines for a product-market strategy

5.11 Johnson and Scholes suggested the following principles and guidelines for product-market planning.

(a) *The potential for improvement and growth.* It is one thing to eliminate unprofitable products and 'has-beens' (dogs) but will there be sufficient growth potential among the products that remain in the product range? Will the elimination of 'dogs' free resources for developing products for growth markets? (This question is not easily answered. In the case of the Serpell report on the British railways network, it was suggested that a severe cutback of the rail network to a much smaller system would create a commercially viable and profitable system. This conclusion, however, is debatable and it is quite possible that a cutback which eliminated existing unprofitable services might send the volume of traffic on the rest of the network into a further spiralling decline. Moreover, this ignores the wider social costs of cutting the rail network.)

(b) *Cash generation.* Since 'stars' require some initial capital expenditure, there must be enough 'cash cows' on the market already to be milked to obtain the cash to invest in the stars. The funds for investment do not come out of thin air, and retained profits are by far the most significant source of new funds for companies. A company investing in the medium to long term which does not have enough current income from cash cows, will go into liquidation, in spite of its future prospects.

(c) *The timing decision for killing off existing products.* There are some situations where 'dogs' should be kept going for a while longer, to provide or maintain a necessary platform for launching new 'stars'. The Triumph TR7 sports car has already been used as an example of a dog product which was eventually axed, but BL deferred the killing off of the model in spite of the losses it was making. It was kept on to preserve BL's dealer network in the important US sports car market, to give BL time to develop an alternative 'star' model.

(d) *The long-term rationale of a product or market development.* Matrix analysis helps to highlight the long term planning justification for a product or market development. In the 1970s, BL cars subjected a newly planned model, the AD088 to a marketing clinic to assess its potential as a star and cash cow. The analysis proved discouraging. BL were faced with the option to pursue a potentially disastrous project, the AD088, in spite of weak competitive advantage, against a background of an urgent need to introduce a new model to the small cars market very quickly. The eventual decision was to change the product concept dramatically; the LC8 model was developed and the AD088 abandoned. The LC8 was eventually launched as the Metro.

(e) *Diversification by acquisition.* It might pay to buy question marks and dogs in a takeover deal. If the product-market strategy includes a policy of diversification, then the products or services which the expanding company should seek to acquire need not be stars or cash cows. It might be preferable to purchase question marks or dogs in the expectation that these products can be revived and turned into stars.

  (i) When BATs acquired the Eagle Star Insurance Company, it purchased a star in the rapidly-growing financial services market.

  (ii) When Trafalgar House acquired Cunard, on the other hand, Cunard was a very prestigious but also unprofitable up-market transport firm which was struggling to survive in a competitive market. Trafalgar House transformed this dog, once a useful tax loss, into a profitable travel operation.

  (iii) In the same way a company run by Rupert Murdoch purchased the predecessor of the ailing Sun newspaper and transformed it over the years into a market-leader.

Closing the profit gap and product-market strategy

5.12 The aim of product-market strategies is to close the profit gap that is found by gap analysis. A mixture of strategies may be needed to do this.

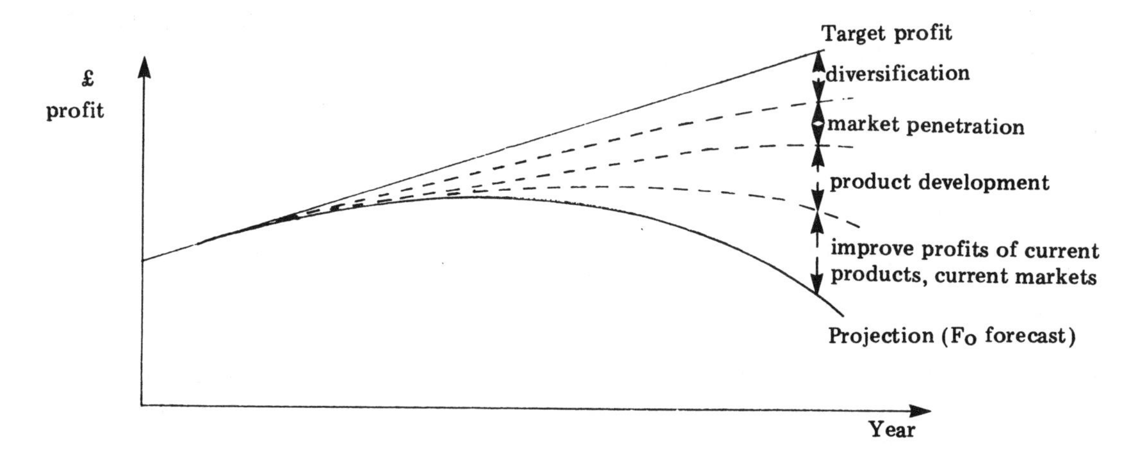

5.13 It is worth remembering that *divestment* is a product-market option to close the profit gap. Cadbury-Schweppes provides a good example. In 1982, Sir Adrian Cadbury was quoted in the Financial Times as holding the view that many companies will be forced to become more specialised in their product range, and shed fringe activities, with the possible creation of a more federated type of organisation, in which large and independent subsidiaries compete in their respective markets. This has now come to pass, with Cadbury Schweppes shedding its non-food activities such as Jeyes fluid, while in March 1986 came the announcement of a management buyout of the food and beverages division (Financial Times 22 March 1986) to enable the organisation to concentrate on the mainstream part of its activities, ie confectionery and soft drinks.

6. THE MANUFACTURING DEVELOPMENT STRATEGY

6.1 A successful product-market strategy depends on a successful strategy for manufacturing the products (or providing the services). The factors to be considered in a manufacturing development strategy are as follows.

(a) The nature and technology of production processes. Are the products mass-produced or custom-made etc? Future product opportunities will probably need to be related to current (and expected) technology and product types.

(b) Changes in production technology. How significant and urgent are these?

(c) What is a *critical mass* of output? Are *economies of scale* significant?

(d) What should *production capacity* be, and how can it be achieved? Is there a need for extra capacity, or for the closure of surplus capacity?

(e) The *utilisation of resources*, and whether there is spare production capacity at the moment. The availability of material and labour etc should also be assessed.

(f) Decisions to switch from manufacturing components in-house to buying them from external suppliers, or vice versa.

(g) How can production costs be reduced and *productivity* improved?

6.2 There are several aspects of manufacturing strategy that we need to consider.

(a) For companies that are planning to expand production capacity, the *capacity fill* that is needed to achieve economies of scale and a satisfactory return.

(b) Systems for improving the planning and utilisation of manufacturing resources, such as the following.

(i) MRP II
(ii) World Class Manufacturing (WCM)
(iii) Just in Time manufacturing (JIT)
(iv) Flexible manufacturing systems (FMS).

Note: although you are not required to have detailed knowledge of thse systems the brief overview provided here should be of assistance when developing corporate strategy or when talking to operations colleagues.

Manufacturing resource planning (MRP II)

6.3 Manufacturing resource planning (MRP II) developed out of material requirements planning (MRP).

(a) MRP was devised in the late 1960s as a system for calculating the total quantities of materials required to manufacture finished products. The aim was stock control, ie to make sure that the materials would be available in sufficient quantities to meet production demand, but that excessive quantities of unwanted items would not be held.

(b) MRPII emerged in the 1970s, and involves the building of a computer model of the manufacturing environment, which provides the following.

(i) Material requirements planning.
(ii) Capacity planning and production scheduling.
(iii) Shopfloor control.
(iv) A reporting system for actual progress.
(v) Control through a comparison of actual achievements and costs against the plan.

6.4 MRPII is used by many companies for manufacturing planning, but with the advent of Just in Time manufacturing (JIT) it has been criticised as a planning system.

'The primary criticism of the MRPII approach is that by modelling the reality of manufacturing plant, it builds in all the bad habits. It takes account of long leadtimes, shopfloor queues, large batch sizes, scrap and quality problems. Instead of accommodating these things, it should be driving towards their elimination. Poor productivity is built into MRPII and planned into the production process.' (Brian Maskell, *Management accounting* January 1989)

6.5 Even so, MRPII has advantages as a system for planning and controlling manufacturing systems, especially when JIT methods are unsuitable.

World Class Manufacturing (WCM)

6.6 World Class Manufacturing (WCM) is a term used by Professor Schonberger in 1986 to describe the fundamental changes taking place in manufacturing companies. WCM is a very broad term, but it can be taken to have four key elements.

(a) *A new approach to product quality.* Instead of a policy of trying to detect defects or poor quality in production as and when they occur, WCM sets out to identify the root causes of poor quality, eliminate them, and achieve zero defects - ie 100% quality. Eliminating waste is likely to involve building better quality into the product.

(b) *Just in Time manufacturing (JIT).* This is a system of manufacturing that aims to eliminate waste. Waste can be described as the use of resources that fail to add value to the product. Wasteful activities include the following.

(i) Inspection of goods.
(ii) Shopfloor queues.
(iii) Re-working of defective items.
(iv) Excessive storage.
(v) Unnecessary movement of materials.

(c) *Managing people.* The aim of WCM is to utilise the skills and abilities of the work force to the full. Employees are given training in a variety of skills, so that they can switch from one task to another. They are also given more responsibility for production scheduling and quality. A *team approach* is encouraged, with strong trust between management and workers.

(d) *Flexible approach to customer requirements.* The WCM policy is to develop close relationships with customers in order to achieve the following.

(i) Know what their requirements are.
(ii) Supply customers on time, with short delivery lead times.
(iii) Change the product mix quickly and develop new products or modify existing products as customer needs change.

6.7 A WCM manufacturer will have a clear *manufacturing strategy* aimed at issues such as the following.

(a) Quality and reliability.
(b) Short lead times.
(c) Flexibility.
(d) Customer satisfaction.

Just in Time manufacturing (JIT)

6.8 Just in Time manufacturing (JIT) is a concept or strategy for manufacturing that began in Japan in the 1970s, and began to emerge in the UK in the 1980s.

6.9 The most well-known feature of JIT is that it is a system for achieving reductions in stocks of raw materials and components, work in progress and finished goods.

6.10 Items should be delivered or produced just in time for when they are needed. Materials of goods sitting around the factory are not making any money and they tie up capital and take up space. So one of the first results of adopting JIT production is a steep fall in inventories.

6.11 However, a JIT manufacturing strategy has other important implications.

(a) A manufacturer that uses JIT will want its *suppliers* to deliver materials and components 'just in time' and in small quantities rather than in large deliveries. This calls for a close relationship with suppliers, and so the manufacturer is likely to have just one or two suppliers for each component or material item.

(b) Keeping stocks of components to a minimum also means that their quality standard must be high, because there is no safety margin if some of them turn out to be defective.

(c) Low levels of work in progress and finished goods have the following implications.

(i) Production quality must be high, because many rejects will halt the production line, and there will be insufficient safety stock of finished goods to meet customer demand.

(ii) The production process may need to be shortened and simplified. Flexible manufacturing systems (FMS) are an example of this. Changing the shopfloor layout to reduce the movement of materials is another.

(iii) The manufacture of components and sub-assemblies needs to be synchronised, so that they are available when they are needed, and neither too soon (causing excess stocks) nor too late (causing delay in production).

(d) Quality may need to be controlled and improved through measures such as:

(i) statistical checks on output quality
(ii) training workers.

(e) '*Training workers* fits in well with another tenet of the JIT philosophy: "total employee involvement". Workers need to have diverse skills so they can move from one task to another keeping production flowing smoothly.'

(Diane Coyle, *Investors chronicle* 5 May 1989)

(f) Production systems must have flexibility, and the workforce contributes to this. '"Kanban" is a system of markers for passing components around the factory - but only when they are needed. One worker cannot produce his next item until the next worker along the line has taken the last one; instead he does something else useful - like sweeping the floor.'

(Diane Coyle)

6.12 The characteristics of JIT were summarised by consultant Martin Cocker *(Management accounting*, March 1989) as follows.

'A just-in-time environment is composed of the following:

- the elimination of waste;
- a move towards zero inventory;
- an emphasis on perfect quality;
- stable production rates;
- increased people responsibility;
- short set-ups;
- moving towards a lot size of one;
- preventative maintenance;
- balanced capacity.'

6.13 An interesting footnote to our discussion of JIT is a report on revisions to the strategy of the Apple Computer company *(Financial Times* 4 October 1990). Apple was an early adopter of JIT and significantly cut its inventory costs by ordering components as they were needed. Now they acknowledge that it is difficult to predict patterns of demand for new products and as a result they are abandoning JIT methods of inventory management in favour of a less rigid approach, despite higher costs.

Flexible manufacturing systems (FMS)

6.14 Flexible manufacturing systems (FMS) are highly-automated computer-controlled manufacturing systems that enable manufacturers to achieve small batch production without the loss of machine operating time caused by set-up times between batches.

6.15 The strategic possibilities of FMS have been excellently described by Anna Kochan in the *Financial Times* (31 May 1989) as follows.

'Small batch production helps to provide the flexibility needed for *just-in-time manufacturing*, which involves producing only to customer order and eliminating stock.

The problem with small batches is the set-up time. Even with the most modern of machine tools, it can take several hours, or several days to prepare a machine before production can start.

The target of an FMS is to avoid this delay by separating the set-up operation from the machining process. While an operator at one station is preparing a pallet, its fixtures and the component for machining, machine tools at other stations are cutting the prepared components.

To keep production going continuously, an FMS has to incorporate tool stores, pallet stores and an automated cart that transfers the pallets between the different stations and stores. The whole operation is computer controlled.

With the automated equipment and the organising software, FMS is a big investment for a company. So although its flexibility makes it the obvious technology for small subcontractors few have adopted it. '

6.16 The high investment cost of switching to an FMS (with compatible computer-controlled equipment) would obviously be a key factor in any manufacturing strategy decision for such a change.

Synergy - the planning bonus

6.17 Synergy is the advantage to a firm gained by having existing resources which are compatible with new products or markets that the company is developing, ie. with *product-market entries*. It can be described as the 2 + 2 = 5 effect, where a firm looks for combined results that reflect a better rate of return than would be achieved by the same resources used independently as separate operations. The combined performance, therefore, is greater than the sum of its parts.

6.18 The greater the synergy a firm can manage to achieve through its selection of products and markets, the more flexible will be its competitive position and the more cost-competitive it will be. This can then be used to advantage in the following ways.

(a) Increasing market share through price reductions.
(b) Making larger investments in research and development than competitors.
(c) Increasing return on investment, thereby increasing the firm's capital base, if some of the extra profits are retained in the business.

6.19 There are different ways in which synergy can be obtained when a company expands its range of products and the markets it sells its products in, or when it diversifies into new products and markets. It is useful to identify different categories of synergy, as follows.

(a) Sales synergy.
(b) Operating synergy.
(c) Investment synergy.
(d) Management synergy.

6.20 *Sales synergy* for products is obtained through use of common marketing facilities such as distribution channels, sales staff and administration, and warehousing. Supplying a range of complementary products increases the productivity of the sales force, an obvious example of which is the range of both dairy and non-dairy products (bread, turkeys, orange juice etc) carried by milk roundsmen. Shared advertising (such as soap powders together with washing machines) sales promotion and corporate image can generate a much higher return than average, per pound spent.

6.21 *Operating synergy* arises from the better use of operational facilities and personnel, bulk purchasing, a greater spread of fixed costs (by producing more items with little or no increase in fixed costs, and so a reduction in unit costs) and the advantages of common learning curves whereby the experience gained by employees in making one product can be transferred to making new products. Thus, if two small firms merge and save fixed costs by moving into the same premises and sharing the same office staff, there will be some cost savings through operating synergy.

6.22 *Investment synergy* can be achieved from the joint use of plant, common raw material stocks, transfer of research and development from one product to another, ie from the wider use of a common investment in fixed assets, working capital or research.

6.23 *Management synergy* is the advantage to be gained where management skills concerning current operations are easily transferred to new operations because of the similarity of problems in the two industries. The converse is also true and there might be negative synergy at a top management level in situations where the problems inherent in new ventures are unrelated to current operations and attempts to solve them in the familiar way lead to incorrect or even disastrous decisions. Over-extending management capabilities is one reason for diseconomies of scale; however, in some circumstances, management synergy might be achievable.

6.24 Synergy is gained by exploiting the strengths within the company, and is closely associated with economies of scale. Although synergy might be acquired by developing the internal resources of a company, it is more commonly sought through mergers and acquisitions. However, the potential synergy is not always realised in mergers and acquisitions because of the difficulty of reconciling the different corporate cultures.

6.25 Corporate planners will seek to develop strategic plans which provide synergy, yet there is a severe danger of misguided optimism. Argenti wrote the following.

> 'It should be noted that synergy is unlikely to occur, or even be negative, when a company attempts a new activity that is not related to a strength. A company with a poor distribution channel for Product A may court disaster by attempting to sell Product B through it as well. (Synergy is popularly described as the 2 + 2 = 5 effect. This equation may be correct for strengths, but for weaknesses it must be -2 - 2 = - 5.)'

Start-up synergy

6.26 Ansoff makes a useful distinction between operating synergy (already described) and start-up synergy.

6.27 When a company launches a new product, enters a new market, or does both at the same time, there will be heavy start-up costs. There are the tangible costs of acquiring plant and machinery, working capital and skilled labour, together with the more intangible costs of early operating inefficiency (as the labour force acquires skills and learning) and management blunders due to inexperience. During this start-up time the firm will be at a disadvantage against well established competitors in the field whose costs ought to be lower.

6.28 Clearly, a firm should look for product-market opportunities where the conditions of entry are not severe, ie start-up costs are lower and the start-up period is relatively short before the new area of business is well established. This is likely to occur where the company already has assets or experience which will minimise the start-up costs and reduce the start-up time, ie where there is 'start-up synergy'.

6.29 Corporate planners looking for new product and market opportunities should attempt to look for areas where both start-up synergy and operating synergy will be strong, or at second best, where one of the following apply.

(a) Start-up synergy is high, and so profits can be made fairly quickly, even though operating synergy is low.

(b) Operating synergy is high, and so the profits obtainable would justify the high initial costs of starting up.

7. CONCLUSION

7.1 Strategies for product-market mix and manufacturing should be developed with a particular view to having a product range sold to various markets and market segments, and produced by methods and in volumes, which will enable the company to achieve its objectives.

(a) The product range must be rejuvenated by continuous new product development.

(b) Markets should be varied and reliance on a few individual customers in each market should be avoided where possible. There is the danger that if a major customer withdraws his custom, sales of the product might fall below breakeven point so that the product would be unprofitable.

(c) Where suitable, profitability should be sought through a manufacturing strategy to cut costs and improve productivity. Even in differentiated markets there is a limit to what buyers will pay, and so cost control or cost reductions will be necessary to ensure that unit costs are low enough to earn a satisfactory profit at prices the markets will bear.

7.2 The company's special sphere of influence and resource skills are generally accepted as forming the base on which strategy is, and should be, developed. Where new products are developed for new markets, the risk element and the cost of entry must be considered.

7.3 The assessment of product, market and manufacturing development strategies from the internal and external appraisal in strategic planning is a complex exercise involving wide areas of experience from all disciplines, particularly marketing and accounting.

At the end of the exercise, however, it is necessary to identify the following.

(a) The existing *product line*, probable deletions in the future and possible additions.
(b) The general *characteristics of the company's products* and its *sphere of influence*.
(c) Current and future *market demand*, and the influence on demand of price, sales promotion, product characteristics and channels of distribution.
(d) The *risk* of new product ventures and the cost of entry into new markets.
(e) The possible *synergy* from new product ideas.
(f) *Profitability* of these product/market ideas.
(g) The scope for *cost reductions*.

TEST YOUR KNOWLEDGE

The numbers in brackets refer to paragraphs of this chapter

1. What is meant by the term segmentation and why is it strategically significant? (1.5, 1.6)
2. What factors need to be considered in product-market development? (1.15)
3. What factors influence the speed at which new products diffuse into a market? (2.12)
4. What is meant by the adoption process? (2.14)
5. Distinguish between a policy of penetration and one of skimming. (2.17)
6. What is PIMS analysis and what does it try to do? (3.4)
7. What is a harvesting stratgy? (3.12)
8. List four types of expansion diversification. (4.18)
9. What are the disadvantages of test marketing? (4.26)
10. What is the purpose of the Boston Matrix? (5.1)
11. What are the advantages of portfolio planning? (5.10)
12. What is just in time manufacturing?

Now try illustrative questions 9 and 10

Chapter 9

OPERATIONAL PLANNING

This chapter covers the following topics.

1. DEVELOPING OPERATIONAL PLANS

1.1 Once developed, the strategic business plan must now be communicated throughout the organisation. Awareness of the plan is not enough: each manager should appreciate the contribution he or she must make if corporate objectives are to be achieved.

1.2 The corporate strategic plan must be translated into terms and objectives which have a meaning at lower levels in the organisation. (There might be a plan for each department, or for each market.) Implicit in the process of developing operational plans is the establishment of control points.

1.3 Operations plans follow on after the definition of corporate and strategic objectives, the formulation and selection of strategies, and the outline development of the corporate plan. Depending on the size and nature of the organisation, operations planning is concerned essentially with *resource allocation* , possibly in the short to medium term, although the distinction between strategic planning and operations planning becomes blurred where major long-term capital investment programmes are planned.

1.4 Linneman defines operations planning as follows.

(a) Deciding what is to be accomplished, by whom and when, and at what cost.
(b) Setting up *control points* and *methods of measuring and monitoring performance.*

This planning process spans plans at the corporate level, for product-market areas (subsidiaries or divisions), for functional areas (functional departments etc) and for lower echelons of management.

1.5 At corporate and functional area levels, operations planning is a three-stage process.

(a) Putting together detailed operational plans.
(b) Preparing a draft balance sheet, profit and loss account and cash flow forecast to reflect the outcome of these plans.
(c) Final adjustments and fine tuning.

Putting together detailed operational plans

1.6 To help you get a clearer picture of what operations planning entails, it is worth stressing at the outset that they are relatively *short* plans. Strategic planning does not require the same kind of 'line by line detail' that annual budgeting demands, although budgeting will be necessary afterwards to add flesh and muscle to the bones of these skeleton operations plans.

1.7 Even so, major items would need to be quantified, such as sales, cost of sales, operating profit, other income, fixed asset details, inventory levels, working capital investment, production targets (if appropriate) etc.

1.8 Plans for functional departments must also be prepared, below the overall corporate level. In a manufacturing company, major functional plans will be for marketing and production. A possible format for the marketing plan is shown below.

Structure of a marketing plan

MARKETING PLAN

1. *Objectives:* levels of sales to be attained.

2. *Situational analysis:* summary of the strengths and weaknesses of the marketing activity, for example:

   (a) poor image on delivery times and availability of spares;
   (b) strong technical reputation and positive corporate image;
   (c) pricing generally above competitors' average.

3. *Environmental forecast:* a statement of the external opportunities and threats which might impact on the marketing activity and function for example key sales staff being poached by competitors, higher interest rates or new competitor entering the market.

4. *Summary outline* of the marketing plan indicating how it relates to the corporate plan and showing the sales forecast for each product area etc.

5. *Detailed plans of action:* this is the area of major planning effort and is the most detailed part of the functional plan. It indicates activities and responsibilities by brand areas or marketing mix responsibilities (see Chapter 9).

6. *Contingency plans*

7. *Resources* required to implement the plan.

1.9 The marketing plan will have given consideration to the portfolio's position on the product life cycle, considered eliminating any declining products (dogs) and forecast demand levels within the range of product-markets in which the company operates. From these estimates of selling quantities the required production programmes can be formulated. These would state what needs to be produced and at what cost, to match the volume and diversity of products which the marketing function expect to sell.

1.10 In this way the manufacturing and marketing plans can be meshed together under the umbrella of the corporate plan. Building such a planning hierarchy ensures that there is synergy in the organisation's activities and that the objectives of one function are well communicated and understood by the others.

1.11 Since the functional plan for marketing relies on the ability of the organisation to produce the goods for sale, production programmes and inventory levels are a necessary element in the marketing operations plan. As you might imagine, there are potential 'snags' in co-ordinating the efforts of the two functions to produce an optimal plan.

(a) Marketing staff are occasionally over-optimistic about what they can sell, and so might ask for too much production. If the goods are produced but not sold, there would be unnecessary stock levels and so an excessive investment in inventory. Furthermore, the production department might be able to produce in the quantities required by marketing, but at an unacceptable cost, where marginal extra production calls for high labour costs (overtime) or high material costs (supply shortages) etc.

(b) The production function might create its own problems too, where there are inefficiencies in manufacture which give rise to unnecessarily high costs. Some consideration should be given to realistic cost reduction which would enable the marketing function to sell at a profit the goods for which there is demand at a given price.

1.12 The functional plans for marketing and production must be prepared in close co-operation: obviously, the manufacturing plan must initially follow on from the marketing plan. However, the manufacturing function may come up with costings which, even allowing for cost reductions, make the sales targets impossible because the product would be uncompetitive at a higher price, or unprofitable at the currently planned one. Such problems need to be resolved by revising sales schedules, or compromising on production schedules and inventory levels, or even by considering whether the product has a worthwhile future.

2. MANAGEMENT BY OBJECTIVES

2.1 An approach to operations planning and control, which can be integrated with a system of budgeting, was described by John Humble in *Improving business results* and *Management by objectives*. During the 1960s, Humble became a leading authority on the application of management by objectives.

2.2 He argues that within the framework of long term corporate plans, the operating and functional units of a company (factories, sales regions, marketing departments etc.) should clarify their own objectives.

(a) Both team objectives and individual managers' objectives must be identified; therefore key tasks must be analysed and performance standards agreed.

(b) These key tasks will be fused together into divisional plans, prepared each year by divisional managers and expressed in strategic terms rather than as short-term budgets.

(c) The divisional plans are reviewed centrally and amended by company or group headquarters, in consultation with divisional managers. Any imbalance between divisional objectives can be adjusted at this stage, ie is one division attempting to do too much, and another too little? Are the divisional plans consistent with each other or is there sub-optimality? If resources are scarce, and the demand by divisions for resources exceed the supply, how should a fair allocation be made between them?

(d) Having agreed annual plans for each division, with key tasks identified and performance indicators established for each team and individual manager within the division, managers identify:

(i) *policies:* guides to making decisions which are in keeping with corporate objectives;
(ii) *procedures:* more specific rules about how decisions should be taken;
(iii) *financial budgets:* a statement in money terms of a plan to achieve certain objectives. Financial budgets are *not* the objectives themselves.

Humble said that each of these three devices (policies, procedures and financial budgets) were necessary for sound management control.

(e) Each division should make a monthly operating report, measuring actual results against key performance indicators. There should also be similar quarterly and annual reviews, after which new divisional plans would be prepared.

2.3 These activities provide a link between corporate planning and executive action. Humble made two further comments about this process.

(a) When the analysis of strengths and weaknesses is made, short-term corrective action should become apparent to management as well as long-term strategic problems. Action to remove weaknesses may require a longer-term strategy but it is just as important (and often effective) to look for short-term plans to deal with them.

(b) One of the most difficult problems for top management is finding the right balance between the conflicting claims of long term and short term results. Shareholders expect dividends every year and will not be content to wait for the long term to receive their returns. On the other hand, large capital-intensive companies are forced to take the long view because they do not have the flexibility to change plans and direction quickly.

'Since any attempt to interlock different levels of objectives in detail is bound to fail, great concentration must be made on selecting a limited number of priorities which *must* be linked from top to bottom of the business.' (Humble)

Interlocking these key objectives must be not only vertical, but horizontal, ie objectives of the production function must be linked with those of sales, warehousing, purchasing, R & D etc.

Short-term objectives can be regarded as intermediate 'staging posts' on the road towards long-term objectives.

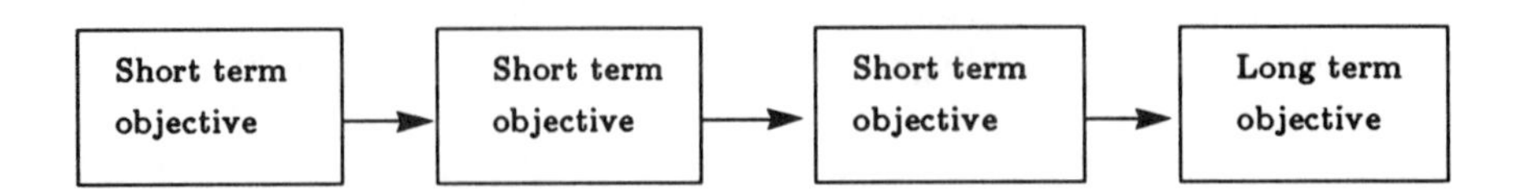

2.4 The hierarchy of objectives which emerges is as follows:

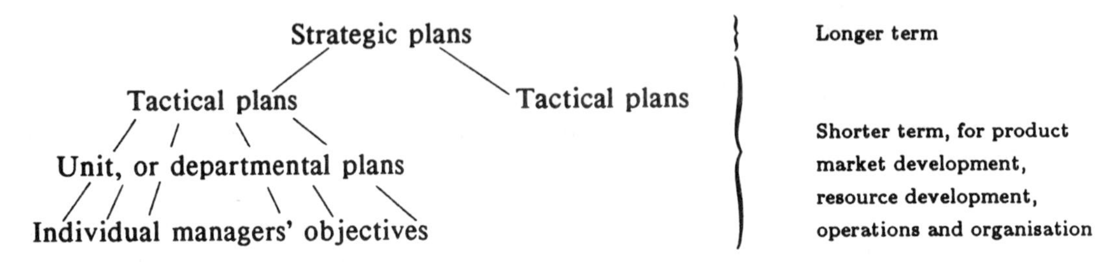

2.5 There are two approaches to establishing the hierarchy of objectives.

(a) Senior managers (perhaps the managing director personally) can tell managers what to do and set up control procedures. Humble comments that this apparently sensible and logical approach often misses the spark of vitality, challenge and involvement on which the real use of human beings depends. It is 'top down' management.

(b) Develop the contribution and motivation of each manager in the business by involving them in the planning process. This approach which Humble called 'improving management performance' introduces an element of 'bottom up' management, organised within the framework of corporate objectives and strategic plans.

2.6 The essential features of Humble's recommended approach are as follows.

(a) Clarify with managers the *key results* and *performance standards* each should individually achieve. These should conform to corporate and divisional objectives, but each manager should contribute to the process of agreeing these key results and performance standards, so as to win commitment to them.

(b) Agree, with each manager, a personal job *improvement plan* which will make a quantifiable and measurable contribution to achievement of the plans for the department, company or group as a whole.

(c) Provide conditions which will help managers to achieve their key results and job improvement plans. For example:
   (i) there must be an efficient and effective management information system to provide feedback of results;
   (ii) there must be an organisation structure which provides managers with sufficient flexibility and freedom of action;
   (iii) there should be a sense of 'team spirit and corporate purpose' within the organisation.

(d) Undertake a systematic *performance review* of each manager's results and the results of each 'unit' of the organisation.

(e) Hold a regular *potential review* for each manager so as to identify the individuals with potential for advancement within the company.

(f) Develop *management training plans* to improve management skills.

(g) Motivate managers by effective *salary, selection and career development* plans.

(h) Ensure there must be a continuity or cycle in the revision of unit and job improvement plans. Annual budgets provide one method of continuity, although at a lower level of management (foreman, chief clerk etc.) a shorter cycle might be more appropriate.

2.7 *Unit objectives* are required for administration and R & D as well as production, marketing, purchasing and distribution. They must be set first of all in terms of primary targets, relating to:

(a) profitability;
(b) level of activity, or turnover;
(c) achievement of production schedules;
(d) the quality of output or services;
(e) safety;
(f) efficiency in the use of resources (labour productivity, material usage);
(g) plant utilisation, etc.

2.8 For each of these primary targets, secondary targets (or sub-targets) will be set. Examples are as follows.

(a) *Profitability:* the contribution required from each individual product, and the method of fixed overhead allocation.

(b) *Quality of output:* the acceptable level of rejected units at inspection should be specified for each type of work and product, and acceptable standards of workmanship identified, target requirements for after-sales service and customer complaints might be set etc.

2.9 Once the unit objectives have been identified, it is then necessary to identify which individual managers within the unit are in a position to influence the achievement of each of them.

2.10 At the same time that unit objectives are formulated, a *key results analysis* is prepared for each individual manager. As the term suggests, the analysis attempts to identify *key* results and does not list all the tasks of each manager. For example, the key results of the data processing operations manager might be as follows.

(a) *Service to users*	To ensure that users get immediate access to processors through on-line terminals, and all batch processing must be done within agreed turn-round schedules.
(b) *Use of resources and efficiency*	Mainframe computers must operate at more than 80% capacity within a two-shift day, six-day week. Breakdown time must not exceed 5%.

(c) *Costs* — The cost per operating hour must not exceed £100 which is the standard cost.

(d) *Quality* — There must be no irretrievable corruption of files and complaints from users must be restricted to an acceptable level (this level must be quantified, if possible).

2.11 Identifying and establishing *performance standards* is an important feature of management control (and also of operational control). Performance standards may be quantitative or qualitative. Examples are as follows.

(a) *Quantitative:* volume of output or sales, market share, levels of scrap and inventory, cost levels, timescales etc. Quantities can be expressed in terms of volume, quality, time, costs and profits.

(b) *Qualitative:* attitudes of employees and customers.

At middle management level, any quantitative performance standards will be largely expressed in terms of money (costs, revenues, profits).

2.12 Performance standards provide a means of both planning and control. Where they are quantitative, control will be initiated by the preparation of a report or control document (for example production cost report, selling cost report, distribution cost report, monthly operating statement, profit and loss account etc.)

2.13 Top management must integrate the unit objectives of each department and the key results analysis of individual managers:

(a) to ensure that unit objectives are consistent with each other and with overall corporate objectives;

(b) to identify common areas for improvement and ensure that the best joint approach is being taken to deal with them;

(c) to assign priorities for improvement schemes and objectives;

(d) to check whether every key area of business performance is the responsibility of one manager, and there are no gaps where control is non-existent;

(e) to check whether there is unnecessary duplication of control work by more than one manager.

2.14 Top management will now make a *unit improvement plan* for each 'unit' of the business, setting out specifically the objectives for improvement, the performance standards and the timescale. Although many of these plans will be given a one-year duration so as to fit within a scheme of budgetary control, some aspects may be longer-term.

2.15 Each unit improvement plan must be approved by the senior manager with overall responsibility for the unit (for example departmental manager, profit centre manager, or managing director of a subsidiary).

2.16 The unit improvement plan is then broken down into a series of results required from the various individual managers within the unit, expressed as *job improvement plans*.

(a) The job improvement plan tells the manager what must be done within given time periods.

(b) Key results analysis tells the manager how achievements can be gauged.

(c) Performance standards for each key result will provide a means of measuring actual results against the plan in each key area.

2.17 'Once it is agreed and issued, the job improvement plan is vitally important. The manager is committed to achieving the results, and the line manager is committed to providing any agreed resources and information'. (Humble)

2.18 A *performance review* must be a formal and disciplined review of the results achieved by each manager, carried out regularly on pre-determined dates. Performance standards in key results areas provide the means of comparison for actual results achieved.

Failure to achieve satisfactory results should initiate control action by the manager with prompting from a superior.

3. RESOURCE PLANNING

3.1 *Resource planning* involves planning the resources (and identifying potential resources) of the undertaking in order that the defined and agreed corporate objectives may be achieved within a given time period. The stages in resource planning are as follows.

(a) Establishing currently available and currently obtainable resources (by category) and details of any which are not available or readily obtainable - making a resource audit.

(b) Estimating what resources would be needed to pursue a particular strategy and deciding whether there would be enough resources to pursue it successfully.

(c) Assigning responsibilities to managers for the acquisition, use and control of resources.

(d) Identifying all constraints and factors exerting an influence on the availability and use of resources (internal and external environments).

3.2 The situation might be explained more simply by means of a Venn diagram.

Some objectives and strategies can be met from existing resources, new resources, or a mixture of existing and new resources in tandem, but the objectives and strategies which cannot be met will have to be deferred until a later time, or abandoned altogether.

3.3 Johnson and Scholes suggest that there are three central questions in operational resource planning that must be resolved.

(a) *Resource identification.* What resources will be needed to implement the strategy? All the required resources should be identified - manufacturing resources, manpower, R & D, finance, marketing mix etc.

(b) *Fit with existing resources.* An assessment must be made of:
   (i) the extent to which the required resources are already in place;
   (ii) to what extent any extra resources that are needed can be built on existing resources;
   (iii) whether there will have to be some changes to existing resources in order to implement the strategy.

(c) *Fit between required resources.* An assessment must also be made, when new resources are required to implement a strategy, of how these resources can be properly integrated with each other.

3.4 The principal resources which have to be planned for are manpower, materials, finance, plant and equipment, though marketers should also be aware of the need to invest in the information resource.

4. BUDGETS

4.1 It is incorrect to suppose that strategic planning is merely an extension of budgeting but the relationship between planning and budgeting is close. A budget as defined by the Chartered Institute of Management Accountants (CIMA) is a 'plan expressed in money. It is prepared and approved prior to the budget period and may show income, expenditure and the capital to be employed.'

> Budgets have a role in the strategic planning process, as a budget is a *consolidated statement of the resources required to achieve the organisation's objectives or to implement the planned strategies.*

4.2 'Budgeting is a planning and control tool relevant to all aspects of management activities.

The primary purposes of budgeting are:

(a) to assist in the assessment and evaluation of different courses of possible action;
(b) to create motivation by expressing a proposed plan of action in terms of personal achievement based upon the involvement and commitment of management;
(c) to monitor the effectiveness of performance being accomplished against the budget and to report deviations.

Budgeting assumes that objectives are defined and strategy developed to achieve them and an organisational structure with designated areas of responsibility.' (CIMA, *Budgeting - a practical framework)*

4.3 It is important that senior managers are clear about and that all documentation shows the following.

(a) The *objective of the organisation* and *the targets set for individuals* in order to achieve the objective.

(b) The *principal underlying assumptions and circumstances* divided between responsibilities for

(i) external factors over which the manager has little influence;
(ii) internal factors over which the manager has substantial influence during the budget period.

4.4 The purpose of a budget is:

(a) to *co-ordinate* the activities of all the different departments of an organisation into a single master plan; in addition, through participation by employees in preparing a budget, it may be possible to motivate them to raise their targets and standards and to achieve better results;

(b) to *communicate* the policies and targets to every manager in the organisation responsible for carrying out a part of that plan;

(c) to establish a system of *control* by having a plan against which actual results can be progressively compared;

(d) to *compel planning*. By having a formal budgeting procedure, management is forced to look to the future instead of 'living hand-to-mouth' without any clear idea of purpose.

The budget manual

4.5 Procedures for preparing the budget are contained in the *budget manual.*

(a) *Which* budgets must be prepared, *when* and *by whom* (for example the order in which they are prepared and when they should be sent to the budget committee.
(b) What each functional budget should contain.
(c) Directions on how to prepare budgets and, where appropriate, the standard forms to use etc.

Use of a budget manual should enable a company to develop improved techniques for forecasting sales and costs. It will be circulated to all those involved in the budget.

The budget committee

4.6 The preparation and administration of budgets is usually the responsibility of a *budget committee.* Every part of the organisation should be represented on the committee, ie there should be a representative from sales, production, marketing etc. Functions of the budget committee include:

(a) co-ordination of the preparation of budgets, which includes the issue of the budget manual;
(b) issuing of timetables for the preparation of functional budgets;
(c) allocation of responsibilities for the preparation of functional budgets;
(d) provision of information to assist in the preparation of budgets;
(e) communication of final budgets to the appropriate managers;

(f) comparison of actual results with budget and investigation of variances;
(g) continuous assessment of the budgeting and planning process, in order to improve the planning and control function.

The budget period

4.7 A budget does not necessarily have to be restricted to a one year planning horizon. The factors which should influence the budget period are as follows.

(a) A plan decided upon now might need a considerable time to be put into operation. Capital budgets must have a planning horizon well in excess of one year. For example a long lead time may elapse between a decision to purchase an item of machinery and getting it manufactured, installed and tested. The long time required to purchase or erect new buildings, to move a company to a different location etc explain why the planning horizon for capital budgets is usually several years, even though expenditure decisions are taken 'now'. In the same way, other budgets may require distant planning horizons because of the delay in obtaining resources or achieving tangible results. A manpower training budget or a research and development programme might cover several years.

(b) A distinction can be made between long-term planning and short-term budgeting according to the 'fixed' or 'variable' nature of the resources of the business.

In the long term, all resources (men, money, machines and materials) are variable in quantity, but in the short-term, although some resources are variable, others are fixed. The fixed nature of these resources, and the length of time which must elapse before they become variable, might therefore determine the planning horizon for budgeting.

(c) All budgets involve some element of forecasting and guesswork, since future events cannot be quantified with accuracy. The more distant the planning horizon, the greater the uncertainty and the wider the margin of error will be.

For example management might predict that cost inflation will be 10% over a one year period, and 21% over a two year period. The one year estimate is likely to be more accurate than the two year estimate. Since budgets are quantified statements of organisational targets, and since they are also used for the control of actual results, the margin of error in the budget should be suitably low. This places a limit on the distance of the planning horizon.

(d) An organisation operates in a continually changing environment. Unforeseen events might occur which transform the commercial situation for an organisation.

Change might involve the closure of a market (for example an embargo on imports by a foreign government) or the opening up of a new market, new products, new production technology, the emergence or disappearance of a competitor etc. Since unforeseen events cannot be planned for, it would be a waste of time to plan in detail too far ahead if these events cause a significant re-appraisal of the future by an organisation's management. The rate of change varies from industry to industry and organisation to organisation. The greater the rate of change that is likely in the future, the nearer the planning horizon should be.

(e) The further into the future budgets are projected, the more costly they will be to prepare.

(f) Most budgets are prepared over a one-year period to enable managers to plan and control financial results for the purposes of the annual accounts. There is a need for management to satisfy shareholders that their company is achieving good results, and for this reason the arbitrary one-year financial period is usually selected for budgeting.

4.8 The preparation of a budget may take weeks or months, and the budget committee may meet several times before the master budget is finally agreed. Functional budgets and cost centre budgets prepared in draft may need to be amended many times over as a consequence of discussions between departments, changes in market conditions, reversals of decisions by management, etc during the course of budget preparation.

The principal budget factor

4.9 The first task in budgeting is to identify the *principal budget factor*. This is also known as the *key budget factor* or *limiting budget factor*. This is the factor which prevents the organisation from expanding indefinitely.

4.10 The principal budget factor is usually sales demand, ie a company is restricted from making and selling more of its products because there would be no sales demand for the increased output at a price which would be acceptable/profitable to the company. Alternatively the principal budget factor could be machine capacity, distribution and selling resources, the availability of key raw materials or the availability of cash etc. Once this factor is defined then the rest of the budget can be prepared. For example if sales are the principal budget factor then the production budget cannot be prepared until after the sales budget is complete.

Budgets and forecasts

4.11 A forecast is an estimate of what might happen in the future. It is a best estimate, made on certain assumptions about the conditions that are expected to apply. For example a sales forecast would be a best estimate of future sales, given certain assumptions about the prices to be charged, market conditions, expenditure on advertising etc.

4.12 In contrast, a budget is a plan of what the organisation would like to happen, and what it has set as a target. A budget should be realistic and so it will be based to some extent on the forecasts prepared. However, in formulating a budget, management will be trying to establish some control over the conditions that will apply in the future. For example in setting a sales budget, management must decide on the prices to be charged and the advertising expenditure budget, even though they might have no control over other market factors.

4.13 When a budget is set the budget will for a short time be the same as the forecasts. However, as actual events progress and the situation develops and changes, new forecasts might be prepared that differ from the budget targets. Management might be able to take control action to bring forecasts back into line with the budget; alternatively, management will have to accept that the budget will not be achieved, or it will be exceeded, depending on what the current forecasts include.

Problems in constructing budgets

4.14 Most of the practical problems in budgeting are, however, not so much the computations themselves, but rather the factors listed below.

(a) It might be difficult to forecast sales with any reliable accuracy.

(b) The availability of resources, especially skilled labour and cash, might be difficult to predict, and so it might be difficult to identify the principal budget factor.

(c) Because of inflation, it might be difficult to estimate future price levels for materials, expenses, wages and salaries.

(d) Managers might be reluctant to budget accurately.

(i) They may overstate their expected expenses, so that by having a budget which is larger than necessary, they will be unlikely to overspend the budget allowance. (They will then not be held accountable in control reports for excess spending). Excess expenditure built into a budget is known as *slack* and zero base budgeting is an attempt to eliminate this.

(ii) They may compete with other departments for the available resources, by trying to expand their budgeted expenditure. Budget planning might well intensify inter-departmental rivalry and the problems of 'empire building'.

(e) Inter departmental rivalries might ruin the efforts towards co-ordination in a budget.

(f) Employees might resist budget plans either because the plans are not properly communicated to them, or because they feel that the budget puts them 'under pressure' from senior managers to achieve better results.

4.15 You will have come across budgets and budgeting in your earlier studies or work experience. It is important to recognise that CIM examiners are increasingly requiring that Diploma students demonstrate their appreciation of the financial aspects and their implications for both marketing and business. You must be prepared to support plans with budgets both in the context of minicases and major case study exercises. These need not be elaborate and detailed as though you were taking accountancy qualifications, but they need:

(a) to indicate your awareness of the process of budgeting and its significance;
(b) to identify key headings and inclusions.

5. CONCLUSION

5.1 Strategies must be converted into operating plans. One type of operating plan is the budget. Another is the marketing plan.

5.2 Management by objectives is a scheme which sets divisional planning within a framework of corporate planning. It is wider-reaching than a more limited control system.

5.3 Operational plans are an effective way of communicating the corporate strategy within the organisation. They have to be developed under the corporate strategy umbrella and with close co-operation between functional areas to ensure synergy.

5.4 Planning is not just an extension of budgeting, but there is a close link between them. A budget is a plan expressed in money terms, representing the resources needed to achieve the objective.

5.5 The principal budget factor should be identified at the beginning of the budgetary process. It is often sales volume and so the sales budget has to be produced before all the others.

5.6 Planning without proper consideration of the resources needed or available is a sterile activity. Marketing managers have to be able to demonstrate their competence in this aspect of planning.

TEST YOUR KNOWLEDGE

The numbers in brackets refer to paragraphs of this chapter

1. What is the purpose of operational planning? (1.3)
2. What are the principal headings for a marketing plan? (1.8)
3. What are the two approaches to establishing a hierarchy of objectives? (2.5)
4. Distinguish between a job improvement plan and a unit improvement plan. (2.14, 2.16)
5. What is the purpose of a budget? (4.4)
6. How long is the budget period? (4.7)
7. What is the principal budget factor? (4.9)

Now try illustrative question 11

Chapter 10

DEVELOPING THE MARKETING PLAN

This chapter covers the following topics.

1. The marketing plan
2. Market segmentation
3. Market positioning
4. Strategies for specific situations
5. The marketing action plan
6. Control of the plan's implementation

1. THE MARKETING PLAN

1.1 In the last chapter we saw how operational plans have to be developed from the corporate objectives and strategy to ensure a synergy of effort across the organisation. We also considered briefly the structure of the marketing plan.

1.2 In this chapter we will examine in more detail the elements of the marketing plan. Although you will be familiar with the marketing content it is important that you are able to produce realistic and credible marketing plans for your diploma examinations.

1.3 The steps involved in developing a marketing plan are the same as those already examined in depth for the corporate level:

- analysis
- objectives
- strategy
- tactics
- control.

1.4 Kotler identifies the formulation of marketing plans as follows.

(a) *The executive summary*. This is the finalised planning document with a summary of the main goals and recommendations in the plan.

(b) *Situation analysis*. This consists of the SWOT analysis and forecasts which have been referred to earlier in this text.

(c) *Objectives and goals*. What the organisation is hoping to achieve, or needs to achieve, perhaps in terms of market share or 'bottom line' profits and returns.

(d) *Marketing strategy*. This considers the selection of target markets, the marketing mix and marketing expenditure levels.

(e) *Action programme*. This sets out how these various strategies are going to be achieved.

(f) *Budgets* are developed from the action programme.

(g) *Controls*. These will be set up to monitor the progress of the plan and the budget.

Formulating strategy

1.5 A *marketing strategy* may be defined as a plan (usually long term) to achieve the organisation's objectives as follows.

(a) By specifying what resources should be allocated to marketing.

(b) By specifying how those resources should be used to take advantage of opportunities which are expected to arise in the future. (Since the organisation's environment is continually changing, new opportunities will emerge as customer needs alter.)

1.6 In the context of applying the *marketing concept*, a marketing strategy would consist of the following.

(a) Identifying target markets and customer needs in those markets.

(b) Planning products which will satisfy the needs of those markets.

(c) Organising marketing resources, so as to match products with customers in the most efficient and effective way possible, ie so as to maximise customer satisfaction and the organisation's profits or sales revenue (or whatever its objectives are!) at the same time.

1.7 Much marketing planning is based on the concepts of segmentation and product positioning.

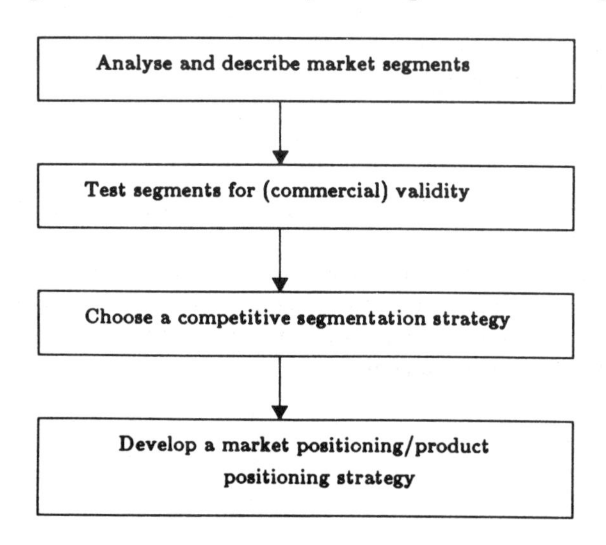

2. MARKET SEGMENTATION

2.1 A market is not a mass, homogeneous group of customers, each wanting an identical product.

> Market segmentation is based on the recognition that every market consists of potential buyers with different needs, and different buying behaviour. These different customer attitudes may be grouped into segments and a different marketing approach will be taken by an organisation for each market segment.

2.2 *Market segmentation* may therefore be defined as 'the subdividing of a market into distinct and increasingly homogeneous subgroups of customers, where any subgroup can conceivably be selected as a target market to be met with a distinct marketing mix'. 'The danger of thinking in terms of single, mass homogeneous markets has been recognised. Market segmentation, as an approach, emerged from the recognition of this danger.' (Tom Cannon *Basic marketing: principles and practice*).

2.3 There are two important elements in this definition of market segmentation.

(a) Although the total market consists of widely different groups of consumers, each group consists of people (or organisations) with common needs and preferences, who perhaps react to 'market stimuli' in much the same way. For example the market for umbrellas might be segmented according to the sex of the consumers; women might seem to prefer umbrellas of different size and weight. The men's market might further be subdivided into age (with some age groups perhaps buying few umbrellas and others buying much more) or occupation (for example professional classes, commuters, golfers). Each sub-division of the market, ie each subsegment etc, will show increasingly common traits. (Golfers, for example, might appear to buy large multi-coloured umbrellas.)

(b) Each market segment can become a target market for a firm, and would require a unique marketing mix if the firm is to exploit it successfully. In other words, recognition of segmentation will enable a company to adopt the proper approach to selling to a given group of potential customers, which will be more successful than an undifferentiating market approach to all customers.

> 'As companies that segment well know, segmentation allows for (1) more precise market definition (2) better analysis of competition (3) rapid response to changing market needs (4) efficient resource allocation and (5) effective strategic planning'. *(Marketing,* Peter D Bennett)

2.4 A total market may occasionally be homogeneous but this is likely to occur only rarely. At one time, for example, the Coca Cola Company successfully sold one type of drink in one bottle size to a mass market (although it has since of course recognised market segments in the soft drinks market). Sometimes consumer differences may exist, but it may be difficult to analyse them into segments. A segmentation approach to marketing succeeds when there are identifiable 'clusters' of consumer wants in the market.

The bases for segmentation

2.5 **An important initial marketing task is the identification of segments within the market.**

There are many different bases on which segments can be analysed; one basis will not be appropriate in every market, and sometimes two or more bases might be valid at the same time. One basis or 'segmentation variable' might be 'superior' to another in a hierarchy of variables; for example market segments may exist on the basis of sex; sub-segments may then be age-group within sex, and sub-subsegments may be geographical region within age group within sex. On the other hand, if a market can be segmented both by marital status (unmarried, married) and by religious sect (say, Protestant and Catholic) then the market might be divisible into a number of separate segments (eg married Protestants; unmarried Protestants; married Catholics and unmarried Catholics), when dealing with individuals or even more if the 'couple' is also considered a unit of its own. The segmentation would thus be: unmarried Protestants; unmarried Catholics; Protestant couples; Catholic couples; mixed couples.

2.6 Segmentation may to some extent be a matter of subjective analysis by marketing management, but typical market segments relate to the following.

(a) *Geographical area:* (the needs and behaviour of potential customers in South East England may differ from those in Scotland or Italy etc). For example commercial radio stations may compete with national radio stations by broadcasting items of local interest; and in the past, the market for beer and cider could be segmented on a regional basis, between for example, the North ('mild' beer) the South (lager) and the South West (cider).

(b) *End use:* for example paper used in offices will vary in quality depending on whether it is used for formal letters and reports, informal working or for typewriter carbon copies. Paper is also bought by consumers, who have their own uses for the product. 'Use' in the consumer market might refer to leisure or work use: for example the men's shirts market can be divided into leisure wear, formal wear and shirts to wear at work etc with suits or jackets.

(c) *Age.* A useful age division might be 0 - 3 years, 4 - 6 years, 7 - 11, 12 - 19, 20 - 34, 35 - 49, 50 - 64 and over 64.

(d) *Sex.*

(e) *Family size or family life cycle:* for example young and single, young and married with no children, with one, two or more children, older and single, older and married with one, two or more children. The age of the children might also be introduced into the segment analysis of the family.

(f) *Income.* The market for housing is partly dependent on income over a period.

(g) *Occupation.* The market for men's suits might be segmented according to occupation.

(h) *Education.* For example segmenting by education may be relevant to the marketing of newspapers.

(i) *Ethnic background.* This might provide a market segment for food or cultural items (imported videos).

(j) *Social class*. The marketing analysis of consumers into socio-economic groupings is an important one because these groupings appear to provide reliable indicators of different consumer attitudes and needs for a wide range of products. More recently developments of computer based models such as ACORN have made this even more specific.

(k) *Life style*. Differences in personality, activities, interests and opinions etc might be condensed into a few categories of life style. It may therefore be possible to segment a market according to these life-style categories (second hand or new motor cars).

(l) *Buyer behaviour*. This includes the usage rate of the product by the buyer, whether purchase will be on impulse, customer loyalty, the sensitivity of the consumer to marketing mix factors, ie price, quality and sales promotion.

(m) *Previous behaviour*. If your previous 'buying' decisions have been recorded, then this itself can be the basis for a marketing effort. For example charities swap mailing lists, so that if you contribute to the Samaritans you might also receive mailshots from Oxfam.

> You should also remember from your early studies that it is important to identify not just the target segment, but also the decision making unit appropriate in that segment.
>
> In both consumer and industrial markets it is often inadequate to talk simply of the consumer (the end user of the product or service). Many others may be involved in the purchase decisions, providing advice, influence, finance or the rationale for the purchase.

2.7 There are other possible bases for segmentation connected with the use or usefulness of the product. The market for various foods, for example, can be segmented into 'convenience foods', for example frozen chips, TV dinners or 'wholesome foods' etc.

Segmentation of the industrial market

2.8 Segmentation applies more obviously to the consumer market, but it can also be applied to an industrial market. An important basis for segmentation is the nature of the customer's business. Accountants or lawyers, for example, might choose to specialise in serving customers in a particular type of business. An accountant may choose to specialise in the accounts of retail businesses, and a firm of solicitors may specialise in conveyancing work for property development companies.

2.9 In much the same way, components manufacturers specialise in the industries of the firms to which they supply components. In the motor car industry, there are companies which specialise in the manufacture of car components, possibly for a single firm.

2.10 It must be stressed that identifying the significant basis or bases for segmentation in any particular market is a matter of 'intuition' or 'interpretation' so that a new company entering a market may be able to identify a potentially profitable target market segment that no other firm has yet recognised.

Testing segment validity

2.11 A market segment will only be valid if it is worth designing and developing a unique marketing mix for that specific segment. Four questions are commonly asked to decide whether or not the segment can be used for developing marketing plans.

(a) *Can the segment be measured*? It might be possible to conceive of a market segment, but it is not necessarily easy to measure it. For example for a segment based on people with a conservative outlook to life, can conservatism of outlook be measured by market research?

(b) *Is the segment big enough?* There has to be a large enough potential market to be profitable.

(c) *Can the segment be reached?* There has to be a way of getting to the potential customers via the organisation's promotion and distribution channels.

(d) *Do segments respond differently?* If two or more segments are identified by marketing planners but each segment responds in the same way to a marketing mix, the segments are effectively one and the same and there is no point in distinguishing them from each other.

Target markets

2.12 Because of limited resources, competition and large markets, organisations are not usually able to sell with equal efficiency and success to the entire market, ie to every market segment. It is necessary for the sake of efficiency to select target markets. The marketing management of a company may choose one of the following policy options.

(a) *Undifferentiated marketing:* this policy is to produce a single product and hope to get as many customers as possible to buy it; segmentation ignored entirely.

(b) *Concentrated marketing:* the company attempts to produce the ideal product for a *single* segment of the market (for example Rolls Royce cars, Mothercare mother and baby shops).

(c) *Differentiated marketing:* the company attempts to introduce several product versions, each aimed at a different market segment (for example the manufacture of different styles of the same article of clothing).

2.13 The major disadvantage of differentiated marketing is the additional costs of marketing and production (more product design and development costs, the loss of economies of scale in production and storage, additional promotion costs and administrative costs etc). When the costs of further differentiation of the market exceed the benefits from further segmentation and target marketing, a firm is said to have 'over-differentiated'. Some firms have tried to overcome this problem by selling the same product to two market segments (for example Johnson's baby powder is sold to many adults for their own use; in the fairly recent past, many hairdressing salons switched from serving women only to serving both sexes).

2.14 The major disadvantage of concentrated marketing is the business risk of relying on a single segment of a single market; for example, the de Lorean sports car firm ran into irreversible financial difficulties in 1981-1982 when the sports car market contracted in the USA. On the other hand, specialisation in a particular market segment can give a firm a profitable, although perhaps temporary, competitive edge over rival firms (for example Kickers specialising in leisure footwear).

2.15 The choice between undifferentiated, differentiated or concentrated marketing as a marketing strategy will depend on the following factors.

(a) The extent to which the product and/or the market may be considered homogeneous. Mass marketing may be 'sufficient' if the market is largely homogeneous (for example safety matches).

(b) The company's resources must not be over extended by differentiated marketing. Small firms may succeed better by concentrating on one segment only.

(c) The product must be sufficiently advanced in its life cycle to have attracted a substantial total market; otherwise segmentation and target marketing is unlikely to be profitable, because each segment would be too small in size.

2.16 The potential benefits of segmentation and target marketing are as follows.

(a) *Product differentiation:* a feature of a particular product might appeal to one segment of the market in such a way that the product is thought better than its rivals. To other customers in different segments of the market, there may be no value in this distinguishing feature, and it would not attempt to buy it in preference to a rival product.

(b) The seller will be more aware of how product design and development may stimulate further demand in a particular area of the market.

(c) The resources of the business will be used more effectively, because the organisation should be more able to make products which the customer wants and will pay for.

3. MARKET POSITIONING

3.1 Target marketing by a company involves the selection of its market (undifferentiated, concentrated or differentiated marketing) and setting as an objective a target share of each market segment (or of the market as a whole, with a policy of undifferentiated marketing).

3.2 If the company wants a leadership position, and cannot lead the entire market, it can attempt to gain the leadership position in a single market segment or in several segments. The market segments selected for a leadership position would ideally have the following characteristics.

(a) There should be potential for future growth.
(b) There should be no direct competitor.
(c) There should be a customer need which is distinct and which can be exploited.
(d) It should be accessible and substantial.

3.3 It is not always possible to identify a market segment where there is no direct competitor, and a marketing problem for the firm will be the creation of some form of product differentiation (real or imagined) in the marketing mix of the product. 'Competitive positioning requires the firm to develop a general idea of what kind of offer to make to the target market in relation to competitors' offers.' (Kotler).

3.4 Theodore Levitt, writing in the Harvard Business Review in September 1965, gave a useful commentary on market positioning in the case of banks.

'. . . no bank can be the best bank for all customers. A bank must choose. It must examine its opportunities and 'take a position' in a market. Positioning goes beyond image-making. The image-making bank seeks to cultivate an image in the customer's mind as a large, friendly or efficient bank . . .. Yet the customer may see the competing banks as basically alike
. . .. Positioning is an attempt to distinguish the bank from its competitors along real dimensions in order to be the preferred bank to certain segments of the market. Positioning aims to help customers know the real differences between competing banks so that they can match themselves to the bank that can be of most value to them.'

Even in high-street banking, there can be differences in service according to cost (ie the cost of services), availability of cash card machines and personal loans, hours of opening etc.

3.5 One simple perceptual map that can be used is to plot brands or competing products in terms of two key characteristics such as price and quality.

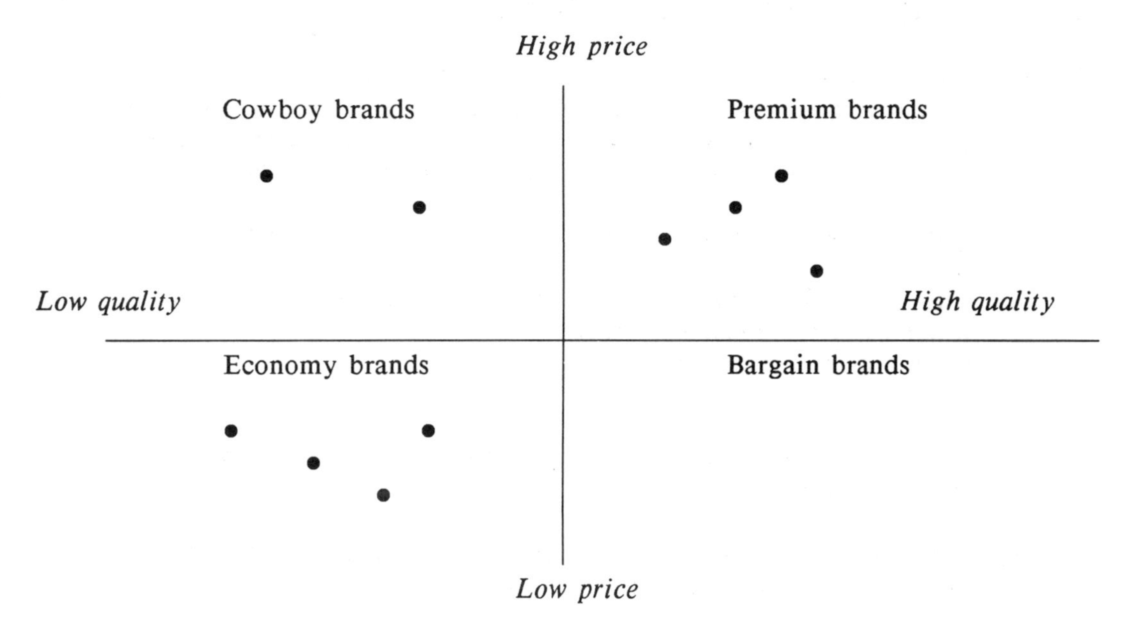

3.6 A perceptual map of market positioning can be used to identify gaps in the market. This example might suggest that there could be potential in the market for a low-price high-quality 'bargain brand'. A company that carries out such an analysis might decide to conduct further research to find out whether there is scope in the market for a new product which would be targeted at a market position where there are few or no rivals.

Competitive positioning

3.7 Competitive positioning concerns 'a general ideal of what kind of offer to make to the target market in relation to competitors' offers' (Kotler). Important considerations in competitive positioning are product quality and price, and Kotler identified a 3 x 3 matrix of nine different competitive positioning strategies. This is a development of the simple 2 x 2 matrix shown in paragraph 3.5.

Product quality	*Product price*		
	High price	*Medium price*	*Low price*
High	Premium strategy	Penetration strategy	Superbargain strategy
Medium	Overpricing strategy	Average-quality strategy	Bargain strategy
Low	Hit-and-run strategy	Shoddy goods strategy	Cheap goods strategy

4. STRATEGIES FOR SPECIFIC SITUATIONS

4.1 Strategy formulation follows on from the situation analysis and deciding objectives, and the choice of strategies will obviously depend on what the organisation's current and forecast situation is. As a general guide to competitive strategy, it might be helpful to list certain points that might be relevant in the following specific situations.

(a) When an industry is threatened by fragmentation into increasing numbers of market segments.
(b) When a new industry/market is emerging and growing.
(c) When a market is reaching maturity.
(d) When a market is in decline.

4.2 Before reading the remainder of this section it will be useful to remind yourself of the following two facts.

(a) Entry into a market or growth in market share can be achieved by organic growth or by takeovers, or a combination of the two.

(b) Pulling out of a market can involve the sale of a business as a going concern, or else by the closure of operations, redundancies in the workforce, and the sale of the individual assets on a 'break-up' basis.

Fragmented industries and market segmentation

4.3 The fragmentation of industries and proliferation of market segments tends to occur when the following conditions apply.

(a) There are low entry barriers, and so new firms can enter the market relatively easily.
(b) There are few economies of scale or learning curve effects, and so it is difficult for big firms to establish a significant overall cost leadership.
(c) Transport and distribution costs are high, and so the industry fragments on a geographical basis.
(d) Customer needs vary widely.
(e) There are rapid product changes or style changes, which small firms might succeed in reacting to more quickly than large firms.

(f) There is a highly diverse product line, so that some firms are able to specialise in one part of the industry.

(g) There is scope for product differentiation, based on product design/quality differences or even brand image.

4.4 If an organisation operates in an industry which is beginning to fragment further, it must make certain strategic choices.

(a) *Does it want to prevent fragmentation?*

(i) If the answer is yes, because the organisation expects to benefit from holding a large share of an undifferentiated market, then it should:

(1) consider whether economies of scale or learning curve benefits are achievable. If so, it should aim to become overall cost leader, and produce a low-price standard product. The acquisition of a competitor might be necessary to build up the required 'critical mass' to benefit from economies of scale;

(2) consider ways of standardising customer needs, perhaps by *adjusting the product* to suit the tastes of different types of customer.

(ii) If the answer is no, the organisation must consider its strategy for fragmentation.

(b) *How can fragmentation and segmentation be planned for?* The answer to this question is that the organisation must decide on its strategic positioning in the industry - ie must select the market segments it wishes to develop, and what market share of each segment it will aim to achieve. The organisation must choose how it will specialise:

(i) by product type or segment;
(ii) by customer type;
(iii) by geographical area;
(iv) by type of order (for example small orders, or big orders only);
(v) low prices for a basic product.

4.5 The organisational implications of a fragmentation strategy might be that there is a need to decentralise the organisation, and give more decision-making authority to product-market divisions.

Growth industries and markets

4.6 There are a number of problems facing an organisation that is planning to compete in an emerging industry.

(a) There will be uncertainty about how technology is going to develop. Products will be non-standard, and of variable quality. Customers will probably be confused about what they want from the product in terms of quality, performance and price, and there is also a likelihood of rapid obsolescence as the technology and customer needs develop.

(b) There will be uncertainty about the strategy that competitors will adopt.

(c) There is a likelihood that new companies will emerge to compete in the industry.

(d) There will be high initial costs (capital investment, initial advertising and sales promotion etc) although unit costs should eventually fall rapidly.

4.7 Customers will be first-time buyers of the product, and there might be a difficult task in persuading them to buy the product. Developing a suitable marketing mix will be crucially important.

4.8 There will be barriers to entry into the new market.

(a) Firms already in the market might have a patent in the product technology.
(b) Getting access to adequate distribution channels might be difficult.
(c) There may also be difficulties in getting access to sources of raw materials or labour of the right quality and at a reasonable price.
(d) Firms already in the industry might already have built up certain cost advantages through learning curve benefits.
(e) The investment in a new industry will be risky and the organisation will be looking for the promise of a high return to compensate for the risk.

4.9 An organisation will have to make estimates of the future growth in the market, the market share it might achieve and the potential profitability.

4.10 Strategic decisions facing an organisation in this situation include the following.

(a) *Timing* its entry into the industry. The longer an organisation waits, the more it might have to catch up on competitors, but the less the uncertainties should be about how the industry is developing.

(b) Deciding how to cope with *competition*. Should there be co-operation between competitors, in developing product technology and building up total market demand? This is essential to a feature of the Japanese methods of marketing.Or should there be aggressive competition and product differentiation from the outset? This has been a problem the computer industry has had to cope with, given the choice between the following.

(i) Co-operation between producers in developing equipment that is compatible with the hardware of other producers; in doing so, the total market demand for computer hardware would build up more quickly. This is evident in the growth of the microcomputer market.

(ii) Developing individual product technologies so that the hardware of one producer is incompatible with the hardware of another. This was evident in the development of mainframe computers.

Industries reaching maturity

4.11 The features of a mature industry and market can be listed as follows.

(a) A slow-down in growth, and so bigger competition for market share.
(b) The customers are repeat-buyers who know what they want from the product.
(c) Competition between firms will be based more on price and service, rather than further product differentiation.

(d) International competition might be increasing.
(e) New product developments for the industry are harder to come by.

An organisation in a mature market will have to expect that lower growth will result in a slow down in profit growth, and perhaps some decline in profits because the competition for market share will squeeze profit margins and raise marketing costs. The organisation might have to make a critical choice between a strategy of overall cost leadership, or creating a differentiated product and segmenting the market. Controls over productivity will also be important.

Industries entering decline

4.12 Decline is caused by technological change which makes existing products obsolete, by changing customer needs, or even by a reduction in the total number of potential customers (for example a regional market would go into decline if the local population dwindled in size).

4.13 The decline phase of an industry's life is characterised by falling sales, falling profit margins, a dwindling product line and a sharp cut-back on R & D and advertising. Porter has written as follows.

'The accepted strategic prescription for decline is a 'harvest' strategy, that is, eliminating investment and generating maximum cash flow from the business, followed by eventual divestment.'

4.14 Alternative strategies in a declining industry, referred to in an earlier chapter on product and market development, are as follows.

(a) *A leadership strategy:* seek market share leadership in the declining industry, and so achieve a reasonable return.

(b) *A niche strategy:* create and defend a strong market position in a segment of the market that is not declining, or declining slowly.

(c) *Quick divestment.*

4.15 The choice of strategy may depend on the following.

(a) Estimates of how quickly the industry will decline (or demand for an individual product will decline).

(b) The cost of pulling out of the market, ie exit barriers.

Improving the performance of an existing product

4.16 If the analysis of existing products suggests that a product has performed badly, for example it has a small market share in a growing market, or costs too much to produce, or is entering into the decline stage of its life cycle, the formulation of a strategy for the individual product might have to consider a variety of alternative options, such as the following.

(a) *Repositioning:* moving the product or brand into a different market segment (for example move up-market, down-market, into a specialist market etc).

(b) *Brand extension:* adding new brand names to the same product in order to widen the overall appeal of the product.

(c) Varying the total marketing expenditure level, or the amount spent on one particular product.

(d) Changing the marketing mix.

5. THE MARKETING ACTION PLAN

5.1 The link between the formulation and the implementation of marketing strategy is the marketing action plan. This is illustrated in the table on the following page.

5.2 The marketing mix is defined by Kotler as 'the set of controllable variables and their levels that the firm uses to influence the target market.' It is of prime importance to marketing management because it represents the *controlled* use of a firm's resources allocated to the marketing budget. The marketing mix choices will be reviewed briefly in the next chapter.

The marketing mix may be simplified into the four Ps.

(a) *Product:* factors concerning the product or service offered are quality, features, fashion, packaging and branding, after sales service, guarantees, durability etc.

(b) *Price:* factors concerning price include not only the level of price, but also credit terms, bulk purchase discounts, discounts for early payment, trade-in allowances etc.

(c) *Place:* factors here include the location of sales outlets and the number and type of sales outlets (shops, supermarkets etc), the location of service departments, stock levels and transportation and delivery services.

(d) *Promotion:* sales promotion includes the work of the sales team, advertising, merchandising and publicity.

5.3 Different marketing mixes will appeal to different market segments in any particular market. In addition to the items listed in (a) to (d) above, we could also add the need to obtain information about consumer preferences; and to forecast the likely demand for a product. A further element in the marketing budget will therefore be expenditure on *market research.*

5.4 The marketing mix for a product must be planned. It should also be reviewed in the light of experience and, if product sales have not been as good as expected, some thought should be given to changing the mix, for example lowering product quality, reducing price and spending more on advertising.

A more detailed marketing plan

5.5 The marketing plan in detail consists of several inter-related parts.

(a) Sales targets: these must be set for each product and each sales division (with sub-targets also set for sales regions, sales areas and individual salespeople). Sales targets may be referred to as sales quotas.

(b) The total marketing budget must be set.

(c) Given an overall marketing budget, resources (cash) must be allocated between:
   (i) salaries of salespeople;
   (ii) above the line expenditure (advertising);
   (iii) below the line expenditure (sales promotion items, price reduction allowances, etc).

(d) The overall sales target set by top management will incorporate *sales price decisions*; but within the formulation of the marketing plan there is likely to be some room for manoeuvre and an element of choice in the pricing decision. In other words, top management will decide on a 'rough pricing zone' and a specific price within this zone will be fixed later within the marketing plan.

(e) Expenditure on marketing will also be allocated to different products or services within the organisation's product or service range. Some products might justify additional marketing expenditure; whereas others, nearing the end of their life cycle, may lose a part of their previous allocation.

The marketing budget

5.6 Strategic marketing decisions are an integral part of the corporate plan. Top management must set an overall sales strategy and a series of sales objectives; only then should a more detailed marketing plan be prepared.

5.7 There are three types of annual budget planning for a marketing budget.

(a) Top-down planning involves the setting of goals for lower management by higher management.

(b) Bottom-up planning exists where employees set their own goals and submit them to higher management for approval.

(c) 'Goals down - plans up' planning is a mixture of the two styles, whereby top management sets overall goals and employees lower in the organisation hierarchy then set plans for achieving those goals. This type of planning is well suited to the formulation of sales budgets.

5.8 Budgeting for sales revenue and selling costs is plagued with uncertainty. The variables are so many and so difficult to estimate, even within a wide tolerance (largely because of competitive action and changing consumer habits and tastes) that both setting budgets and budgetary control on the marketing side are different from the more 'mechanical' approach which can be adopted with other budgets.

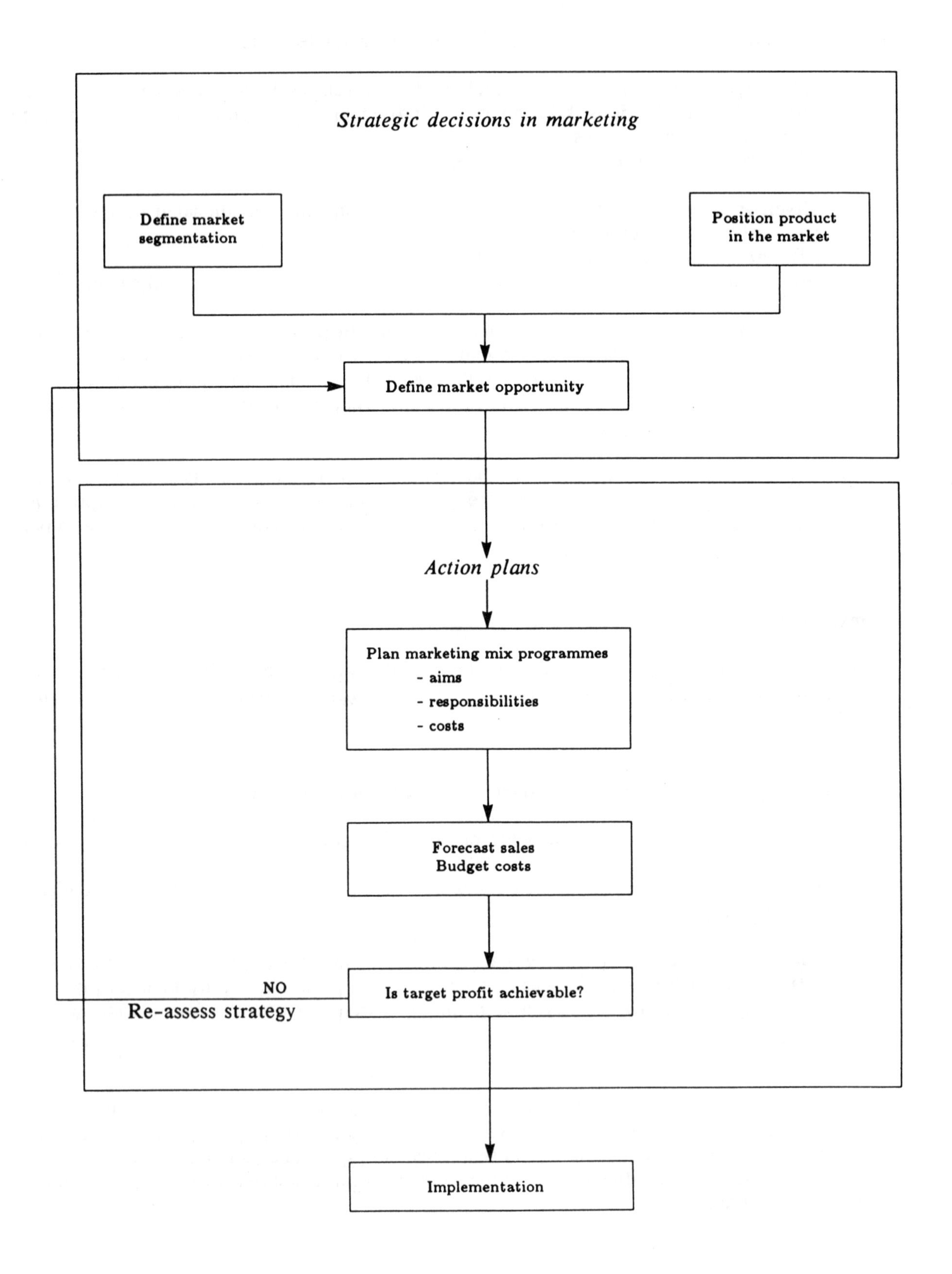
Strategic decisions in marketing
Define market segmentation
Position product in the market
Define market opportunity
Action plans
Plan marketing mix programmes
- aims
- responsibilities
- costs
Forecast sales
Budget costs
Is target profit achievable?
NO
Re-assess strategy
Implementation

5.9 It is plainly unsatisfactory to engage in minute cost-control systems in production, and then hope that all other costs (such as research, distribution, sales) will look after themselves. A sales and marketing budget is necessary for the following reasons.

(a) It is an element of the overall strategic plan of the business (the master budget) which brings together all the activities of the business.

(b) Where sales and other non-production costs are a large part of total costs, it is financially prudent to forecast, plan and control them.

(c) The very uncertain nature of factors which influence selling makes the need for good forecasts and plans greater, and it can be argued that if budgets are to be used for control, the more uncertain the budget estimates are, the more budgetary control is necessary.

Matching forecast demand with estimated available capacity

5.10 One of the problems in setting budgets is matching the forecast demand from customers with the estimated available capacity. There are three aspects to this problem as follows.

(a) It is difficult to make an accurate forecast of demand.

(b) It is difficult to predict available capacity accurately too, given uncertainties about the following.

(i) Efficiency and productivity levels.
(ii) The availability of staff, or cash.
(iii) The likely down-time or time lost through industrial action.
(iv) Whether overtime or double-shift working will be available.
(v) The likelihood that changes in equipment (for example introduction of new equipment and replacement equipment) will take place in the budget period.

(c) There are often practical difficulties in matching demand with capacity. Demand might be seasonal, and if services or non-standard products are required, it will not be possible to build up inventories in periods of slack demand in anticipation of periods of high demand.

5.11 In order to match demand with capacity, management must be flexible, and be prepared to take action to achieve the following.

(a) To suppress demand if it exceeds capacity, for example by raising prices.

(b) To stimulate demand if there is excess capacity, for example by advertising or price reductions.

(c) To reduce excess capacity by selling off surplus assets.

(d) To supplement production when there is under-capacity by sub-contracting work to other organisations, and perhaps to take steps to increase capacity (by acquiring new premises, equipment and labour, or by negotiating for more overtime from existing employees).

The advertising budget decision

5.12 This is an important feature of the marketing budget. The theory behind setting an advertising budget is the theory of diminishing returns, ie for every extra £1 of advertising spent, the company will earn an extra £x of profit. Further expenditure on advertising is justified until the marginal return £x diminishes to the point where £x < £1.

Unfortunately, the marginal return from additional advertising cannot be measured easily in practice for the following reasons.

(a) Advertising is only one aspect of the overall marketing mix.

(b) Advertising has some long-term effect, which goes beyond the limits of a measurable accounting period.

(c) Where the advertising budget is fixed as a percentage of sales, advertising costs tend to follow sales levels and not vice versa.

5.13 Research has shown that in the UK, most advertising budgets are fixed by some rule-of-thumb, non-scientific methods, such as the following.

(a) A percentage of the previous year's sales.
(b) A percentage of the budgeted annual sales.
(c) A percentage of the previous year's profit.

There is no reason, however, why advertising costs should relate directly to either total turnover or profits. Given that large amounts of expenditure may be incurred on advertising, these arbitrary guesswork systems reveal an alarming lack of proper financial control and an equally alarming lack of understanding of the nature of advertising's impact on the purchase decision.

5.14 Other methods of setting the advertising budget include the following.

(a) *Competitive parity*, ie fixing advertising expenditure in relation to the expenditure incurred by competitors. (This is unsatisfactory because it presupposes that the competitor's decision must be a good one).

(b) The *task method (or objective and task method)*. The marketing task for the organisation is set and an advertising budget is prepared which will help to ensure that this objective is achieved. A problem occurs if the objective is achieved only by paying out more on advertising than the extra profits obtained would justify.

(c) *Communication stage models*. These are based on the idea that the link between advertising and sales cannot be measured directly, but can be measured by means of intermediate stages (for example increase in awareness, comprehension, and then intention to buy). An example of such a model is Colley's *DAGMAR* model (Defining Advertising Goals for Measured Advertising Results). A major problem with the use of such models is that it is not yet clear how the use of indices of customer opinion will enable management to set an effective advertising budget.

(d) *All you can afford*. Crude and unscientific, but commonly used. The firm simply takes a view on what it thinks it can afford to spend on advertising given that it would like to spend as much as it can.

5.15 Recommended practice for fixing advertising cost budgets would be the use of the following.

(a) Empirical testing (for example in a mail order business or in retail operations). It may be possible to measure the effect of advertising on sales by direct observation.

(b) Mathematical models using data about media and consumer characteristics, desired market share, and using records of past results. Regression analysis can be conducted to find out the likely cost of advertising (through several media) to achieve a given target.

6. CONTROL OF THE PLAN'S IMPLEMENTATION

6.1 Once the plan has been implemented, the task of management is to control the use of resources. Aspects of control include the following.

(a) A comparison of actual sales against the budget.

(b) A comparison of actual marketing costs against the budgeted expenditure levels and against actual sales.

(c) Analysis of the profitability of individual products, and distribution outlets.

(d) Strategic control, ie checking whether the company's objectives, products and resources are being directed towards the correct markets.

6.2 Control will be dealt with more fully in a later chapter, but two aspects of strategic controls that will be mentioned here are the problems with apportioning shared costs, and marketing audits.

Allocation of costs

6.3 The allocation of direct selling costs to products, or type of outlet, etc is fairly straightforward, but indirect costs must be allocated on an arbitrary basis (for example to products by value of sales). This aspect of cost allocation should be carefully considered when deciding whether to eliminate an unprofitable expenditure from selling or distribution.

(a) The cost of distributing goods to a distant area may seem unprofitable; but if, by not selling the goods in this area, there will be unused production capacity, the products which are produced and sold will have to bear a higher proportion of fixed costs.

(b) The allocation of fixed selling costs to products may make a product seem unprofitable, but the product may still be making a contribution to those fixed costs.

6.4 Eliminating unprofitable selling and distribution expenditure is sound commercial practice, but the concept of avoidable and unavoidable costs should be used in deciding what is unprofitable. If the removal of one part of selling costs relieves a company of a cost which is higher than the contribution to profit gained from it, then this part of selling activity can and should be eliminated. The unavoidable fixed costs of production as well as selling and distribution should be taken into account in any such decision.

Marketing audits

6.5 Top management is responsible for ensuring that the company is pursuing optimal policies with regard to its products, markets and distribution channels. Carrying out this responsibility is known as strategic control of marketing, and the means to apply strategic control is the marketing audit.

> 'A marketing audit is a *comprehensive, systematic, independent and periodic* examination of a company's - or business unit's - marketing environment, objectives, strategies and activities with a view of determining problem areas and opportunities and recommending a plan of action to improve the company's marketing performance.'
> (Kotler, Gregor and Rodgers, 1977)

6.6 A marketing audit does not exist in the compulsory formal sense that an external financial audit does. For proper strategic control, however, a marketing audit should have the following features.

(a) It should be conducted *regularly*, for example once a year.

(b) It should take a *comprehensive* look at every product, market, distribution channel, ingredient in the marketing mix etc. It should not be restricted to areas of apparent ineffectiveness (for example an unprofitable product, a troublesome distribution channel, low efficiency on direct selling etc).

(c) It should be carried out according to a set of predetermined, specified procedures, ie it should be *systematic*.

The audit procedure

6.7 Marketing audits have been covered in more detail in an earlier chapter. To recap however, a marketing audit should consider the following areas.

(a) *The marketing environment*
- (i) What are the organisation's major markets, and what is the segmentation of these markets; what are the future prospects of each market segment?
- (ii) Who are the customers, what is known about customer needs, intentions and behaviour?
- (iii) Who are the competitors, and what is their standing in the market?
- (iv) Have there been any significant developments in the broader environment (for example economic, or political changes, population or social changes etc).

(b) *Marketing objectives, strategies and plans*
- (i) What are the organisation's marketing objectives and how do they relate to overall objectives? Are they reasonable?
- (ii) Are enough (or too many) resources being committed to marketing to enable the objectives to be achieved; is the division of costs between products, areas etc satisfactory?
- (iii) Is the share of expenditure between direct selling, advertising, distribution etc an optimal one?
- (iv) What are the procedures for formulating marketing plans and management control of these plans; are they satisfactory?
- (v) Is the marketing organisation (and its personnel) operating efficiently?

(c) *Marketing activities: organisation, systems and productivity*
   (i) A review of sales price levels should be made (for example supply and demand, customer attitudes, the use of temporary price reductions etc).
   (ii) A review of the state of each individual product (ie its market 'health') and of the product mix as a whole should be made.
   (iii) A critical analysis of the distribution system should be made, with a view to finding improvements.
   (iv) The size and organisation of the personal sales force should be studied, with a view to deciding whether efficiency should be improved (and how this could be done).
   (v) A review of the effectiveness of advertising and sales promotion activities should be carried out.

6.8 The marketing audit for control brings us back round to situation analysis for marketing planning, and the cycle of planning and control should be continuous.

7. CONCLUSION

7.1 The steps in marketing planning can be defined as follows.

(a) Analysis of the current situation and forecasting based on the current situation.

(b) Identification of objectives.

(c) The formulation of strategies and plans to meet the stated objectives. Marketing strategies should recognise target markets, market segments, target market position, the state of the market (growth, decline etc).

(d) Control to ensure that plans are achieved.

7.2 As a final conclusion to this chapter, we will bring together all of the points covered in an example. See what your ideas would be for a marketing strategy in the following example of an institute of higher education.

> 'An Institution of Higher Education is concerned at a falling trend in applications. What steps should it take to develop a strategy to halt this trend?'

Suggested outline solution

7.3 *Step 1: Analysis*

The reasons for the falling trend in applications should be discovered. Possible reasons might be as follows.

(a) The courses are no longer attractive to students, because their content or quality is not up to the standard expected by them.

(b) Other institutions of higher education, with a higher academic status, are beginning to offer similar courses.

(c) The qualifications students obtain are no longer sufficient to guarantee graduates a job at the end of the course.

(d) The costs of the course are now so high that they deter applicants.

(e) The size of the target market is falling.

7.4 *Step 2: Objective*

The Institution's objective is assumed to be to improve the appeal of its courses, and so to increase applications by a targeted quantity, ie to maintain next years' enrolments at year x level.

7.5 *Step 3: Strategy*

Having identified the probable reasons for declining applications and an objective for strategic planning, the Institution can begin to develop a strategy to improve the situation, insofar as it has the power to do so (for example the costs of courses might be controlled by government, not by the Institution itself).

(a) If the courses have an inadequate content or quality, new or improved courses must be designed. Student needs should be investigated.

   (i) What sort of courses do they need? Both the structure of the courses (full time, block release, day release etc) and academic content should be reviewed.

   (ii) What quality of teaching (and teaching equipment) is required? If existing staff are unable to teach the subjects required, some re-planning or re-training of manpower will be necessary.

   The product should be capable of satisfying student needs before it can be sold.

(b) If qualifications are no longer sufficient to guarantee graduates a job, the needs of potential employers should also be investigated. Courses should be designed so as to produce graduates whom employers would prefer to recruit in preference to other people with different qualifications, or even with no qualifications at all.

7.6 Any new courses which are designed must conform to the objectives of the Institution, ie to offer education of a particular type and standard.

7.7 *Step 4: More detailed planning*

Having identified student needs and employer needs, the next step in a marketing strategy should be as follows.

(a) Design courses to suit customer needs better.

(b) Allocate marketing resources to a campaign to attract applicants. Possible elements in a marketing mix would be as follows.
   (i) Better advertising or communication. If students are recruited from schools, better information about courses should be supplied to schools careers advice staff etc.
   (ii) Lower prices.
   (iii) Improving the quality image of the Institution's academic standards, perhaps through the acquisition of new staff or facilities.

7.8 *Step 5: Control*

Any marketing strategy should have a quantified target (for example to raise applications by x% per annum for the next five years) and there should be some procedure or *control mechanism* whereby actual results are monitored, compared against the strategic plan, and evaluated.

TEST YOUR KNOWLEDGE

The numbers in brackets refer to paragraphs of this chapter

1. What are the steps involved in developing a marketing plan? (1.3)
2. Suggest six ways in which markets could be segmented. (2.6)
3. What are the criteria for a useful segment? (2.11)
4. What are the three policy options in selecting target markets? (2.12)
5. What is market positioning? (3.3, 3.4)
6. What strategies could a firm adopt in a declining industry? (4.13, 4.14)
7. Describe how advertising budgets might be set. (5.13 to 5.15)
8. What is a marketing audit? (6.5)

Now try illustrative questions 12 and 13

Chapter 11

THE MARKETING MIX

This chapter covers the following topics.

1. The marketing mix
2. Product
3. Price
4. Place
5. Promotion

1. THE MARKETING MIX

1.1 In the last chapter we considered the process of marketing planning. The marketing mix decisions are an important part of marketing action plans and at Diploma level you will be expected to be familiar with the strategic choices involved at these more tactical levels. This chapter provides an overview of the marketing mix issues which need to be considered the developing the marketing strategy. You should already be familiar with much of this marketing detail from your earlier studies.

1.2 The term 'marketing mix' was coined by Borden of the Harvard Business School to show the range of marketing decisions and elements which must be balanced to achieve maximum effect. 'The marketing mix refers to the apportionment of effort, the combination, the designing, and the integration of elements of marketing into a program or 'mix' which on an appraisal of the market forces, will best achieve the objectives of an enterprise at a given time.' (N H Borden). Thus, according to Borden, the marketing manager is 'a mixer of ingredients, one who is constantly engaged in fashioning creatively a mix of marketing procedures and policies to produce a profitable enterprise.'

1.3 Kotler defines it more briefly as follows. 'Marketing mix is the set of controllable variables and their levels that the firm uses to influence the target market.' McCarthy's definition of marketing mix as the four Ps of product, place, price and promotion is the convenient way we categorise the marketing mix.

(a) *Product*. The success of a new product will be improved if the product has certain distinguishing characteristics and features.

(i) If it is an innovative product, it must appeal to certain consumer needs in a way that no other product can do as well.

(ii) If there are rival products, it should have features which give it some edge, such as a better quality/price mix, new technology or be 'environmentally' safe etc. In the case of some products (for example cars) a favourable product report in a consumer magazine could be very important for a new product.

(b) *Place.* The producer must plan for the availability of the product, and the distribution channels to be used. The product must be readily available where consumers would expect to find it. A new product launch should therefore not take place until adequate stocks have been built up to meet anticipated demand.

(c) *Price.* If the consumer's buying decisions are strongly influenced by price factors, a new product must be launched:

(i) at an attractive price;
(ii) where appropriate, with suitable available credit facilities (for example as with household furniture).

(d) *Promotion.* Advertising and sales promotion are critical aspects of a successful product launch, to build up customer awareness. Depending on the nature of the product, factors to be taken into account should be as follows.

(i) The scope of advertising and the advertising message.
(ii) Special sales promotions when the product is first launched.
(iii) Brand image.
(iv) Coinciding the product launch with the date of an important exhibition (for example a well publicised Motor Show).

Elements in the marketing mix

1.4 Elements in the marketing mix can be listed as follows.

(a) The *selling mix,* which consists of:
(i) advertising;
(ii) special promotions;
(iii) branding;
(iv) packaging;
(v) personal selling;
(vi) dealer relationships;
(vii) merchandising;
(viii) distribution policy.

(b) The balance between a 'push' and a 'pull' policy of selling.

(i) A *push* policy is concerned with moving goods out to wholesalers and retailers who then have the task of selling to customers, ie getting dealers to accept goods.

(ii) A *pull* policy is one of influencing final consumer attitudes so that a consumer demand is created which dealers are obliged to satisfy; a pull policy usually involves heavy expenditure on advertising, but holds the promise of stimulating a much higher demand.

(iii) A proper balance between 'push' and 'pull' is necessary to optimise sales.

(c) Price policy including discounts.

(d) Product design and quality.

(e) Credit policy.

(f) After sales service.

1.5 It might be useful to consider some examples of how the marketing mix might be variable.

(a) A manufacturer of chairs might wish to sell to both the consumer market and the industrial market for office furniture. The marketing mix selected for the consumer market might be low prices with attractive dealer discounts, sales largely through discount warehouses, modern design but fairly low quality and sales promotion relying on advertising by the retail outlets, together with personal selling by the manufacturing firm to the reseller. For the industrial market, the firm might develop a durable, robust product which sells at a higher price; selling may be by means of direct mail-shots, backed by personal visits from salespeople.

(b) An interesting comparison can be made between different firms in the same industry; for example, Avon and Yardley both sell cosmetics, but whereas Avon relies on personal selling in the consumer's own home, Yardley rely on an extensive dealer network and heavy advertising expenditure.

Choosing the marketing mix

1.6 The 'design' of the marketing mix will be decided on the basis of management intuition and judgement, together with information provided by marketing research. It is particularly important that management should be able to understand the image of the product in the eyes of the customer, and the reasons which make customers buy a particular product. As an example, a newspaper publisher must try to understand the image of its paper; thus the Financial Times tries to sell on the basis of well-informed opinions on world and financial affairs, the Guardian tries to sell on the basis of lively and witty reporting, and the Sun has prospered on its 'page three' image.

1.7 It is nevertheless likely to be the case that elements in the marketing mix act as substitutes for each other. For example, a firm can raise the selling price of its products if it also raises product quality or advertising expenditure; equally, a firm can perhaps reduce its sales promotion expenditure if it is successful in achieving a wider range and larger numbers of sales outlets for its product, etc. Kotler suggests that the rate of 'substitutability' to achieve a given volume of sales is variable.

1.8 If a firm has a fixed marketing budget which it can use to offer price discounts or spend on advertising, there will obviously be different combinations of expenditure-sharing which are possible; however, for every £1 extra spent on advertising and taken away from the sales discounts budget, the effect on sales volumes will be subject to increasing and then diminishing returns. The diagram shows the possible combinations of price discounts and advertising expenditure on the budget line BB. The iso-sales curves I_1 I_2 and I_3 show the different combinations of price discounts and advertising expenditure which will achieve a given sales volume.

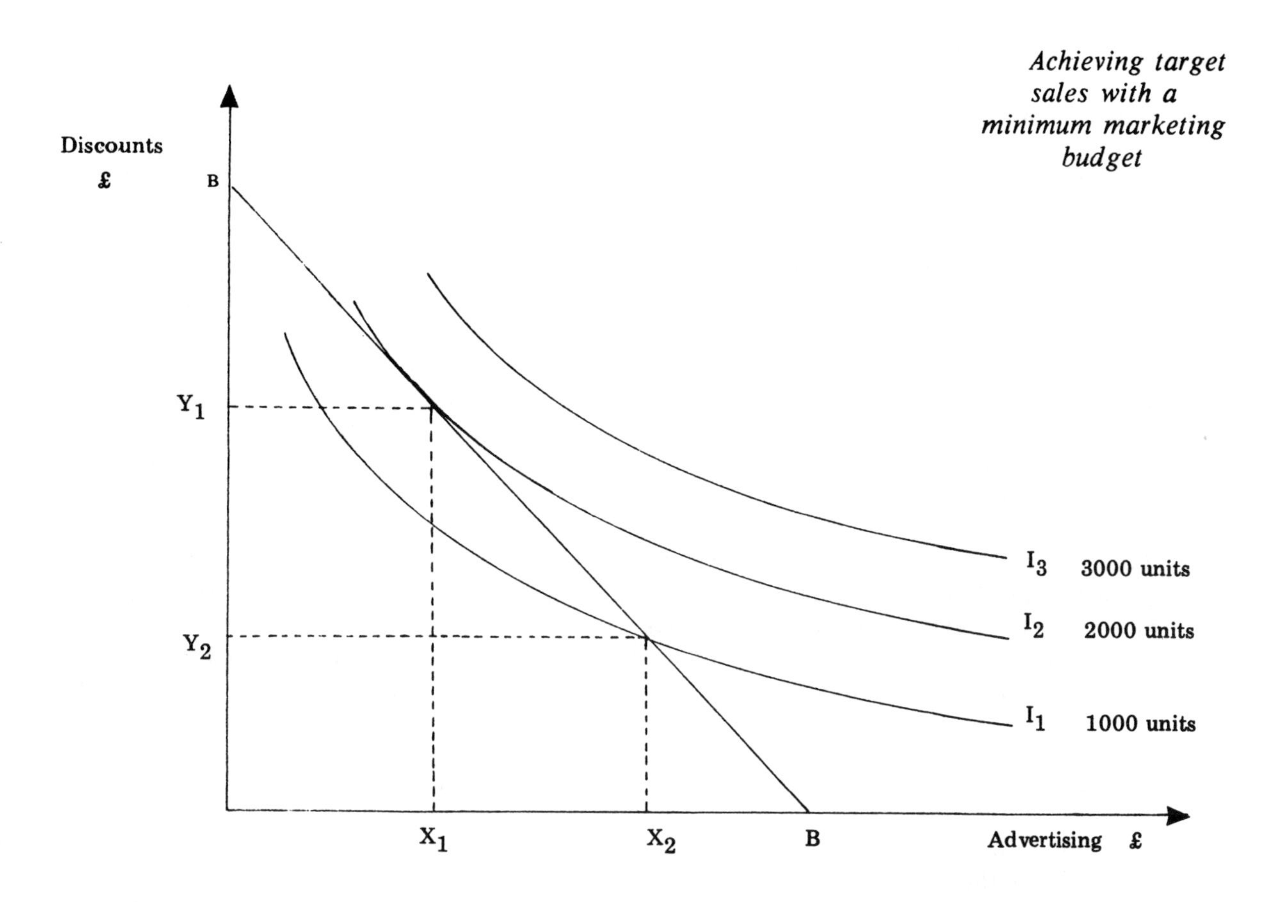

1.9 Suppose that a firm wants to sell 2,000 units of a product, but has a limited marketing budget. The budget line BB shows that marketing expenditure will be insufficient to sell 3,000 units; but is sufficient to sell up to 2,000 units. Y_1 spent on discounts and X_1 on advertising will provide a mix capable of selling 2,000 units, whereas a mix of Y_2 and X_2, with the same total marketing cost, would only sell 1,000 units. The optimal marketing mix to achieve 2,000 units of sale is therefore Y_1, X_1.

1.10 The stages in the formulation of a marketing mix might be as follows.

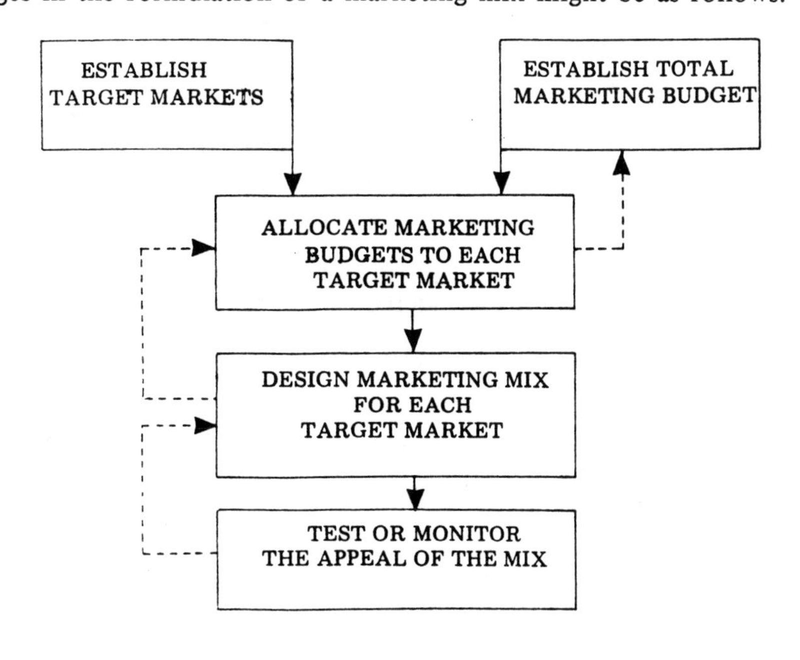

Other aspects of the marketing mix

1.11 Other aspects of the marketing mix design which should be noted are as follows.

(a) A manufacturer of consumer goods will need a marketing mix for the consumer, and an additional marketing mix for the resellers.

(b) The optimum marketing mix will change over time as the marketing environment changes. The growth of discount stores and warehouses, for example, might persuade some manufacturers to switch to lower prices for selling through these outlets. The time of year might also be relevant to the mix; manufacturers of fires and central heating equipment might have to reduce prices in the summer months, and increase advertising expenditure but reduce the product range on offer in order to achieve a reasonably profitable sales volume. In a recession, some manufacturers (for example home improvements) might develop a stronger policy of door to door selling and mailshots, etc.

(c) The marketing mix will also change over time as the product goes into different stages of its life cycle. When a product is in its 'growth' stages of life, the marketing mix might emphasise the development of sales outlets and advertising, in its 'mature' phase, there might need to be more concern for product quality, and to postpone the eventual decline, it may be necessary to reduce prices and spend more on advertising.

1.12 The ideal marketing mix is one which holds a proper balance between each of these elements.

(a) One marketing activity in the mix will not be fully effective unless proper attention is given to all the other activities. For example if a company launches a costly sales promotion campaign which emphasises the superior quality of a product, the outlay on advertising, packaging and personal selling will be wasted if the quality does not live up to customer expectations. Expensive packaging and advertising will be wasted if distribution inefficiency reduces the availability of goods to the consumer, or the price is too high to attract buyers.

(b) A company might also place too much emphasis on one aspect of the marketing mix, and much of the effort and expenditure might not be justified for the additional returns it obtains. It might for example, place too much importance on price reductions to earn higher profits, when in fact a smaller price reduction and greater spending on sales promotion or product design might have a more profitable effect.

1.13 The marketing mix must be customer orientated and the main principle behind the marketing mix (and the smaller selling mix) is that the arrangement and allocation of resources should be such as to maximise returns per unit of outlay.

1.14 The ideal mix for a convenience good (requiring a heavy emphasis on distribution and sales promotion) will be different from that for an industrial good (where price, design, quality and after-sales service are more important).

2. PRODUCT

2.1 The role of product in the marketing mix involves developing products of the right quality that customers will want to buy, ie product design, development and testing, the recognition of the product life cycle, and ensuring that products are made to the intended quality.

Quality policy

2.2 This is an important policy consideration. The mix of price and quuality in a target market strategy is important in the product's positioning. Customers do not necessarily want the best quality of goods, and there may be a market potential for a lower quality as well as a higher quality article. When a market is dominated by established brand names, a means of getting into a market might be to tap the potential demand for a lower quality (cheaper, or fashion) item.

2.3 Customers do not always know properly what they are buying, and tend to judge the quality of an article by its price. One aspect of quality policy may therefore be to decide a price and then manufacture a product to the best quality standard that can be achieved for the price, ie rather than making a product of a certain quality and then deciding what its price should be.

2.4 Quality should also be determined by the expected physical, technological and social life of the product for the following reasons.

(a) There is no value in making one part of a product good enough to have a physical life of five years, when the rest of the product will wear out and be irreplaceable within two years (unless this part with the longer life has an emotional or irrational appeal to customers, for example a leather covering may be preferred to plastic).

(b) If technological advances will make a product obsolete within a certain number of years, there is little value in producing an article which will last for a longer time.

(c) If social tastes determine the life of a product, the quality required need only be sufficient to cover the period of demand; the quality of fashion clothes, for example, is usually governed by their fashion life.

2.5 Quality policy must be carefully integrated with sales promotion, which will have poor success if a product is branded and advertised as having a certain quality which customers then find is not actually true. The quality of a product (involving its design, production standards, quality control and after-sales service) must be properly established and maintained before a sales promotion campaign can use it as a selling feature.

3. PRICE

3.1 Price is another element in the marketing mix that needs a great deal of attention. Prices must be competitive and consistent with image but high enough to cover costs and maximise demand given the stage of the product life cycle.

3.2 As a general point products will not sell unless they are priced in such a way that customers are prepared to buy them. This has the following implications.

(a) Pricing should be consistent with making the required profits at the expected level of demand.
(b) A suitable balance should be found between price and quality.
(c) Prices should be reviewed in the context of a product's stage in its life cycle.
(d) Pricing should be consistent for the organisation's product range.

Elasticity of demand

3.3 The concept of price elasticity is important. You may remember from your earlier economics studies that price elasticity is measured as

$$\frac{\text{\% change in sales demand}}{\text{\% change in sales price}}$$

(a) When elasticity is greater than 1 (ie elastic), a change in price will lead to a change in total revenue so that the following statements apply.

   (i) If the price is lowered, total sales revenue would rise, because of the large increase in demand.
   (ii) If the price is raised, total sales revenue would fall because of the large fall in demand.

(b) When elasticity is less than 1 (ie inelastic) the following will happen.

   (i) If the price is lowered, total sales revenue would fall, because the increase in sales volume would be too small to compensate for the price reduction.
   (ii) If the price is raised, total sales revenue would go up in spite of the small drop in sales quantities.

Marketing management needs to be able to estimate the likely effects of price changes on total revenue and profits. 'Price elasticity of demand gives precision to the question of whether the firm's price is too high or too low. From the point of view of maximising revenue, price is too high if demand is elastic and too low if demand is inelastic. Whether this is also true for maximising profits depends on the behaviour of costs'. (Kotler)

When do price decisions arise?

3.4 The need to make a price decision arises in the following circumstances.

(a) When a new product is launched on the market.
(b) When the organisation decides to initiate a price change, perhaps:
   (i) due to cost increases;
   (ii) to have a loss leader;
   (iii) for a sales promotion;
   (iv) due to a change in the product's 'age' in its life cycle;
   (v) to reconsider discount policy.
(c) When there is a price change by competitors.
(d) When the organisation wishes to decide on a price policy for an entire product line.

New product pricing: market penetration and market skimming

3.5 J Dean (in *Fundamentals of marketing* Taylor, Robb and New, 1979) has suggested that there are three elements in the pricing decision for a new product. These are as follows.

(a) Getting the product accepted.
(b) Maintaining a market share in the face of competition.
(c) Making a profit from the product.

3.6 When a firm launches a new product on to the market, it must decide on a pricing policy which lies between the two extremes of *market penetration* and *market skimming*.

3.7 *Market penetration* pricing is a policy of low prices when the product is first launched in order to gain sufficient penetration into the market. It is therefore a policy of sacrificing short-run profits in the interests of long-term profits.

The circumstances which favour a penetration policy are as follows.

(a) The firm wishes to discourage rivals from entering the market.
(b) The firm wishes to shorten the initial period of the product's life cycle, in order to enter the growth and maturity stages as quickly as possible. (This would happen if there is high elasticity of demand for the product).
(c) There are significant economies of scale to be achieved from a large output.

3.8 *Penetration prices* are prices which aim to secure a substantial share in a substantial total market. They will be relatively low and the view of management is that it is worthwhile forgoing current profits in order to achieve good long-term profits. A firm might therefore deliberately build excess production capacity and set its prices very low; as demand builds up, the spare capacity will be used up gradually, and unit costs will fall; the firm might even reduce prices further as unit costs fall. In this way, early year losses will enable the firm to dominate the market and have the lowest costs.

3.9 *Market skimming* involves the following.

(a) Charging high prices when a product is first launched.
(b) Spending heavily on advertising and sales promotion to win customers.
(c) As the product moves into the later stages of its life cycle (growth, maturity and decline) progressively lower prices will be charged. The profitable 'cream' is thus 'skimmed' off in progressive stages until sales can only be sustained at lower prices.

3.10 The aim of market skimming is to gain high unit profits very early on in the product's life. Conditions which are suitable for such a policy are as follows.

(a) Where the product is new and different, so that customers are prepared to pay high prices so as to be 'one up' on other people who do not own one.

(b) Where demand elasticity is unknown. It is better to start by charging high prices and then reducing them if the demand for the product turns out to be price elastic than to start by charging low prices and then attempting to raise them substantially when demand turns out to be price inelastic.

(c) High initial prices might not be profit-maximising in the long run, but they generate high initial cash flows. A firm with liquidity problems may prefer market-skimming for this reason.

(d) Skimming may also enable the firm to identify different market segments for the product, each prepared to pay progressively lower prices. If product differentiation can be introduced, it may be possible to continue to sell at higher prices to some market segments.

3.11 *Skimming prices* are at the opposite end of the spectrum to penetration prices in the range of prices that are possible. Some firms set a high initial price to achieve high unit profits, knowing that a certain number of customers will buy at the high price. (This is possible where rival firms are not expected to undercut these high prices, where the fixed costs of output are fairly low, so that economies of scale are relatively insignificant and where the customer believes that high prices signify a quality product). In due course of time, the firm will lower its prices in order to attract more price-elastic segments of the market; however, these price reductions will be gradual. The firm aims to skim the cream off the top of the market to obtain the highest unit price that the customer will offer and to recoup some of the R & D costs in the product's development.

3.12 Another method of new product pricing is the use of introductory offers to attract an initial customer interest. Introductory offers are temporary price reductions, after which the price is then raised to its normal 'commercial' rate.

3.13 The price decision might also be to charge an amount which covers the cost of sale plus an element for profit (cost plus pricing), or to set a price which follows the existing market. These methods of pricing are common to established products as well as to new products.

Product line pricing

3.14 When a firm sells a range of related products, or a product line, its theoretical pricing policy should be to set prices for each product which maximise the profitability of the line as a whole. A firm may therefore have a pricing policy for an entire product line.

(a) There may be a brand name which the manufacturer wishes to associate with high quality but high price, or reasonable quality and low price, etc. All items in the line will be priced accordingly. For example all major supermarket chains have an 'own brand' label which it uses to sell goods at a slightly lower price than the major named brands.

(b) If two or more products in the line are complementary, one may be priced as a loss leader in order to attract more demand for all of the related products.

(c) If two or more products in the line share joint production costs (ie joint products) the prices of the products must be considered as a single decision. For example if a common production process makes one unit of joint product A for each one unit of joint product B, a price for A which achieves a demand of, say, 17,000 units, will be inappropriate if associated with a price for product B which would only sell, say 10,000 units. 7,000 units of B would be unsold and wasted.

Other pricing tactics

3.15 In the prolonged period of inflation in the 1970's, price increases caused by increased costs to the manufacturer became common. The effect of cost inflation on price decisions was very noticeable and different organisations reacted in different ways as follows.

(a) Some firms raised their prices regularly, for example car manufacturers often raised their prices every three or six months.

(b) Other firms gave advance warning of price rises, especially in an industrial market. Customers might then be persuaded to advance their purchases in order to avoid paying the higher price at a later date.

(c) A firm which did not raise its prices was in effect reducing its prices in real terms.

3.16 A *loss leader* is a product or service sold at margins lower than normal (probably at a loss) in order to attract customers who might then buy other items at normal prices. Loss leaders have usually been associated with supermarkets which might offer several products at very low, loss making prices. Shoppers attracted by the bargains will then be expected to do all their shopping in the supermarket, so that the profits earned from the normally priced items will more than pay for the losses on the loss leader items.

3.17 Loss leader pricing is therefore a form of sales promotion and it is also an example of a pricing policy which recognises the inter relationship between the price and demand for one product and the price and demand for other products.

3.18 *Promotional prices* are short-term price reductions or price offers which are intended to attract an increase in sales volume. (The increase is usually short term for the duration of the offer, which does not appear to create any substantial new customer loyalty). Loss leaders are a form of promotional pricing, but 'money off' coupons are perhaps just as well known to you.

3.19 A temporary price cut (ie a promotion) may be preferable to a permanent reduction because a permanent reduction will boost sales once before the new price becomes the 'natural' one, whereas a temporary reduction (or bonus offer) can be ended without unduly offending customers and can be reinstated later to give a repeated boost to sales.

3.20 A firm may need to consider whether the price of a product should be changed according to its 'age' and the stage it has reached in its life cycle.

(a) When it has reached its maturity (non-growth) stage, a price reduction might be advisable to extend the product's mature life.

(b) Further reductions may be necessary to slow down a product's decline. On the other hand, price increases might speed up the decline.

(c) In the 'senile' stage of its life, a product might be sold at knock down prices simply to clear stocks.

3.21 A firm may lower its prices to try to increase its market share; on the other hand, a firm may raise its prices in the hope that competitors will quickly do the same (ie in the expectation of tacit price collusion). The purpose of such competitive initiatives will presumably be to raise profits or the firm's market share; however, in established industries dominated by a few major firms, it is generally accepted that a price initiative by one firm will be countered by a price reaction by competitors. In these circumstances, prices tend to be fairly stable, unless pushed upwards by inflation or strong growth in demand. Thus in industries such as breakfast cereals (dominated in Britain by Kelloggs, Nabisco and Quaker) or canned soups (Heinz, Crosse and Blackwell and Campbells) a certain price stability might be expected without too many competitive price initiatives, except when cost inflation pushes up the price of one firm's products with other firms soon following in line.

3.22 If a rival firm cuts its prices in the expectation of increasing its market share, a firm has the following options.

(a) Maintaining its existing prices. This would be done if the expectation is that only a small market share would be lost, so that it is more profitable to keep prices at their existing level. Eventually, the rival firm may drop out of the market or be forced to raise its prices.

(b) Maintaining its prices but responding with a non-price counter-attack. This is a more positive response, because the firm will be securing or justifying its current prices with a product change, advertising, or better back-up services, etc.

(c) Reducing its prices. This should protect the firm's market share so that the main beneficiary from the price reduction will be the consumer.

(d) Raise its prices and respond with a non-price counter-attack. The extra revenue from the higher prices might be used to finance an advertising campaign or product design changes. A price increase would be based on a campaign to emphasise the quality difference between the firm's own product and the rival's product.

4. PLACE

4.1 'Place' as an element in the marketing mix is largely concerned with the selection of distribution channels and with the physical distribution of goods.

4.2 In selecting an appropriate marketing channel for a product, a firm has the following options.

(a) Selling direct to the customer. Consumer goods can be sold direct with mail order catalogues, telephone selling, door-to-door selling of consumer goods, or selling 'off the page' with magazine advertisements. Industrial goods are commonly sold direct by sales representatives, visiting industrial buyers.

(b) Selling through agents or recognised distributors, who specialise in the firm's products. For example a chain of garden centres might act as specialist stockists and distributors for the products of just one garden shed manufacturer.

(c) Selling through wholesalers or to retailers who stock and sell the goods and brands of several rival manufacturers.

4.3 The choice of a suitable marketing channel will depend on many factors, including the following.

(a) The customers' motivation mix, and the importance of distribution channel in the mix (for example whether the good is a convenience, shopping or specialty good).
(b) How rival products are distributed.
(c) Whether there is a 'gap' in the market for exploiting a new or different marketing channel.

4.4 The distribution dilemma facing management in place strategy is that of the trade-off between cost and control. The shorter the distribution channel the more control managers have over the marketing of the products, but the higher their distribution costs. Long distribution channels cut the costs but also reduce the firm's control.

5. PROMOTION

5.1 In the context of marketing and strategic planning, communication is essential to the success of any strategy or plan, since eventually, something has to be 'sold', and a customer has to be told about its availability and attributes.

The theory of communication is concerned with the general principles of how a producer gets a customer to buy his products or services.

5.2 Kotler suggests that all the four 'P's of the marketing mix are tools of communication, but recognises that the most obvious one is the promotional aspect, where the message of the organisation is communicated to the consuming public. He identifies four categories of promotional activity as follows.

(a) *Advertising*, defined as any paid form of non-personal presentation and promotion of ideas, goods or services by an identified sponsor.

(b) *Sales promotion* to encourage through incentives, over a short term period, the purchase of the good or service.

(c) *Personal selling*, ie the oral presentation of the goods or services, either to actually make a sale, or to create goodwill to improve the prospects of sales in the future.

(d) *Publicity*, which unlike advertising, cannot be bought and it might be thought of as unpaid advertising. Although organisations will spend large sums of money on publicity, they do not formally buy space in a newspaper or time on television or radio. Nor do they usually control the content of the publicity message, and so some publicity can be bad rather than good.

The role of communication in the marketing mix

5.3 Communication in the marketing mix is two-way. Firms must find out what customers' needs are before telling them about the products they have developed which will satisfy those needs.

However, communications are generally considered in the more restricted context of advertising and sales promotion, and the purpose of such messages might be as follows.

(a) To increase sales.
(b) To maintain or improve market share.
(c) To create or improve brand image.
(d) To create a favourable customer climate for future sales.
(e) To inform and educate the market.
(f) To create a competitive difference from other products.
(g) To improve the efficiency of a sales promotion activity.
(h) To remind customers of the benefits of the product or service.

5.4 Bell *(Marketing: concepts and strategy)* identifies five key conditions in which advertising or sales promotion is likely to be most effective as an element in the marketing mix.

(a) When there is already a favourable trend in sales demand.
(b) When products are clearly differentiated.
(c) When product qualities are hidden.
(d) When emotional buying motives exist.
(e) When adequate funds are available for the promotion.

5.5 'Promotion' is one of the four major categories in the marketing mix. It is concerned with *communication* between the seller and the buyer and is controlled by the seller who seeks to promote his products. There are different methods of promotion as follows.

(a) Advertising.
(b) Sales promotion activities, also known as *below the line* activities.
(c) Publicity or public relations.
(d) The activities of the sales force.

5.6 Firms will use a combination of these promotion methods and the optimal *communications mix* will depend on the nature of the product, the market and the customer. For example a manufacturer of industrial goods will rely more heavily on direct selling and sales literature, whereas a consumer goods manufacturer will use more advertising and sales promotion devices.

6. CONCLUSION

6.1 In this chapter we have reviewed the concept and role of the marketing mix as a set of controllable variables which management can alter to influence demand.

6.2 The exact components of the marketing mix need to be put together with judgement and creativity. Every product, market and every stage in the product's life will require a different balance of the marketing mix ingredients.

6.3 Over time the demand for a product changes and the external environment changes. Therefore the marketing mix needs to be adjusted throughout the product's life.

6.4 Marketing managers need to be familiar with all the mix elements to enable them to recommend appropriate strategies and tactics.

TEST YOUR KNOWLEDGE

The numbers in brackets refer to paragraphs of this chapter

1. Who defined the marketing mix as the 4P's? (1.3)
2. How would you distinguish between a push and pull policy of selling? (1.4)
3. How is the balance of design of the marketing mix for a product decided? (1.6)
4. What are the stages in formulating a marketing mix? (1.10)
5. In what ways is quality an important policy consideration? (2.2-2.5)
6. When do managers need to make pricing decisions? (3.4)
7. What is meant by the term market skimming? (3.9)
8. When would product line pricing be an appropriate pricing strategy? (3.14)
9. What are the main factors which will influence a manager's choice of distribution channel? (4.3)
10. Describe the five conditions identified by Bell in which advertising or sales promotion are likely to be an effective marketing mix ingredient. (5.4)

Now try illustrative questions 14 and 15

PART D
STRATEGIC IMPLEMENTATION AND CONTROL

Chapter 12

IMPLEMENTATION

> **This chapter covers the following topics.**
>
> 1. Implementation of plans
> 2. Internal marketing
> 3. Managing the process of change

1. IMPLEMENTATION OF PLANS

1.1 Having determined objectives, appraised strategy and formulated plans, it is time to put the corporate plan into action. Everyone involved should know what is required and when, and should be committed to the successful accomplishment of the plan.

1.2 It could be argued that this is where senior management should 'back off' and leave it to their juniors to finish off the work by putting the plans into effect. This argument has a number of flaws.

(a) Senior managers have the ultimate responsibility for ensuring that the organisation achieves its objectives. Senior managers have responsibility for both planning and control. The corporate plan is a statement of what they intend to do. Having made a plan, they must keep in touch with how things are going, to carry out the control function. Senior managers stand accountable for their success or failure - even if initially, they are only accountable to themselves at board level. Monitoring actual results is thus an essential ingredient of the control cycle.

(b) Control action by senior management includes a need to keep their juniors up to the mark. Lower levels of management almost invariably, when left to themselves, spend their time on short term or pressing issues, rather than dealing with the less immediate problems of the corporate plan.

(c) The performance appraisal of middle and junior management is based on achieving short-term or budgeted tasks and targets. These managers will therefore concentrate on doing well in those areas where they are judged and rewarded, rather than give much attention to longer-term targets for which performance appraisal is less frequent, and, unless senior management does something about it, less important to them personally.

1.3 Successful implementation of the corporate plan demands the continued interest of senior management and involves the following tasks.

(a) Converting strategic plans into action plans, ie operations plans and budgets.

(b) Allocating responsibilities and giving authority to individual managers to use resources, for example spend sufficient money to allow them to achieve their individual targets.

(c) Establishing checkpoints to monitor activities.

(d) Exerting pressure for control action where necessary, to ensure that things get done according to the aims of the corporate plan.

1.4 *Control checkpoints* should monitor factors such as the following.

(a) Have deadlines been met and are future deadlines going to be met?
(b) Are any targets in danger of being missed?
(c) Will the required resources be available to make the products/services?
(d) Will the products be available in sufficient numbers to achieve the aims of the marketing plan?

1.5 There are always unforeseen events to deal with, some of them controllable and others uncontrollable and unavoidable. There might be adverse tax changes in a government's budget; there might be a long strike; a competitor might introduce a rival product which captures much of the company's market; weak or inept management might be unable to meet their targets.

1.6 Events must be monitored by senior management, to keep results on course for achieving the planned targets. But monitoring at this level does not need large procedure manuals or sophisticated and unwieldy measuring and reporting systems. The plan should instruct management on what should be monitored and should perhaps indicate 'variance' levels beyond which action will have to be taken.

2. INTERNAL MARKETING

2.1 Planning implies change. It is one thing to put intentions down on paper. It is another thing altogether to manage the implementation of a plan so that it is actually put into effect.

2.2 Today the emphasis is increasingly focusing on the implementation skills of the manager. Many are turning to the marketer's approach and using a similar process to help them market plans and intended change effectively to colleagues and staff. This approach is referred to as internal marketing.

2.3 The principles of internal marketing are as follows.

(a) The implementation of plans needs planning.

(b) Staff needs must be identified and benefits of the plan must be presented to them.

(c) Those who influence the organisation and decision makers must be identified and targeted. They represent the equivalent of the *innovators* in a product's life cycle, and must be sold the plan first.

(d) Plans need packaging and promoting. Resources may be needed to achieve this.

(e) Managers must make use of informal networks of communication within the organisation. It is not sufficient to rely wholly on the formal networks which are the result of the prevailing organisation structure.

2.4 Internal marketing plans should be based on research to identify the relevant decision making unit and their needs and concerns.

2.5 The internal marketing mix can be described in terms of the 4P's.

(a) *Product:* this is the plan or change which management wants to implement.

(b) *Price:* there will be a price tag. The costs and benefits to staff need to be clearly assessed. As with any product their may need to be negotiation, but managers must be clear what the costs and benefits are. For example a move to a new office block may entail a longer journey to work, but offers improved working conditions. A change in the sales commission package may depress potential earnings in exchange for a higher average salary.

(c) *Place:* in marketing, place represents when and where the product is available. The timing of the announcement of plans can have a dramatic effect on the way they are received and this needs careful consideration.

(d) *Promotion:* poor communication is probably the biggest single failure when evaluating internal company problems. The grapevine tends to work quickly and not always very accurately. Therefore when plans are announced they are often met by hostility and antagonism. Improving the communication of plans is an essential step to ensuring that they are owned and supported by those who have to implement them. Communication should be two way and meetings and discussions to take account of staff's views and thoughts at an early stage will help implementation later.

2.6 Internal marketing is about the manner in which plans and change are 'sold' to those they affect. The right manner is important in creating a motivated and successful team at whatever level the plan is being implemented.

3. MANAGING THE PROCESS OF CHANGE

3.1 As we have seen, it is management's responsibility to prepare the organisation for the future. We have also seen that the future will inevitably bring change. Organisations have to adapt and modify if they are to survive in the environment of the future.

We have already seen how *strategic management* and corporate planning are essential in identifying and meeting the needs *for* change and brought about *by* change. Change in the environment creates opportunities and threats: the organisation must respond with internal change in order to maximise its strengths and minimise its weaknesses.

3.2 Change, in the context of organisation and management, could involve any of the following.

(a) *Changes in the 'environment'*
These could be changes in what competitors are doing, what customers are buying, how they spend their money, changes in the law, changes in social behaviour and attitudes, economic changes, and so on.

(b) *Changes in the products the organisation makes, or the services it provides*

These are made in response to changes in customer demands, competitors' actions, new technology, and so on.

(c) *Changes in how products are made (or services provided) or by whom. Changes in working methods*

These changes are also in response to environmental change, for example new technology, new laws on safety at work etc.

(d) *Changes in management and working relationships. Cultural change*

These include changes in leadership style, and in the way that employees are encouraged to work together. Changes in training and staff development are also relevant here.

(e) *Changes in organisation structure or size*

These might involve creating new departments and divisions, greater delegation of authority or more centralisation, changes in the way that plans are made, management information is provided and control is exercised, and so on. Organisation re-structuring will be made in response to changes in (a), (b), (c) or (d) above.

3.3 Earlier we considered how important both the organisational framework and culture were in facilitating change.

Charles Garfield *(Peak performers: the new heroes in business)* writes of the change in ethos which now celebrates innovation and adaptability, opportunism and flair - the attributes of the entrepreneur.

> 'Entrepreneurs and intrapreneurs (the internal entrepreneurs who pull together diverse strengths within their organisations to promote innovation) are the new stars'.

3.4 Peters and Waterman, in their influential anecdotal study of successful American companies, *In search of excellence,* define 'excellent' as 'continually innovative'. They, too, note that the promotion of exploration, experimentation, willingness to change, opportunism and internal competition create an entrepreneurial 'culture' or 'climate' in organisations that keeps them adaptive to their environment and enables consistent success.

3.5 Management can give encouragement to innovation in a number of ways.

(a) By giving it financial backing, by spending on market research and risking capital on following through viable new ideas.

(b) By giving employees the opportunity to work in an environment where the exchange of ideas for innovation can take place. Management style and organisation structure can help here.

(i) Management can actively encourage employees and customers to put forward new ideas. Participation in development decisions might encourage employees to become more involved with development projects and committed to their success.

(ii) Development teams can be set up and an organisation built up on project team-work.

(iii) Quality circles and brainstorming groups can be used to encourage creative thinking about work issues.

(c) Where appropriate, recruitment policy should be directed towards appointing employees with the necessary skills for doing innovative work. Employees should be trained and kept up to date.

(d) Certain managers should be made responsible for obtaining information from outside the organisation about innovative ideas, and for communicating this information throughout the organisation.

(e) Strategic planning should result in targets being set for innovation, and successful achievements by employees should be rewarded if possible.

3.6 Management can also create conditions in which risk-taking, creativity and enthusiasm for change is impossible. The Financial Times of 25 June 1986 reported the ideas of Rosabeth Moss Kanter on how to *stifle* innovation.

1. Regard any new idea from below with suspicion.
2. Insist that people who need your approval first go through several other levels of management.
3. Get departments/individuals to challenge each other's proposals.
4. Express criticism freely, withhold praise, instill job insecurity.
5. Treat identification of problems as signs of failure.
6. Control everything carefully. Count everything in sight - frequently.
7. Make decisions in secret, and spring them on people.
8. Do not hand out information to managers freely.
9. Get lower-level managers to implement your threatening decisions.
10. Above all, never forget that you, the higher-ups, already know everything important about the business.

Evaluating change management

3.7 The effectiveness of change management can be evaluated in a number of ways.

(a) The impact of the change on organisational goals: has the change contributed to the overall objectives of the organisation as defined by the corporate plan?

(b) The success of the change in meeting its specified objective (and short-term targets set for progress measurement): has the change solved the problem?

(c) The behaviour of people in the organisation: has the change programme resulted in the behavioural changes planned (for example higher output, better teamwork, more attention to customer care)?

(d) The reaction of the people in the organisation: has the change programme been implemented without arousing hostility, fear, conflict, and its symptoms (absenteeism, labour turnover etc)?

3.8 There are many reasons why an organisation might fail to manage change successfully.

(a) Failure to identify the *need* to change (typically a failure to pay attention to change in the environment).

(b) Failure to identify the *objectives* of change, so that the wrong areas are addressed.

(c) Failure to identify correctly the strategy required, out of all the options, to achieve the objectives. The result is that change takes place, but not in the relevant direction. New technology, for example, is sometimes regarded as a universal solution to organisational problems, but it will not necessarily improve productivity or profitability if the product/market strategy or the workforce is the real problem.

(d) Failure to commit sufficient resource to the strategy.

(e) Failure to identify the appropriate method of implementing change, for the situation and the people involved (typically, failing to anticipate resistance to change).

(f) Failure to implement the change in a way that secures acceptance, because of the leadership style of the person managing the change (typically, failure to consult and involve employees).

3.9 The first four of the above reasons for failure are to do with strategic planning generally: they are potential shortcomings in any planning exercise. The peculiar difficulties of introducing change, however, are human factors. When implementing plans or changes, managers must never lose sight of the fact that their success depends on people.

3.10 Before commencing their internal marketing of plans, managers must recognise the behavioural factors which might influence people to welcome or resist change.

3.11

Reasons for resisting change	*Reasons for welcoming change*
(a) Fear of personal loss - security - money (eg. travelling costs to work, when a change of office location is proposed) - pride and job satisfaction - friends and contacts - freedom - responsibility - authority/discretion - good working conditions - status	(a) Expectations of personal gain
(b) Can't see the need for change	(b) Change provides a new and welcome challenge
(c) Believes change will do more harm than good	(c) Change will reduce the boredom of work
(d) Lack of respect for the person initiating the change	(d) Likes/respects the source of the change
(e) Objection to the manner in which the planned change was communicated	(e) Likes the manner in which the change was suggested
(f) No participation 'We weren't asked'	(f) Participation in the decision
(g) Negative attitude to the job	(g) Wants the change
(h) Belief that the change is a personal criticism of what the individual has been doing	(h) The change improves the employee's future prospects
(i) The change requires effort	(i) The change comes at a good time
(j) The change comes at a bad time 'We have enough on our plate already'	
(k) Challenge to authority in the act of resisting change	

3.12 Good managers will be looking out for change and they will be in a position to plan for it. In this way they are able to market change to their staff so that it is welcomed and not resisted.

4. CONCLUSION

4.1 Plans cannot be forgotten by senior managers once they have been prepared. The implementation of plans requires the continued interest of senior managers and their involvement in the progress.

4.2 The effective implementation of plans requires that they are marketed to staff. The process of internal marketing is the same as marketing to external customers and should be taken as seriously.

4.3 Plans involve change and managing that process of change is an important responsibility. Managers can encourage innovation by their attitude and behaviour.

TEST YOUR KNOWLEDGE

The numbers in brackets refer to paragraphs of this chapter

1. Why should senior managers not simply leave the implementation of plans to subordinates? (1.2)
2. What is internal marketing? (2.2)
3. What are the main principles of internal marketing? (2.3)
4. What kind of organisation and management changes might it be necessary to implement? (3.2)
5. How would you judge the effectiveness of the management of change? (3.7)
6. Why might organisations fail to manage change successfully? (3.8)
7. List five reasons why change may be resisted. (3.11)
8. List five reasons why change may be welcomed. (3.11)

Now try illustrative question 16

Chapter 13

CONTROL

This chapter covers the following topics

1. Control and performance measurement
2. Setting targets
3. Other aspects of performance
4. Measuring the effectiveness of the marketing mix

1. CONTROL AND PERFORMANCE MEASUREMENT

1.1 You should already be very familiar with the idea that once plans have been made and put into action, management must exercise controls to try to ensure that the planning targets are achieved.

Control information may be obtained from sources outside the organisation itself, but much is obtained internally, and is referred to as *feedback*.

1.2 In broad terms, control information consists of a comparison between actual results and planned results. The differences are analysed and suggested explanations are given indicating, if possible:

(a) which of these reasons are attributable to non-controllable factors;
(b) which of the differences can be rectified because they are due to controllable causes.

1.3 In terms of strategic planning and marketing, planned results often comprise the following.

(a) Targets for the overall financial objective, for each year over the planning period, and other financial strategy objectives such as productivity targets.

(b) Subsidiary financial targets.

(c) Financial targets in the annual budget (including the sales budget and marketing expenditures budget).

(d) Product-market strategy targets.

(e) Targets for each element of the marketing mix.

The nature of control

1.4 Control and monitoring can be defined as follows.

> 'The continuous comparison of actual results with those planned, both in total and for separate sub-divisions and taking management action to correct adverse variances or to exploit favourable variances.'

1.5 This definition of control includes the three main underlying components of the control process.

(a) Setting *targets or standards* which serve as guidelines for performance.
(b) The *measurement and evaluation* of actual performance.
(c) Corrective action where it is needed in the form of a control decision.

1.6 Performance measurement, item (b) above, is therefore an essential bridge between planning (item (a)) and control (item (c)).

Performance measurement is an integral part of the planning and control cycle. A measurement of past performance is valuable not only to control current activities but also to provide data for making future plans. Plans for the future cannot be made without a realistic assessment of what has happened in the past.

Setting targets or standards

1.7 Targets and standards of performance stem from a decision about what the objectives of the organisation should be. The overall corporate objectives adopted in the planning process serve as a foundation for all subsidiary quantified targets from divisional and departmental targets down to the performance standards for every echelon of manager and employee in the organisation. We will look at the setting of targets and standards in more detail in the next section of this chapter.

Measurement and evaluation of performance

1.8 Performance can be measured by a management accounting system and other formal reporting systems within an organisation, or by personal observation. The latter is usually the most convenient method for a *qualitative* evalution of human performance. An experienced supervisor, for example, will be able to judge the pace of the production line, personally inspect the quality of work in progress and also assess workers' morale and motivation by observing their behaviour. Conversely, it is easy for the eye to be deceived and for qualitative judgement to be wrong. Formal reporting systems, such as management accounting systems, provide a much more objective quantitative assessment than the human observer and, once systems are set up, can be much less time-consuming for the controller.

1.9 Where performance is below the standard set or objectives are not being achieved, the reason for the 'poor showing' will not necessarily be obvious.

Before taking corrective action, therefore, it is important to determine the apparent reason for any unsatisfactory performance and whether the reason is one which will lend itself to control action or whether it is an uncontrollable matter. For example if sales in a particular region are low, increasing the sales supervision or sending the representative on additional sales training programmes will be of little effect if the cause of the poor sales is exceptionally high unemployment in the area.

1.10 Performance should be measured and judged by obtaining data about actual results for a direct comparison with the targets or standards set. Performance measures must therefore have the following characteristics.

(a) They must be measurable, in quantitative or qualitative terms. Not all results are easily measured. For example if a company sets itself an aim of improving customer goodwill, how can the strength of such goodwill be judged, except by relying on the opinion, probably biased, of sales management? Unless an assessment of performance is made, managers will have no information with which to decide whether or not any control action is needed. Ideally, such an assessment should be measured as objectively as possible.

(b) They must relate directly to the targets or standards set in the plan.

1.11 Targets or standards might be for the long term or short term. Long term targets for achievement will relate to the organisation's *objectives* and *strategic plans*. Short term targets and standards will be for operational planning and control at a junior management level, and for medium-term planning and budgeting, and budgetary control by middle management.

1.12 The control measures and analytical techniques that might be relevant for control at a strategic level are as follows.

Type of analysis	*Used to control*
1. *Financial analysis*	
Ratio analysis	Elements of profitability
Variance analysis	Costs or revenue
Cash budgeting	Cash flow
Capital budgeting and capital expenditure audit	Investment
2. *Market/sales analysis* - overall consideration of size and growth of market segments and corporate market share	
Demand analysis Market share or penetration	Competitive standing
Sales targets	Sales effectiveness
Sales budget	Efficiency in use of resources for selling
3. *Physical resource analysis*	
Capacity fill	Plant utilisation
Yield	Materials utilisation
Product inspection	Quality
4. *Human resources analysis*	
Work measurement Output measurement	Productivity
Labour turnover	Workforce stability

Type of analysis	*Used to control*
5. *Analysis of systems*	
Management by objectives	Implementation of strategy
Network analysis	Resource planning and scheduling

Financial control information

1.13 Management control information is often expressed in monetary terms because money is a common denominator which everyone throughout the organisation understands.

The other advantages of expressing control information in monetary terms are as follows.

(a) It allows direct performance comparisons of completely different functions and activities: the relative costs and profit contributions of, say, a purchasing manager and sales manager cannot readily be compared without a universal monetary basis.

(b) It facilitates the processing of technical information by non-technical personnel because monetary terms can be understood but technical terms might be meaningless to them.

(c) It is the commonly accepted measure by which corporate and departmental performance is gauged because profitability is probably the most important criterion.

1.14 The disadvantages of using monetary information include the following.

(a) Where absorption costing techniques are used, the process of apportioning and absorbing overhead costs is somewhat arbitrary and meaningless.

(b) There is a tendency to assume that all costs charged to a product or department are controllable by the manager in charge, whereas this is not the case. A manager of a production department, for example, cannot control the prices of raw materials, nor the amount of production overhead charged to the department.

(c) Costs and profits are not necessarily a useful way of comparing the results of different parts of a business, and ratio analysis (or productivity etc) might be more useful.

(d) Managers who are not accountants may prefer to quantify information in non-monetary terms, for example:
   (i) the sales manager may look at sales volume in units, size of market share, speed of delivery, volume of sales per sales representative or per call etc;
   (ii) a stores manager might look at stock turnover periods for each item, volume of demand, the speed of materials handling, breakages, obsolescence etc.

(e) Although much management information is quantitative, some information is *qualitative* and impossible to measure in money terms. Where qualitative factors (notably human behaviour and attitudes) are important, monetary information is less relevant. This is one reason why strategic planning information, which relies more heavily on both external and qualitative factors, is generally more imprecise and not necessarily expressed in money terms.

Communication in planning and control activity

1.15 We have discussed in the last chapter that if planning is to function effectively, there must be effective communication, and certain essential principles should be followed.

(a) There should be a formal reporting structure, based on the company's organisation structure, and defined by:
(i) function; or
(ii) product or service; or
(iii) geographical area;
or even a combination of all three.

(b) Duties must be broadly identified, and for control purposes, reporting procedures should be set up. It is necessary to communicate plans so that they can be carried out, but it is also necessary to communicate results, so that achievements can be monitored and reviewed.

1.16 The following outline diagram is derived from *Accountancy, Computers and MIS* by Professor D H Li.

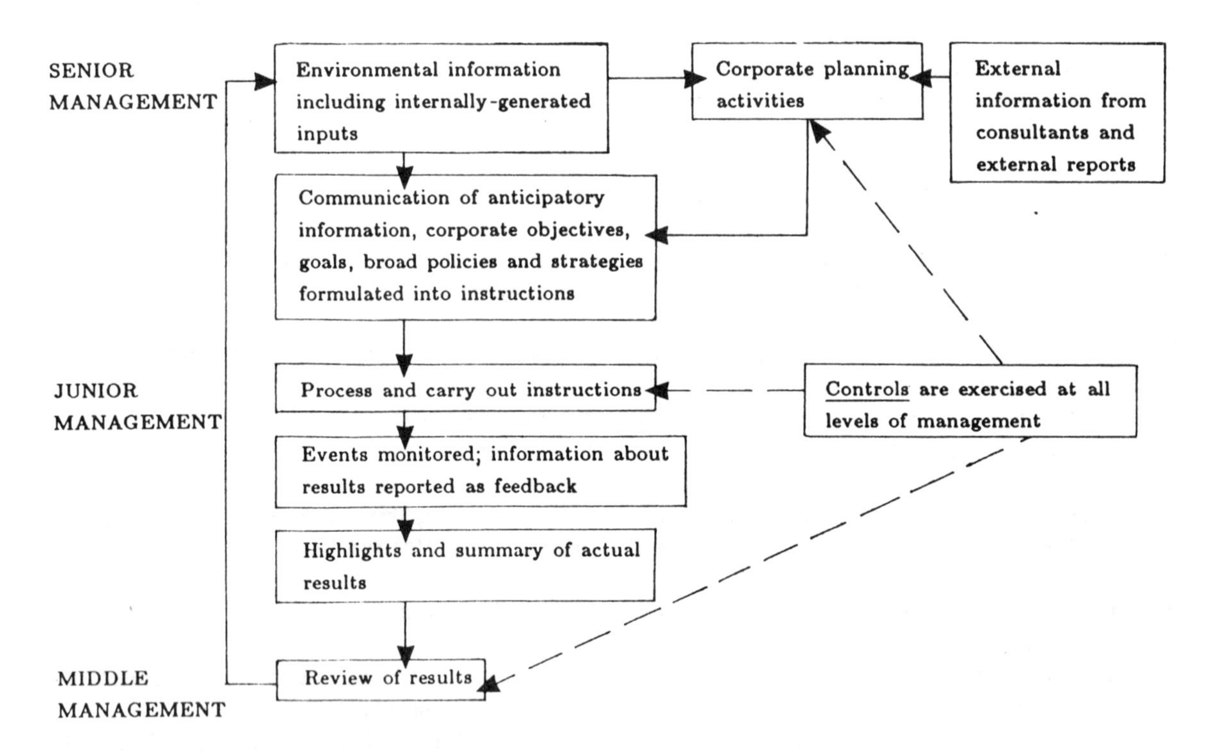

Guidelines for basic strategic control

1.17 Control should take place at three levels - the strategic level, the management control (or tactical) level and the operational control level. Control must influence the behaviour of individuals and groups towards the implementation of the corporate strategy and towards progressive change. Six guidelines can be usefully followed.

(a) Distinguish between control at different levels in the management hierarchy. When managers take control action, they ought to be aware of what they are trying to achieve, ie is their control measure intended to have an immediate impact (for example 'firefighting' at an operational control or budgetary level) or will it take time for the measure to have a tangible effect because it is for longer-term strategic benefits?

(b) Individual managers should be identified as having the responsibility for certain matters, and authority to take control measures. At a budget level, responsibility centres should be established for accounting purposes and budgetary control reporting: these responsibility centres might be revenue centres, cost centres, profit centres or investment centres. In other words, there must be an *organisation structure* for control.

(c) The *key factors for control* should be identified. Managers responsible for taking control action must be informed about what the key factors are, and why they are critical.

(d) Control reporting should be *timed* sensibly. Depending on the level of control (strategic, budgetary, or operational) control reports should vary from occasional to regular and frequent.

(e) Suitable targets and standards should be applied. For example, it might be reasonable to set profit targets for all the products in a company's product range, but well-established, thriving products ('cash cows') ought to have a different profit target from new products. Targets should be tailored to suit individual circumstances, and control applied accordingly.

(f) Control reports should contain relevant information for the manager receiving the report, and should not contain unnecessary details about irrelevant items. A production report, for example, should not include unnecessary details about sales volumes and deliveries, and selling costs, because these will be of no interest to the production manager receiving the report. However, some sales details might be relevant if production delays are affecting sales levels and profits.

Some of these guidelines warrant closer attention.

1.18 *The need for selective reporting*
Control in strategic planning should not spawn a large batch of enormously detailed control reports. If there were detailed control reports, control of the corporate plan would become a paper chase, exhibiting all the worst features of a two-tier fire-fighting budgetary control system with the corporate plan sitting on top of the budget and control being confused by a tangle of inter-related targets in the two plans. Reporting for control in strategic planning must therefore be selective.

1.19 Selective reporting means identifying key points for control.

(a) In the product-market plan, there will be products identified as question marks or potential stars. New products will be planned. The position of each product in the product-market matrix will suggest how much close watching the product needs. High risk/high potential projects should require the greatest amount of monitoring.

(b) A product which performs inconsistently might need close watching and control. However, there is a danger of 'overkill' in monitoring and control of inconsistent performers. Excessive or intensive monitoring in unlikely to change an outcome that is more or less a foregone conclusion. An activity which now appears to have a high probability of indifferent success might respond weakly to control measures, and the product concerned might be drifting into the 'dog' category so that the most appropriate control measure may be to let the product die quietly.

(c) Information and control reporting cost money. The sense of keeping control information down to a minimum is that it saves time and money, and provided that key control measures are identified, nothing is lost by omitting subsidiary detail (which is probably available anyway in routine budgetary control reports). For example if the objectives of the finance function are expressed in terms of profit and reductions in working capital, these are control items to be reported. Subsidiary information such as interest savings, debtors' turnover periods, credit levels and gearing levels are no doubt very interesting to management, but it is debateable whether information of this kind is necessary for control reporting at the level of the corporate plan. Similarly, in the case of marketing, the objective will be sales volume and contribution towards fixed overheads and profit. Sales growth will probably depend mainly on the performance of 'stars' in the product range and so control reporting should emphasise the achievements of the stars (sales and contribution earned).

1.20 If there is a single corporate objective, say profit, this will generate objectives for each divisional function of the organisation and these sub-objectives in turn will be turned into sub-sub-objectives for smaller units of the organisation. There is a clear danger here that the number of key control points will 'mushroom' and so become excessive. If, because of the scale of the organisation's operations, the number of key items is high, the answer is to be even more selective in choosing the critical items which matter more than any others. For example if the key item is to get a new factory built and commissioned, the timing of this project should have control priority over everything else, even current sales levels.

1.21 The key item might be more 'qualitative'. For example within the production function it might be considered vitally important that there should be a rapid and significant improvement in employee commitment and productivity, time lost through stoppages and labour turnover. Control reporting at the corporate planning level should therefore emphasise these points, and shift back to matters such as equipment, tooling and production quantities and costs at a later time, when appropriate.

Tolerance limits for variances

1.22 No corporate plan has the detail or 'accuracy' that a budget has. Consequently, the tolerance limits giving 'early warning' or deviations from the plan should be wider. For example if tolerance limits in budgetary control are variance ± 5% from standard, then corporate planning tolerance limits might be set at ± 10% or more from targets.

1.23 Whatever the tolerance limits are, the reporting of results which go outside the limits must be prompt. If sales have dropped well below target, the reasons must be established quickly and possible solutions thought about. Tolerance limits should be set on both the favourable and the adverse side of the planning targets. For example if a company's products unexpectedly gain second highest market share, the questions that should be asked are as follows.

(a) How did it happen?
(b) Can profitability targets be maintained or exceeded at the sales volumes supporting that market share?
(c) Can second place be maintained, and if so, what needs to be done to secure the position?
(d) Can the market leader be toppled? (And if so, is this profitable?)

Revising forecasts

1.24 Data about actual results can be used to revise forecasts about what is likely to happen in the future. Managers need information about whether actual results so far show that short term targets have been met. They also need to know whether longer term targets are likely to be met.

1.25 Control at a strategic level calls for the continuous revision of forecasts. A simple numerical example might help to explain this. Suppose that in 19X1, a company forecasts its future return on capital employed, year by year for the next five years, as follows.

Year	*19X2*	*19X3*	*19X4*	*19X5*	*19X6*
Return	12%	13.5%	15%	16%	17%

In 19X2, the forecast might be revised in view of actual results in 19X2, as follows.

Year	*19X2 (actual result)*	*19X3 (forecast)*	*19X4*	*19X5*	*19X6*	*19X7*
Return	11.5%	12.5%	14%	15.5%	16.5%	17%

The revised forecast in 19X2 would show that the forecast return each year will be less than originally planned in 19X1, and that a return of 17% would not now be achieved until 19X7.

1.26 This revised forecast could be used in two ways.

(a) Either to take control action to try to improve the forecast return each year, back to the levels that were originally planned in 19X1.
(b) Or to revise the strategic planning targets.

1.27 Control at a strategic level, and the review of strategic plans, should therefore be an iterative process, with revised forecasts for the future being an important part of the control information.

The efficiency and effectiveness of performance

1.28 Efficiency and effectiveness are two fundamental ways of measuring performance (preferably in quantitative terms).

Drucker wrote: 'Efficiency is concerned with doing things right. Effectiveness is doing the right thing'... Even the healthiest business, the business with the greatest effectiveness, can die of poor efficiency. But even the most efficient business cannot survive, let alone succeed, if it is efficient in doing the wrong things, ie if it lacks effectiveness. No amount of efficiency would have enabled the manufacturer of buggy whips to survive.'

1.29 Efficiency is defined as the ratio of output quantities to input resources.

Efficiency and inefficiency are measures along the same scale, with 'efficiency' referring to a higher ratio of output to input than the norm or standard and 'inefficiency' referring to a lower ratio.

1.30 The fact that most organisations try to achieve certain objectives with limited resources gives rise to the concept of *efficiency* or *productivity.*

Compare two companies both making widgets. Company A uses 100 tonnes raw material and 100 man hours of labour to produce 1,000 widgets. Company B produces exactly the same product widgets, in the same numbers (1,000), but only uses 99 tonnes of materials and 99 man hours of labour' *All other things being equal*, Company B is more efficient and productive. This analysis begs a lot of questions (eg we haven't mentioned the *cost* of the raw materials, which is a measure of resource consumption: Company A might use lower quality raw materials which are cheaper).

1.31 Inputs are *all* factors which contribute to the production of organisational outputs. Drucker points out that efficiency or productivity is now less related to the productivity of manual labour or machinery, and more related to the increasing role of 'knowledge work' ie the work of managers, researchers, planners, designers and innovators - those parts of the organisation often accounted for as 'overheads.'

1.32 Effectiveness is defined as success in producing a desired result.

1.33 There are two approaches to measuring organisational effectiveness.

(a) *The goal model approach*: this is to express effectiveness in terms of goal attainment, ie. the more an organisation's goals are met or surpassed, the greater is its effectiveness. However, one difficulty with this approach is that most organisations aspire to a number of goals simultaneously and problems arise where realisation of one goal is at the expense of another. Thus, even if an organisation is effective in reaching most of its goals, it may still not be completely effective. Where several goals co-exist, an acceptable ranking of goals must be worked out. When a choice must be made between achieving one goal or another, when it is not possible to achieve both together because resources are insufficient, the ranking process would indicate which goal has priority.

(b) A second approach to organisational effectiveness focusses on the relationship between the organisation and its environment. This so-called *systems resource approach* defines effectiveness as the degree to which an organisation is successful in acquiring and utilising scarce and valued resources. Organisations take in resources from their environment and 'return' them as output with an economic value. The more effective organisations survive because they can maintain a greater intake of resources than is required to produce their output. An important difficulty with this approach is that it fails to provide guidance as to which resources might be relevant in the assessment of an organisation's effectiveness. For example the coal industry can arguably say it has increased productivity. However, if there are high stocks of unsold coal this would reflect the industry's failure to gear activity to existing demand or to find new markets or even effectively compete in the market place against other fuel sources.

1.34 The goal approach and the systems resource approach are not incompatible and it can be argued that both views should be taken into account simultaneously. To be effective in the long run, organisations need to be concerned not only with the attainment of internally established objectives (the emphasis of the goal approach) but also with the manner in which objectives are achieved (the emphasis of the systems resource approach).

1.35 Effectiveness can be measured *internally* within an organisation by establishing whether or not it has achieved the targets set for itself in its planning processes. However, one organisation might set itself easier targets than another and so it might be *effective* in terms of its own targets but not effective when compared with other organisations. This, in fact, highlights the key difference between the goal approach and systems resource approach to measuring effectiveness. If we take the view that comparisons of the effectiveness of different organisations would be useful measures for control purposes, how should yardsticks for measuring effectiveness be set?

1.36 Various factors have been suggested as criteria for measuring organisational effectiveness, including, for example, adaptability, profitability, growth, employee retention, productivity, stability etc. Unfortunately, no widely acceptable measures have been found and many analyses are judgemental and subjective.

1.37 In addition, there are several more general unsolved problems of measuring effectiveness.

(a) *Effectiveness over time.* Effectiveness has to be measured over time as the organisation and its environment change. The problem is essentially one of how best to balance short term considerations against long term interest.

(b) *Measurements of effectiveness which relate to the organisation as a whole* are not entirely satisfactory because they ignore the vital role played by individual sub-units of the organisation.

(c) *Different organisations have different characteristics and goals* and this fact suggests that different criteria of effectiveness ought to apply to different types of organisation. Furthermore, even with similar types of organisation, the appropriate measure of effectiveness may vary according to the stage of development that an organisation has reached or even to the nature of the ownership (for example a public company or a state-owned business etc).

2. SETTING TARGETS

2.1 We have seen already in this chapter that the organisation objectives provide the basis for setting targets and standards. Each manager's targets will be directed towards achieving the company objectives.

2.2 The purpose of setting targets or standards is as follows.

(a) To tell managers what they are required to accomplish, given the authority to make appropriate decisions.

(b) To indicate to managers how well their actual results measure up against their targets, so that control action can be taken where it is needed.

2.3 It follows that in setting standards for performance, *it is important to distinguish between controllable or manageable variables and uncontrollable ones.* Any matters which cannot be controlled by an individual manager should be excluded from their standards for performance.

2.4 This is a basic principle of responsibility accounting, ie placing responsibilities fairly and squarely on the right person. Ultimately, it is argued, all costs and revenues are someone's responsibility and so all items of expenditure and income should be appropriately monitored. This is especially important in the long-term corporate planning area when even the most ostensibly uncontrollable 'fixed' cost, such as rent, becomes a subject for scrutiny because in the long term, it is negotiable and controllable.

Long term and short term targets

2.5 Consider the case of a small manufacturing company which had a £6 million turnover in 1986. An objective was established to increase profits through higher sales, and so a target was set to increase sales in real terms to £10 million by 1990. To achieve this it had to do the following.

(a) Ensure sales growth of around 15% per annum. This required introducing new products, maintaining existing markets and developing new ones.

(b) Invest additional capital in new equipment to increase operational capacity, requiring several million pounds.

(c) Obtain the additional space to accommodate this extra capacity, again requiring substantial investment.

(d) Rationalise an old and inefficient site - not only for the cost saving, but also to generate funds for reinvestment elsewhere.

2.6 The agreement of the overall four year sales target set in motion the development of subsidiary targets necessary for achievement of the plan.

(a) The overall target was to increase sales to £10 million at 1986 prices by 1990.

(b) Subsidiary targets for the appropriate departmental managers were to obtain and install extra capacity, to obtain new accommodation, to rationalise the existing plant, to develop new products, to develop new markets and to sustain sales of current products in existing markets. These targets must be *quantified.*

(i) How much extra capacity should be bought and at what maximum cost?
(ii) How much extra sales must be generated by new products or by new markets?
(iii) What should the annual sales growth be between 1986 and 1990?

They must also be given a *time scale* for achievement. Obviously, the time scale for subsidiary targets must be shorter than the time scale for the overall target, for example the extra capacity and growth in sales had to build up before 1990.

(c) These subsidiary targets might lead to the following targets in the hierarchy of targets and standards.

  (i) Product development targets, to introduce a given number of new products by a given date.
  (ii) Budgets for income and expenditure.
  (iii) Within the framework of the budget, there should be efficiency standards for labour times, machine times and material usage etc, for the new and existing products.

2.7 Professor Higgins makes the point that as additional shorter term 'objectives' are established, lower levels of the management hierarchy become involved. Each subsidiary 'objective' becomes the standard or benchmark of performance for the manager responsible for its achievement. Additionally, the timing of these events, coupled to the costs involved, add further benchmarks by which to judge actual performance against target.

2.8 Different companies, of course, might take slightly different approaches, although the overall features of a hierarchy of targets remain the same. For example a company might set the less rigid objective of achieving a 15% return on shareholders' capital by a certain date, without specifying how it should be achieved (for example by increasing sales). Managers would then be given a free hand to establish subsidiary targets in order to achieve the 15% ROSC.

2.9 Managers at the appropriate level in the company's hierarchy would thus select their own targets and perhaps also be more flexible in their approach to altering the targets as their business circumstances changed (for example as new opportunities for making profits arise). However, they would still be targets for achievement, and these in turn would enable targets and standards to be set for *their* subordinate managers.

2.10 Having set targets or standards for a certain timescale, actual results should be measured with sufficient frequency so that the manager responsible for achieving the targets is aware of the progress being made. He should then be able to take control action in good time, so that adverse results can be corrected and the targets still achieved.

2.11 Performance measures should therefore be taken more frequently for targets and standards with a short time scale, and less frequently for longer term targets.

The trade off between short term and long term for control action

2.12 It is often the case that in order to rectify short-term results, control action will be at the expense of long-term targets. Similarly, controls over longer-term achievements might call for short-term sacrifices. This conflict between controls for achieving short-term and long-term targets, and the need to keep a balance between the short term and long term, is sometimes referred to as the S/L trade-off, which we referred to in an earlier chapter.

2.13 Very often managers are under pressure to produce good short term results (for example immediate profitability) in order to get their next promotion. The successfully promoted manager then goes on to another job where again he succeeds only if he produces good short term results. And so it goes on up the management scale, with managers being rewarded for short term results, even if they damage long term prospects in the process.

2.14 Examples of the need for S/L trade offs are as follows.

(a) A company has a target of building up its market share for a new product to 30% within four years. It has decided to do this with a low price market penetration strategy. As a short term target, it wants the product to earn a small profit (£100,000) in the current year. Actual results after three months of the year indicate that the market share has already built up to 18%, but that the product will make a £50,000 loss in the year.

The S/L trade off involves a decision about what to do about short term profitability (raise prices? cut back on advertising? reduce the sales force?) without sacrificing altogether the long term market share target. A manager who is hoping for promotion at the end of the year would be tempted to concentrate his control actions on trying to achieve the short term profit target.

(b) *Capital expenditure.* K Bhattacharya has written *(Accountancy,* September 1985) as follows.

> 'This is one of the most vulnerable areas for detrimental S/L trade-offs. The horizon for returns is most certainly more than a year off, yet costs associated with the implementation of the programme can easily reduce short term profits. Postponements can almost always release capital and manpower resources needed to generate immediate operating profit.'

(c) *Research and development.* This is another area where short term profitability is boosted, by cutting back on R & D expenditure at the expense of the longer term need to continue to develop new products.

2.15 Bhattacharya argues that there are times when the long-term targets must be adversely affected by the need for short-term controls, but there should be a control mechanism to ensure that the S/L trade off is properly judged and well balanced.

2.16 He recommends the following.

(a) An organisation should recognise whether or not S/L trade offs in control action could be a serious problem for it.

(b) Managers should be aware that S/L trade offs take place.

(c) Controls should exist to prevent or minimise the possibility that short term controls can be taken which damage long term targets, without an appraisal of the situation by senior management.

(d) Senior management must be given adequate control information for long term as well as short term consequences.

(e) The planning and review system should motivate managers to keep long-term goals in view.

(f) Short-term goals should be *realistic.* Very often, the pressure on managers to sacrifice long term interests for short term results is caused by the imposition of stringent and unrealistic short term targets on those managers in the first place.

(g) Performance measures should reflect both long-term and short-term targets. There might be, say, quarterly performance reviews on the achievement of strategic goals.

Quantitative and qualitative targets

2.17 Performance measurements might be quantitative or qualitative.

(a) *Quantitative*: ie expressed in figures, and given as cost levels, units produced per week, delay in delivery time, market penetration per product etc.

(b) *Qualitative*: sometimes called 'judged', which, although not actually and directly measurable in quantitative terms, may still be verified by judgement and observation.

2.18 Where possible performance should be measured in quantitative terms because these are less subjective and biased. Qualitative factors such as employee welfare and motivation, protection of the environment against pollution, and product quality might all be gauged by quantitative measures (for example by employee pay levels, labour turnover rates, the level of toxicity in industrial waste, reject and scrap rates etc).

3. OTHER ASPECTS OF PERFORMANCE

Market share performance

3.1 When a market manager is given responsibility for a product or a market segment, the product or market segment will be a profit centre, and measures of performance for the centre will include profits and cost variances etc. However, another useful measure of performance would be the market share obtained by the organisation's product in the market.

3.2 Professor Kenneth Simmonds of the London Business School has suggested that a market share performance report draws attention to the following.

(a) The link between cost and profit and market performance in both the short term and the long term.
(b) The performance of the product or market segment in the context of the product life cycle.
(c) Whether or not the product is gaining or losing ground, as its market share goes up or down.

3.3 Changes in market share have to be considered against the change in the market as a whole, since the product might be increasing share simply when the market is declining, but the competition is losing sales even more quickly. The reverse may also be true. The market could be expanding, and a declining market share might not represent a decline in absolute sales volume, but a failure to grab more of the growing market.

Simmonds concedes that while it may be difficult initially to define the market and the market share of the organisation's products, the approach may be less fraught with theoretical problems than, say, defining capital employed and measuring ROCE.

Monitoring competitor performance

3.4 Budgetary control comparisons will tell the management of an organisation whether the established targets are being achieved, but this sort of comparison can tend to be very inward looking. When an organisation operates in a competitive environment, it should try to obtain information about the financial performance of competitors, to make a comparison with the organisation's own results. It might not be possible to obtain reliable competitor information, but if the competitor is a public company it will publish an annual report and accounts. This will give figures for overall profits and capital employed, and also a business segment analysis.

3.5 Financial information which might be obtainable about a competitor from published sources might be as follows.

(a) Total profits, sales and capital employed.

(b) ROCE, profit/sales ratio, cost/sales ratios and asset turnover ratios.

(c) The increase in profits and sales over the course of the past twelve months (and prospects for the future, which will probably be mentioned in the chairman's statement in the report and accounts).

(d) Sales and profits in each major business segment that the competitor operates in.

(e) Dividend per share and earnings per share.

(f) Gearing and interest rates on debt.

(g) Share price, and P/E ratio (stock exchange information).

3.6 A more detailed comparison of financial performance might be obtainable when there is a scheme of interfirm comparison for the industry.

3.7 Benchmaking, as an approach, identifies what a company's most efficient competitor can achieve, and sets this as a minimum target. The Rover Group, for example, has recently proposed restructuring industrial relations on the Japanese lines to achieve Japanese levels of productivity and quality, as Japanese motor companies are reputedly the most productive and efficient (in terms of car per employee per year).

Monitoring customers

3.8 In some industrial markets or reseller markets, a producer might sell to a small number of key customers. The performance of these customers would therefore be of some importance to the producer: if the customer prospers, he will probably buy more and if he does badly, he will probably buy less. It may also be worthwhile monitoring the level of profitability of selling to the customer.

3.9 Key customer analysis calls for six main areas of investigation.

(a) *Key customer identity*. Name of each key customer. Location. Status in market. Products they make and sell. Size of firm (capital employed, turnover, number of employees).

(b) *Customer history*
- (i) First purchase date.
- (ii) Who makes the buying decision in the customer's organisation?
- (iii) What is the average order size, by product?
- (iv) What is the regularity/ periodicity of the order, by product?
- (v) What is the trend in size of orders?
- (vi) What is the motive in purchasing?
- (vii) What is the extent of the customer's knowledge of the firm's products and of competitors' products?
- (viii) On what basis does the customer reorder? How is the useful life of the product judged?
- (ix) Were there any lost or cancelled orders? For what reason?

(c) *Relationship of customer to product*
- (i) Are the products purchased to be resold? If not, for what purpose are they bought?
- (ii) Do the products form part of the customer's service/product?

(d) *Relationship of customer to potential market*
- (i) What is the size of the customer in relation to the total end-market?
- (ii) Is the customer likely to expand, or not? Diversify? Integrate?

(e) *Customer attitudes and behaviour*
- (i) What interpersonal factors exist which could affect sales by the firm and by competitors?
- (ii) Does the customer also buy competitors' products?
- (iii) To what extent may purchases be postponed?
- (iv) What emotional factors exist in buying decisions?

(f) *The financial performance of the customer*
How successful is the customer in his own markets? Similar analysis can be carried out as with competitors.

(g) *The profitability of selling to the customer*
This is an important part of key customer analysis, and must provide answers to questions such as the following.
- (i) What profit/contribution is the organisation making on sales to the customer, after discounts and selling and delivery costs?
- (ii) What would be the financial consequences of losing the customer?
- (iii) Is the customer buying in order sizes that are unprofitable to supply?
- (iv) What is return on investment in plant used? (This will require valuation of the plant and equipment involved in supplying each customer. The valuation might be at historical book value or current cost);
- (v) What is the level of inventory required specifically to supply these customers?
- (vi) Are there any other specific costs involved in supplying this customer, for example technical and test facilities, R & D facilities, special design staff?
- (vii) What is the ratio of net contribution per customer to total investment on both a historic and replacement cost basis?

Such an evaluation would be a part of research into potential market opportunities. Smaller customers should not be ignored and there should be a similar analysis of the organisation's other customers, although a separate analysis for each individual customer may not be worthwhile, and customers may be grouped, for example on the basis of order sizes or another such characteristic such as a geographical basis.

Market performance ratios

3.10 An organisation should study information not only about its share of a particular market, but also the performance of the market as a whole.

(a) Some markets are more profitable than others. The reasons why this might be so (rivalry among existing firms, the threat of new entrants, the bargaining power of buyers, the bargaining power of suppliers and the threat from substitute products or services) were discussed in an earlier chapter.

(b) Some markets will be new, others growing, some mature and others declining. The stage in the product's life cycle might be relevant to performance analysis.

Information about market performance is needed to enable an organisation to plan and control its product-market strategy.

4. MEASURING THE EFFECTIVENESS OF THE MARKETING MIX

4.1 Marketing managers are responsible for monitoring their progress towards the agreed targets and objectives. To do this it is necessary to evaluate the effectiveness of the marketing mix.

4.2 This section will consider ways of assessing the effectiveness of four of the mix elements.

(a) Personal selling.
(b) Advertising and sales promotions.
(c) Pricing.
(d) Channels of distribution.

Personal selling

4.3 The effectiveness of personal selling can be measured in three different ways.

(a) For the sales force as a whole.

(b) For each group of the sales force (for example each regional sales team, or the 'special accounts' sales staff etc).

(c) For each individual salesperson.

If there is a telephone sales staff, their performance should be measured separately from the 'travelling' sales staff.

4.4 Measures of performance would compare actual results against a target or standard, and might include any of the following:

(a) sales, in total, by customer, and by product;
(b) contribution, in total, by customer and by product;
(c) selling expenses (budget versus actual), if selling expenses exceeded budget, did actual net sales exceed budgeted sales by a corresponding amount?
(d) customer call frequency;
(e) average sales value per call;
(f) average contribution per call;
(g) average cost per call;
(h) average trade discount;
(i) number of new customers obtained;
(j) percentage increase in sales compared with previous period;
(k) average number of repeat calls per sale;
(l) average mileage travelled per £1 sales.

4.5 The type of performance standards in this list might seem fairly obvious and sensible. However, you ought to remember that actual performance is measured in order to compare it against a standard, and it is not an easy task to decide what the standards should be. How should an individual's sales quota be set, for example? The standards or budget might be strict or lax. One person might be given an easy quota and another a difficult one to achieve. There is rarely an objectively 'correct' standard or target which seems fair to everyone concerned.

4.6 There can be a big difference between (a) net sales (ie sales after returns and discounts) and (b) profits or contribution. The costs of selling and distribution can be a very large proportion of an organisation's total costs, and so the performance of a sales force should be based on productivity and profitability, rather than sales alone.

'In recent years the cost of fielding a sales force has increased dramatically ... Faced with such large and continually rising costs, many firms set expense goals all the way down to the territory level. Moreover, although representatives and sales managers tend to focus on the 'top line' (net sales), more and more firms are using profitability and productivity goals (the 'bottom line') to help evaluate the performance of their sales force.'

(P Bennett *Marketing*)

The effectiveness of advertising

4.7 It is difficult, if not impossible, to measure the success of an advertising campaign, although volume of sales may be a short-term guide.

A campaign to launch a new product, however, may have to be judged over a longer period of time (ie to see how well the product establishes itself in the market). A comparison of the relative efficiency of different sales promotion methods (price cuts, personal selling, advertising etc.) is also difficult to make, since a combination of different methods is necessary for any successful sales promotion campaign, ie there must be a selling mix, and advertising alone will not sell a product. Shop window displays, for example, may be an important reminder to consumers who have seen a television advertisement. Advertising's main purpose in the communication mix is to create awareness and interest.

4.8 The effectiveness of advertising is therefore usually measured by marketing researchers in terms of customer attitudes or psychological response. Kotler, writing in an American context, commented that 'most of the measurement of advertising effectiveness is of an applied nature, dealing with specific advertisements and campaigns. Of the applied part, most of the money is spent by agencies on *pre-testing* the given advertisement or campaign before launching it into national circulation. Relatively less tends to be spent on *post-testing* the effect of given advertisements and campaigns.'

4.9 Post-testing involves finding out how well people can recall an advertisement and the product it advertises, and whether (on the basis of a sample of respondents) attitudes to the product have changed since the advertising campaign. Post-testing can be conducted over a long period of time, to establish how customer attitudes change over time in response to advertising. This might be particularly relevant in the case of advertising a corporate image:post-testing would help to establish whether an organisation is succeeding in getting the corporate image it is trying to build up in the public mind.

4.10 It would seem sensible too, to try to consider the effectiveness of advertising in terms of cost, sales and profit, but only if the aim of an advertising campaign was directed towards boosting sales. If there is a noticeable increase in sales volume as a result of an advertising campaign, it should be possible to estimate the extent to which advertising might have been responsible for the extra sales and contribution, and the extra net profit per £1 of advertising could be measured.

4.11 Another aspect of the effectiveness of advertising is the choice of media. Should a TV campaign be national, or limited to certain regions? Would it be better to use repeat ads in national newspapers or magazines? Or to use radio advertising? and so on.

4.12 A special mention should be made of the cut-out reply coupon in some newspaper and magazine advertisements. If either of these media is used, the advertiser can invite would-be customers to fill in an order coupon (or a coupon requesting further details of the advertiser's services), and over a period of time, the effectiveness of the advertising can be measured fairly well (although by no means exactly - not all people like to fill in ready-made coupons) by the number of coupons sent in.

The effectiveness of sales promotions

4.13 There is often a direct link between below-the-line advertising (sales promotions) and short-term sales volume. For example the consumer sales response to the following is readily measurable.

(a) Price reductions as sales promotions (for example introductory offers).
(b) Coupon 'money-off' offers.
(c) Free sendaway gifts.
(d) On-pack free gift offers.
(e) Combination pack offers.

4.14 It might also be possible to measure the link between sales and promotions for industrial goods, for example special discounts, orders taken at trade fairs or exhibitions and the response to trade-in allowances.

However, there are other promotions where the effect on sales volume is indirect and not readily measurable, for example sponsorship, free samples, catalogues, point-of-sale material and inducements.

4.15 A further problem with measuring the effectiveness of promotions is that they may go hand in hand with a direct advertising campaign, especially in the case of consumer products, and so the effectiveness of the advertising and the sales promotions should then be considered together.

4.16 One problem with sales promotion is its potential expense, if it is not properly controlled. Since many manufacturers have to sell the bulk of their products through supermarket chains or other similar powerful intermediaries, a sales promotion campaign must be planned in consultation with the major intermediaries. Manufacturers will obviously want to restrict their costs, whereas intermediaries might try to persuade the manufacturers to improve their offers (spend more money) in order to make the promotion more attractive to potential consumers.

4.17 There are a number of ways in which a manufacturer can try to control sales promotion costs.

(a) By setting a time limit to the campaign (for example money off coupons, free gift offers etc must be used before a specified date).
(b) By restricting the campaign to certain areas or outlets.
(c) By restricting the campaign to specific goods (for example to only three or four goods in the manufacturer's product range, or only to products which are specially labelled with the offer).

Pricing

4.18 It might seem odd that the effectiveness of pricing should need measuring. Nevertheless, there are several aspects to pricing which should be reviewed. These include discount policy, sales volume, product-market strategy and market positioning.

4.19 *Discount policy* should be directed towards either of the following two aims.

(a) Encouraging a greater volume of sales.
(b) Obtaining the financial benefits of earlier payments from customers, which ought to exceed the costs of the discounts allowed.

4.20 Sales prices are set with a view to the total *volume of sales* they should attract.

(a) New product pricing policy might be to set high 'skimming' prices or low 'penetration' prices. The effectiveness of such pricing policies should be judged in the light of the following.

    (i) For skimming prices, whether they have been too high, because the market has grown faster than anticipated, leaving the organisation with a low market share because of its high prices.

    (ii) For penetration prices, whether the price level has succeeded in helping the market to grow quickly and the organisation to grab its target share of the market.

(b) Decisions to raise prices or lower prices will be based on assumptions about the elasticity of demand. Did actual increases or decreases in demand exceed or fall short of expectation?

4.21 An aspect of *product-market strategy* is the mixture of product quality and price (both aspects of the marketing mix). An organisation might opt for a *high price and high quality* strategy, or a *low price and average quality* strategy etc. Actual price performance can be judged:

(a) by comparing the organisation's prices with those of competitors, to establish whether prices were comparatively low, average or high, as planned;

(b) by judging whether the mix of product quality and price appears to have been effective.

Channels of distribution

4.22 Some organisations might use channels of distribution for their goods which are unprofitable to use, and which should either be abandoned in favour of more profitable channels, or made profitable by giving some attention to cutting costs or increasing minimum order sizes.

4.23 It might well be the case that an organisation gives close scrutiny to the profitability of its products, and the profitability of its market segments, but does not have a costing system which measures the costs of distributing the products to their markets via different distribution channels.

4.24 A numerical example might help to illustrate this point.

Let us suppose that Biomarket Ltd sells two consumer products, X and Y, in two markets A and B. In both markets, sales are made through the following outlets.

(a) Direct sales to supermarkets.
(b) Wholesalers.

Sales and costs for the most recent quarter have been analysed by product and market as follows.

	Market A			*Market B*			*Both markets*		
	X	*Y*	*Total*	*X*	*Y*	*Total*	*X*	*Y*	*Total*
	£'000	£'000	£'000	£'000	£'000	£'000	£'000	£'000	£'000
Sales	900	600	1,500	1,000	2,000	3,000	1,900	2,600	4,500
Variable production costs	450	450	900	500	1,500	2,000	950	1,950	2,900
	450	150	600	500	500	1,000	950	650	1,600
Variable sales costs	90	60	150	100	100	200	190	160	350
Contribution	360	90	450	400	400	800	760	490	1,250
Share of fixed costs (production, sales, distribution, administration)	170	80	250	290	170	460	460	250	710
Net profit	190	10	200	110	230	340	300	240	540

4.25 This analysis shows that both products are profitable, and both markets are profitable. But what about the channels of distribution? A further analysis of market A might show the following.

	Market A		
	Supermarkets £'000	*Wholesalers* £'000	*Total* £'000
Sales	1,125	375	1,500
Variable production costs	675	225	900
	450	150	600
Variable selling costs	105	45	150
Contribution	345	105	450
Direct distribution costs	10	80	90
	335	25	360
Share of fixed costs	120	40	160
Net profit/(loss)	215	(15)	200

4.26 This analysis shows that although sales through wholesalers make a contribution after deducting direct distribution costs, the profitability of this channel of distribution is disappointing, and some attention ought perhaps to be given to improving it.

5. CONCLUSION

5.1 Controls are essential to ensure that planning targets are achieved and much of this information is provided internally in the form of feedback.

5.2 The control signposts can be easily identified from the quantified objectives. To prevent managers being swamped with data, they need to establish a system of exception reporting where only result which vary by more than agreed tolerance levels are brought to their attention for corrective actions.

5.3 Control information should also be used to inform strategic planners of the need to revise longer term forecasts.

5.4 The whole process of planning and control must be a continual loop, a dynamic exercise and not a routine academic one. Managers given targets to achieve must also have the authority to make the changes necessary to ensure that the targets are met.

5.5 At marketing management level controls are equally important to ensure efficient and effective use of the marketing budget. Marketing practitioners need to be familiar with measures appropriate for evaluating the elements of the marketing mix, whilst recognising that it is how the variables are used in combination which brings about changes in demand.

TEST YOUR KNOWLEDGE

The numbers in brackets refer to paragraphs of this chapter

1. How would you define the process of control? (1.4)
2. How are targets or standards derived? (1.7)
3. Why is management control information often expressed in monetary terms? (1.13)
4. Why is there a need for selective reporting in a control system? (1.18)
5. What is the difference between efficiency and effectiveness? (1.29, 1.32)
6. What is the purpose of setting targets? (2.2)
7. What financial information might be obtainable about a competitor? (3.5)
8. What areas should be investigated when undertaking an analysis of key customers? (3.9)
9. Why is it necessary for an organisation to consider how a market is performing? (3.10)
10. List eight measures of performance which could be used to evaluate the effectiveness of personal selling. (4.4)

Now try illustrative questions 17 and 18

PART E
THE MARKETING PLANNING AND CONTROL EXAMINATION

Chapter 14

MINICASES IN THE EXAMINATION

This chapter covers the following topics.

1. WHAT IS A MINICASE?

1.1 A minicase in the examination is a 500-word long description of an organisation at a moment in time. You first see it in the examination room and so you have a maximum of 90 minutes to read, understand, analyse and answer the minicase.

If you have taken the certificate examinations you will already be familiar with the minicase from the Practice of Marketing/Sales Management paper.

1.2 The minicase is a feature of all the Diploma examinations, with the exception of Analysis and Decision, which is of course a major case study exercise in itself. It is therefore worth spending some time mastering the technique of the minicase. The approach is the same for all the subjects and so practice in one area will benefit your other Diploma subjects.

1.3 The minicase (Section I of the paper) carries 50% of the available marks in the examination and students *must* pass this part of the paper to pass this paper overall. It is worth noting that a good result on the minicase can be used to compensate for a weaker performance in part B of the paper.

1.4 As minicases are fundamental to your exam success, you should be absolutely clear about what minicases are, CIM's purpose in using them, what the examiners seek and then, in context, to consider how best they should be tackled.

The purpose of the minicase

1.5 Diploma examiners require students to demonstrate not only their knowledge of marketing management, but also their ability to use that knowledge in a commercially credible way in the context of a 'real' business scenario.

1.6 You cannot pass part of the paper by regurgitating theory. You must be able to apply the theory to real problems. The minicase is included to test your competence in analysing information and making clear and reasonable decisions.

The Examiner's requirements

1.7 The examiners are the 'consumers' of your examination script. You should remember first and foremost that they need a paper which makes their life easy. That means well laid out, with plenty of white space and neat readable writing. All the basic rules of examination technique must be applied, but because communication skills are fundamental to the marketer, the ability to communicate clearly is particularly important.

1.8 The examination is your opportunity to market yourself to the examiner, in this case as a marketing professional competent in the skills of planning and control. As actions speak louder than words, a candidate who has failed to plan the answers or who has run out of the resource *time*, is unlikely to impress.

1.9 Management skills are commonly ignored by candidates who fail to recognise their importance. Management is more about thinking than knowing, more about decision than analysis. It is about achieving action through persuasive communication. It is about meeting deadlines. It is therefore about clear, logical analysis under time pressure, which leads to decisive recommendations presented in simple, clear Business English.

1.10 The six key factors from the above paragraph are:

(i) thinking;
(ii) logical analysis;
(iii) decision;
(iv) action;
(v) persuasive communication;
(vi) Business English.

All must be demonstrated to the examiners, especially in the case and minicase study elements of the Diploma examinations.

1.11

> If you are entering the Diploma by exemption, take particular note of the examiner's requirements. Certificate holders will have encountered minicases before. They should note the change in emphasis from the learning of marketing to its management.

1.12 Examiners' reports note the reasons why candidates fail. It makes depressing reading to go back over a series of reports because year after year the examiners make the same points and year after year many candidates ignore them! No examiner can understand why candidates refuse to take notice of their requirements. In everyday life we do what our manager instructs, or we leave the job (one way or another). If candidates would only think of the examiners as senior managers at work, and address them accordingly, the pass rate would shoot up.

Examiners' comments

1.13 The *Planning and Control*, *Marketing Communications* and *International Marketing* examiners' reports on minicases for recent years all repeatedly stress the same points.

(a) Relate the time allocated to the answer to the marks available.
(b) Answer the question asked. Never use a question as a pretext to answer a different one.
(c) Time planning is crucial to success.
(d) Quality and insight are worth more than quantity and detail.
(e) It is essential to write in role.
(f) Intelligently apply knowledge of theory to a marketing problem.
(g) Do not repeat chunks of the minicase in the answer.
(h) Do not show any analytical work (for example SWOT).
(i) Presentation must be of management quality. Spelling and grammar are important, only a certain laxity will be allowed for the pressures of the exam room.

1.14 Direct quotes from examiners' reports reinforce the points made in the previous paragraph.

(a) 'The commonest "self-destruct" faults are:

(i) bad time management;
(ii) using the question as a pretext to answer a different one;
(iii) poor presentation.'

(b) 'Your examiners regard badly constructed and unrealistic case solutions as a particularly serious failing among candidates for the *professional* diploma of a *chartered* institute.'

(c) 'The gap between question answering and case solving abilities continues to be very marked.'

(d) 'A wider spread of up-to-date knowledge (greater than Coca-Cola and McDonald's) would give the examiner greater confidence in your competence.'

(e) 'Management of any sort, and particularly marketing management, is about thinking rather than knowing. It is for example about selecting the best strategy rather than simply knowing the range of options available.'

(f) 'Preparation time should be spent in practising techniques as much as in learning content.'

(g) 'Diploma candidates not only need to demonstrate their ability to communicate succinctly as a subsidiary test of marketing awareness but in their own interests of scoring higher marks by getting more valid points across in the limited time available in the exam situation.'

(h) 'It is a shame that such basic mistakes mar what are often otherwise diligent and enthusiastic efforts.'

The expectations of examiners

1.15 Examiners are experienced marketing managers. They know that minicases give only limited information and that candidates are working under a tight time constraint. They do not, therefore, require considered, fully rounded answers. There is insufficient data and time. The successful candidate learns to work with what is available, to make reasonable assumptions that help in the decision making process, and to present an answer cogently and concisely.

1.16 The examiner can only mark within the criteria that have been established. The requirements are set out very clearly. It is not difficult to satisfy them. The well prepared candidate should not fail the minicase. Since the information is limited, the time is very constrained, and the examiner is looking for evidence of a managerial approach, any candidate that makes reasonable assumptions about the case, takes clear and sensible decisions, and communicates these succinctly must pass.

1.17 Also remember that minicases are set for all candidates. Some will know absolutely nothing about the industry, some will work in it and be expert. Candidates take the examinations in centres across the world. Therefore the examiner will not ask technical questions about the industry, nor any tied to a specific culture or economy. Questions have to be more general, more open, less specific. However, you will be expected to have acquired a level of business appreciation and marketing knowledge from your other studies.

1.18 *Summary*

The requirements are as follows.

Quality	not	Quantity
Insight	not	Detail
Decision	not	Analysis
Report	not	Essay.

Management reports in CIM minicases

1.19 A management report is a specialised form of communication. It is the language used in business. It is not difficult to learn to write in report style, but it does require practice to become fluent. Minicases must *always* be answered in report style.

1.20 Management reports are *action planning documents* and are generally written in the third person. Their role is to make positive recommendations for action. Situational analysis is included only if it is needed to clarify an ambiguity. Examiners complain that many candidates do little more than produce a SWOT analysis as their response to a minicase. Support material is often included, but as appendixes to the body of the report. In CIM minicase work it is exceptional to include an appendix.

1.21 *Management reports - the basic rules*

(a) Always head a report with the name of your organisation.
(b) State to whom it is addressed, from whom it comes, and give the date.
(c) Head the report (for example 'Marketing research plan for 1991/92').
(d) Number and sub-number paragraphs. Head them if appropriate.
(e) Present the contents in a logical order.
(f) Include diagrams, graphs, tables only if they have positive value.
(g) Include recommendations for action that are written as intention against time.

1.22 If you are forced to use appendixes there are two further rules to remember.

(a) Refer to them within the body of the report (eg 'See Appendix A').
(b) Indicate when the report concludes (.../ends).

1.23 Management reports are written in crisp, no-nonsense business English. There is no room for superlatives, flowery adjectives nor flowing sentences. You are not trying to entertain, simply to present facts as clearly as possible. Think about the style you would adopt if writing a report to senior managers at work.

1.24 As we have already said, presentation is of key importance in CIM examinations. The rules are as follows.

(a) Use a black or a blue pen, never red or green.
(b) Start your first answer on the facing page of the answer book, never inside the cover.
(c) Make the first three pages as neat and well laid out as possible, to impress.
(d) Use plenty of space. Do not crowd your work.
(e) Number your questions above your answers. Never write in either margin.
(f) Leave space (four or five lines) between sections of your report.

2. AN APPROACH TO MINICASES

2.1 Minicases are easy once you have mastered the basic techniques. The key to success lies in adopting a logical sequence of steps which with practice you will master. You must enter the exam room with the *process* as second nature, so you can concentrate your attention on the *marketing* issues which face you.

2.2 Students who are at first apprehensive when faced with a minicase often come to find them much more stimulating and rewarding than traditional examination questions. There is the added security of knowing that there is no single correct answer to a case study.

2.3 You will be assessed on your approach, style, creativity and commercial credibility, but you will not be judged against a single 'correct' answer. Treat the minicase as though it were happening in real life, at work or at a social meeting with a friend. Most of the minicase is *narrative;* it tells a story or paints a picture. If a friend says over a drink 'I've got a problem at work' the most usual answer is 'Tell me about it'. The listener will need background information to establish frame reference and to understand the problem. That is what the case narrative is doing. Most of it is background, and it should be read just to grasp the context and flavour of the situation.

2.4 It helps to pretend to yourself that the examiner needs your advice. The questions posed indicate the advice which is being sought.

(a) Just as your friend would not be impressed if you spent half an hour pontificating on how he or she got themselves into this situation, neither will the examiner reward you for analysis of how the situation arose.

(b) Neither will the examiner be impressed with a long list of 'you could do this ....' 'but on the other hand....' Identify the alternatives, but make a clear recommendation if you want to win friends and influence examiners.

2.5 You will be faced with limited information, less than would be available to you in the real world. This is one of the limitations of case study examinations, but everyone is faced with the same constraint. You are able to make assumptions where it is necessary.

2.6 A *reasonable* assumption is *logically possible* and *factually credible*. (This excludes winning the pools as a means of increasing your available marketing budget!) You may need to make and clearly state two or three assumptions in order to tackle a case.

2.7 Some students feel uncomfortable that there is no bedrock (an easy, well defined question) on which to build. They feel all at sea and panic.

2.8 Preparation is the answer. It is important to practise the technique of handling a minicase. There are three later in this chapter, and they should be taken individually. For each there are careful instructions and a time guide is given. After you have completed these it will still be necessary for you to develop speed, but the principles needed for success in the examination will have been established. Minicase scenarios are also included as one of the data sheets in the CIM's *Marketing success* and these will provide you with regular new material on which to practise.

2.9 *Minicase method*

		Time Minutes
(a)	Read the case through very quickly. Skim it.	2
(b)	Read the questions carefully. Identify exactly what is asked.	5
(c)	Read the case again, but carefully. Digest every sentence, pause to consider, re-read sentences where necessary.	5
(d)	Go through for the last time, making brief notes of significant material - use SWOT.	5
(e)	Put the case on one side and turn to your notes. What do they contain? A clear picture of the situation? (Go back if necessary and look at the part of the case that has the detail needed.)	4
(f)	Identify the potential actions and note if there is sufficient evidence in the case to allow you to make decisions.	5
(g)	Make any assumptions that are needed. (Production capacity is sufficient for an expansion, allowing you to recommend a market extension programme - OR - production capacity is limited and so you will recommend a quality/price upgrade, and a re-positioning of the product.)	5

(h)	Make decisions. Be certain there is clear reason for them. Ensure that control exists, or that it can be recommended.	4
(i)	Plan the report so that it answers *all* the questions.	5
(j)	Write the *report.*	40
(k)	Read through and correct errors.	10
		90

A good answer will be a document on which a competent manager can take action.

Notes

(i) It is not seriously suggested that you can allocate your time so rigorously! The purpose of showing detailed timings is to demonstrate the need to move *with purpose and control* through each stage of the process.

(ii) Take time to get the facts into your short term memory. Making decisions is easier once the facts are in your head.

(iii) Establish a clear plan and you will find that writing the report is straightforward.

(iv) Some candidates will be writing answers within five minutes. The better candidates will ignore them and concentrate on planning. This is not easy to do, but management of your examination technique is the key to your personal success.

2.10 *Presentation* is crucial. You must take time to set the report out properly. It must be headed and addressed, it must use space to full advantage, and it should be signed. It should be written as a final draft that would go to typing. If the typist could understand every word and replicate the layout, then the examiner will be delighted and it will be marked highly.

2.11 Do not provide logos for your consultancy/division/department. They take time and do not impress. Similarly do not waste time with an introductory letter. It will be taken for granted that your work would, in real life, be typed, bound and submitted under cover of an appropriate letter or memo.

3. SOME EXAMPLES OF MINICASES

3.1 The first minicase example is taken from the December 1989 paper and is worked through stage by stage to show you the process. The second two examples are provided for you to attempt yourself and we have provided tutorial notes as a guide and prompt.

3.2 Read through the minicase quickly and identify what the case is about.

Direct Lounge Furniture Ltd (DLF)

3.3 DLF is owned by two entreprenuers each of whom built up a separate direct marketing business, one in the East Midlands and one in the West Midlands over a period of some 15 years, before merging three years ago. The main advantages of the merger were joint advertising, wider product ranges, more flexible production and less reliance upon one person. The two owners are good friends and work well together, meeting at least once a week.

Both the two constituent businesses comprise showrooms mainly featuring upholstered three-piece suites finished in Dralon cloth, in a wide variety of styles and colours. This furniture is manufactured in two small factories, each of which has an adjoining showroom.

Sales are achieved by advertising in free newspapers delivered to Midlands households. These advertisements illustrate the furniture on offer, strongly emphasise the lower prices available to the public by buying *direct from the manufacturers* and of course invite readers to visit the showrooms without obligation.

Upon visiting the showroom the public can look around the products on offer, discuss their individual requirements with a salesperson and be shown round the factory to emphasise the quality of the workmanship, wooden frames etc.

This marketing formula works very well and sales/profits are booming. Customers feel they are involved in the design of their own furniture and that they are getting good value. DLF enjoy high proportions of recommendations and repeat sales.

Buying behaviour patterns are however changing. People are tending to buy individual items rather than the standard three-piece suite (two armchairs plus a 2/3/4 seater settee) and to seek co-ordination with curtains, carpet etc. In partial response to this the East Midlands showroom offers made-to-measure curtains in Dralon to complement or match the upholstery. Another change in the industry is in the foam used for upholstering which was formerly highly flammable and when on fire gave out dense black smoke causing many deaths. Legislation has now been passed enforcing the use of safer foam.

The media exposure of the fire hazard has caused the public to be more careful when choosing furniture and increasing affluence has also resulted in a move up-market by more households.

DLF are well aware that their formula appeals mainly to the more price-conscious households, who have been tolerant of the somewhat less than sophisticated showroom and factory conditions associated with direct marketing of this nature.

Question

3.4 You have been called in by DLF as a consultant to advise on expansion options. After conducting a marketing audit and a SWOT analysis you are now evaluating the options for:

(a) product development only;
(b) market development only; and
(c) a combination of both product and market development.

Submit your report giving the advantages and disadvantages of each of these three options in more detail, stating what control techniques you would recommend in each case.

Analysis

3.5 You should immediately identify the following characteristics about the business.

(a) DLF is a small business.
(b) They operate in a local market.
(c) They specialise in the direct marketing of consumer durables.

3.6 These characteristics should start to inform your thinking about the case and the nature of the business, for example you can now make the following connections.

(a) *Small business:* may mean limited resources.
(b) *Local market:* local communication media.
(c) *Direct marketing:* control over marketing mix but cost of storage and delivery, credit provision etc.
(d) *Consumer durables:* infrequent purchase, influenced strongly by style, colour, not brand names etc.

3.7 The secret of case study questions is to really play the role you have been given. You need to be able to picture this business, its products and showrooms. As soon as you have a mental picture you will be able to fit easily into the role of marketing consultant.

3.8 Now read through the case again and identify the key points, strengths, weaknesses etc. You can do this on the examination paper to save time. You need to really think about the narrative and what it is telling you.

3.9 Alternatively, or in addition, you can convert the information onto a SWOT chart to help clarify the picture. Remember that you are not presenting this to the examiner, so use a page at the back of your answer book and do not waste too much time on it.

> Remember that weaknesses can always be converted into strengths and that threats can usually be turned to opportunities. Do not waste time worrying about how to categorise an element. It is usually more important that you have identified it.

3.10 *SWOT of Direct Lounge Furniture Ltd*

Strengths	*Weaknesses*
• Owners are friends	Could be a weakness if they fall out; may imply informal systems and procedures
• Established	
• Financially strong; sales and profits high	Resources for expansion limited for a small business
• Good reputation - price - workmanship	Perceived as bottom end of market
	• Limited geographic market • Two unsophisticated showrooms • Product oriented • Limited product portfolio • Little marketing activity

Opportunities

- Higher customer incomes
- Safety awareness pushing demand towards higher value products
- New materials and production techniques which may become available

Threats

- Legislation
- Changing customer needs and attitudes
- Increased standard of living amongst current customers
- Possibility of increased competition

3.11 Marketing audit is an assessment of the current marketing activity of DLF. We have uncovered some clues when developing the corporate SWOT.

(a) The company is product oriented not marketing oriented.

(b) There is advertising activity but no evidence of a co-ordinated marketing function, therefore no marketing procedures, plans etc.

(c) We can do a SWOT on the marketing mix.

- *Product*

  Strength: good workmanship, low prices, range of suites
  Weakness: not a varied product portfolio, one material used, traditional ideas of customer needs

- *Promotion*

  Weakness: limited to local advertising, not targeted or controlled. Product oriented by featuring pictures of products.

  Strengths: good local image and reputation for value for money.

- *Place*

  Weakness: limited to two showrooms. No information on waiting lists etc.

- *Price*

  Strength: current pricing policy is a strength while market is price conscious, but the market is changing.

3.12 Marketing opportunities do exist and some have been identified for us.

(a) To diversify into new products:
- curtains;
- other furniture.

(b) To develop a wider market.

(c) To develop new segments in the current geographic market.

(d) To reposition DLF as a quality product provider.

3.13 Review the question carefully. We have done the SWOT and the marketing audit. Our response should be based on our analysis of the company. It should *not* be just a presentation of the analysis.

3.14 We are required to evaluate three options and to submit a *report* indicating the advantages, disadvantages and control techniques in each case.

> It is important that you attempt all parts of this question if you want a chance to gain the maximum marks. In this case the question requirements give you an automatic structure to your report.

Before going further you will find it useful to spend 40 minutes preparing your own answer to the question. Compare it with the suggested solution we have provided. Remember that there is no single right answer. Use our solution only as a guide and as an indicator of the process involved.

3.15 *Suggested solution*

Report to: Managing Directors
Direct Lounge Furniture Ltd

From: A Consultant

Date: 5 April 19XX

Subject: Evaluation of product/market opportunities for DLF Ltd.

1. **Background**

1.1 Following our initial analysis of DLF's current situation we have found that although the company is in a secure financial position, with no doubt about short-term survival, the medium-term picture is rather bleak.

1.2 The DLF product range is limited to lounge suites, traditionally configurated and covered in one fabric, Dralon. This type of lounge furniture is probably in the mature stage and possibly in the decline stage of its life cycle. The DLF position has been weakened by the following macroenvironmental changes.

(a) Changing customer needs and expectations in home furnishings.
(b) Higher incomes making demand increasingly price inelastic.
(c) Safety fears encouraging customers to trade up.

1.3 We would therefore confirm your personal assessment that for DLF to thrive in the medium and long term, positive action must be taken to develop new product/market strategies. It is important that this action is undertaken before declining demand has an adverse impact on profitability and erodes the resources necessary for exploiting a new opportunity.

The options

2. **Product development only**

2.1 Product development could cover any activity from modification of the existing product (lounge suites), to adding new products to the range. We will assume that the option is basically the former.

2.2 *Advantages*

(a) This would be a market oriented development, allowing products to be designed to meet identified customer needs.

(b) You are experienced in the business, its production and operational requirements, materials etc.

(c) You have an established reputation in the business of lounge furniture.

(d) Product development would allow ranges and lines to be developed to meet the needs of a variety of market segments and would provide a number of opportunities to develop and enhance the business. The workmen have the skills to develop a quality 'made to order' package.

2.3 *Disadvantages*

(a) You are positioned at the 'value for money' end of the market. Repositioning for a new segment of the market would require a considerable marketing effort and may be easier with a new kind of product, for example dining room furniture.

(b) Proliferation of product choice would increase the costs of stockholding, requiring a greater variety of raw materials etc.

(c) Existing showrooms may be unsuitable for attracting a different group of customers.

(d) Product portfolio is limited. Recession and declining demand for lounge furniture affects the whole business.

2.4 *Controls*

(a) Enquiry and sales data by product line would be important to assess the profitability of new products offered.

(b) If the product range was extended to provide all lounge furnishings, for example curtains, cushions, and tables, it would be important to measure the scale of 'value added' sales, by customers purchasing additional items.

(c) Information on customers would help to identify whether target markets are being attracted. As most products will be delivered, it should be relatively easy to monitor geographic locations and possibly develop a simplified process for classifying residential neighbourhoods.

(d) There should be controls on production activities such as average stock levels. Order times etc would also be important to monitor efficiency of the operations as a more customer oriented product policy was developed.

3. Market development only

3.1 This would involve looking for new customers for the existing product range. It would imply increasing the geographic spread of the business.

3.2 *Advantages*

(a) It would require no change to the existing operation at production level.

(b) It would allow the profitable 'value for money' target customer base to be extended. These are customers who DLF already know well.

(c) It would require no additional investment in the production resources.

3.3 *Disadvantages*

(a) It would leave the company product oriented, looking for customers for products, instead of developing products for customers. In the long run this approach will make DLF very vulnerable to competition.

(b) Although this strategy may boost sales in the short run, we know that customer needs and wants are changing and that this low price, traditional product is in decline.

(c) It would require investment in distribution to set up either showrooms or agencies in new areas. These may prove difficult to control.

3.4 *Controls*

(a) Controls would need to focus on any new distribution channels and salespeople established. Cost of sales and conversions of enquiries would help DLF establish the rate at which the new market became aware of their products.

(b) Given the indicators of general decline in DLF's market, control information would be needed to monitor average customer purchases (two sofas and no chairs), demand for matched curtains, average spend and other purchase patterns. This would provide valuable control information for sales forecasting.

4. Product and market development

4.1 At its extreme, for example moving into high quality kitchen units, product and market developments could be a major diversification, involving not only products but also customers with whom DLF is unfamiliar. However, diversifying into TV cabinets and coffee tables for a made to measure premium market would involve less risk.

4.2 *Advantages*

(a) It allows DLF to have an effective new start, researching the market to identify product/market opportunities which could be developed.

(b) Assuming that the current cash cow business will be retained at least in the short run, this strategy would diversify the business and so reduce the risk of sudden changes in demand caused by external variables.

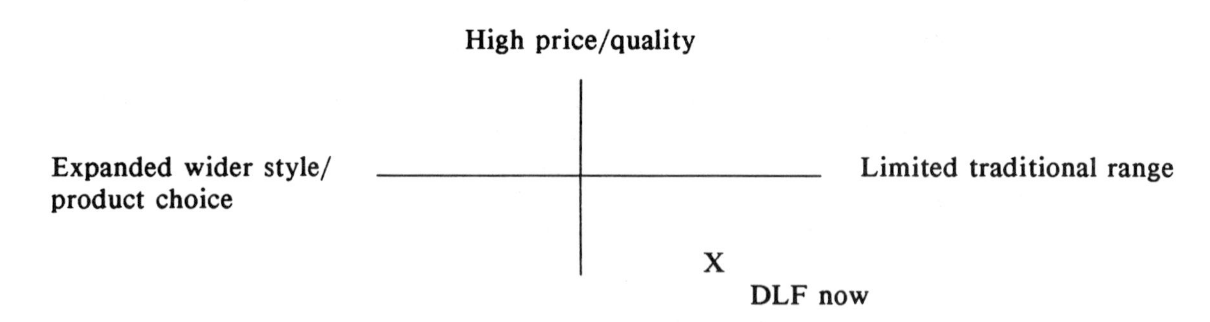

A product/market development would allow DLF to completely reposition themselves in the furniture market.

4.3 *Disadvantages*

(a) The strategy would be risky. The extent of the diversification would indicate how much risk is involved.

(b) It would be expensive, involving investment in both marketing and production.

(c) There is a danger of attempting to develop too many opportunities simultaneously, losing sight of the core business and over-extending resources.

4.4 *Controls*

(a) Such a major shift in strategy would require close control. New product sales levels would need to be monitored as would the value of business from new market segments.

(b) New distribution channels and promotional activities would probably be needed and these would also require evaluating to assess their effectiveness.

(c) Plans and budgets for the separate parts of the business would need establishing, together with administrative systems and procedures. These are unlikely to exist in the current small scale operation.

5. **Conclusions and recommendations**

(a) Action is needed to ensure the medium term survival of DLF.

(b) The business has the strengths to extend its product range to meet the needs of new customer segments, in particular high quality, made to order products at premium prices. This extension of the product portfolio should be developed after careful research of the target market.

(c) The company should clearly review its mission and should establish financial objectives for the operation. Corporate and marketing plans must be developed as well as a management information system.

A. Consultancy will be happy to offer any further assistance to DLF in this activity.

Crafted Foundary Products Ltd (CFP)

3.16 Here is an example for you to attempt yourself. It was set in December 1988. This time we have not provided a full suggested solution, but our tutorial notes are designed to guide and prompt you in preparing your own answer.

3.17 CFP, an old-established foundry in the heart of the industrial Midlands, got into difficulties in late 1985 when its major customer went into liquidation, owing considerable debts. CFP were obliged to drastically reduce their work-force and rapidly started to make losses, finding they were unable to cover fixed costs with the small amount of business coming in from remaining customers.

Early in 1986 CFP accepted a management buy-out offer by two of its most able managers John Irons (production manager) and Jim Steel (customer relations).

Owing to over-dependence on one major customer CFP had never felt the need for a sales force or a formal sales/marketing manager. However, it had two major strengths, one of which was the extremely high quality of its castings which owed much to the efforts of John Irons. The other major strength had been built up by Jim Steel in the form of a design and estimating service. This enabled potential customers to get their own rough sketches or ideas turned into design drawings by CFP for estimating purposes, CFP adding their suggestions for improvements against design/cost/installation criteria. By this means CFP had consistently been able to please customers by turning out castings of considerably higher quality/utility than customers had originally envisaged.

At the time of the buy-out offer Jim Steel was negotiating the supply of street furniture to their local city authority as part of a campaign to improve the image of the city as a tourist attraction. The street furniture designs being discussed covered litter bins incorporating the city coat of arms, 'olde-worlde' street signs, street posts and benches, finished in black and gold paint. As an additional inducement CFP were offering to finish the street furniture with a new rubber based paint which resisted corrosion and chipping, plus a maintenance service so that the street furniture was always clean and new looking.

In 1988, CFP's position had greatly improved. Considerable orders were coming in from their local authority for street furniture, profits were being made and the work-force had expanded. However, CFP still had spare production capacity at their own foundry and could, of course, subcontract casting to a number of other foundries capable of high quality work.

After attending a CIM branch meeting where you met Jim Steel, you have accepted a part-time marketing consultancy contract for the next 12 months for CFP. After completing situational/SWOT analyses, CFP have decided upon a corporate objective of steady profitable growth using the company's product and service strengths to build up a stronger customer base, ie a combined strategy of product and market development.

(a) Draw up an outline tactical plan to fulfil these strategies.
(b) What controls would you incorporate in your tactical plan?

Minicases become easier with practice. Go through CFP following the same process as previously. Allow yourself two to two and a half hours and when you have finished, turn to our comments to help you assess your performance.

CFP Tutorial notes

3.18 (a) This is another fairly small business, this time in an industrial market but with a realistic objective of organic profit growth.

(b) You are required to produce a *tactical* plan to deliver the corporate strategy, ie a marketing plan. Refer back to our outline of a marketing plan and make sure that your answer is laid out appropriately.

(c) We would recommend that you start with quantified marketing objectives, for example :

(i) to introduce two new council clients to the company within 12 months;
(ii) to increase sales by 50% by.... etc.

Remember that the examiner is looking for *process*. As long as your objectives are reasonable and credible that is all that matters.

(d) You must make tactical recommendations concerning the following.

(i) Necessary research to be conducted.
(ii) Product.
(iii) Promotion.
(iv) Price.
(v) Place.

(e) You should give an indication of budget requirements and the time scales involved in implementing the plan.

(f) Controls would be required to evaluate the effectiveness of the marketing activity in total, ie progress against objectives and targets, variances against budget etc. There should also be controls to evaluate the elements of the marketing mix, for example pricing, any promotional activity and the effectiveness of the sales force.

Pax and Porter (P&P)

3.19 This is the third example for you to tackle, taken from the December 1990 examination. Again follow the same procedure but try and complete the exercise in one and a half hours, before turning to our tutorial notes.

3.20 P&P is a large manufacturer of packaging materials with a range of products and services, which tries to satisfy the needs of a wide variety of industries in the UK.

Towards the end of the last financial year, the marketing director elected to spend some marketing budget surplus on commissioning communications research through their PR agency. The method used was the drawing up by P&P's salesforce of a list of important companies in the market containing the names of packaging buyers. An independent marketing research company then telephoned these buyers to seek their cooperation in completing a postal questionnaire. About two thirds agreed while one third declined saying it was against company policy. In the event a proportion of those who agreed did not comply despite telephone and written reminders. It was also found on telephoning that the named respondent was not always the packaging buyer or specifier and that there were errors in other details on the list provided.

However, a sufficient number of responses was received to enable meaningful analysis to be conducted, with the following results.

1. P&P scored quite highly on those questions testing awareness of packaging suppliers.

2. Buyers/specifiers were not unduly influenced by advertising but took considerable note of editorials/articles - a factor on which P&P's score was relatively low.

3. Although some importance was attached to suppliers' literature, buyers/specifiers preferred to deal personally with suppliers' representatives.

4. Quality and service were the most highly rated buying motives overall, with price third and technical support fourth.

5. Recall of packaging suppliers who had exhibited at packaging industry exhibitions was relatively high compared with advertising recall. It was also apparent that buyers were visiting exhibitions on the continent as well as the UK.

6. In some industries such as food, the buyers reported reading other trade journals as well as the standard packaging media. For the food industry, reliability of delivery and flexibility were key buying motives.

7. It was found that most but not all buyers who were responsible for specifying suppliers were also responsible for specifying packaging requirements.

8. Very few buyers had actually visited packaging suppliers to view their production/ distribution facilities at first hand.

9. Most buyers were receptive to the use of modern communication techniques despite these not being used by the packaging suppliers.

Questions

3.21 (a) What are the implications of this information for marketing planning and control decisions?

(b) Provide a list of further information you would ideally require in order to draw up your marketing communications plan for the medium term.

(Both questions carry equal marks)

P&P tutorial notes

3.22 Use these notes to see whether your answer would have included the main points.

(a) The two questions carry equal marks. Have you allocated your time equally between them? If not you are automatically at a disadvantage.

(b) The first point is the obvious lack of the customer data base before the survey and the errors in compiling a list from the sales force. The implication is that all the information generated was news to P&P, indicating that there is no control information on current marketing activities.

(c) The communications activity is currently developed in an ad hoc way. Communication objectives for awareness targets, through to sales objectives need to be established and an integrated communication strategy developed.

(d) It would be very useful to have a detailed profile of the packaging decision making units, industry by industry if there are significant variations. This should include details of relevant trade publications and exhibitions for the industry.

(e) A competitor analysis and research survey to confirm customer needs and the relative perceived strengths and weaknesses of any players in the market would be helpful in designing a promotional platform.

(f) A well researched client data base is needed.

(g) Details of all relevant exhibitions, media and their costs must be established.

4. CONCLUSION

4.1 This chapter has explained the nature and purpose of a minicase. We have used examples from past examination papers to demonstrate how to use our recommended technique and extracts from examiners' reports have illustrated the examiners' requirements and common mistakes made by candidates.

TEST YOUR KNOWLEDGE

The numbers in brackets refer to paragraphs of this chapter

1. What are the six key management skills that you must demonstrate to the examiner? (1.10)

2. Summarise the requirements of a minicase examination answer. (1.18)

3. What are the basic rules for management reports? (1.21)

ILLUSTRATIVE QUESTIONS AND SUGGESTED SOLUTIONS

ILLUSTRATIVE QUESTIONS

1. The process of management is often described as comprising planning, organising, directing and controlling. Describe each of these activities and comment on their inter-relationship.

2. What is corporate planning and why is it carried out? Describe and show the relationship between its different components at strategic, tactical and operational levels.

3. Illustrate with examples the essential differences between strategic, tactical and contingency planning. *CIM June 1990*

4. Describe the role of marketing in a firm in response to factors in the environment, with particular reference to:

   - environmentalism
   - high rates of inflation
   - economic recession
   - supply shortages of raw materials or energy.

5. Evaluate the different purposes of a full marketing audit on the one hand and a SWOT analysis on the other. *CIM December 1989*

6. Write an outline market research plan to identify the market for a proposed new product/service.

7. Organisations which claim to be 'market oriented' attempt to define the nature of the business in which they are operating.

   (a) Discuss the relevance of such a definition to an organisation which has its objective stated other than in profit terms.

   (b) Outline the 'business' or 'businesses' in which a public library service may be said to be operating.

8. Accurate sales forecasting demands considerable human and financial resources. Defend the need for accuracy to the financial director of your company seeking cost reductions.

9. (a) How might a small volume producer manage to compete with a larger-volume producer? Evaluate the likely differences in the product-market strategies of each.

   (b) Discuss the factors that might enable each producer to increase market share at the expense of the other:
   (i) in the short term;
   (ii) in the long term.

10. In what ways can the concept of the product life cycle be of assistance to the marketing planning process? *CIM June 1988*

11. (a) Discuss the behavioural arguments for and against involving those members of management who are responsible for the implementation of the budget in the annual budget setting process.

    (b) Explain how the methods by which annual budgets are formulated might help to overcome behavioural factors likely to limit the efficiency and effectiveness of the budget.

12. (a) Outline the major stages in the development of a marketing plan.

    (b) Draw up a hypothetical marketing plan showing the likely features to be considered at each stage for a national tourist board.

13. (a) What is the purpose of dividing a market into segments?

    (b) Describe the likely ways in which:

    (i) a manufacturer of diesel engines; and
    (ii) a manufacturer of breakfast cereals;

    might segment their markets.

14. Explain why pricing can be one of the most difficult elements of the marketing mix to plan and control. *CIM December 1989*

15. (a) What are the objectives of sales promotion activities?

    (b) At whom are sales promotion activities aimed, what forms can they take and how can their success be evaluated?

16. In what ways can marketing planning and control contribute to corporate planning? *CIM June 1989*

17. The Warmex Organisation manufactures domestic and industrial heaters, the domestic variety being a range of standard items and the industrial heaters made specifically to meet customer requirements. There are two different sales forces employed, one for each activity. How would you measure the performance of each of these sales forces?

18. The chief executive of your company has asked you to co-ordinate an attempt to appraise both qualitatively and financially the various channels of distribution used for the company's products.

    (a) Outline the financial information you would supply.

    (b) List the other factors which should be included in the appraisal and state the sources of your information.

SUGGESTED SOLUTIONS

1. *Tutorial note:* you might find it easier to provide a detailed discussion of the control process after you have read chapter 2.

   (a) *Planning* is involved with the establishment of objectives, and the strategies, policies, programmes and procedures for achieving them at all levels of the organisation. Long-term strategic planning occurs at the top level of management and is concerned primarily with objective setting and strategic development; operational planning is carried out at the lower levels of management, and is concerned with day-to-day decisions and the implementation of tactical action plans.

   Planning is a function of all managers. It precedes all other management functions: an organisation must have an idea of its objectives and tactics before management can determine the organisational structures, leadership styles, resources and standards of performance necessary to achieve them. Plans are also mechanisms for the co-ordination of individual and group effort to a stated end.

   (b) According to Cole, 'If planning is considered as providing the route map for the journey, then *organising* is the means by which you arrive at your chosen destination'.

   Organising is not the same as 'organisation' ie the actual grouping or network of relationships, but is the *process* whereby organisation is formed and put into action. Organising involves the following tasks.

   (i) Identifying, grouping and giving structure to the activities the organisation needs to perform in pursuit of its objectives (ie forming functions, departments etc).

   (ii) Determining 'roles' which will be needed for the performance of those grouped activities (ie allocating responsibility for functional areas).

   (iii) Delegating authority and establishing accountability for performance.

   (iv) Devising systems, procedures and rules for efficient working.

   In other words, organising is the putting in motion of purposeful activity, in order to put plans into effect.

   (c) *Directing* (sometimes known as 'commanding') involves giving instructions to subordinates to carry out tasks over which the manager has authority for decisions and responsibility for performance. Once the organisation has planned its activity and created structures and systems to accomplish them, the people must be mobilised to perform specific roles, functions and tasks. Information must be given to employees that will enable them to perform their tasks, and will indicate the standard to which they must perform their tasks.

   Some theorists have argued with Fayol's term 'commanding', suggesting that 'leading', 'persuading' and 'motivating' are more true to the interpersonal nature of management, and the manager's dependence on his subordinates for co-operation in fulfilling plans.

   (d) *Control* is the process which ties all the above together, establishes whether the organisation, leadership and co-ordination are contributing to fulfil effectively and efficiently the plans made - and indicates corrective action, or adjusted plans, if they are not. According to Fayol himself '...control consists in verifying whether everything occurs in conformity with the plan adopted, the instructions issued and the principles established. It has for object to point out weaknesses and errors in order to rectify them and prevent recurrence. It operates on everything; things, people, actions.'

The basic control process or control cycle in management has six stages.

(i) Making a plan; deciding what to do and identifying the desired results. Without plans there can be no control.

(ii) Recording the plan formally or informally, in writing or by other means, statistically or descriptively. The plan should incorporate standards of efficiency or targets of performance.

(iii) Carrying out the plan, or having it carried out by subordinates; and measuring actual results achieved.

(iv) Comparing actual results against the plans. This is sometimes referred to as the provision of 'feedback'.

(v) Evaluating the comparison, and deciding whether further action is necessary to ensure the plan is achieved.

(vi) Where corrective action is necessary, this should be implemented.

2. Corporate planning is the continuing process of planning the activities of a business. It consists of the following.

(a) Identifying what business an organisation is in.
(b) Identifying what its objectives should be.
(c) Formulating strategic plans to achieve those objectives. The strategic planning period might be five or ten years, or even longer.
(d) Formulating budget plans within the longer-term corporate planning strategies and objectives.
(e) Formulating operating plans to carry out budget plans and day-to-day activities.
(f) Establishing policies, procedures and rules for the organisation.

In other words, it is the formulation of objectives at all levels of organisational activity.

The reasons why corporate planning is carried out are as follows.

(a) The organisation needs to look at the future, to identify its current direction and how it may need to change direction to adapt to changes in the environment, ie it needs a sense of purpose, which takes into account possible threats and opportunities in the future.

(b) The organisation has to pursue its chosen objectives in an efficient manner, co-ordinating its many components and tasks into a directed effort. Planning provides a framework within which the many and varied business resources can be integrated.

The strategic component

The strategic component of corporate planning may be divided into three basic stages.

(a) *Identification of the corporate 'mission', or 'purpose':* ie 'What business are we in?' This is deceptively simple: in fact, it may necessitate a fundamental reappraisal of the organisation. The Hollywood film industry, for example, defined itself as being in the movie picture business, and adopted a strategy of competition with television, with nearly disastrous results. Only after a re-definition of itself as being in the entertainment business did Hollywood realise the vast growth market for its products that was offered by television and video.

(b) *Setting objectives.* Corporate objectives are the broad targets to which the firm as a whole directs its efforts: they should be refined regularly as the environment changes, performance feedback is obtained etc. Objectives might be related to finance (for example profitability, return on capital employed), market position (for example market share, growth of sales), product development (for example quality level at a certain price, develop new range), technology, employment (for example to pay wages above industry average, to reduce labour turnover), organisation (for example to implement MBO, quality circles), or public responsibility (for example to support the local community, improve ecological controls).

These objectives enable management to direct the organisation towards its primary goal; They are the framework for strategies, tactics, budgets etc and the yardstick against which they are measured.

(c) *Strategic planning* is the formulation of means to reach objectives, the organisational 'game plan'. This will involve identification of the purpose of organisational functions, the nature of the environment (threats, opportunities, stability etc) and the strengths and weaknesses of the organisation itself. The organisation will then be able to decide where its best options lie for fulfilling its objectives: for example if its objective is profitability it will still have much to decide about what markets or market segments to operate in, what processes to use, whether to be market-orientated, product-orientated, how resources are to be used etc. Strategic plans will still be in fairly general terms, but should be genuine, identifiable plans against which actual performance can be measured.

The tactical component

Tactical planning is the next 'stratum' of planning, at functional/departmental level. It develops strategic plans in more detail, by considering the following.

(a) Which alternative courses of action, within the chosen strategy, the organisation should take. Detailed options will be sought, evaluated and selected, using modelling, forecasting, market research etc.

(b) How the resources of the organisation can be used effectively and efficiently in the accomplishment of strategic plans. For example how to allocate resources between different functional activities, how to price a new product etc.

(c) In the pursuit of effectiveness, what performance on budgetary targets should be set, ie the basic aims, criteria and standards of control systems for operational activities.

(d) Formulation of policies, ie guidelines for response to a range of standard or recurrent eventualities. These guarantee a consistency of response, and save time on decision-making in routine situations.

The operational component

Operational planning is designed to ensure that specific tasks are carried out effectively and efficiently within the defined framework of strategic and tactical plans. Tactics 'harden' into detailed, quantified plans, including the following.

(a) *Procedures*, ie a chronological sequence of actions required to perform a given task.

(b) *Rules*, specific, definite courses of action that must be taken in a given situation.

(c) *Programmes*, ie co-ordinated groups of plans, procedures, etc.

(d) *Budgets*, ie formal statements of expected results, set out in numerical terms, and summarised in monetary values. Budgets are the 'nitty gritty' of corporate planning, used to allocate resources, set standards and timescales, and compare actual performance with planned performance.

3. Planning is an everyday activity with which we are all familiar and at which to a greater or lesser extent we are all expert. We plan shopping trips and holidays and we plan our careers and dinner parties. Planning is simply a way of allocating our available resources, for example time or money, in a way which will achieve a desired outcome, whether the desired outcome is a goal or an objective.

In the work environment, faced by limited time and budgetes, it is hardly surprising that most of us adopt a planning framework to the tasks we are required to do. We use the jargon of planning easily, talking about objectives, strategies and tactics. It is this common use of the tools and language of planning which then causes some confusion when considering the formal framework of corporate planning.

To be certain about the actual level and contribution any planner is making it is important to clarify the position within the management hierarchy from which he or she is working. The managing director, marketing manager and sales manager are all equally likely to talk about their strategy. To each a strategic plan is a broad statement of how resources are to be co-ordinated to achieve the overall objective.

It has been asserted that, in the business context, a strategic approach need only be used at a corporate level, as it is used to identify the broad approach which the organisation has decided to adopt in pursuit of agreed objectives. For example a company wishing to increase its profitability could adopt a strategy of cost reduction or revenue expansion, or perhaps some combination of the two.

The strategic plan ensures that everyone in the operation not only knows the overall goal, but is also co-ordinating efforts in achieving it in the same way. Companies like Hanson have successfully achieved a steady growth in earnings per share through an aggressive policy of acquisition, whilst Marks & Spencer have adopted a strategy of steady organic growth.

Once the strategy plan is agreed, it has to be put into effect. That requires much planning at a more detailed level. The action planning and budgeting activity associated with implementing the strategy is the *tactical planning stage*.

From the *corporate* viewpoint the operational marketing and finance plans are tactics. To the marketing director the sales strategy is tactics. At whatever level you work in the management structure, the delegated detailed planning represents your tactical planning.

Strategic plans are longer term tactical ones. Strategy is required to provide the sense of direction and focus for the organisation. Tactical plans provide the checks and balances which allow progress to be made towards those long term goals and which allow progress to be measured and assessed.

The problem with planning is that by definition it is dealing with the future, which is always uncertain. The further ahead you are planning the more chance there is of getting it wrong. Planners at all levels of business require controls to allow progress to be monitored and plans to be modified in the light of new information and changing circumstances.

Behaving in this way, managers are being 're-active' and this is often the only option available when faced with dramatic changes which could not be forecast, for example war, political unrest, natural disasters.

Nevertheless, the speed with which organisations can respond to such events is often crucial to gaining or maintaining competitive advantage. Big organisations often have complex planning cycles and decision-making processes which do not lend themselves to quick reactions. Investing in contingency planning is one way round this. Contingency plans are 'what if' plans. They allow managers to prepare in advanced of the unexpected. If needed the plans can be implemented 'off the shelf', cutting down reaction time.

Contingency plans can be made at a strategic level (for example the company's response to a hostile takeover bid or a dramatic rise in interest rates). Alternatively they can deal with tactical level (for example what to do if there is an increase in a competitor's sales effort, or a serious accident involving customers). Contingency planning is an investment in forward thinking. It provides an opportunity for more planning practice and can be particularly valuable in dynamic global markets.

Planning does not guarantee future success, but if it is co-ordinated and thoroughly undertaken and implemented, it does increase the chances of success.

4. The implications of environmental factors for marketing might be 'negative' in the sense that they will impose constraints on the quality, quantity or price of goods offered, but they also provide 'positive' marketing opportunities which can be exploited.

   (a) Environmentalists believe that firms must not pollute the environment, damage the ecology or reduce the 'quality of life' in any similar way. The success of environmental pressure against certain industries has given rise amongst other things to smoke-free zones, low-phosphate detergents, lead-free petrol, bio-degradable packaging, regulations to control the effluence of harmful wastes from factories etc. Many companies have regarded environmentalism as a threat to low cost production and have attempted to resist change. Positive marketing, however, might enable a firm to take advantage of the pressures to protect the environment.

      (i) By looking for products, such as bio-degradable packaging, unbleached disposable nappies etc, which can be marketed to customers as being beneficial to the environment or to health.

      (ii) By developing equipment which controls pollution or re-cycles waste, for sale to other industrial firms.

      (iii) By employing market researchers to monitor customer attitudes to pollution-free products.

   (b) The role of marketing in a period of high inflation should be to protect the profits of the firm by obtaining information about the effects of government anti-inflation policies and consumer response to price rises. In product design and development work, an effort should be made to hold down costs by introducing cheaper substitute materials without unintentionally affecting product quality. The company should seek to move into markets where profit margins are higher; low profit or loss-making products may have to be axed. Price increases should be sufficient, but should not be so high as to drive away customers; discounts and other price deals might be used more favourably to price initiatives in a period of inflation; and advertising messages should perhaps emphasise 'value for money'. Cost reductions might be achieved by switching to low-cost channels of distribution. Salespeople should be trained and educated to explain the reasons for price increases to customers. If inflation persuades customers to buy products of a poorer quality at a lower price, a firm may need to develop cheap varieties of its products if these do not already exist.

(c) Similarly, in a recession, consumers will probably try to economise. For example they may switch from branded goods to the cheaper 'own brand' goods of supermarkets, or from buying in local shops to buying at large discount warehouses. There is also likely to be 'trading down' from more expensive products to cheaper substitutes (for example from beef to chicken or from chicken to sausages and eggs). Demand is likely to increase for do-it-yourself items or secondhand goods, and for durable products. Impulse buying and the purchase of inessential products will also decline.

The task of marketing is to identify these changes and adapt to them by developing a marketing mix which offers cheaper products in low-cost sales outlets with greater durability. If the firm can offer goods or services which satisfy customer needs, it should be profitable, even in a recession.

(d) Supply shortages of raw materials and energy give rise to the prospect of insufficient output to satisfy current and future demand. The response of firms might be to secure whatever sources of raw materials that it can, at a higher cost, and to raise prices to customers significantly. The increase in sales prices would be intended to offset the consequent loss of sales volume, thereby sustaining profit levels. High prices might then be sufficient to dampen demand, but the cost would be in terms of lost customers or lost goodwill.

An alternative marketing strategy would be 'strategic marketing' as follows.

(i) The purchasing department should be strengthened, and given the task of finding alternative sources of supply under long-term controls.

(ii) The product development programme should be geared towards seeking substitute products which use materials in plentiful supply (for example central heating equipment manufacturers might switch from oil to gas or coal-fired systems, etc).

(iii) Sales representatives should be trained in the role of customer counselling, after-sales service and information gathering as much as in the art of salesmanship. In other words, the role of selling will be less important when supply falls well short of potential demand.

(iv) Advertising should be reduced, or switched to products which are in over-supply or to substitute products. Alternatively, advertising can be used to inform the public of what is being done to overcome the shortage problems.

5. There is often confusion between a marketing audit and a SWOT analysis yet there is a very clear distinction between them.

   (a) A marketing audit is a process or activity carried out periodically, usually annually, to assess the effectiveness of the organisation's marketing activity.

   (b) SWOT analysis is a management tool or technique, used to help sort information and clarify the current situation.

   The marketing audit is a review of current marketing activity. It involves a systematic, thorough and analysis of the whole marketing operation. It should include an assessment of the company's attitude to marketing and the marketing philosophy on the one hand and on the other a review of the marketing organisation, methods and procedures. A rigorous evaluation should be made of the marketing objectives, policies and the effectiveness of strategies to achieve them. A marketing audit attempts to assess the marketing process and how well it performs. It could be seen as the equivalent of an annual 'MOT test' for marketing. A marketing audit is therefore best undertaken by an independent outsider who can review the marketing activity objectively. It can be undertaken by a consultant or perhaps by someone in the company who does not work in the marketing function.

   A marketing audit should be undertaken at the start of the planning cycle. It represents an important element of the corporate situational analysis.

   SWOT stands for Strengths, Weaknesses, Opportunities and Threats.

   (a) Strengths and weaknesses represent internal controllable factors which management can influence.

   (b) Opportunities and threats represent external, uncontrollable factors which influence the business but cannot be controlled by management.

   This simple technique provides a method of organising information and identifying a possible strategic direction. The basic principle of SWOT analysis is that any statement about an organisation or its environment can be classified as a Strength, Weakness, Opportunity or Threat. An opportunity is simply any feature of the external environment which creates conditions which are advantageous to the firm in relation to a particular objective or set of objectives. By contrast, a threat is any environmental development which will present problems and may hinder the achievement of organisational objectives. What constitutes an opportunity to some firms will almost invariably constitute a threat to others. An increased presence in domestic financial markets by overseas banks might be regarded by them as the pursuit of an opportunity but will be perceived as a threat by domestic banks. By contrast, the recent changes relating to State pension schemes might be regarded as an opportunity for building societies, banks and insurance companies in relation to personal customers.

   A strength can be thought of as a particular skill or distinctive competence which the organisation possesses and which will aid it in achieving its stated objectives. These may relate to experience in specific types of markets or specific skills possessed by employees. A strength may also refer to factors such as a firm's reputation for quality or customer service. A weakness is simply any aspect of the company which may hinder the achievement of specific objectives such as limited experience of certain markets/technologies, extent of financial resources available. The lack of experience within building societies of money transmission facilities could be regarded as a weakness when considering the development of current accounts, while banks may consider their experience in wholesale money markets to be a strength in relation to the development of mortgage services.

This information would typically be presented as a matrix of strengths, weaknesses, opportunities and threats. Effective SWOT analysis does not simply require a categorisation of information, it also requires some evaluation of the relative importance of the various factors under consideration. In addition, it should be noted that these features are only of relevance if they are perceived to exist by the consumers. Listing corporate features that internal personnel regard as strengths/weaknesses is of little relevance if they are not perceived as such by the organisation's consumers. In the same vein, threats and opportunities are conditions presented by the external environment and they should be independent of the firm.

SWOT analysis

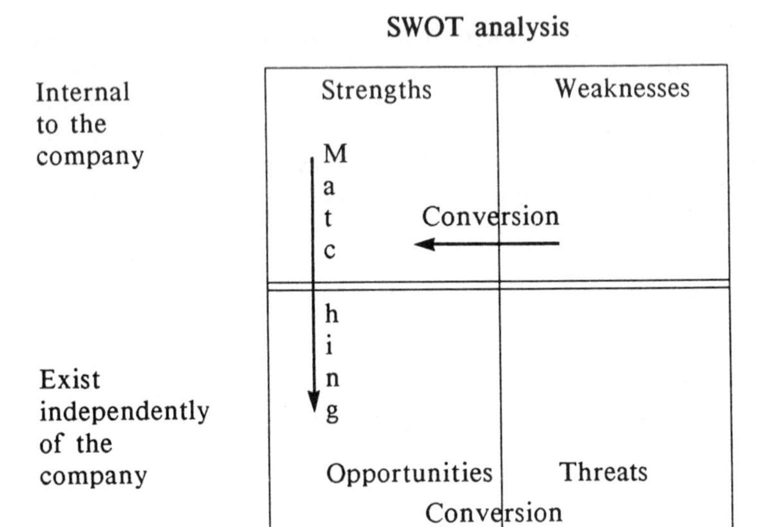

Having constructed a matrix of strengths, weaknesses, opportunities and threats with some evaluation attached to them, it then becomes feasible to make use of that matrix in guiding strategy formulation. The two major options are as follows.

(a) *Matching*
This entails finding, where possible, a match between the strengths of the organisation and the opportunities presented by the market. Strengths which do not match any available opportunity are of limited use while opportunities which do not have any matching strengths are of little immediate value from a strategic perspective.

(b) *Conversion*
This requires the development of strategies which will convert weaknesses into strengths in order to take advantage of some particular opportunity, or converting threats into opportunities which can then be matched by existing strengths.

Although SWOT provides some guidance on developing a match between the organisation's environment and its strategic direction, it is also necessary to consider more specific aspects of strategies such as how best to compete, how to grow within the target markets etc. To aid this process there are a number of analytical techniques which can be used; the role of these techniques is not to offer definitive statements on the final form that a strategy should take, but rather to provide a framework for the organisation and analysis of ideas and information.

6. Market research is the activity undertaken to generate information in order to aid management decision making. Market research activities should not be undertaken lightly, it can be an expensive process which takes time and if not planned carefully can fail to generate information which really reduces the decision-making risk.

All research proposals should be evaluated in terms of their costs compared with the benefit of obtaining more information. The launch of a new product/service is certainly a major decision which may involve the organisation in substantial investment in development and in providing increased capacity. A marketing oriented company would more normally be expected to identify a customer need and then develop a product. However, when moving into overseas markets or as a result of research and development activities it is feasible that a new product/service opportunity is identified and it is then necessary to research a possible market for it.

The market research plan

Background (where are we now?)
The research plan would start with a brief statement of the background

- about the product - features and benefits
- similar products we have knowledge of
- any research information already available.

Objectives/brief (where are we going?)
It is important that research is conducted against a clear framework of objectives - what information is needed, to make what decision, within what time period.

All the constraints involved in the research need to be clearly identified here, including costs, the accuracy levels required and any time or security constraints.

(a) To identify two market segments each of which is forecast to generate a minimum of x units of demand for this new product.

(b) To establish a detailed profile of each of these segments.

(c) To undertake the necessary research within six months and a budget of £y.

Research proposal (how do we get there?)
The research proposal will be developed by the researcher, either an internal member of the marketing team or a consultant.

It will indicate the research method, sample size and population to be investigated.

For a new product evaluation the following stages and recommendations may be adopted.

	Time
(a) *Secondary data* Search of internal and external sources to provide any further information on similar products, competitors and buyer behaviour.	Month 1
(b) *Qualitative research* Group discussions across a range of potential segments to identify key target markets. *Note:* product concept boards or prototypes can be tested with these groups to help assess those most interested in the new product.	Month 2

(c) *Quantitative research* Month 3
Questionnaire follow up on a quota sample basis within the targets identified, to confirm the group's receptiveness to the product and provide data for the quantification of sales forecasts.

(d) *Test marketing option* Month 4-6
If further information is required a test market could be established to evaluate consumer response, profiles and sales levels in a real market situation.

7. (a) 'Market orientation' is a management philosophy which holds that the key task of an organisation is to identify the needs and wants of customers in a target market, and to adapt the organisation to satisfying them effectively and efficiently. An organisation whose objective is to make profits would be market-oriented in order to satisfy customers and thereby be more profitable than it could by means of any other policy. An organisation which does not have a profit objective may be a charity, an organisation formed to promote a cause (for example a political party) or an organisation which is established to provide a certain non-commercial service (for example a club or a government department). These organisations have 'target markets' and 'customers' with needs to satisfy, therefore a market-oriented approach by the management of the organisation is a feasible proposition.

A definition of the nature of the business in which an organisation operates is useful because it diverts attention away from particular products towards the interests of the consumer. For example, as profit-making organisations, Hollywood film companies eventually realised that they were not film-makers but firms in the entertainment market. As a result, instead of competing unsuccessfully with television, they switched profitably into the production of television programmes.

A similar market-orientation might help non-profit-motivated organisations to re-assess their future. For example, the fire department of a local authority might redefine its purpose from fighting fires to 'being in the business of minimising injury and damage through fire or other accidents'. This redefinition, if it is in keeping with the needs of customers, would extend the activities of the department to fire prevention, rescuing victims from accidents etc.

Another example might be a public swimming pool, which defines its business, not as providing a facility for swimming but as swimming for general recreation and life protection. In this way, the pool's management might extend its activities into swimming classes, life-saving classes, opening a swimming club for sports competition etc.

As a final example, a charitable organisation might define itself, not in terms of raising funds and providing food to help a starving population in an overseas country, (product or service orientation) but in terms of the business of providing for the health and security of the population in the short term and for the improvement of the population's well-being in the longer term (ie market orientation). In this way the charity's management might actively seek ways, not only of providing food and medical supplies etc, but also of providing funds for education and investment in agricultural machinery or even a social infrastructure of roads, communications etc for the country concerned.

The essence of market orientation is to find out what the customer needs and attempt to satisfy those needs, rather than to devise a product or service and then offer it for use.

(b) A public library may be said to operate in several businesses. A product-orientated view would be that a library lends books, records and cassettes and offers a reading room and reference section. A market-oriented approach would consider that a library is in the following businesses.

(i) *Entertainment:* currently, entertainment is provided by a lending service for books, records and cassettes. However, if customers' entertainment needs change, a library with a marketing outlook might seek to develop its services into the lending of video cassettes or computer programs for home computers, etc.

(ii) *Information provision:* if a library is currently restricted to providing information by means of reference books and books for lending, or by means of a public notice board, a marketing approach might help management to identify new areas for growth to satisfy changing customer needs. In particular, libraries might offer the use of computer terminals to the public, or Prestel equipment, or provide archives of information on microfiche.

(iii) *Education:* one purpose behind lending books is to encourage people, especially children, to read. However, education services can be extended into activities such as reading groups for children, run by a member of the library staff.

A marketing approach would encourage library management to consider what the education, information and entertainment needs of customers are, how 'competitors' attempt to satisfy these needs and whether the library can extend its services to satisfy 'unsatisfied' needs or to satisfy needs more effectively and efficiently than the competition.

8. To: Financial Director
From: A marketing person
Re: Sales forecast

Sales forecasting by its very nature is never accurate no matter how much in terms of resources is committed to it. It is impossible to predict every eventuality, as some events affecting sales have nothing directly to do with the company.

Given that a degree of error must inevitably be tolerated, the temptation to be satisfied with forecasts that are even less accurate than what are usually produced is understandable, especially as there would be cost savings in the production of the forecasts. There would be a reduction in management time, and staff could be redeployed elsewhere.

From the marketing point of view, that assumption appears shortsighted. Financial benefits would only accrue in the immediate future after which time the reduced quality of the forecast information would have an adverse effect on the quality of planning and decision making. Waste, lost opportunities and adverse profit effects would almost certainly result.

The purpose of a sales forecast is not only to forecast the level of sales but also to plan the level of production to meet those sales. The sales forecast is ultimately the basis of the production plan, so that enough is produced at the right times to meet demand.

Unmet demand, if we produce too little, means lost sales revenue, and dissatisfied customers who might resent the wait. Excess of demand over supply would mean that the business is selling fewer products for a given amount of marketing resources than it could.

Too little demand for goods produced implies an excess of capacity. The business is incurring costs which are not matched by revenue. If surplus goods are perishable, they must be written off, meaning that none of the cost can be recovered, or alternatively they must be sold at a low price. The same principle applies to services too. An unsold seat on a flight is potential income forever lost to the airline. Even if products are stored, the costs of holding stocks and the capital held up in stocks is extensive. This might lead to higher bank borrowings and interest payments, as more working capital is illiquid.

Although sales forecasts are never accurate, the more accurate they are, the closer we come to matching demand with supply, not only in aggregate, but for each individual product and in each area.

Making decisions without such information means that planning and budgeting becomes a matter of guesswork, and the satisfaction of organisational objective is subject to the whims of chance.

Simply reducing costs in the short term would have the long term effect of reducing profitability. However, if long-term cost reductions are required, investment in forecasting systems might be the way forward.

9. (a) A small volume producer might manage to compete with larger-volume producers in a number of different ways.

(i) He or she should look for a small niche in the market in which to be 'big' and dominate the selected niche or segment. 'It is more profitable to be a niche-picking dominator than to enter a big market and be a follower.' (report by L Light, Chairman of advertising agency Backer Spielvogel Bates, 1989).

(ii) He or she might provide a better or more specialised product or service. A small hotel or group of hotels, for example, might compete against giants such as THF by emphasising smallness, a more personal service, a more homely or local atmosphere or outstanding cuisine.

(iii) Small producers might combine informally to gain economies of scale. For example small shopkeepers have maintained a competitive edge against cut-price giants by combining into groups to centralise their purchasing and so benefit from bulk-buying discounts.

(iv) He or she might extend the market, and gain a share of the growing total market demand. Laker Airways, for example, in the period of its existence, never intended to dislodge PanAm, TWA or British Airways from the transatlantic air routes. Rather, the Laker Skytrain service was a 'no-frills' form of travel designed to bring transatlantic travel to the masses.

(v) He or she might survive in a market where economies of scale are difficult to achieve. Such markets include those based on 'brainpower' (for example computer programming or tax consultancy) where individuals work well on their own, and markets based on design ability (for example fashion goods) where consumers might prefer exclusive designs to mass-produced fashions.

The likely differences in product-market strategies between small volume and large volume producers are as follows.

(i) A strategy based on small-scale operations, as opposed to a strategy based on larger volumes and economies of scale.

(ii) A strategy based on quality of service as opposed to one based on volume, a large network of sales outlets, easy availability and perhaps lower price.

(iii) A strategy based on seeking to appeal to a new class of customer, rather than one based on enlarging the share of existing markets.

(iv) A marketing strategy based on an appeal to individuality and exclusiveness as opposed to one based on offering a standardised service or product.

(v) A growth strategy based on 'in-house' development rather than growth through takeover.

(b) The factors that might enable a small volume producer to increase his market share at the expense of a large volume producer *in the short term* are as follows.

(i) *Price.* In the short term, a small producer might be able to underprice a large volume producer without provoking a competitive response, and still make a profit.
(ii) *The creation of new specialised market segments.* By creating new variations of a product or service, a small firm might be able to attract customers away from the major market segments.
(iii) *Lower costs.* Small firms can expand up to a certain size without significantly increasing overheads. However, beyond a certain size, overhead costs might rise sharply.
(iv) *Precise segmentation.* Keep the size of the specialised market segment sufficiently small for large volume producers not to be attracted into direct competition.

The factors which might enable a large volume producer to increase his market share at the expense of small producers *in the short term* are as follows.

(i) Increased marketing expenditure to boost sales.
(ii) Lower prices to undercut small producers.

In the long term, small producers might increase their market share at the expense of larger producers as follows.

(i) By investing in cost-saving equipment, which enables the small producer to be more competitive on cost against large scale producers.

(ii) In the long term a smaller organisation might grow by simply providing a better quality of product or service, so that its clients or customers are increasingly attracted to it. Queens Moat started by operating hotels around the Essex area: growth came from the provision of a high standard of service enabling realistic competition with THF and Ladbrokes. This formed a basis for acquisition of further hotel units but also some spectacular growth, largely at the expense of Grand Metropolitan and Hilton. Clearly, there was a profit potential from being a quality small 'producer' in a market sector with an aversion to large organisations.

(iii) Good service coupled with good marketing can also provide a situation for growth. In the airline business, despite 'smallness' handicaps, Singapore Airlines have a growth record at the expense of the competition arising from their marketed claims of superior standards of service. Avis, the car rental firm, competed equally successfully by 'trying harder'.

(iv) Continuing to innovate and develop new products and new market segments.

In the long term, however, larger producers can gain market share at the expense of smaller producers as follows.

(i) By pursuing a policy of acquisition of successful small producers. Many small business entrepreneurs are willing to be 'bought out'.

(ii) By pursuing an investment policy and to enlarge market demand so as to achieve economies of scale in production and reduce prices to levels where small producers are unable to compete as effectively.

(iii) By investing further in research and development so as to be more innovative than small producers.

(iv) By copying the small producers and trying to offer the quality of service or individuality which small producers are more naturally capable of. For example, in the UK, small real ale producers gained a substantial market share at the expense of big brewery companies which then responded by introducing their own localised real ales to satisfy the change in consumer demand.

10. The product life cycle (PLC) concept is based on the idea that the life of a product, as seen through its sales graph, follows a distinctive pattern.

    The analogy can be drawn between the stages of a human life cycle from cradle to grave, with the product's stages of introduction, through growth and maturity to decline.

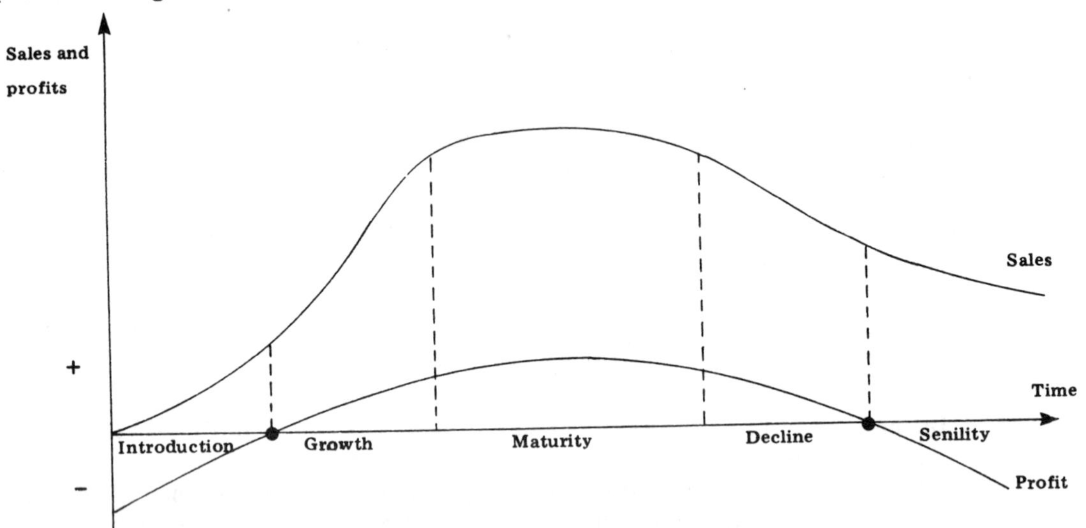

This pattern of sales may not be universal, but it does provide planners with a framework for forecasting and planning which can be very valuable.

Undoubtedly the PLC concept has its practical limitations. Even though it is intended to predict the broad shape of the sales graph it provides no clues as to its dimensions, neither the time each stage will last nor the quantity which will be sold. Nonetheless it does provide a general guide as to what might be expected.

- For example as the product enters the growth stage a period of rapid sales growth can be forecast. The planners know they must be geared up to meet this increase in demand from stocks or from available capacity. Typically it is at this stage that competitors are likely to enter the marketplace, so competitive strategies can be ready for implementation.

A slowing down in the growth rate of sales is the first indication that the product is entering maturity. Although sales may be maintained at this level for years, the PLC tells marketing planners that extension of this product's positive financial contribution will require specific strategies. These may involve modifying the product, developing new market opportunities or changing the marketing mix.

Any such marketing strategy can be better planned and more effectively implemented if the marketer is developing a clear picture of the product's life cycle.

The marketing planner knows that each stage of the product's life is characterised by a different market scenario. The level of demand and supply will change and the degree of competition and profitability will fluctuate. The target innovative customers attracted to a product in its introductory stage will be very different from the brand loyal customers established in its mature years.

Knowing this, the PLC concept forces planners to accept the need for a dynamic and flexible approach to developing a marketing strategy. It reduces the tempotation of setting a price and promitional campaign in year one which will last an unmodified product until it is withdraw from the market. This encourages planners to constantly monitor the product's performance, forecast its future and implement creative strategies for both the short and long term.

In this way each product can maximise its contribution to the organisation's profits and revenues.

Besides providing a framework for planning an individual product's life, the PLC encourages planners to think about the balance of products in their portfolio. Getting the timing right in product planning is as much an art as a science and decisions about when to launch a new product or delete and old one can be critical to a firm's financial health.

The PLC ensures that every marketer understands the need to have growth products in the wings ready to replace declining ones and not to wait until too late to be faced by the cash drains of developing or launching a new product whilst sales revenues fall from a 'cash cow' entering decline.

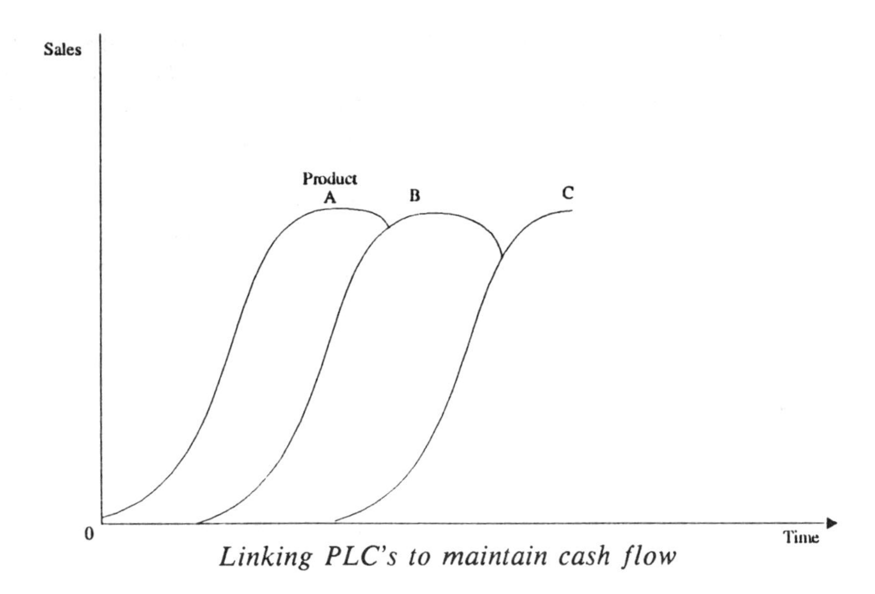

Linking PLC's to maintain cash flow

Despite its limitations and generalisations, the product life cycle is a simple but valuable tool in the marketing planner's toolbox.

11. (a) *Behavioural arguments for involving managers in budget preparation*

(i) Managers will be more likely to adopt budget targets as realistic goals if they have been involved in setting them.

(ii) Motivation may improve as the result of a 'team spirit' developing through the involvement of more managers.

(iii) Managers are encouraged to think more innovatively and use their own initiative if they are involved in the planning process, as opposed to having budgets imposed on them.

(iv) Managers who feel aggrieved by imposed budgets may under-perform intentionally, in order to discredit the budget.

(v) Goal congruence - where an individual's personal goals are congruent with those of the organisation - is more likely to exist in a participatory system. Involving managers in setting their budgets enables individual aspiration levels to be taken into account.

Behavioural arguments against involving managers in budget preparation

(i) Managers may try to build unnecessary expenditure - budgetary slack - into their budgets, in order to reduce the risk of overspending.

(ii) Communication problems can arise if too many managers are involved.

(iii) It is difficult to develop co-ordination if several managers are involved in the process, each having a different personal perspective of the business and its environment.

(iv) There is a danger that participation will be cosmetic only, because managers are 'consulted' about something that in reality has already been decided. Such pseudo-participation can only generate cynicism.

(v) Individual managers may not be able to take the wider view of the whole business which is required in the budget setting process. There is a danger that 'empire building' will develop, with managers attempting to secure resources for their own budgets without considering the effect on other parts of the business.

(b) Many of the behavioural factors which limit the effectiveness and efficiency of budgets can be overcome with the use of zero base budgeting. Traditional budgetary planning processes often use the current year's budget as a starting point for the budget for the following year. This leads to many problems including the following.

(i) Overspending to prevent subsequent year's budgets from being reduced.

(ii) The inclusion of unnecessary expenditure in the budget as a cushion against overspending.

(iii) Continuation of expenditures and practices from one year to another, without questioning their validity.

(iv) Lack of incentive for managers to be forward thinking and innovative.

Zero base budgeting practices can overcome these problems because each budget is started from scratch without being based on the previous year. Managers are required to quantify the benefits to be received from expenditure in their budgets, and resources are allocated according to a cost-benefit ranking.

12. (a) The question does not indicate whether the plan is a long term corporate plan or an annual budget. The solution which follows incorporates the approach to developing both.

The first stage in a marketing plan should be to identify the separate products or product lines for which separate plans will be prepared. For each product, management must then analyse the current and prospective market situation. This 'situation analysis' will consider the trend of sales in recent years, the growth or decline in market share for the product, changes in the unit selling price and variable costs over the same period, together with turnover, gross contribution, advertising, sales promotion and distribution costs. Together with a consideration of 'threats' or 'opportunities' in the market which offer the prospect of a decline or an expansion of the total market and product sales, management should then be able to assess where the product stands and what its future is likely to be.

The situation analysis for each product in the company's range can then be brought together, so that management can assess the total sales, gross contribution, selling and distribution costs etc based on the current situation. This assessment should be compared with the long term objectives of the company, which should be stated in terms of return on shareholder capital, or market share etc. If there is any discrepancy between strategic objectives and the forecast derived from the situation analysis, management must consider ways of improving product performance or developing new products quickly.

An 'action programme' can then be developed in which individual managers are given strategic tasks to accomplish (for example to raise the sales of product X, to achieve a 20% share of the market for product Y etc). This action programme must then be converted into a budget for short term planning and control.

For each product or new product development, management must now consider the marketing mix, in order to produce a budget for sales volume and turnover, gross contribution, selling and distribution costs (analysed into budgets for direct selling, advertising, promotions etc).

The budget for each product, as developed in accordance with the action programmes, should then be sufficient, in combination, to enable the company to plan to achieve its strategic objectives.

(b) A marketing plan could be developed by a national tourist board in the way described above, as follows.

For each tourist region of the country, and for each major resort within each region, a situation analysis would consider trends over recent years in the number and type of hotels, the number of beds in hotels, the number and capacity of caravan sites and camping sites, the actual 'occupancy' of hotels, caravan and camping sites, the amount of foreign exchange and travellers' cheques spent by foreign visitors to the country, attendances at major tourist attractions, the amount of money spent on advertising at home and abroad by the tourist board etc.

An analysis of threats and opportunities might concern the economic aspects of a world recession on the tourist trade in general. As another example, it appears that the chaos at Britain's airports during the summer of 1988, when thousands of holiday-makers faced long delays to their flights abroad, led to a much stronger demand for holidays in the UK in 1989.

The situation analysis for each resort or region can then be brought together to provide a picture of the expected situation in the tourist industry in the immediate and longer-term future. This should be compared with the strategic objectives of the tourist board (for example to raise the money spent on tourism to an amount equivalent to x% of the GNP etc).

An action programme can then be developed which attempts to improve performance in the tourist industry or to develop new tourist areas. Individual managers may be given the tasks, for example, of increasing hotel accommodation in the South West region by 10% in the next five years, increasing the number of visitors to the North by 20% next year, increasing the number of Japanese visitors by 20% over the next two years etc.

These action programmes must then be converted into a detailed plan, ideally within the framework of an annual budget. The tourist board will need to consider, within the limitations of its budget and available resources, how to produce a marketing mix which will enable it to achieve its targets. The marketing mix will consist of advertising expenditure at home and in overseas countries, expenditure on tourist offices, tourist literature and guides, advisory services to hotels etc.

The plan will be finalised as a series of expenditure budgets and achievement targets. Means of monitoring and controlling performance should, if possible, be built into the plan.

13. (a) Segmentation, an aspect of product policy, is the variation of the design of a single basic product (or service) so that different types of the same product (or service) are produced and marketed. Each variation is intended to appeal to a different sort of customer (and therefore different market segments) within the total market for the product or service.

Segmentation is based on the desire or need to maintain markets large enough to achieve a unit cost of output which enables the product to be sold at a profit. High fixed costs of production (a feature of modern manufacturing) make it necessary to sell high levels of output to be profitable. As the same equipment and administration can be used for all segment products, segmentation is a means of increasing total demand without increasing fixed costs (or increasing them only a little).

Changing demand may also call for the development of variations on a product (for example high/lower quality and price) and adaptation to changing demand may be necessary to stay in business in the face of competition from rival manufacturers who adapt to the changes themselves.

The purpose of market segmentation is therefore to identify potentially profitable target markets. The firm can then develop a product which will appeal to the target market as having a tangible differential advantage over the products of competing firms, so that consumers in the target market will buy the product offered. Target marketing may concentrate on a single product (or small range of products) and single market segment, or it may select a few different target markets and develop 'unique' products for each (differentiated marketing). Target marketing should enable a firm to achieve a competitive position in a market, and by this strategy sustain adequate sales volumes and profits in both the longer as well as the shorter term.

(b) (i) Diesel engines are an industrial good, so a manufacturer would probably segment the market on a 'typical' industrial basis, namely by industrial user segments or by individual customers. Diesel engines are used in a variety of industries, such as mining and quarrying, vehicles, mechanical engineering, marine engineering etc. Different types of diesel engine will be required in each industry, so that a manufacturer can product 'specialist' machines for each segment of the market. The industries mentioned above can also be divided into sub-categories, so that market segments and sub-sub-segments could be identified and established as target markets.

An alternative form of segmentation might occur if the market for diesel engines is dominated by a few major buyers. If this is the case, the engine manufacturer might decide to identify each major buyer as an individual target market.

(ii) Breakfast cereals are consumer goods, therefore segmentation of the market will be according to perceived sub-groupings of consumers. Possible segments might be on the basis of any of the following.

(1) *Age:* it is possible that many households buy cereals in order to feed children, although some cereals could be clearly targeted at adults.

(2) *Family life cycle:* large families may consume cereals quickly and market segmentation on family size had led to the sale of 'family-sized' and 'economy' packets.

(3) *Geographical area:* there may be a preference for certain cereals over others in each geographical region. It is possible, for example, that porridge oats are more popular in Scotland than in the rest of Britain.

(4) *Occupation:* people in some occupations may breakfast more regularly than others and therefore eat cereals more frequently. Conceivably, segmentation based on occupation might help a firm to identify a target market.

(5) *Race or nationality:* the eating preferences of different nationalities are likely to create variations in taste for cereals. A firm might be able to produce a cereal product which appeals particularly to one country's population or to one racial group.

(6) *Usage rate:* this is perhaps a similar basis for segmentation as item (2) above. Large users may want 'family-size' packets, whereas occasional users may prefer small one-meal packets of cereal.

(7) *Customer buying habits:* market segments may relate to brand loyalty or those consumers who buy on impulse. Groups which are not brand loyal might become the target market of cheaper cereal brands (for example supermarket's own brand labels), and groups which buy on impulse might become a target market by means of sales promotion and display planning.

(8) *Life-style:* high-fibre low-sugar cereals are fashionable amongst healthy eaters.

14. Pricing can be described as the most important element in the marketing mix as well as one of the most difficult. The price set will directly determine the revenue generated and so affect the financial health of the organisation. However, price setting is not a simple process. There is no straightforward formula which can be applied. Instead pricing decisions have to take into account a wide variety of factors and variables. Pricing decisions, though critical, are more of an art than a science.

    Price has to be high enough so that all the costs of the business are covered. Costs then become the price floor according to traditional practice. Some Japanese companies, on the other hand, discover the price at which a good can be sold, and *then* squeeze down the costs to meet this. However not all the products sold have to make the same contribution to costs, as long as in combination all costs are covered. Some situations will warrant a marginal pricing approach, for example a hotel with empty rooms at the weekend may accept a rate below average costs as long as variable costs are covered. A supermarket chain may actually sell a product below its variable cost (ie at a loss) if it attracts additional spending to the store.

    The customer demand, that is what the market will bear, represents the price ceiling. The nature of demand gives marketers an indication of how customers will respond to price, ie whether demand is price sensitive/elastic, or whether customers use price as an indicator of quality. In this case pricing decisions become very important in the strategic positioning of the product in the market place. Research can provide an insight into the nature of demand, but that position the situation is constantly changing throughout the product's life cycle. Planning for these changes is not always easy or precise as it is based on forecasted sales volume and market changes.

    In the middle of these two extremes is the price range, within which the firm has to consider competitors' pricing and predict how, when and if they are likely to change price and the implications for the business of any such moves.

    Added to these considerations are other aspects which include the impact of price on corporate image, the financial objectives of the firm, the need to offer discounts, the credit to be offered, pricing of other products in the range and any international dimensions of price, such as exchange rate requirements.

    With all these variables involved, planning the price becomes very difficult and complex. However managers have to pay particular attention to planning price, because price influences demand, which in turns changes unit costs in the long run.

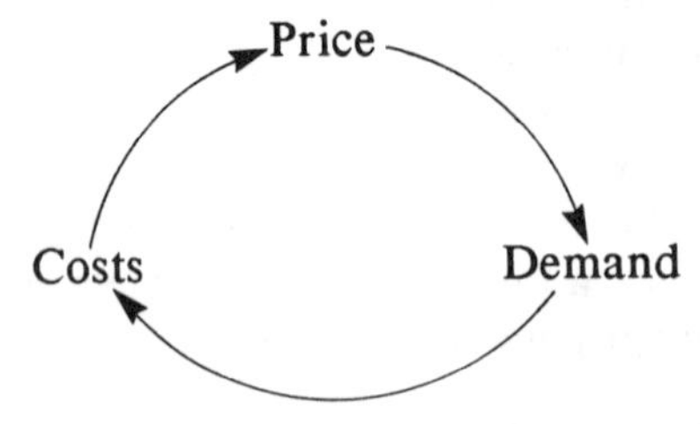

    Sales prices need to be set with a view to the total volume of sales they will attract, but the following points must also be borne in mind.

    (a) This is not always an accurate assessment and so the decision may need to be modified in the light of improved feedback.

    (b) The sales price is not always the price customers pay. Retailers may vary the end price and sales people may offer discounts etc. Both of these possibilities must be assessed and monitored.

(c) Unexpected events, for example the government increasing the rate of VAT, can suddenly change price to the customer and is an event which is outside the firm's control.

15. (a) The basic objective of sales promotion is to increase sales of a product. Whereas media advertising can create customer awareness and interest in the product, inertia often prevents the customer from actually buying the product. A further incentive might be needed to make the sale, and this is provided by sales promotion. The objective may be to improve sales over a long period of time, but promotions are generally considered to be effective only for the duration of the promotion campaign.

An alternative objective to increasing sales might be to counter the tactics of a competitor, and thereby simply maintain sales volume. For example if a competitor launches a new product in a mass advertising campaign, a counter action might be a money-off voucher campaign or a premium offer campaign.

A list of sub-objectives of sales promotion can now be itemised. These are as follows.

(i) If the promotion is aimed at the consumer, the aim will be to encourage more frequent buying or faster usage by existing users, and to encourage trial use by previous non-users or users of other brands.

(ii) If the promotion is aimed at the retailer, the aim will be to encourage the holding of larger stocks, or stocks of new items and so gaining entry to new retail outlets.

(iii) If the promotion is aimed at the company's own sales force, the objective might be to encourage support for a new product, to encourage salespeople to prospect for new customers or to stimulate sales in a low period for sales.

(b) Sales promotions are aimed at consumers, industrial customers, resellers or the company's own sales force. The forms they take may also be listed, as follows.

(i) For consumers, promotions may be free samples, coupon offers, price reductions, competitions, free sendaway premiums, combination pack offers, samples, catalogues, on-pack offers, trading stamps, exhibitions or demonstrations.

(ii) For industrial customers, promotions might be attractive sales literature and catalogues, special discounts, exhibitions, trade fairs, trade-in allowances, events such as a day's golfing contest or inducements such as diaries and calendars.

(iii) For resellers, promotions might be merchandising facilities, extended credit facilities, or contests for shop assistants.

(iv) For the sales force, promotions might be contests between staff, bonuses or gifts linked to sales achievements.

The success of a promotion must be evaluated according to its specific objective and the nature of the promotion. The benefits obtained must be considered in relation to the costs of the promotion, and marketing managers can also probably make some evaluation by comparing the effects of one promotion with those of other previous promotions.

The success of a promotion for retailers will be measurable in terms of the volume of goods delivered to existing reseller customers and new customers during the period of the promotion, and perhaps for some time thereafter. The increase in deliveries might then be attributed to the promotion. Similarly, effectiveness might be measured in terms of shelf-space allocation in stores (or the amount of co-operative advertising or sales promotions jointly funded by resellers and the manufacturer).

Consumer promotions are more difficult to evaluate, although any increase in sales volume during the promotion campaign might be considered as attributable to the campaign. The profitability can then be calculated in terms of extra contribution less incremental direct costs of the campaign. A measurement of the number of money-off coupons used, competitions entered or premium offers taken up etc will not be a direct indicator of the effect of a promotion on sales, although it would indicate the level of consumer interest in the promotion itself. An alternative method of evaluation would be to use a consumer panel, or to conduct a survey, in order to find out how a promotion has changed the buying patterns of a sample of consumers. A more complex evaluation technique might be to have two different promotions, one in each of two similar 'matched' areas; the difference in consumer response in each area would then indicate the comparative success of each promotion method.

Promotions to industrial customers are more difficult to evaluate, and much 'evaluation' may be the subjective views of the sales force about customer response to events, inducements or sales literature. The response to exhibitions and trade fairs can be measured in terms of actual sales or 'leads' to follow up later.

The effect of sales force promotions should be measured in terms of the increase in sales volume and therefore contribution.

The evaluation of sales promotions might not be a wholly accurate assessment, but it should be sufficient to give some indication as to whether the costs of the promotions were justified in terms of extra sales and profits. It is perhaps useful to add, as a final point, that the promotion should be well conceived and should not create bad publicity or bad will (which might then have an adverse effect on sales). For example early in 1982 a competition (in a continuing series) run by the Daily Mail with a £35,000 prize had thousands of simultaneous winners, instead of just one winner, as expected. The effect of the bad publicity (from news reports of claimants for the big-money prize) on sales volumes thereafter would need to have been measured in order to gauge the full effect of the promotion by the newspaper.

16. Marketing can and should play a very significant part in the corporate planning process of a market-oriented organisation. In such a business the needs of the customers will be central to all decisions and so they are an essential starting point from which all plans should evolve. As marketing information and research provides the bridge between the customer and the firm, so its role can be seen as fundamental.

    However we should recognise that not all companies are market driven. In some, finance or operations or R&D may represent the driving force. In these more product-oriented cultures, the role of marketing in the corporate planning process is likely to be much more re-active than pro-active.

    With that caveat we can consider in more detail the possible role that marketing planning and control may adopt.

The corporate planning process can be split into a number of stages.

(a) Where are we now?
(b) Where are we going?
(c) How can we get there?
(d) Which is the best route?
(e) Developing our plan.
(f) Implementation and control.

We need to evaluate the contribution of marketing at each of these stages.

Where are we now?
The audit stage is based on information about the current strengths and weaknesses of the orgnaisation, including its market position and image etc, and opportunities and threats. This environmental audit is most likely to be informed by marketing information systems which have been set up to monitor the market place and the evolving market opportunities and threats.

Where are we going?
Although set normally in financial terms of profit and return, the activity of corporate objective setting of 'ehre are we going' should be influenced by all the functions. Perhaps most importantly, marketing will provide the sales forecasts which will ensure that corporate objectives are realistic and perceived to be achievable.

How can we get there?
Identifying alternative strategies and selecting the one best suited to the organisation's strenth and weaknesses is also likely to be strongly influenced by marketing. An organisation which wants to develop and change has options related to product/market opportunities as illustrated by the Ansoff matrix.

		Products	
		Existing	New
Markets	Existing		
	New		

Quantification and calculation of the potential benefits of each of the identified opportunities will be the responsibility of marketing, informed by the information available from marketing research.

Developing our plan
Developing the plan means turning corporate objectives and strategy into operational plans. With other functions, marketing has a part to play in developing a marketing plan which is designed to deliver the agreed corporate objectives.

Implementation and control
The success of the corporate and marketing plans is determined by the skill of the managers implementing them. Communciation is essential at this stage and marketing has an increasingly important part to play in developing plans to ensure the effective internal marketing of corporate plans and changes.

Control is the feedback of actual performance results to allow the modification of plans as the environment changes and as better information becomes available. The acid test will be the market reaction to the company's offering, therefore marketing control is critical to ensuring that the demand can be satisifed by the firm's capacity to supply.

Marketing's role as the voice of the customer within the organisation puts it in a special position, able to influence, inform and contribute to the success of the corporate planning process.

17. To monitor the sales representatives' performance, the following data would be useful:

(a) the number of locations of the accounts to be visited/contacted;
(b) the 'call frequency' relating to the various types/groups of customer;
(c) achievement of mean call rates;
(d) time spent in selling;
(e) call rates for existing/new customers;
(f) time expended on repeat/new business;
(g) the number of working days available to each representative;
(h) time allowed for travelling, contact, report writing.

Such quantitative measurements do help in making some form of comparison in relation to predetermined targets (or other sales representatives). Nevertheless, we have to realise there are also specific qualitative elements which can influence performance: personality, methods of selling, differing market characteristics in geographical locations, the judgment of the representative (in understanding when and how to take longer on a potential sale or not).

Having collated individual information, as far as the sales team is concerned, we might be able to use the total number of units sold and total sales value of these, the resultant market share, and/or profits derived on units sold.

Even so, there may be considerable incompatibility in performance targets. The largest number of units of products sold may not always create the largest profits (perhaps lower quantities of units at a high price are more profitable than larger quantities of standardised lower price items). This also suggests that, because there may be conflicting objectives here for the team, it may not be possible to 'maximise performance'.

In the case of this particular company, there are further problems. Comparison of the two sales teams could be rendered impossible since there are major distinctions between domestic and industrial heating needs. For one thing, order size will differ, and so will the degree of technical service required per customer. There are, of course, similarities in the two teams, but the distinctions give rise to incompatibility and inability to make comparisons between them, or even between two time periods for the same team.

For the reasons outlined, the two markets need to be separately controlled. Probably the standard domestic heater would be sold through retail outlets rather than direct selling. Thus the call frequency control system would relate to time spent visiting the various outlets. A further refinement might be type of outlet, since high volume outlets such as stores and discount houses may require bigger discounts.

If there is a sufficient justification, a split of the representatives between type of outlet and area may be a useful help in creating a reliable measure of performance. If there is selling either through mail order or telephone, then the same criteria can be used.

In the case of the non-standard industrial heaters first of all territory should be identified. The criteria based on individual calls, possibly based on initial canvassing by mail or telephone, can be brought in.

Most sales will require costing and estimating support, so the cost of the back up will be important and performance based possibly on standard contribution for representatives compared with the costs of keeping the representative in the field, and the cost of support for each representative.

As in many other areas, there are external influences on the market and the head of each sales team may be quite unable to identify various sorts of influences which can and do affect his team's performance. These would include, say, the activities of competitors and their sales campaigns (free offers in the area?) and the general state of the economy as a whole. Even the quality of the product being sold, or the presence of a design fault, can destroy chances of reaching targets. Due consideration must be given, when judging sales performance, to such factors.

This cannot be taken to mean that performance evaluation of either team should not be attempted, but only that great care must be taken when, as a result of monitoring and control, comparisons are being made.

18. A channel of distribution is the means by which a company's products reach their customers/ buyers. An appraisal of existing channels should be concerned with the following.

    (a) Cost efficiency.
    (b) Making profits from the sale of products through each channel.
    (c) Quality of service, and efficiency of operation. The various channels of distribution should provide goods to customers in the place, at the time and in the condition that the customers want them.

    Management must therefore make a balance between cost efficiency and profitability on the one hand and quality of service on the other. A higher standard of service is likely to be more costly and so less profitable in the short run.

    The financial information will be quantitative. It will be mainly concerned with costs, cost efficiency (for control purposes) and profitability, although information about incremental costs and benefits of providing more or fewer channels of distribution should also be made available to management on request.

    (a) *Financial information*

        (i) For each category of distribution channel, the direct costs of operations, for example costs of:
            - warehousing;
            - transportation;
            - discounts to resellers;
            - insurance;
            - handling costs and charges.

            Direct costs should be analysed into fixed and variable costs.

(ii) For each category of distribution channel, the volume of each type of product sold per period and the contribution from those sales.

(iii) The gross profit from each distribution channel, being the difference between the contribution in (ii) and direct costs in (i).

(iv) The distribution cost of products sold.

(v) For each category of distribution channel, *budgeted* direct costs, sales volumes, contribution and gross profit.

(vi) Supplementary to this information would be details of any share of central promotion costs (if relevant). For example marketing and advertising may be centrally organised, but its activities may relate to specific channels of distribution, and as a consequence this should be brought into the information.

(vii) Ratio analysis, indicating the returns on capital employed per product before and after the deduction of the already-analysed distribution costs; also ROCE per distribution channel.

(viii) The value of stocks still owned by the company and held unsold in each distribution channel.

From this, management will be able to appraise the returns and profits generated by their products in the respective markets and what it is costing to service those markets. From such information, decisions can be taken about the financial viability of the various products in the market, and the viability of individual distribution channels.

The cost information should help to provide a basis for budgeting future costs and actual costs compared with budget will provide information for *control*.

(b) *Non financial information*
This will mostly come from the marketing department which in turn might obtain it from other sources such as market research agencies, or trade associations. It will include the following.

(i) Details of market shares in the various sectors.
(ii) Details of the strength of the competition.
(iii) An appraisal of how much scope there is for price adjustments.
(iv) Implications of price and volume sensitivity of the product.
(v) Sales volume/goodwill implications of withdrawing a distribution channel.
(vi) Implications of stepping up activity - the probability of a damaging price war.
(vii) Implications on production of withdrawals or loss of volume.
(viii) Information from production about capacity for increased production, potential unit cost savings at higher output levels and potential efficiency savings to create better margins.
(ix) Details of how any economies could be achieved in distribution (marketing).
(x) The volume and nature of customer complaints.

The non-financial information will be necessary in order to do the following.

(i) Consider fully the quantitative/financial implications of a decision to increase or reduce the number of distribution channels.
(ii) Consider the qualitative aspects of the company's distribution service.

APPENDIX: DISCOUNT FACTORS

PRESENT VALUE TABLE

Present value of 1 ie $(1 + r)^{-n}$ Where r = discount rate, n = number of periods until payment.

Discount rates (r)

Periods (n)	*1%*	*2%*	*3%*	*4%*	*5%*	*6%*	*7%*	*8%*	*9%*	*10%*	
1	0.990	0.980	0.971	0.962	0.952	0.943	0.935	0.926	0.917	0.909	1
2	0.980	0.961	0.943	0.925	0.907	0.890	0.873	0.857	0.842	0.826	2
3	0.971	0.942	0.915	0.889	0.864	0.840	0.816	0.794	0.772	0.751	3
4	0.961	0.924	0.888	0.855	0.823	0.792	0.763	0.735	0.708	0.683	4
5	0.951	0.906	0.863	0.822	0.784	0.747	0.713	0.681	0.650	0.621	5
6	0.942	0.888	0.837	0.790	0.746	0.705	0.666	0.630	0.596	0.564	6
7	0.933	0.871	0.813	0.760	0.711	0.665	0.623	0.583	0.547	0.513	7
8	0.923	0.853	0.789	0.731	0.677	0.627	0.582	0.540	0.502	0.467	8
9	0.941	0.837	0.766	0.703	0.645	0.592	0.544	0.500	0.460	0.424	9
10	0.905	0.820	0.744	0.676	0.614	0.558	0.508	0.463	0.422	0.386	10
11	0.896	0.804	0.722	0.650	0.585	0.527	0.475	0.429	0.388	0.350	11
12	0.887	0.788	0.702	0.625	0.557	0.497	0.444	0.397	0.356	0.319	12
13	0.879	0.773	0.681	0.601	0.530	0.469	0.415	0.368	0.326	0.290	13
14	0.870	0.758	0.661	0.577	0.505	0.442	0.388	0.340	0.299	0.263	14
15	0.861	0.743	0.642	0.555	0.481	0.417	0.362	0.315	0.275	0.239	15

	11%	*12%*	*13%*	*14%*	*15%*	*16%*	*17%*	*18%*	*19%*	*20%*	
1	0.901	0.893	0.885	0.877	0.870	0.862	0.855	0.847	0.840	0.833	1
2	0.812	0.797	0.783	0.769	0.756	0.743	0.731	0.718	0.706	0.694	2
3	0.731	0.712	0.693	0.675	0.658	0.641	0.624	0.609	0.593	0.579	3
4	0.659	0.636	0.613	0.592	0.572	0.552	0.534	0.516	0.499	0.482	4
5	0.593	0.567	0.543	0.519	0.497	0.476	0.456	0.437	0.419	0.402	5
6	0.535	0.507	0.480	0.456	0.432	0.410	0.390	0.370	0.352	0.335	6
7	0.482	0.452	0.425	0.400	0.376	0.354	0.333	0.314	0.296	0.279	7
8	0.434	0.404	0.376	0.351	0.327	0.305	0.285	0.266	0.249	0.233	8
9	0.391	0.361	0.333	0.308	0.284	0.263	0.243	0.225	0.209	0.194	9
10	0.352	0.322	0.295	0.270	0.247	0.227	0.208	0.191	0.176	0.162	10
11	0.317	0.287	0.261	0.237	0.215	0.195	0.178	0.162	0.148	0.135	11
12	0.286	0.257	0.231	0.208	0.187	0.168	0.152	0.137	0.124	0.112	12
13	0.258	0.229	0.204	0.182	0.163	0.145	0.130	0.116	0.104	0.093	13
14	0.232	0.205	0.181	0.160	0.141	0.125	0.111	0.099	0.088	0.078	14
15	0.209	0.183	0.160	0.140	0.123	0.108	0.095	0.084	0.074	0.065	15

INDEX

INDEX

INDEX

CIM - MARKETING PLANNING AND CONTROL

Name: ______________________________

How have you used this text?

Home study (book only) ☐ With 'correspondence' package ☐

On a course: college__________________ ☐ Other ______________________

How did you obtain this text?

From us by mail order ☐ From us by phone ☐

From a bookshop ☐ From your college ☐

Where did you hear about BPP texts?

At bookshop ☐ Recommended by lecturer ☐

Recommended by friend ☐ Mailshot from BPP ☐

Advertisement in __________________ ☐ Other ______________________

Your comments and suggestions would be appreciated on the following areas.

Syllabus coverage

Illustrative questions

Errors (please specify, and refer to a page number, if you've spotted anything!)

Presentation

Other (index, cross-referencing, price - whatever!)

Please send to: BPP Publishing Ltd, FREEPOST, London W12 8BR